BLOOM'S PERIOD STUDIES

American Naturalism
The American Renaissance
The Eighteenth-Century English Novel
Elizabethan Drama
English Romantic Poetry
Greek Drama
The Harlem Renaissance
The Italian Renaissance
Literature of the Holocaust
The Victorian Novel

BLOOM'S PERIOD STUDIES

Greek Drama

Edited and with an introduction by
Harold Bloom
Sterling Professor of the Humanities
Yale University

CHELSEA HOUSE
PUBLISHERS
A Haights Cross Communications Company
Philadelphia

Printed and bound in the United States of America.

10 9 8 7 6 5 4 3 2 1

Library of Congress Cataloging-in-Publication Data
Greek drama / edited and with an introduction by Harold Bloom.
    v. cm. — (Bloom's period studies)
  Includes bibliographical references and index.
  Contents: The use of the chorus in tragedy / Friedrich Schiller —
Introduction to ten Greek plays / Lane Cooper — Poetics / Aristotle —
The criticism of Greek tragedy / William Arrowsmith — Sophocles's
electra : the Orestes myth rephrased / John Jones — The birth of
tragedy / Friedrich Nietzsche — Tragedy and Greek archaic thought / R.
P. Winnington-Ingram — The antidote of comedy / C. M. Bowra —
From Aristophanes to Menander / W. Geoffrey Arnott — Greece : the forms of
Dionysus / E. T. Kirby — I know you by your rags : costume and
disguise in fifth-century drama / Frances Muecke — Fear and suffering
in Aeschylus and Euripides / Jacqueline de Romilly — Aristophanes and
his rivals / Malcolm Heath — The tragedians and popular religion / Jon
D. Mikalson — Knowledge that is sad to have to know / Ruth Padel —
The fabrication of comic illusion / Niall W. Slater — Myth into
muthos : the shaping of tragic plot / Peter Burian.
  ISBN 0-7910-7894-9
  1. Greek drama—History and criticism. I. Bloom, Harold. II. Series.
PA3133.G655 2004
882'.0109—dc22

                                                         2003028162

Chelsea House Publishers
1974 Sproul Road, Suite 400
Broomall, PA 19008-0914

http://www.chelseahouse.com

Contributing Editor: Pamela Loos

Cover designed by Keith Trego

Layout by EJB Publishing Services

Contents

Editor's Note

My Introduction meditates upon the *Oresteia* of Aeschylus, the *Oedipus* and *Electra* of Sophocles, the *Bacchae* of Euripides, and *The Birds* of Aristophanes.

The sequence of essays begins with Friedrich Schiller, Goethe's friend and fellow poet-dramatist, remarking perceptively on how the tragic chorus "gives life to the language" and "repose to the action."

Lane Cooper gives the backgrounds, historical and theatrical, that are necessary for understanding the four great Athenian dramatists.

The essential sections of Aristotle's *Poetics* for the study of Greek drama are followed by their worthy complement in William Arrowsmith's admirable excursus on the criticism of Athenian tragedy, in which he restores "turbulence" to its proper place as a quality that most critics pass over.

John Jones reads the *Electra* of Sophocles in contrast to Aeschylus' *Oresteia*.

Nietzsche's *The Birth of Tragedy*, his first book, is represented by central extracts that give the still vital range of perceptions he brought to the tragic art.

The difficult matter of the relation between Athenian tragedy and the earliest Greek speculations is explored by R.P. Winnington-Ingram, after which Sir Maurice Bowra exuberantly presents Aristophanes as comic antidote for the ills of Athens.

Old Comedy and New Comedy, the movement from Aristophanes to Menander, is presented by W.G. Arnott, while E.T. Kirby searches for the origins of theater in the forms of Dionysus.

Frances Muecke usefully searches out the grotesque in the costumes of disguise in Athenian drama, after which Jacqueline de Romilly gives a brief, strong account of lamentation and anguish in Aeschylus and Euripides.

The lost rivals of Aristophanes, Eupolis and Cratius, are the subject of Malcolm Heath's skilled conjectures, while Jon Mikalson compares the neglect of popular religion by Aeschylus and Sophocles with the support given to it by Euripides.

Ruth Padel traces the elements of tragic madness, after which Niall Slater shows the growth of a consistent dramatic illusion in the change from Old to New Comedy.

In this volume's final essay, Peter Burian sees tragic plot as the interplay between repetition and innovation.

HAROLD BLOOM

Introduction

Aeschylus

When Odysseus encounters the ghost of Agamemnon in the underworld (*Odyssey*, Book XI) the embittered shade memorably recalls his slaughter by his extraordinary wife:

> As I lay dying the woman with the dog's eyes would not close my
> eyes for me as I descended into Hades.

One recalls that Faulkner took the title for his most original novel from those first four words, but Aeschylus created an Agamemnon who is less imposing than Homer's. Selective in his use of the story, Homer omits any mention of the sacrifice of Iphigeneia by Agamemnon, and does not tell us that the Furies harried Orestes for his matricide. The *Odyssey* intimates that Clytemnestra was hateful, but does not elaborate. Aeschylus, who somehow gives me the uncanny notion that he is more archaic than Homer, certainly more primordial, portrays a Clytemnestra far more vivid than any other role in the *Oresteia*.

Clytemnestra's hatred for her husband appears to transcend his ritual sacrifice of Iphigeneia, and pragmatically represents a desire to usurp the kingdom. Aeschylus could not have been unaware of the negative splendor with which he had endowed Clytemnestra. One hesitates to call her a heroine-villain, though the mixed metaphor of lioness-serpent, mother of the lion Orestes whom she calls a serpent, certainly applies to her.

Since Clytemnestra is dramatically and imaginatively stronger than

1

Agamemnon, his slave-mistress Cassandra, and the avenging Electra and Orestes, she certainly is the most memorable figure not only in the trilogy, but in all of Aeschylus that has survived. She is superbly flamboyant, and fascinates us because she exults outrageously in her slaughter of Agamemnon, and also in her wholly gratuitous butchery of the innocent Cassandra. I employ here the translation of Richmond Lattimore (1947), to give Clytemnestra's speech as she stands over the bodies of Agamemnon and Cassandra:

> Much have I said before to serve necessity,
> but I will take no shame now to unsay it all.
> How else could I, arming hate against hateful men
> disguised in seeming tenderness, fence high the nets
> of ruin beyond overleaping? Thus to me
> the conflict born of ancient bitterness is not
> a thing new thought upon, but pondered deep in time.
> I stand now where I struck him down. The thing is done.
> Thus have I wrought, and I will not deny it now.
> That he might not escape nor beat aside his death,
> as fishermen cast their huge circling nets, I spread
> deadly abundance of rich robes, and caught him fast.
> I struck him twice. In two great cries of agony
> he buckled at the knees and fell. When he was down
> I struck him the third blow, in thanks and reverence
> to Zeus the lord of dead men underneath the ground.
> Thus he went down, and the life struggled out of him;
> and as he died he spattered me with the dark red
> and violent driven rain of bitter savored blood
> to make me glad, as gardens stand among the showers
> of God in glory at the birthtime of the buds.
>
> These being the facts, elders of Argos assembled here,
> be glad, if it be your pleasure; but for me, I glory.
> Were it religion to pour wine above the slain,
> this man deserved, more than deserved, such sacrament.
> He filled our cup with evil things unspeakable
> and now himself come home has drunk it to the dregs.

Few utterances in drama before Shakespeare have so stunning a force. The third blow is a shocker, but less so than the image of the murderess as gardens gloried by the rain of her husband's blood. Even in Shakespeare's panoply of Lady Macbeth, Goneril, and Regan, there is no woman of similar violence. To go beyond this might seem unlikely, but Aeschylus surpasses it in Clytemnestra's sadistic delight at having added Cassandra to the orgiastic slaughter:

> Now hear you this, the right behind my sacrament:
> By my child's Justice driven to fulfilment, by
> her Wrath and Fury, to whom I sacrificed this man,
> the hope that walks my chambers is not traced with fear
> while yet Aegisthus makes the fire shine on my hearth,
> my good friend, now as always, who shall be for us
> the shield of our defiance, no weak thing; while he,
> this other, is fallen, stained with this woman you behold,
> plaything of all the golden girls at Ilium;
> and here lies she, the captive of his spear, who saw
> wonders, who shared his bed, the wise in revelations
> and loving mistress, who yet knew the feel as well
> of the men's rowing benches. Their reward is not
> unworthy. He lies there; and she who swanlike cried
> aloud her lyric mortal lamentation out
> is laid against his fond heart, and to me has given
> a delicate excitement to my bed's delight.

It is wonderfully clear that Clytemnestra's hatred for Agamemnon is sexual, a woman's resentment of a male weaker than herself, who rules over her only because of gender. Her pride in her double-murder is exuberant, and her hatred extends both to Zeus and to Cassandra. Ironically extending reverence to Zeus as "lord of dead men underneath the ground," she implies a hatred towards him as well, presumably as supreme male. But why does she relish her murder of Cassandra, a captive? There is a sexual element in this hatred also: it is as though Clytemnestra has manned herself in unmanning Agamemnon.

Her final outcry is made to Orestes, just before he takes her inside the house to kill her:

> You are the snake I gave birth to, and gave the breast.

Her defiance and bitterness, her refusal of guilt or remorse, remains compellingly steadfast.

SOPHOCLES

I

Whether there is a "tragic flaw", a *hamartia*, in King Oedipus is uncertain,
though I doubt it, as he is hardly a figure who shoots wide of the mark.
Accuracy is implicit in his nature. We can be certain that he is free of that
masterpiece of ambivalence—Freud's Oedipal complex. In the Age of Freud,
we are uncertain what to do with a guiltless Oedipus, but that does appear to
be the condition of Sophocles' hero. We cannot read *Oedipus the King* as we
read the *Iliad* of Homer, where the gods matter enormously. And even more,
we know it is absurd to read Oedipus as though it were written by Yahwist,
or the authors of Jeremiah or Job, let alone of the Gospels. We can complete
our obstacle course by warning ourselves not to compound Oedipus with
Hamlet or *Lear*. Homer and the Bible, Shakespeare and Freud, teach us only
how not to read Sophocles.

When I was younger, I was persuaded by Cedric Whitman's eloquent
book on Sophocles to read Oedipus as a tragedy of "heroic humanism." I am
not so persuaded now, not because I am less attracted by a humanistic
heroism, but because I am uncertain how such a stance allows for tragedy.
William Blake's humanism was more than heroic, being apocalyptic, but it
too would not authorize tragedy. However the meaning of Oedipus is to be
interpreted in our post–Nietzchean age, the play is surely tragedy, or the
genre will lose coherence. E.R. Dodds, perhaps assimilating Sophocles to the
Iliad, supposed that the tragedy of Oedipus honored the gods, without
judging them to be benign or even just. Bernard Knox argues that the
greatness of the gods and the greatness of Oedipus are irreconcilable, with
tragedy the result of that schism. That reduces to the Hegelian view of
tragedy as an agon between right and right, but Knox gives the preference to
Oedipus, since the gods, being ever victorious, therefore cannot be heroic. A
less Homeric reading than Dodds's, this seems to me too much our sense of
heroism—Malraux perhaps, rather than Sophocles.

Freud charmingly attributed to Sophocles, as a precursor of
psychoanalysis, the ability to have made possible a self–analysis for the
playgoer. But then Freud called *Oedipus* an "immoral play," since the gods
ordained incest and patricide. Oedipus therefore participates in our universal
unconscious sense of guilt, but on this reading so do the gods. I sometimes
wish that Freud had turned to Aeschylus instead, and given us the
Prometheus complex rather than the Oedipus complex. Plato is Oedipal in
regard to Homer, but Sophocles is not. I hardly think that Sophocles would
have chastised Homer for impiety, but then, as I read it, the tragedy of

Oedipus takes up no more skeptical stance than that of Plato, unless one interprets Plato as Montaigne wished to interpret him.

What does any discerning reader remember most vividly about *Oedipus the King*? Almost certainly, the answer must be the scene of the king's self–blinding, as narrated by the second messenger, here in David Grene's version:

> You did not see the sight.
> Yet in so far as I remember it
> You'll hear the end of our unlucky queen.
> When she came raging into the house she went
> straight to her marriage bed, tearing her hair
> with both her hands, and crying upon Laius
> long dead—Do you remember, Laius,
> that night long past which bred a child for us
> to send you to your death and leave
> a mother making children with her son?
> And then she groaned and cursed the bed in which
> she brought forth husband by her husband, children
> by her own child, an infamous double bond.
> How after that she died I do not know,—
> for Oedipus distracted us from seeing.
> He burst upon us shouting and we looked
> to him as he paced frantically around,
> begging us always: Give me a sword, I say,
> to find this wife no wife, this mother's womb,
> this field of double sowing whence I sprang
> and where I sowed my children! As he raved
> some god showed him the way—none of us there.
> Bellowing terribly and led by some
> invisible guide he rushed on the two doors, —
> wrenching the hollow bolts out of their sockets,
> he charges inside. There, there, we saw his wife
> hanging, the twisted rope around her neck.
> When he saw her, he cried out fearfully
> and cut loose the dangling noose. Then, as she lay,
> poor woman, on the ground, what happened after,
> was terrible to see. He tore the brooches—
> the gold chased brooches fastening her robe—
> away from her and lifting them high
> dashed them on his own eyeballs, shrieking out

such things as: they will never see the crime
I have committed or had done upon me!
Dark eyes, now on the days to come, look on
forbidden faces, do not recognize
those whom you long for—with such imprecations
he struck his eyes again and yet again
with the brooches. And the bleeding eyeballs gushed
and stained his beard—no sluggish oozing drops
but a black rain and bloody hail poured down.
So it has broken—and not on one head
but troubles mixed for husband and wife.
The fortune of the days gone by was true
good fortune—but today groans and destruction
and death and shame—of all ills can be named
not one is missing.
(1.1238–86.)

The scene, too terrible for acting out, seems also too dreadful for
representation in language. Oedipus, desiring to put a sword in the womb of
Jocasta, is led by "some god" to where he can break through the two doors
(I shudder as I remember Walt Whitman's beautiful trope for watching a
woman in childbirth, "I recline by the sills of the exquisite flexible doors").
Fortunately finding Jocasta self–slain, lest he add the crime of matricide to
patricide and incest, Oedipus, repeatedly stabbing his eyes with Jocasta's
brooches, passes judgment not so much upon seeing as upon the seen, and so
upon the light by which we see. I interpret this as his protest against Apollo,
which brings both the light and the plague. The Freudian trope of blinding
for castration seems to me less relevant here than the outcry against the god.

To protest Apollo is necessarily dialectical, since the pride and agility of
the intellect of Oedipus, remorselessly searching out the truth, in some sense
is also against the nature of truth. In this vision of reality, you shall know the
truth, and the truth will make you mad. What would make Oedipus free?
Nothing that happens in this play, must be the answer, nor does it seem that
becoming an oracular god later on makes you free either. If you cannot be
free of the gods, then you cannot be made free, and even acting as though
your daemon is your destiny will not help you either.

The startling ignorance of Oedipus when the drama begins is the *given*
of the play, and cannot be questioned or disallowed. Voltaire was scathing
upon this, but the ignorance of the wise and the learned remains an ancient
truth of psychology, and torments us every day. I surmise that this is the true

force of Freud's Oedipus complex: not the unconscious sense of guilt, but the necessity of ignorance, lest the reality–principle destroy us. Nietzsche said it not in praise of art, but so as to indicate the essential limitation of art. Sophoclean irony is more eloquent yet:

> CREON: Do not seek to be master in everything, for the
> things you mastered did not follow you throughout
> your life.
>
> *(As Creon and Oedipus go out.)*

> CHORUS: You that live in my ancestral Thebes, behold
> this Oedipus,—him who knew the famous riddles
> and was a man most masterful; not a citizen who
> did not look with envy on his lot—see him now
> and see the breakers of misfortune swallow him!
> Look upon that last day always. Count no mortal
> happy till he has passed the final limit of his life se-
> cure from pain.
>
> (1. 1521–30)

II

Sophocles was a child of three or four when Aeschylus presented his first tragedy, in 499 B.C.E. At twenty-eight, Sophocles won the first prize competing against Aeschylus, and until 456, when Aeschylus died, there must have been many contests between the two. Sophocles's *Electra* has a complex relation to Aeschylus's *Libation-Bearers*, which was the second play of a trilogy; in Sophocles's case, *Electra* stood alone.

I intend to contrast *Electra* and the *Libation-Bearers*, employing Richmond Lattimore's version of the Aeschylus, and the new translation of the Sophocles by the Canadian poet Anne Carson. Carson, a major poet and a classical scholar, cites Virginia Woolf's essay, "On Not Knowing Greek," from *The Common Reader*. Woolf remarks that Electra's cries "give angle and outline to the play," and Carson (who shows a dark affinity for Electra) writes a remarkable foreword, emphasizing Electra's horror of the evil in her life, a horror virtually beyond measure: "she is someone off the scale." Strikingly comparing the Electra of Sophocles to Emily Dickinson's "equally private religion of pain," Carson observes that: "They touch a null point at the centre of the woman's soul."

Woolf, Dickinson, and Carson perhaps have only their literary greatness in common, and yet Carson's translation teaches us to uncover the

Sophoclean Electra in the novelist and in both poets. Electra's grief is passionately personal in Sophocles, as John Jones noted in his *On Aristotle and Greek Tragedy*. "Personal" seems not strong enough, because we have debased the word, as when we speak of a "personal letter." That is too far from "Electra's private language of screams," as Carson phrases it, and too far also from Woolf's *Three Guineas*, Dickinson's Master poems, and Carson's tangos, *The Beauty of the Husband*.

In the *Libation-Bearers*, Electra is perhaps more angry than pained, a princess who fiercely resents her debasement, and who centers her love upon Orestes. The Electra of Sophocles has a death-absorbed imagination, as Carson says, and suffers the negation of her own sexuality. Here is Aeschylus's Electra, craving revenge, and unwilling to abandon life:

> Almighty herald of the world above, the world
> below: Hermes, lord of the dead, help me; announce
> my prayers to the charmed spirits underground, who watch
> over my father's house, that they may hear. Tell Earth
> herself, who brings all things to birth, who gives them strength,
> then gathers their big yield into herself at last.
> I myself pour these lustral waters to the dead,
> and speak, and call upon my father: Pity me;
> pity your own Orestes. How shall we be lords
> in our house? We have been sold, and go as wanderers
> because our mother bought herself, for us, a man,
> Aegisthus, he who helped her hand to cut you down.
> Now I am what a slave is, and Orestes lives
> outcast from his great properties, while they go proud
> in the high style and luxury of what you worked
> to win. By some good fortune let Orestes come
> back home. Such is my prayer, my father. Hear me; hear.
> And for myself, grant that I be more temperate
> of heart than my mother; that I act with purer hand.
>
> Such are my prayers for us; but for our enemies,
> father, I pray that your avenger come, that they
> who killed you shall be killed in turn, as they deserve.
> Between my prayer for good and prayer for good I set
> this prayer for evil; and I speak it against Them.
> For us, bring blessings up into the world. Let Earth
> and conquering Justice, and all gods beside, give aid.

Such are my prayers; and over them I pour these drink
offerings. Yours the strain now, yours to make them flower
with mourning song, and incantation for the dead.

This woman contrasts sharply to the Sophoclean Electra:

Alright then, you tell me one thing—
at what point does the evil level off in my life?
you say ignore the deed—is that right?
Who could approve this?
It defies human instinct!
Such ethics make no sense to me.
And how could I nestle myself in a life of ease

while my father lies out in the cold,
outside honor?
My cries are wings:
they pierce the cage.
For if a dead man is earth and nothing,
if a dead man is void and dead space lying,
if a dead man's murderers
do not give
blood for blood
to pay for this,
then shame does not exist.
Human reverence
is gone.

Electra is believed to have come late in Sophocles's career, and the
celebrated irony of *Oedipus Tyrannus* seems far away. The dramatic ironies of
Electra turn upon freedom, rather than knowledge. Orestes frees Electra
from her immediate torments, but he has arrived too late to save her from
the negativity that has become her nature. Knowledge cannot liberate
Oedipus: to know the truth causes the agony in which he blinds himself. It
may even be that pity in Sophocles is only another irony. Electra, in Carson's
version, cannot be said to have suffered and then broken free. Throwing the
corpse of Aegisthus to the dogs will not cut the knot of evils inside Electra.
Her irony is simply that there is no correcting the past, least of all for
women.

EURIPIDES

E.R. Dodds, in his splendid edition of the *Bacchae* (1944, 1960), explains not only the nature of Dionysiac religion, but remarks also the particular place of the play in the work of Euripides. The poet, over seventy, left Athens for Macedonia in 408 B.C.E., and never returned, dying in the winter of 407–406. In abandoning Athens, Euripides may well have felt defeated by public taste and poetic satirists. At least he did not have to endure the *Frogs* of Aristophanes, presented at Athens the year after his death. In the *Frogs*, Dionysus goes down into Hades in order to bring back a tragic poet-playwright, severely lacking in Athens after the death of the three great figures: Aeschylus, Sophocles, Euripides. Poor Euripides is savaged by Aristophanes, though nowhere near so viciously as Socrates was debased in the *Clouds*.

Dodds, still the authority upon the Greeks and the irrational, reads the *Bacchae* as being beyond any single stance by Euripides upon the Dionysiac. Euripides presents Dionysus as soft and sinister, a fatal androgyne of a god. Pentheus, the god's destined victim, also receives an equivocal representation. Neither the god nor the tyrant moves our sympathy as audience or readers.

The *Bacchae* was not presented in Athens until after the death of Euripides. We do not have a complete text of the play, but what is missing is not necessarily central. In the Hellenistic period and in Rome, the *Bacchae* was very popular, and still seems the masterpiece of Euripides's nineteen extant tragedies. William Arrowsmith, whose turbulent, wonderful translation I will employ here, compares the *Bacchae* in eminence to Sophocles's *Oedipus Tyrannus* and Aeschylus's *Agamemnon*. Like those plays, the *Bacchae* makes us into what Shakespeare called "wonder-wounded hearers." Oedipus and Clytemnestra find their rival in Euripides's uncanny Dionysus, who is a triumph of representation: disturbing, fascinating, ultimately terrifying.

Dionysiac worship came late to Hellas, and did not attempt to supplant the Olympian pantheon. In Hellenistic Alexandria and in Rome, Dionysus became Bacchus the wine-god, but in earlier Hellas he was a more comprehensive divinity, emblematic of natural abundance, of flowering life, the Power in the tree. The Maenads in the *Bacchae* have drunk no wine (Pentheus is wrong about this) but are ecstatic through mountain-dancing, a shamanistic practice, restricted in Hellas to women's societies, and still carried on by certain group of women in the United States today. Dodds is eloquent on Dionysiac dance:

... he is the cause of madness and the liberator from madness ...
To resist Dionysus is to repress the elemental in one's own nature;
the punishment is the sudden complete collapse ... when the
elemental breaks through...

This Dionysiac dance of enthusiastic women culminated in a *sparagmos*,
in which an animal body was torn apart and devoured raw, thus repeating the
Titanic act of rending and consuming the infant Dionysus. The women who
destroy Pentheus think he is a lion; more usually the Bacchantes ripped
asunder and ate a bull, whose innate strength of resistance testifies to the
daemonic ferocity imparted by Dionysus to his Maenads. There is some
evidence of human sacrifice and ritual murder associated with Dionysiac
celebration in the classical world. The Bacchantes achieved both the vitality
of animal life and the group ecstasy in which individual consciousness
vanished, for a time.

The origins of this shamanism may have been in Thrace, but in any
rate it was tamed in Hellas, until the dark times of the Peloponnesian War,
when it returned under the name of various mystery gods: Attis, Adonis, and
Sabazius, to be deprecated and attacked by Plato, among others.

Dodds categorizes the *Bacchae* as the most severely formalized of
Euripides's plays, and warns us against seeing it either as an exaltation of
Dionysus or as an enlightened protest against orgiastic religions, since
Penthues is very hard to like, and Dionysus is absolutely beyond human
moral categories. There is a renewed force in the aged, self-exiled Euripides
of the *Bacchae*, but it is neither Dionysiac nor counter-Dionysiac. Euripides,
at the end, perfected his own art as poet-dramatist. It is as though he
answered his enemy Aristophanes in advance, by demonstrating that, in his
own way, he could raise himself to the Sublime measure of Sophocles and of
Aeschylus.

William Arroswmith was a great humanist, who died in 1992, fighting
heroically against the tides of Resentment that since have totally drowned
humanism in the universities of the English-speaking world. I mourn him
still, as we were close friends, and he restored my spirits, each time we met. A
lover of both Euripides and Aristophanes, he refrained from translating the
Frogs, while giving us superb version of the *Birds* and the *Clouds*, and of the
Bacchae and four other tragedies by Euripides. Arrowsmith saw in the *Bacchae*,
as in *Hippolytus* and in *Heracles*, an unique Euripidean compassion: "the pity
that is born from shared suffering." To Arrowsmith, this was Euripidean
humanism: "that faith and that fate which, in Euripides, makes man human,
not mere god." Whether Arrowsmith, in his moral generosity and genial

humaneness, imparted his own qualities to Euripides seems to me something of a question. Here is the close of the play, in Arrowsmith's version:

AGAVE:
I pity you, Father.

CADMUS:
    And I pity you, my child,
    and I grieve for your poor sisters. I pity them.

AGAVE:
    Terribly has Dionysus brought
    disaster down upon this house.

DIONYSUS:
    I was terribly blasphemed,
    my name dishonored in Thebes.

AGAVE:
    Farewell, Father.

CADMUS:
    Farewell to you, unhappy child.
    Fare well. But you shall find your faring hard.
    (Exit Cadmus)

AGAVE:
    Lead me, guides, where my sisters wait,
    poor sisters of my exile. Let me go
    where I shall never see Cithaeron more,
    where that accursed hill may not see me,
    where I shall find no trace of thyrsus!
    That I leave to other Bacchae.
    (Exit Agave with attendants.)

CHORUS:
    The gods have many shapes.
    The gods bring many things
    to their accomplishment.
    And what was most expected

has not been accomplished.
But god has found his way
for what no man expected.
So ends the play.

I hear ironies that are far stronger than the traumatized pity exchanged by Cadmus and his daughter Agave, who has led the Bacchantes in slaying her own son, Pentheus. Were I a director, I would be at a loss to tell the actor playing Dionysus how to speak his frightening lines: perhaps tonelessly, or at least matter-of-fact? An actress can do virtually anything with the blinding irony of: "That I leave to other Bacchae." Since the chorus are Asian Maenads, they are no problem: their tone is triumphant, if no longer ecstatic. Tragic irony is stronger in Euripides than is any humanism. If Aristophanes attended the *Bacchae*, he would have had his view of Euripidean nihilism confirmed. But that is what I find most Shakespearean about Euripides, whose own uncanniness somehow gets into the Shakespeare of *Troilus and Cressida*.

ARISTOPHANES

"There is a God, and his name is Aristophanes"
—*Heinrich Heine*

Of the eleven extant comedies of Aristophanes, the *Birds* seems best of all to me, perhaps because it is even more outrageous than the *Clouds* and the *Frogs*. Aristophanes, outraged by his Athens and his Hellas, turned outrageousness into all but the highest art, to be surpassed only by the greatest of the Shakespearean comedies. Fortunately, we have a superb version of the *Birds* by the late William Arrowsmith, which is the text I will rely upon here.

Arrowsmith avoids the deep pit into which so many of the translators of Aristophanes have tumbled, which is to make the *Birds* or the *Clouds* ring forth like Gilbert and Sullivan. Though imperial Athens in 414 B.C.E. had its parallels with Victorian Britain, W.S. Gilbert's England was not treading near disaster. In 415–414, when Alcibiades and his Athenian fleet sailed off to the Sicilian catastrophe, Athens was a place of hysteria, political frenzy, McCarthyite witch-hunting, and balked aggressivity. Aristophanes therefore sends forth his two confidence men, the daemonic Pisthetairos (let us call him "Plausible," which his name means) and his accomplice Euelpides ("Hopeful") to the wilderness of the Birds. There they suborn Hoopoe, who helps persuade all the other Birds to join in the Plausible-Hopeful project of building a New City, Cloudcuckooland. This City of the Birds will usurp the air-space between Olympus and Athens and so will come to dominate both. At the play's end, Plausible (who should have been played by the late Zero Mostel) is crowned King of the cosmos, displacing Zeus, and marries Miss Universe. The wedding feast is a delicious stew of jailbirds, victims of the Athenian-style "democracy" of King Plausible.

Any summary of outrageousness necessarily fails, particularly because Aristophanes, in an antithetical reaction to Athenian disaster, is in hilarious high spirits throughout the *Birds*. Moses Hadas usefully remarks that Aristophanes "erases the world that is and constructs another," which is in part what Heine meant when he proclaimed: "There is a God and his name is Aristophanes." As befits God, Aristophanes in the *Birds* avoids bitterness, happy to escape with us to Cloudcuckooland.

Prometheus, being a Titan and so anti-Olympian, arrives to offer pragmatic counsel to Plausible:

PROMETHEUS:
But give me your attention. At present these Triballoi gods
have joined with Zeus to send an official embassy
to sue for peace. Now here's the policy you must follow:
flatly reject any offers of peace they make you
until Zeus agrees to restore his sceptre to the Birds
and consents to give you Miss Universe as your wife.

PISTHETAIROS:
But who's Miss Universe?

PROMETHEUS:
A sort of Beauty Queen,
the sign of Empire and the symbol of divine supremacy.
It's she who keeps the keys to Zeus' thunderbolts
and all his other treasures—Divine Wisdom,
Good Government, Common Sense, Naval Bases,
Slander, Libel, Political Graft, Sops to the Voters—

PISTHETAIROS:
And *she* keeps the keys?

PROMETHEUS:
   Take it from me, friend.
   Marry Miss Universe and the world is yours.
   —You understand
   why I had to tell you this? As Prometheus, after all,
   my philanthropy is proverbial.

PISTHETAIROS:
   Yes, we worship you
   as the inventor of the barbecue.

PROMETHEUS:

                                   Besides, I loathe the gods.

PISTHETAIROS:
               The loathing's mutual, I know.

PROMETHEUS:

                                   Just call me Timon:
   I'm a misanthrope of gods.

                                   —But I must be running along.
   Give me my parasol. If Zeus spots me now,
   he'll think I'm an ordinary one-god procession. I'll pretend
   to be the girl behind the boy behind the basket.

PISTHETAIROS:
   Here—take this stool and watch yourself march by.

   Exit Prometheus in solemn procession, draped in his blanket, the
   umbrella in one hand, the stool in the other. Pisthetairos and the
   Attendants retire.

This is the *Birds* in miniature, wonderfully relevant to the present-day
United States, where Plausible II rules as our court-selected President. The
sop to the Voters is of course the six-hundred-dollar-tax-rebate, even though
the equivalents of Miss Universe tempted our previous ruler. Aristophanes is
at his most amiable when he ends with the apotheosis of Plausible. We live
in Cloudcuckooland, and why should we not?

FRIEDRICH SCHILLER

The Use of the Chorus in Tragedy

A poetical work must vindicate itself:—if the execution be defective, little aid can be derived from commentaries.

On these grounds, I might safely leave the Chorus to be its own advocate, if we had ever seen it presented in an appropriate manner. But it must be remembered that a dramatic composition first assumes the character of a whole by means of representation on the stage. The poet supplies only the words, to which, in a lyrical tragedy, music and rhythmical motion are essential accessories. It follows, then, that if the Chorus is deprived of accompaniments appealing so powerfully to the senses, it will appear a superfluity in the economy of the drama—a mere hindrance to the development of the plot—destructive to the illusion of the scene, and wearisome to the spectators.

To do justice to the Chorus, more especially if our aims in poetry be of a grand and elevated character, we must transport ourselves from the actual to a possible stage. It is the privilege of art to furnish for itself whatever is requisite, and the accidental deficiency of auxiliaries ought not to confine the plastic imagination of the poet. He aspires to whatever is most dignified, he labours to realise the ideal in his own mind—though in the execution of his purpose he must needs accommodate himself to circumstances.

The assertion so commonly made, that the public degrades art, is not well founded. It is the artist that brings the public to the level of his own

From *The Maid of Orleans, The Bride of Messina, Wilhelm Tell, Demetrius,* translated by Sir Theodore Martin, Anna Swanwick, and A. Lodge. © 1903 by John C. Nimmo, Ltd.

conceptions; and, in every age in which art has gone to decay, it has fallen through its professors. The people need feeling alone, and feeling they possess. They take their station before the curtain with an unvoiced longing, with a multifarious capacity. They bring with them an aptitude for what is highest—they derive the greatest pleasure from what is judicious and true; and if, with these powers of appreciation, they design to be satisfied with inferior productions, still, if they have once tasted what is excellent, they will, in the end, insist on having it supplied to them.

It is sometimes objected that the poet may labour according to an ideal—that the critic may judge from ideas, but that mere executive art is subject to contingencies, and depends for effect on the occasion. Managers will be obstinate; actors are bent on display—the audience is inattentive and unruly. Their object is relaxation, and they are disappointed if mental exertion be required, when they expected only amusement. But if the theatre be made instrumental toward higher objects, the pleasure of the spectator will not be increased, but ennobled. It will be a diversion, but a poetical one. All art is dedicated to pleasure, and there can be no higher and worthier end than to make men happy. The true art is that which provides the highest degree of pleasure; and this consists in the abandonment of the spirit to the free play of all its faculties.

Every one expects from the imaginative arts a certain emancipation from the bounds of reality: we are willing to give a scope to fancy, and recreate ourselves with the possible. The man who expects it the least will nevertheless forget his ordinary pursuits, his every-day existence and individuality, and experience delight from uncommon incidents:—if he be of a serious turn of mind, he will acknowledge on the stage that moral government of the world which he fails to discover in real life. But he is, at the same time, perfectly aware that all is an empty show, and that, in a true sense, he is feeding only on dreams. When he returns from the theatre to the world of realities, he is again compressed within its narrow bounds; he is its denizen as before—for it remains what it was, and in him nothing has been changed. What, then, has he gained beyond a momentary illusive pleasure which vanished with the occasion?

It is because a passing recreation is alone desired, that a mere show of truth is thought sufficient. I mean that probability or vraisemblance which is so highly esteemed, but which the commonest workers are able to substitute for the true.

Art has for its object not merely to afford a transient pleasure, to excite to a momentary dream of liberty; its aim is to make us absolutely free; and this it accomplishes by awakening, exercising, and perfecting in us a power to remove to an objective distance the sensible world; (which otherwise only burdens us as rugged matter and presses us down with a brute influence); to transform it into the free working of our spirit, and thus acquire a dominion over the material by means of ideas. For the very reason also that true art requires somewhat of the objective and real, it is not satisfied with a show of truth. It rears its ideal edifice on truth itself—on the solid and deep foundations of nature.

But how art can be at once altogether ideal, yet in the strictest sense real;—how it can entirely leave the actual, and yet harmonise with nature, is a problem to the multitude:—and hence the distorted views which prevail in regard to poetical and plastic works; for to ordinary judgments these two requisites seem to counteract each other.

It is commonly supposed that one may be attained by the sacrifice of the other:—the result is a failure to arrive at either. One to whom nature has given a true sensibility, but denied the plastic imaginative power, will be a faithful painter of the real; he will adapt casual appearances, but never catch the spirit of nature. He will only reproduce to us the matter of the world, which, not being our own work, the product of our creative spirit, can never have the beneficent operation of art, of which the essence is freedom. Serious, indeed, but unpleasing, is the cast of thought with which such an artist and poet dismisses us;—we feel ourselves painfully thrust back into the narrow sphere of reality by means of the very art which ought to have emancipated us. On the other hand, a writer, endowed with a lively fancy, but destitute of warmth and individuality of feeling, will not concern himself in the least about truth; he will sport with the stuff of the world, and endeavour to surprise by whimsical combinations; and as his whole performance is nothing but foam and glitter, he will, it is true, engage the attention for a time, but build up and confirm nothing in the understanding. His playfulness is, like the gravity of the other, thoroughly unpoetical. To string together at will fantastical images, is not to travel into the realm of the ideal; and the imitative reproduction of the actual cannot be called the representation of nature. Both requisites stand so little in contradiction to each other that they are rather one and the same thing; that art is only true insomuch as it altogether forsakes the actual, and becomes purely ideal. Nature herself is an idea of the mind, and is never presented to the senses. She lies under the veil of appearances, but is herself never apparent. To the art of the ideal alone is lent, or, rather, absolutely given, the privilege to grasp the spirit of the all, and bind it in a corporeal form.

Yet, in truth, even Art cannot present it to the senses, but by means of her creative power to the imaginative faculty alone; and it is thus that she becomes more true than all reality, and more real than all experience. It follows from these premises that the artist can use no single element taken from reality as he finds it—that his work must be ideal in all its parts, if it be designed to have, as it were, an intrinsic reality, and to harmonise with nature.

What is true of art and póetry, in the abstract, holds good as to their various kinds; and we may apply what has been advanced to the subject of tragedy. In this department, it is still necessary to controvert the ordinary notion of the natural, with which poetry is altogether incompatible. A certain ideality has been allowed in painting, though, I fear, on grounds rather conventional than intrinsic; but in dramatic works what is desired is illusion, which, if it could be accomplished by means of the actual, would be, at best, a paltry deception. All the externals of a theatrical representation are opposed to this notion; all is merely a symbol of the real. The day itself in a theatre is an artificial one; the metrical dialogue is itself ideal; yet the conduct of the play must forsooth be real, and the general effect sacrificed to a part. Thus the French, who have utterly misconceived the spirit of the ancients, adopted on the stage the unities of time and place in the most common and empirical sense; as though there were any place but the bare ideal one, or any other time than the mere sequence of the incidents.

By the introduction of a metrical dialogue an important progress has been made toward the poetical tragedy. A few lyrical dramas have been successful on the stage, and poetry, by its own living energy, has triumphed over prevailing prejudices. But so long as these erroneous views are entertained little has been done—for it is not enough barely to tolerate as a poetic license that which is, in truth, the essence of all poetry. The introduction of the Chorus would be the last and decisive step; and if it only served this end, namely, to declare open and honourable warfare against naturalism in art, it would be for us a living wall which Tragedy had drawn around herself, to guard her from contact with the world of reality, and maintain her own ideal soil, her poetical freedom.

It is well known that the Greek tragedy had its origin in the Chorus; and though, in process of time, it became independent, still it may be said that poetically, and in spirit, the Chorus was the source of its existence, and that without these persevering supporters and witnesses of the incident a totally different order of poetry would have grown out of the drama. The abolition of the Chorus, and the debasement of this sensibly powerful organ into the characterless substitute of a confidant, is by no means such an improvement in tragedy as the French, and their imitators, would have it supposed to be.

The old tragedy, which at first only concerned itself with gods, heroes and kings, introduced the Chorus as an essential accompaniment. The poets found it in nature, and for that reason employed it. It grew out of the poetical aspect of real life. In the new tragedy it becomes an organ of art which aids in making the poetry prominent. The modern poet no longer finds the Chorus in nature; he must needs create and introduce it poetically; that is, he must resolve on such an adaptation of his story as will admit of its retrocession to those primitive times, and to that simple form of life.

The Chorus thus renders more substantial service to the modern dramatist than to the old poet—and for this reason, that it transforms the commonplace actual world into the old poetical one; that it enables him to dispense with all that is repugnant to poetry, and conducts him back to the most simple, original, and genuine motives of action. The palaces of kings are in these days closed—courts of justice have been transferred from the gates of cities to the interior of buildings; writing has narrowed the province of speech; the people itself—the sensibly living mass—when it does not operate as brute force, has become a part of the civil polity, and thereby an abstract idea in our minds; the deities have returned within the bosoms of mankind. The poet must reopen the palaces—he must place courts of justice beneath the canopy of heaven—restore the gods, reproduce every extreme which the artificial frame of actual life has abolished—throw aside every factitious influence on the mind or condition of man which impedes the manifestation of his inward nature and primitive character, as the statuary rejects modern costume:—and of all external circumstances adopts nothing but what is palpable in the highest of forms—that of humanity.

But precisely as the painter throws around his figures draperies of ample volume, to fill up the space of his picture richly and gracefully, to arrange its several parts in harmonious masses, to give due play to colour, which charms and refreshes the eye—and at once to envelop human forms in a spiritual veil, and make them visible—so the tragic poet inlays and entwines his rigidly contracted plot and the strong outlines of his characters with a tissue of lyrical magnificence, in which, as in flowing robes of purple, they move freely and nobly, with a sustained dignity and exalted repose.

In a higher organisation, the material, or the elementary, need not be visible; the chemical colour vanishes in the finer tints of the imaginative one. The material, however, has its peculiar effect, and may be included in an artistical composition. But it must deserve its place by animation, fulness, and harmony, and give value to the ideal forms which it surrounds, instead of stifling them by its weight.

In respect of the pictorial art, this is obvious to ordinary apprehension, yet in poetry likewise, and in the tragical kind, which is our immediate subject, the same doctrine holds good. Whatever fascinates the senses alone is mere matter, and the rude element of a work of art:—if it take the lead it will inevitably destroy the poetical—which lies at the exact medium between the ideal and the sensible. But man is so constituted that he is ever impatient to pass from what is fanciful to what is common; and reflection must, therefore, have its place even in tragedy. But to merit this place it must, by means of delivery, recover what it wants in actual life; for if the two elements of poetry, the ideal and the sensible, do not operate with an inward mutuality, they must at least act as allies—or poetry is out of the question. If the balance be not intrinsically perfect, the equipoise can only be maintained by an agitation of both scales.

This is what the Chorus effects in tragedy. It is, in itself, not an individual but a general conception; yet it is represented by a palpable body which appeals to the senses with an imposing grandeur. It forsakes the contracted sphere of the incidents to dilate itself over the past and future, over distant times and nations, and general humanity, to deduce the grand results of life, and pronounce the lessons of wisdom. But all this it does with the full power of fancy—with a bold lyrical freedom which ascends, as with godlike step, to the topmost height of worldly things; and it effects it in conjunction with the whole sensible influence of melody and rhythm, in tones and movements.

The Chorus thus exercises a purifying influence on tragic poetry, insomuch as it keeps reflection apart from the incidents, and by this separation arms it with a poetical vigour; as the painter, by means of a rich drapery, changes the ordinary poverty of costume into a charm and an ornament.

But as the painter finds himself obliged to strengthen the tone of colour of the living subject, in order to counterbalance the material influences—so the lyrical effusions of the Chorus impose upon the poet the necessity of a proportionate elevation of his general diction. It is the Chorus alone which entitles the poet to employ this fulness of tone, which at once charms the senses, pervades the spirit, and expands the mind. This one giant form on his canvas obliges him to mount all his figures on the cothurnus, and thus impart a tragical grandeur to his picture. If the Chorus be taken away, the diction of the tragedy must generally be lowered, or what is now great and majestic will appear forced and overstrained. The old Chorus introduced into the French tragedy would present it in all its poverty, and reduce it to nothing; yet, without doubt, the same accompaniment would impart to Shakespeare's tragedy its true significance.

As the Chorus gives life to the language—so also it gives repose to the action; but it is that beautiful and lofty repose which is the characteristic of a true work of art. For the mind of the spectator ought to maintain its freedom through the most impassioned scenes; it should not be the mere prey of impressions, but calmly and severely detach itself from the emotions which it suffers. The commonplace objection made to the Chorus, that it disturbs the illusion, and blunts the edge of the feelings, is what constitutes its highest recommendation; for it is this blind force of the affections which the true artist deprecates—this illusion is what he disdains to excite. If the strokes which tragedy inflicts on our bosoms followed without respite—the passion would overpower the action. We should mix ourselves up with the subject matter, and no longer stand above it. It is by holding asunder the different parts, and stepping between the passions with its composing views, that the Chorus restores to us our freedom, which would else be lost in the tempest. The characters of the drama need this intermission in order to collect themselves; for they are no real beings who obey the impulse of the moment, and merely represent individuals—but ideal persons and representatives of their species, who enunciate the deep things of humanity.

Thus much on my attempt to revive the old Chorus on the tragic stage. It is true that choruses are not unknown to modern tragedy; but the Chorus of the Greek drama, as I have employed it—the Chorus, as a single ideal person, furthering and accompanying the whole plot—is of an entirely distinct character; and when, in discussion on the Greek tragedy, I hear mention made of choruses, I generally suspect the speaker's ignorance of his subject. In my view the Chorus has never been reproduced since the decline of the old tragedy.

I have divided it into two parts, and represented it in contest with itself; but this occurs where it acts as a real person, and as an unthinking multitude. As Chorus and an ideal person it is always one and entire. I have also several times dispensed with its presence on the stage. For this liberty I have the example of Æschylus, the creator of tragedy, and Sophocles, the greatest master of his art.

Another license it may be more difficult to excuse. I have blended together the Christian religion and the Pagan mythology, and introduced recollections of the Moorish superstition. But the scene of the drama is Messina—where these three religions either exercised a living influence, or appealed to the senses in monumental remains. Besides, I consider it a privilege of poetry to deal with different religions as a collective whole, in which everything that bears an individual character, and expresses a peculiar mode of feeling, has its place. Religion itself, the idea of a Divine Power, lies under the veil of all religions; and it must be permitted to the poet to represent it in the form which appears the most appropriate to his subject.

LANE COOPER

Introduction to *Ten Greek Plays*

The air is pure and cool; it is a sunbright morning near the end of March, at Athens, and the year, let us say, 429 B.C. Three days ago began the great annual feast of the City Dionysia, most impressive of the festivals of Bacchus; an ancient image of the god, patron of the tragic and comic drama, was taken from his shrine, escorted in a grand and colorful procession to a grove in the country, and, after a day of feasting and merriment for young and old, brought back by torch-light to Athens to be set up in the orchestra of his theatre, there to witness the dithyrambic choral contests which ended yesterday, and the dramatic contests of to-day, to-morrow, and the day thereafter. Over one hundred years ago (535 B.C.) Thespis took part in the earliest competition of tragic poets that was authorized by the State. Seventy years ago (499) Aeschylus began competing; fifty-five years ago (484), at the age of fortyone, he first won the coveted prize, an honor that fell to him thirteen times, all told, before he died. In 484 Sophocles was thirteen years old, Euripides an infant of one year; when he was a child of four, the Greeks overthrew the Persians in the seafight at Salamis. Thirty-nine years ago (468) Aeschylus lost the prize to Sophocles, who then began to compete. Ten years later (458) Aeschylus, on his last appearance, won with the Orestean trilogy; he died in 456, the year before Euripides first had plays accepted for presentation. In the year 429, therefore, Euripides and Sophocles have been rival tragic poets for a quarter of a century. They will be rivals for a quarter

From *Ten Greek Plays*, translated by Gilbert Murray and others. © 1929 by Oxford University Press.

25

of a century more with the watchful eye of Aristophanes upon them; we may suppose that he is in the audience to-day, a stripling sixteen years of age. Sophocles is now sixty-eight years old, still at the height of his powers; and this morning we may imagine that among the four plays he will present will be *Oedipus the King*. As a rule, on each of three successive mornings there are a satyr-drama and three tragedies; on the first two afternoons corresponding there will be two comedies, on the third, but one. In the days of Aeschylus, a group of three plays, a trilogy, might deal with phases of the same tragic story, and if the fourth play, the satyr-drama which then followed, dealt with that theme in a humorous way, we should have a tetralogy proper. Sophocles does not thus link his plays together; at times, following ancient custom, he does act in them, though taking but some minor part. In the dramatic competitions, then, three tragic poets have been, and are, engaged, as authors, trainers, and actors; and, similarly, five comic poets, each presenting one comedy. This will not, we predict, be one of the twenty occasions on which Sophocles is victor in tragedy, for the group of plays including *Oedipus the King* will be adjudged second to the group exhibited by Philocles, nephew of Aeschylus. Two years ago the *Medea* of Euripides fared even worse. There may be five judges for tragedy, as there are five for comedy; the selection of them is an elaborate affair, partly by lot.

Open to the sky, the great theatre of Dionysus lies in his precinet and near his shrine, on the southern slope of the Acropolis, below the Parthenon. The wooden seats, arranged as a vast amphitheatre, will accommodate thousands of spectators, or a good share of the voting population of the city, with a number of boys, probably some women, some of the better-educated slaves, and many of the visitors who throng to Athens at this season. At the winter festival of the Lenaea, when the seas are inclement, fewer alien faces would be seen, and a comic poet would feel freer than he will to-day to ridicule the foibles of the city. The audience is brilliant and lively, and critical; it will audibly reveal its pleasure or displeasure in the action or the actors. It is equally sensitive to false cadence and to expressions of impiety, and is suspicious of improbabilities in the sequence of incident. Though capable of misjudging a play, and of attributing to an author the sentiment he utters as an actor in the imagined scene, it is the most intelligent audience a poet could hope for; or it will be such after Aristophanes and his fellows have shown on the comic stage what is out of proportion in Greek tragedy. For three generations this audience has been tutored by Aeschylus, Sophocles, Euripides, and their rivals. Many of the spectators have sung in a dithyrambic contest; many, in fact, have been members of a dramatic chorus, so that some actually have been trained by Aeschylus and Sophocles in the recitation and music of their plays. The influence of music and the drama has permeated the domestic and communal life of Athens.

Far beneath the topmost row of seats lies the orchestra, a circle 88 feet in diameter, where the actors and chorus jointly perform the play. Nearest to this circle, and to the statue of Dionysus, is the seat of his priest; in neighboring seats are the judges, other civic worthies, and notable visitors from other city-states. In the middle of the orchestra is an altar; at the rear, a long, low, wooden structure which serves for background, for entrance and exit, and for other ends of stage-presentation.

A Greek tragedy or comedy, we perceive, is in the nature of a civic religious rite, celebrated in a building that is devoted to a god. True, if the impulse from Dionysiac worship was strong in the beginnings of the drama, the natural human impulse to imitate was stronger in the end. Yet the choral Attic drama seems never wholly to have lost its original character; herein, therefore, it differs from the modern secular drama, which soon enough forgot its mediaeval origins in the Mass, in the service for Easter. Aeschylus took tragedy from the market-place to the precinct and theatre of Dionysus, and comedy later followed thither. The modern drama left the cathedral for the market-place; ultimately, it found abode in a type of building that descended through Rome from the Greek theatre. Greek tragedy took origin, it seems, from the improvising leaders of the early Bacchic dithyramb; it seems that the leader split off from the chorus to become an actor, the protagonist. In the chorus he was replaced by a new leader, who in turn was withdrawn by Aeschylus, and converted into a second actor. In various ways Aeschylus diminished the part taken by the chorus. The dithyrambic chorus was large, later numbering fifty; his dramatic chorus numbered twelve. And he drew plots not only from the tales of Dionysus, the satyrs, and Thebes, but from the entire epic cycle, taking 'slices,' as he said, 'from the great banquet of Homer.' Sophocles added a third to the complement of actors, an innovation that was adopted by Aeschylus, as in his *Agamemnon*, where indeed, for the last episode, one of the chorus may be temporarily a fourth actor; ordinarily three actors could fill a half-dozen or more parts. Sophocles, then, has subtracted a third person from the chorus, but, by a kind of restoration, has increased the tragic chorus from twelve to fifteen members. Moreover, in the time of Aeschylus, he developed scene-painting, and Aeschylus seems to have learned to do something for himself with that, too. Both these masters of a very complex art have taught the age much even about the affair of spectacle and outward presentation. Sophocles' weak voice will not let him take a leading part, as did Aeschylus at first, in his own plays; but, like Shakespeare and Moliére of later days, he is his own stagemanager.

He has trained his chorus and actors, and, with the help of a costumer, attended to their garb, masks, padding, and foot-wear. In the great theatre, his persons must be of heroic mould and stature. They have been carefully drilled in declamation, for they must be heard by an immense, and sometimes noisy, audience. Apart, however, from the noise and bustle in the seats, the acoustic function of this outdoor theatre is well-nigh perfect. Careful modulation of spoken words and choral song need not be lost. The note of tragedy is not too often strident; more often its voices are tense, its tones are dreary. When the audience is quiet with pity and fear, a sigh in the orchestra may be heard in the topmost seats.

The meaning of the words will not be concealed by the music, for, in this art, poetry, music, and rhythmical action unite to assist the understanding, as they combine to produce one emotional effect. If the dithyramb proper, as it developed side by side with tragedy, came to be something like a modern oratorio, then tragedy itself, say *Oedipus the King*, has its nearest counterpart in the best modern opera. There is this difference, however, that in Greek tragedy music in the stricter sense was intermittent, being supplied by the chorus and one flutist. The actors spoke most of their lines, yet delivered some others in an intoned chant, and sang the more lyrical passages as solos, or in duets or trios; or, again, they joined with the chorus in a song, for example, of lamentation. Since we know very little about Greek music, we can only infer its beauty in the drama from the verbal and metrical beauty of the choral odes and other songs in the extant works of the tragic poets and Aristophanes; these dramatists were, in truth, the greatest of the ancient lyrical poets. And we can but partly conceive the effect of a play in which the chorus was a group of finished dancers. Their statuesque poses and measured evolutions had the greatest share in producing the whole amazing spectacle of an Attic drama. The orchestra, or place of dancing, was the centre of the entire wheel.

The dramatist, then, had to be poet, musician, and expert in pantomimic dancing as well, a Molière and a Mozart in one. Sophocles was all these things, and more; we have seen that he was also a painter. He and Aeschylus were the chief developers of this inclusive poetic art from a choral dance into a form more comprehensive than is drama or opera in our modern sense; in modern opera the poetic art is feeble. And in modern times this art receives virtually no support from the State. In the age of Pericles all the arts received public encouragement. Painting, sculpture, architecture, music, flourished with all the rest, but drama above all others. The efforts of the poets were directly favored by the government, and by wealthy citizens. In particular, the cost of staging the play, and of supplying and training the chorus, was borne by a private citizen who, unless he volunteered for the service, was chosen by lot, and obliged to serve as 'choregus.' Perhaps the choregus for *Oedipus the King* was unwilling, and a niggard, and the group of plays failed through his parsimony. The rich choregus Antisthenes, who knew nothing about the arts, was always successful in his contests because he never shirked any expense in the preparations.

A poet is often thought to be a man with a singular gift of diction, with a flow of metaphor, and with a knack of composing in metre. The diction and metres of the Greek drama need not be discussed at length in a volume of translations. Aeschylus, apparently more than any one else, elevated the style of tragedy above the level of the old dithyrambic plays. The language of Sophocles is clearer than his, with no loss of dignity or beauty; witness the ode on mankind sung by the Theban Elders in *Antigone.* The diction of Euripides is closer to the language of conversation. But perhaps most natural and beautiful of all is the utterance, clear and bright, of Aristophanes, when he is not distorting his medium for comic ends; he was also the most versatile metrist of antiquity.

But a poet is more than an adept in figures of speech and metrical composition. In a drama, from beginning to end he is framing speeches, which must be suited to the persons of his story, and must fit and promote the march of the action. The Greek dramatists learned much about the art of eloquence and dialogue, and of characterization, from the narrative poems of Homer with their speakers impassioned or subtle. Further, if Aeschylus did not know the Sicilian art of rhetoric at first hand, Sophocles would know it when it came to Athens. As for Athenian eloquence, all four of the great dramatists could have heard Pericles; and all but Aeschylus could have talked with Socrates as a man; all must have known some of the leading Sophists. All seem expert, too, in forensic speaking; Euripides certainly had to defend himself in court, and Sophocles and Aeschylus are said to have done the like. The great trial-scene in the *Eumenides* may have started the tradition about Aeschylus. But of course the dramatic contests themselves fostered the rhetoric of poetry. Actor-managers learned how to weave speeches through declamation, through training their players, and, as did Aeschylus and Sophocles, from each other. Euripides was self-centred, but could deliberately adapt and improve a line from Aeschylus; he was also infected with sophistical rhetoric. It is easy to find fault with him, yet it has always been hard to escape his hold upon our emotions. Aristotle praised his tragic quality, referring, however, not to the speeches, but to the unhappy ending of plays like *Medea.* The same critic thinks extremely well of *I phigenia in Tauris* for its construction and emotional effect, and withal because the deed of horror is avoided.

It is Euripides rather than Aeschylus who should pass for the type of enthusiastic poet, giving utterance to his own thoughts and emotions. Aeschylus, according to Sophocles, did right as an artist without knowing why; but Aeschylus, after forty years of practice on the stage, is, in *Agamemnon*, for example, more adroit than is Euripides in *Medea*. With Greek reticence, he yet depicts the cold, hard, verbal sparring between unfaithful husband and faithless, murderous wife when they meet after a long separation. In this scene there is an element of that dramatic irony of which Sophocles is thought to be the first and great master, and Euripides master at times. Aeschylus is adroit also in making Clytemnestra a wily deceiver; a difficulty in the play is solved if we interpret her account of the fire-signals as a calculated lie. Euripides is the framer of poignant speeches, and of tragic fantasy; his own personality is not unified, and hence, though it intrudes itself into his plays, it is baffling to study. Sophocles, in devising speeches, as in other points of art, did right, knowing why. Although antiquity found some of his plays to be very inferior, to us his art at its best seems infallible. His heart and head operated in conjunction. The result has the outward finish of sculpture in marble; within, it lives and moves and glows. He seems to have had from nature what Aeschylus must labor for, the plastic ability to enter into one personality after another—an Oedipus, an Ajax, Creon, Antigone—for the ends of artistic representation. Aeschylus gave us men and women of colossal stature. Euripides depicted human nature as it is? So said Sophocles, while affirming that he himself drew men as they should be drawn in tragedy. With acts of will that are distinct and intelligible, the characters of Sophocles are true to type, true to life, and self-consistent; whoever thinks him inferior to Shakespeare in the life-like delineation of personality should read both poets in the original or both in translation. In spite of the flaws which his personages must reveal if there is to be tragedy, we are struck with their nobility and their desire for justice. Antigone appeals to the higher law; Oedipus and Creon speak like statesmen. Low, petty, and ridiculous motives, bare egoism, pure malignity, are banished from the Sophoclean stage; thus the poet hits the mark at which his two great rivals generally aimed, and is typical of his age and race. The debasement of humanity, noticeable in recent American novels and dramas, will not be learned from Attic tragedy or comedy. Of course we have to reckon with comic foible as well as tragic error. But there is nothing painful or corrupting about the ludicrous characters in the *Frogs*; while the errors of Antigone and Oedipus are often to the modern reader concealed by their virtues. Note, however, that Antigone perishes, not because she buries her brother the first time, or even the second; she taunts her uncle who has power of life and death over her, and finally she is a suicide.

Meanwhile, if the virtues of Creon are often overlooked, so also is the fact that his errors are tragic. Oedipus, again, is often considered the generous victim of fate. There is not a word about fate in Aristotle's remarks on tragedy, and hardly as much fatalism in Euripides as in Shakespeare. The characters of Aeschylus will and perform acts which they attribute to ancestral curses. It is Roman tragedy, with its modern offspring, that is fatalistic. In Sophocles' work, one should examine, at each point, which moves first, the hero or his fate. Young Oedipus kills an old man, whom he should have revered, in a dispute over the right of way, and thus unknowingly slays his own father. Unpremeditated murder, under provocation, was done in hot blood. Upon this act, which is anterior to the play, more light is thrown by the repeated bursts of anger from Oedipus in the play, and particularly by his violence to old men, of whom this tragedy has a large share.

Out of the choices of the agents grow dramatic actions. Creon decides that his nephew Polynices, dead foe of the State, shall lie unburied; Antigone, self-appointed instrument of the 'higher law,' resolves to bury the corpse of her brother. The situation is the more piteous because the clash of wills is between members of a family; and the results are deeds of horror. Of seven tragedies by Sophocles, four begin with words like, 'Sister, mine own dear sister!' and, 'Son of him who led our hosts at Troy!' In *Agamemnon* the husband with great effrontery brings home as concubine Cassandra, poor fatalist, now in love with him; here is the ultimate exasperation to guilty Clytemnestra, who would justify her slaughter of Agamemnon by dwelling on his part, ten years before, in the death of their child Iphigenia, at Aulis. By keeping the hateful paramour Aegisthus in the background, Aeschylus makes an ugly domestic situation, of four persons, less ugly. Scholars who do not observe these facts of life, idealized, miss the pity of it, and wonder why the dramatist brings in Cassandra at all. Some think that love has small place in Greek tragedy; oddly enough, they mean the wholesome romantic love that belongs to comedy, and forget the tragic love awry in Clytemnestra and Medea.

That the families concerned are of high estate, while a matter of less importance than is inward nobility, was important enough to the democratic Athenian audience. The stories are about ancient houses, the members of which associate with the gods, and have birth, wealth, power, and physical excellences, so that their tragic humiliation is impressive. In general they have imagination and eloquence with which to signify their glory and bewail its loss; how many of the tragic heroes seem like poets who have gone to wreck! The ever happy and fortunate Sophocles had a genius for representing this type of hero, winning prizes with his ruin.

One may divide the stories into those which deal with Dionysus and

those which do not. Perhaps the essential first step in Greek tragedy was taken
when its themes widened out from Dionysiac associations with goat-like and
equine satyrs so as to include all the story of Thebes and the whole body of
Greek myth. At an early date, says Aristotle, the tragic poets took any subjects
that came to hand. If so, they had an ample range of selection in the richest
mythology any race has possessed. Later, he says, they narrowed down to the
legends of a few houses. And that is the effect the surviving tragedies have
upon us; the themes seem limited. We have seven plays of Aeschylus, out of
ninety; seven of Sophocles, out of one hundred and twenty; eighteen or
nineteen of Euripides, out of ninety-two. Of these surviving thirty-three
plays, sixteen deal with aspects of the Trojan cycle, and six with the story of
Thebes. But this preponderance is accidental; the choice of plays from
Sophocles, for example, three on Thebes, three from the Trojan cycle, and
one about Heracles, was made by grammarians at Alexandria for study in the
schools. The fragments and titles of lost plays indicate a wider range than that
of Elizabethan and classical French tragedy. There were themes from the
other two great centres of Grecian story, the Calydonian Hunt and the tale of
the Argonauts. To this last cycle belongs the *Medea* of Euripides. If other
poets were as prolific and varied as he and Aeschylus, the tragedies of the great
age must have numbered perhaps fifteen hundred or two thousand, drawn
from many sources besides the four main ones we have noted. The comedies
were not quite equally numerous. The eleven we have from Aristophanes,
added to thirty-two tragedies plus Euripides' satyric *Cyclops*, give us forty-four
surviving plays in all, or, with the fragments from Sophocles' *Trackers*, another
satyr-drama, say forty-five that can be studied in some detail. The ten in this
volume will fairly introduce the reader to the rest.

Turning to the comedies here included, we see that they throw light
upon tragedy, which influenced them, and can be studied in that influence.
Of primitive comedy we know little. The comic drama had developed far in
Sicily before it made much progress at Athens. Here it first received support
from the State in the year 486 B.C. The 'Old Comedy' began to flourish
about the year 450, reached maturity with Aristophanes, and in his hands was
turning into something else when he closed his career. Aristophanes, born
about 444, first exhibited, at the Lenaea, in 427; produced the *Frogs* in 405
soon after the death of Sophocles, hardly a year after that of Euripides; and
himself died some time after the *Plutus* was exhibited in 388, perhaps after
375. Before he was born, the use of three comic actors had been taken over
from tragedy, possibly by Cratinus from Sophocles; and Crates had improved
and universalized comic plots. But Aristophanes was the great developer of
the Old Comedy, in the *Clouds* (423), *Birds* (414), and *Frogs* (405); his *Women*

in Council (392) and *Plutus* (388) set a standard for the Middle Comedy; thereafter, in two plays now lost, or in the last of them, he struck out the type which ultimately matured in the New Comedy of Philemon and Menander. The variety and opulence of Aristophanes, his deep intuitions, and the strange, vivid beauty with which he invests comic ideas, make it difficult to speak of him in brief. Some knowledge of external nature belonged to the Old Comedy in relation to the Dionysiac cult of fertility, but in his amazing knowledge of it Aristophanes doubtless surpassed his rivals. The *Birds* gathers up all the poetry of its subject, and more than we have on birds from Chaucer, Shakespeare, and Wordsworth conjoined. Plays like the *Birds* and the *Frogs*, again, gave rare opportunities for elaborate and fantastic spectacle; an imperfect notion of the feathered Chorus may be had from certain remains of vase-painting. But doubtless what we chiefly now miss in the plays of Aristophanes is the music—in the *Frogs*, the music of both flute and harp. All told, the poet had many means of embellishment, and a genius not only for comic distortion. Moreover, an orderly element in the composition of his dramas atones for any seeming lawlessness in them. The metrical scheme, and the elaboration of parts like the *parabasis* and *agon*, offered special difficulties to the poets of the Old Comedy. These and other difficulties the good sense and good taste of Aristophanes turned to the advantage of his art. He takes credit to himself for diminishing the traditional element of phallic worship in comedy, and for limiting the indecency of the comic dance. In *Plutus*, jokes at the expense of well-known individuals have virtually disappeared. Indeed, in the *Frogs* the poet attacks no one; in a literary comedy he makes two great tragic poets attack each other. His choice of contestants for this *agon* marks his good sense. Even in more improbable situations he has an eye to probability. He laughingly draws attention to what is important and real. Like Molière, once having attained artistic maturity, Aristophanes virtually never makes a mistake in the comic art. His sure skill may be noted in his avoidance of actual pain as a comic motive, and in his way of leading us from familiar circumstance into the world of imagination.

His hold upon reality and his power of imagination make Aristophanes a great political economist and a great literary critic. Ruskin admits a heavy debt in his concepts of poverty and wealth to the *Plutus;* and the other comedies likewise have their subject-matter in the realm of political ideas. It is this, as much as anything else, that distinguishes even the *Plutus* from the later domestic comedy of Greece and Rome. And these political concepts are sound; by skilfully throwing things out of proportion Aristophanes reveals their true proportions. The *Birds* is his comic Utopia, the State as a whole. In the *Frogs* he anticipates a problem of the Platonic Utopia, the function of the poet in the State; this problem he displays in an action that travesties an entire Dionysiac festival.

In the *Persians* (472 B.C.) Aeschylus had celebrated the crushing defeat (480) by the Greeks of their Asiatic foe. The *Frogs* appeared when Athens was exhausted by her last effort in the Peloponnesian war, a few months before her overthrow at Aegospotami; within a year starvation forced the surrender of the city (404), and ended the war. The comedy, however, looks like an expensive one to produce; at all events the poet had an elaborate object to travesty if he was minded at the Lenaea to offer a mock City Dionysia. The parts of the festival are present, adapted to the scheme of a comedy. The wanderer Dionysus becomes the wanderer Heracles for a new harrowing of hell; his labor is to bring back a tragic poet to Athens, for the great age of tragedy has ended. On the way he first has a dithyrambic contest with the Frogs. Then comes the procession, by torch-light, of the initiated, and then the contest of tragic poets, duly closed by an official decision. With unerring intuition Aristophanes anticipates the judgment of all time respecting the three leaders. The *agon* of a comedy, however, is a contest between two opponents; for this he chooses Aeschylus and Euripides. They are extremes in a proportion, where Sophocles doubtless is the golden mean. The comic contrasts between Aeschylus and Euripides betray a profound literary criticism in which Aristophanes is a worthy precursor of Aristotle.

Plutus (388) is (save perhaps the undatable *Rhesus*) the latest extant play of the great Greek drama. In it the difficult features of the Old Comedy are hardly discernible. The structure is simplified, political satire is absent, local allusions are few, and the theme, completely generalized, is intelligible to all. *Plutus* was long the most popular of Aristophanes' works in England. This comedy of Wealth was given when Athens was poor, and depends less than the *Frogs* upon spectacular effect. In time, however, stage and theatre recovered their well-being. In the latter half of the fourth century the old theatre was rebuilt, with Peiraic limestone. In this theatre, before an audience of perhaps 17,000 persons, the successors of Euripides and Aristophanes exhibited their tragedies and comedies; in it Aristotle (died 322 B.C.) doubtless studied the emotions of pity and fear, and mirth, in the spectators; and here the comedies of Menander (342–291) and his fellows were presented. Meanwhile theatres of the Attic type had begun to spread; the Romans built the like, even an additional one in Athens; and first and last such buildings have been erected in various parts of the world from the shores of the Black Sea to a sunlit spot in Berkeley, California. They are monuments to the effect of the Attic drama upon the mind of the civilized world.

ARISTOTLE

Poetics

V.

As for comedy, it is (as has been observed) an imitation of men worse than the average—worse, however, not as regards any and every sort of fault, but only as regards one particular kind, the ridiculous, which is a species of the ugly. The ridiculous may be defined as a mistake or deformity not productive of pain or harm to others. The mask, for instance, that excites laughter, is something ugly and distorted without causing pain.

Though the successive changes in tragedy and their authors are not unknown, we cannot say the same of comedy. Its early stages passed unnoticed, because it was not as yet taken up in a serious way. It was only at a late point in its progress that a chorus of comedians was officially granted by the archon; they used to be mere volunteers. It had also already certain definite forms at the time when the record of those termed comic poets begins. Who it was who supplied it with masks, or prologues, or a plurality of actors and the like, has remained unknown. The invented fable, or plot, however, originated in Sicily with Epicharmus and Phormis. Of Athenian poets Crates was the first to drop the comedy of invective and frame stories of a general and non-personal nature, in other words, fables or plots.

Epic poetry, then, has been seen to agree with tragedy to this extent, that of being an imitation of serious subjects in a grand kind of verse. It differs from it, however, (1) in that it is in one kind of verse and in narrative

From *The Poetics and Longinus of the Sublime*. © 1930 by The Macmillan Company.

form; and (2) in its length, which is due to its action having no fixed limit of time, whereas tragedy endeavours to keep as far as possible within a single circuit of the sun, or something near that. This, I say, is another point of difference between them, though at first the practice in this respect was just the same in tragedies as in epic poems. They differ also (3) in their constituents, some being common to both and others peculiar to tragedy. Hence a judge of good and bad in tragedy is a judge of that in epic poetry also. All the parts of an epic are included in tragedy; but those of tragedy are not all of them to be found in the epic.

VI.

Reserving hexameter poetry and comedy for consideration hereafter, let us proceed now to the discussion of tragedy. Before doing so, however, we must gather up the definition resulting from what has been said. A tragedy, then, is the imitation of an action that is serious and also, as having magnitude, complete in itself; in language with pleasurable accessories, each kind brought in separately in the parts of the work; in a dramatic, not in a narrative form; with incidents arousing pity and fear[1], where-with to accomplish its catharsis of such emotions. Here by 'language with pleasurable accessories' I mean that with rhythm and harmony or song superadded; and by 'the kinds separately' I mean that some portions are worked out with verse only, and others in turn with song.

As they act the stories, it follows that in the first place the spectacle (or stage-appearance of the actors) must be some part of the whole; and in the second melody and diction, these two being the means of their imitation. Here by 'diction' I mean merely this, the composition of the verses; and by 'melody,' what is too completely understood to require explanation. But further, the subject represented also is an action; and the action involves agents, who must necessarily have their distinctive qualities both of character and thought, since it is from these that we ascribe certain qualities to their actions. There are in the natural order of things, therefore, two causes, character and thought, of their actions, and consequently of their success or failure in their lives. Now the action (that which was done) is represented in the play by the fable or plot. The fable, in our present sense of the term, is simply this, the combination of the incidents or things done in the story; whereas character is what makes us ascribe certain moral qualities to the agents; and thought is shown in all they say when proving a particular point or, it may be, enunciating a general truth. There are six parts consequently of every tragedy, as a whole, that is, of such or such quality, viz. a fable or plot, characters, diction, thought, spectacle and melody; two of them arising from the means, one from the manner, and three from the objects of the dramatic imitation; and there is nothing else besides these six. Of these, its formative elements, then, not a few of the dramatists have made due use, as every play, one may say, admits of spectacle, character, fable, diction, melody, and thought.

The most important of the six is the combination of the incidents of the story. Tragedy is essentially an imitation not of persons, but of action and life, of happiness and misery. All human happiness or misery takes the form of action; the end for which we live is a certain kind of activity, not a quality. Character gives us qualities, but it is in our actions—what we do—that we are happy or the reverse. In a play accordingly they do not act in order to portray the characters; they include the characters for the sake of the action. So that it is the action in it, i.e. its fable or plot, that is the end and purpose of the tragedy; and the end is everywhere the chief thing. Besides this, a tragedy is impossible without action, but there may be one without character. The tragedies of most of the moderns are characterless—a defect common among poets of all kinds, and with its counterpart in painting in Zeuxis as compared with Polygnotus; for whereas the latter is strong in character, the work of Zeuxis is devoid of it. And again, one may string together a series of characteristic speeches of the utmost finish as regards diction and thought, and yet fail to produce the true tragic effect; but one will have much better success with a tragedy which, however inferior in these respects, has a plot, a combination of incidents, in it. And again, the most powerful elements of attraction in tragedy, the peripeties[2] and discoveries, are parts of the plot. A further proof is in the fact that beginners succeed earlier with the diction and characters than with the construction of a story; and the same may be said of nearly all the early dramatists. We maintain, therefore, that the first essential, the life and soul, so to speak, of tragedy is the plot; and that the characters come second. Compare the parallel in painting, where the most beautiful colours laid on without order will not give one the same pleasure as a simple black-and-white sketch of a portrait. We maintain that tragedy is primarily an imitation of action, and that it is mainly for the sake of the action that it imitates the personal agents. Third comes the element of thought, i.e. the power of saying whatever can be said or what is appropriate to the occasion. This is what, in the speeches in tragedy, falls under the arts of politics and rhetoric; for the older poets make their personages discourse like statesmen, and the moderns like rhetoricians. One must not confuse it with character. Character in a play is that which reveals the moral purpose of the agents, i.e. the sort of thing they seek or avoid, where that is not obvious. Hence there is no room for character in a speech on a purely indifferent subject. Thought, on the other hand, is shown in all they say when proving or disproving some particular point, or enunciating some universal proposition. Fourth among the literary elements is the diction of the personages, i.e. as before explained, the expression of their thoughts in words, which is practically the same thing with verse as with prose. As for the two remaining parts, the melody is the greatest of the pleasurable accessories of tragedy. The spectacle, though an attraction, is the least artistic of all the parts, and has least to do with the art of poetry. The tragic effect is quite possible without a public performance and actors; and besides, the getting-up of the spectacle is more a matter for the costumer than the poet.

VII.

Having thus distinguished the parts, let us now consider the proper construction of the fable or plot, as that is at once the first and the most important thing in tragedy.[3] We have laid it down that a tragedy is an imitation of an action that is complete in itself, as a whole of some magnitude; for a whole may be of no magnitude to speak of. Now a whole is that which has beginning, middle, and end. A beginning is that which is not itself necessarily after anything else, and which has naturally something else after it; an end is that which is naturally after something itself, either as its necessary or usual consequent, and with nothing else after it; and a middle, that which is by nature after one thing and has also another after it. A well-constructed plot, therefore, cannot either begin or end at any point one likes; beginning and end in it must be of the forms just described. Again to be beautiful, a living creature, and every whole made up of parts, must not only present a certain order in its arrangement of parts, but also be of a certain definite magnitude. Beauty is a matter of size and order, and therefore impossible either (1) in a very minute creature, since our perception becomes indistinct as it approaches instantaneity; or (2) in a creature of vast size—one, say, 1000 miles long—as in that case, instead of the object being seen all at once, the unity and wholeness of it is lost to the beholder. Just in the same way, then, as a beautiful whole made up of parts, or a beautiful living creature, must be of some size, a size to be taken in by the eye, so a story or plot must be of some length, but of a length to be taken in by the memory. As for the limit of its length, so far as that is relative to public performances and spectators, it does not fall within the theory of poetry. If they had to perform a hundred tragedies, they would be timed by water-clocks, as they are said to have been at one period. The limit, however, set by the actual nature of the thing is this; the longer the story, consistently with its being comprehensible as a whole, the finer it is by reason of its magnitude. As a rough general formula, 'a length which allows of the hero passing by a series of probable or necessary stages from misfortune to happiness, or from happiness to misfortune,' may suffice as a limit for the magnitude of the story.

VIII.

The unity of a plot does not consist, as some suppose, in its having one man as its subject. An infinity of things befall that one man, some of which it is impossible to reduce to unity; and in like manner there are many actions of one man which cannot be made to form one action. One sees, therefore, the mistake of all the poets who have written a *Heracleid*, a *Theseid*, or similar poems. They suppose that because Heracles was one man, the story also of Heracles must be one story. Homer, however, evidently understood this point quite well, whether by art or instinct, just in the same way as he excels the rest in every other respect. In writing an *Odyssey* he did not make the poem cover all that ever befell his hero. It befell him, for instance, to get wounded on Parnassus and also to feign madness at the time of the call to arms; but the two incidents had no probable or necessary connexion with one another. Instead of doing that, he took an action with a unity of the kind we are describing as the subject of the *Odyssey*, as also of the *Iliad*. The truth is that, just as in the other imitative arts one imitation is always of one thing, so in poetry the story, as an imitation of action, must represent one action, a complete whole, with its several incidents so closely connected that the transposal or withdrawal of any one of them will disjoin and dislocate the whole. For that which makes no perceptible difference by its presence or absence is no real part of the whole.

IX.

From what we have said it will be seen that the poet's function is to describe not the thing that has happened, but a kind of thing that might happen, i.e. what is possible as being probable or necessary. The distinction between historian and poet is not in the one writing prose and the other verse. You might put the work of Herodotus into verse, and it would still be a species of history. It consists really in this, that the one describes the thing that has been, and the other a kind of thing that might be. Hence poetry is something more philosophic and of graver import than history, since its statements are of the nature rather of universals, whereas those of history are singulars. By a universal statement I mean one as to what such or such a kind of man will probably or necessarily say or do, which is the aim of poetry, though it affixes proper names to the characters; by a singular statement, one as to what, say, Alcibiades did or had done to him. In comedy this has become clear by this time; it is only when their plot is already made up of probable incidents that they give it a basis of proper names, choosing for the purpose any names that may occur to them, instead of writing like the old iambic poets about particular persons. In tragedy, however, they still adhere to the historic names, and for this reason; what convinces is the possible. Now whereas we are not yet sure as to the possibility of that which has not happened, that which has happened is manifestly possible; else it would not have come to pass. Nevertheless even in tragedy there are some plays with but one or two known names in them, the rest being inventions; and there are some without a single known name, e.g. Agathon's *Antheus*, in which both incidents and names are of the poet's invention; and it is no less delightful on that account. So that one must not aim at a rigid adherence to the traditional stories on which tragedies are based. It would be absurd, in fact, to do so, as even the known stories are only known to a few, though they are a delight none the less to all. It is evident from the above that the poet must be more the poet of his stories or plots than of his verses, inasmuch as he is a poet by virtue of the imitative element in his work, and it is actions that he imitates. And if he should come to take a subject from actual history, he is none the less a poet for that, since some historic occurrences may very well be in the probable and possible order of things, and it is in that aspect of them that he is their poet.

Of simple plots and actions the episodic are the worst. I call a plot episodic when there is neither probability nor necessity in the sequence of its episodes. Actions of this sort bad poets construct through their own fault, and good ones on account of the players. His work being for public performance, a good poet often stretches out a plot beyond its capabilities, and is thus obliged to twist the sequence of incident.

Tragedy, however, is an imitation not only of a complete action, but also of incidents arousing pity and fear. Such incidents have the very greatest effect on the mind when they occur unexpectedly and at the same time in consequence of one another. There is more of the marvellous in them then than if they happened of themselves or by mere chance. Even matters of chance seem most marvellous if there is an appearance of design as it were in them; as for instance the statue of Mitys at Argos killed the author of Mitys' death by falling down on him when a looker-on at a public spectacle; for incidents like that we think to be not without a meaning. A plot, therefore, of this sort is necessarily finer than others.

X.

Plots are either simple or complex, since the actions they represent are naturally of this twofold description. The action proceeding in the way defined as one continuous whole I call simple when the change in the hero's fortunes takes place without peripety or discovery; and complex, when it involves one or the other, or both. These should each of them arise out of the structure of the plot itself, so as to be the consequence, necessary or probable, of the antecedents. There is a great difference between a thing happening *propter hoc* and *post hoc.*[4]

XI.

A peripety is the change from one state of things within the play to its opposite of the kind described, and that too in the way we are saying, in the probable or necessary sequence of events; as it is for instance in *Oedipus.* Here the opposite state of things is produced by the messenger, who, coming to gladden Oedipus and to remove his fears as to his mother, reveals the secret of his birth. And in *Lynceus,* just as he is being led off for execution, with Danaus at his side to put him to death, the incidents preceding this bring it about that he is saved and Danaus put to death. A discovery is, as the very word implies, a change from ignorance to knowledge, and thus to either love or hate, in the personages marked for good or evil fortune. The finest form of discovery is one attended by peripeties, like that which goes with the discovery in *Oedipus.* There are no doubt other forms of it; what we have said may happen in a way in reference to inanimate things, even things of a very casual kind; and it is also possible to discover whether some one has done or not done something. But the form most directly connected with the plot and the action of the piece is the first-mentioned. This, with a peripety, will arouse either pity or fear, actions of that nature being what tragedy is assumed to represent; and it will also serve to bring about the happy or unhappy ending. The discovery, then, being of persons, it may be that of one party only to the other, the latter being already known; or both the parties may have to discover themselves. Iphigenia, for instance, was discovered to Orestes by sending the letter; and another discovery was required to reveal him to Iphigenia.

Two parts of the plot, then, peripety and discovery, are on matters of this sort. A third part is suffering, which we may define as an action of destructive or painful nature, such as murders on the stage, tortures, woundings, and the like. The other two have been already explained.

XII.

The parts of tragedy to be treated as formative elements in the whole were mentioned in a previous chapter. From the point of view, however, of its quantity, i.e. the separate sections into which it is divided, a tragedy has the following parts: prologue, episode, exode, and a choral portion, distinguished into parode and stasimon; these two are common to all tragedies, whereas songs from the stage and *commoe* are only found in some. The prologue is all that precedes the parode of the chorus; an episode, all that comes in between two whole choral songs; the exode, all that follows after the last choral song. In the choral portion the parode is the whole first statement of the chorus; a stasimon, a song of the chorus without anapaests or trochees; a *commos*, a lamentation sung by chorus and actor in concert. The parts of tragedy to be used as formative elements in the whole we have already mentioned. The above are its parts from the point of view of its quantity, or the separate sections into which it is divided.

XIII.

The next points after what we have said above will be these: (I) what is the poet to aim at, and what is he to avoid, in constructing his plots? and (2) what are the conditions on which the tragic effect depends? We assume that for the finest form of tragedy the plot must be not simple but complex, and further that it must imitate actions arousing pity and fear, since that is the distinctive function of this kind of imitation. It follows, therefore, that there are three forms of plot to be avoided. (I) A good man must not be seen passing from happiness to misery, or (2) a bad man from misery to happiness. The first situation is not fear-inspiring or piteous, but simply odious to us. The second is the most untragic that can be; it has no one of the requisites of tragedy; it does not appeal either to the human feeling in us, or to our pity, or to our fears. Nor on the other hand should (3) an extremely bad man be seen falling from happiness into misery. Such a story may arouse the human feeling in us, but it will not move us to either pity or fear. Pity is occasioned by undeserved misfortune, and fear by that of one like ourselves; so that there will be nothing either piteous or fear-inspiring in the situation. There remains, then, the intermediate kind of personage, a man not pre-eminently virtuous and just, whose misfortune, however, is brought upon him not by vice and depravity, but by some error of judgement, of the number of those in the enjoyment of great reputation and prosperity; e.g. Oedipus, Thyestes, and the men of note of similar families. The perfect plot, accordingly, must have a single, and not (as some tell us) a double issue; the change in the hero's fortunes must be not from misery to happiness, but on the contrary from happiness to misery; and the cause of it must lie not in any depravity, but in some great error on his part; the man himself being either such as we have described, or better, not worse, than that. Fact also confirms our theory. Though the poets began by accepting any tragic story that came to hand, in these days the finest tragedies are always on the story of some few houses, on that of Alcmeon, Oedipus, Orestes, Meleager, Thyestes, Telephus, or any others that may have been involved, as either agents or sufferers, in some deed of horror. The theoretically best tragedy, then, has a plot of this description. The critics, therefore, are wrong, who blame Euripides for taking this line in his tragedies, and giving many of them an unhappy ending. It is, as we have said, the right line to take. The best proof is this: on the stage, and in the public performances, such plays, properly worked out, are seen to be the most truly tragic; and Euripides, even if his execution be faulty in every other point, is seen to be nevertheless the most tragic certainly of the dramatists. After this comes the construction of plot which some rank first, one with a double story (like the *Odyssey*) and an opposite issue for the good and the bad personages. It is ranked as first only through the weakness of the audiences. The poets merely follow their public, writing as its wishes dictate. But the pleasure here is not that of tragedy. It belongs rather to comedy, where the bitterest enemies in the piece (e.g. Orestes and Aegisthus) walk off good friends at the end, with no slaying of any one by any one.

XIV.

The tragic fear and pity may be aroused by the spectacle; but they may also be aroused by the very structure and incidents of the play; which is the better way and shows the better poet. The plot in fact should be so framed that, even without seeing the things take place, he who simply hears the account of them shall be filled with horror and pity at the incidents; which is just the effect that the mere recital of the story in *Oedipus* would have on one. To produce this same effect by means of the spectacle is less artistic, and requires extraneous aid. Those, however, who make use of the spectacle to put before us that which is merely monstrous and not productive of fear are wholly out of touch with tragedy. Not every kind of pleasure should be required of a tragedy, but only its own proper pleasure.

The tragic pleasure is that of pity and fear, and the poet has to produce it by a work of imitation; it is clear, therefore, that the causes should be included in the incidents of his story. Let us see, then, what kinds of incident strike one as horrible, or rather as piteous. In a deed of this description the parties must necessarily be either friends, or enemies, or indifferent to one another. Now when enemy does it on enemy, there is nothing to move us to pity either in his doing or in his meditating the deed, except so far as the actual pain of the sufferer is concerned; and the same is true when the parties are indifferent to one another. Whenever the tragic deed, however, is done within the family, when murder or the like is done or meditated by brother on brother, by son on father, by mother on son, or son on mother, these are the situations the poet should seek after. The traditional stories, accordingly, must be kept as they are, e.g. the murder of Clytaemnestra by Orestes and of Eriphyle by Alcmeon.

At the same time even with these there is something left to the poet himself; it is for him to devise the right way of treating them. Let us explain more clearly what we mean by 'the right way.' The deed of horror may be done by the doer knowingly and consciously, as in the old poets, and in Medea's murder of her children in Euripides. Or he may do it, but in ignorance of his relationship, and discover that afterwards, as does the Oedipus in Sophocles. Here the deed is outside the play; but it may be within it, like the act of the Alcmeon in Astydamas, or that of the Telegonus in *Ulysses Wounded*. A third possibility is for one meditating some deadly injury to another, in ignorance of his relationship, to make the discovery in time to draw back. These exhaust the possibilities, since the deed must necessarily be either done or not done, and either knowingly or unknowingly.

The worst situation is when the personage is with full knowledge on the point of doing the deed, and leaves it undone. It is odious and also, through the absence of suffering, untragic. Hence it is that no one is made to act thus except in some few instances, e.g. Haemon and Creon in *Antigone*. Next after this comes the actual perpetration of the deed meditated. A better situation than that, however, is for the deed to be done in ignorance, and the relationship discovered afterwards, since there is nothing odious in it, and the discovery will serve to astound us. But the best of all is the last; what we have in *Cresphontes*, for example, where Merope, on the point of slaying her son, recognizes him in time; in *Iphigenia*, where sister and brother are in a like position; and in *Helle*, where the son recognizes his mother, when on the point of giving her up to her enemy. This will explain why our tragedies are restricted, as we said just now, to such a small number of families. It was accident rather than art that led the poets in quest of subjects to embody this kind of incident in their plots. They are still obliged, accordingly, to have recourse to the families in which such horrors have occurred. On the construction of the plot, and the kind of plot required for tragedy, enough has now been said.

XV.

In the characters there are four points to aim at. First and foremost, that they shall be good. There will be an element of character in the play, if, as has been observed, what a personage says or does reveals a certain moral purpose, and a good element of character if the purpose so revealed is good. Such goodness is possible in every type of personage, even in a woman or a slave, though the one is perhaps an inferior, and the other a wholly worthless being. The second point is to make them appropriate. The character before us may be, say, manly; but it is not appropriate in a female character to be manly, or clever. The third is to make them like the reality, which is not the same as their being good and appropriate, in our sense of the term. The fourth is to make them consistent and the same throughout. Even if inconsistency be part of the man before one for imitation as presenting that form of character, he should still be consistently inconsistent. We have an instance of baseness of character, not required for the story, in the Menelaus in *Orestes*; of the incongruous and inappropriate in the lamentation of Ulysses in *Scylla*, and in the (clever) speech of Melanippe; and of inconsistency in *Iphigenia at Aulis*, where Iphigenia the suppliant is utterly unlike the later Iphigenia. The right thing, however, is in the characters just as in the incidents of the play to endeavour always after the necessary or the probable; so that whenever such-and-such a personage says or does such-and-such a thing, it shall be the probable or necessary outcome of his character; and whenever this incident follows on that, it shall be either the necessary or the probable consequence of it. From this one sees (to digress for a moment) that the dénouement also should arise out of the plot itself, and not depend on a stage-artifice, as in *Medea*, or in the story of the (arrested) departure of the Greeks in the *Iliad*.[5] The artifice must be reserved for matters outside the play: for past events beyond human knowledge, or events yet to come, which require to be foretold or announced, since it is the privilege of the gods to know everything. There should be nothing improbable among the actual incidents. If it be unavoidable, however, it should be outside the tragedy, like the improbability in the *Oedipus* of Sophocles. But to return to the characters, as tragedy is an imitation of personages better than the ordinary man, we in our way should follow the example of good portraitpainters, who reproduce the distinctive features of a man, and at the same time, without losing the likeness, make him handsomer than he is. The poet in like manner, in portraying men quick or slow to anger, or with similar infirmities of character, must know how to represent them as such, and at the same time as good men, as Agathon and Homer have represented Achilles. All these rules one must keep in mind throughout, and further, those also for such points of stage-effect as directly depend on the art of the poet, since in these too one may often make mistakes. Enough, however, has been said on the subject in one of our published writings.

XVI.

Discovery in general has been explained already. As for the species of discovery, the first to be noted is (I) the least artistic form of it, of which the poets make most use through mere lack of invention, discovery by signs or marks. Of these signs some are congenital, like the 'lance-head which the Earth-born have on them,' or 'stars,' such as Carcinus brings in in his *Thyestes*; others acquired after birth, these latter being either marks on the body, e.g. scars, or external tokens, like necklaces, or to take another sort of instance, the ark in the discovery in *Tyro*. Even these, however, admit of two uses, a better and a worse. The scar of Ulysses is an instance. The discovery of him through it is made in one way by the nurse and in another by the swineherds. A discovery using signs as a means of assurance is less artistic, as indeed are all such as imply reflexion; whereas one bringing them in all of a sudden, as in the *Bath Story*, is of a better order. Next after these are (2) discoveries made directly by the poet, which are inartistic for that very reason; e.g. Orestes' discovery of himself in *Iphigenia*. Whereas his sister reveals who she is by the letter, Orestes is made to say himself what the poet rather than the story demands. This, therefore, is not far removed from the first-mentioned fault, since he might have presented certain tokens as well. Another instance is the 'shuttle's voice' in the *Tereus* of Sophocles. (3) A third species is discovery through memory, from a man's consciousness being awakened by something seen or heard. Thus in *The Cyprioe* of Dicaeogenes, the sight of the picture makes the man burst into tears; and in the *Tale of Alcinous*, hearing the harper, Ulysses is reminded of the past and weeps, the discovery of them being the result. (4) A fourth kind is Discovery through reasoning; e.g. in *The Choephoroe:* 'One like me is here; there is no one like me but Orestes; he, therefore, must be here.' Or that which Polyidus the Sophist suggested for *Iphigenia*, since it was natural for Orestes to reflect: 'My sister was sacrificed, and I am to be sacrificed like her.' Or that in the *Tydeus* of Theodectes: 'I came to find a son, and am to die myself.' Or that in *The Phinidae:* on seeing the place the women inferred their fate, that they were to die there, since they had also been exposed there. (5) There is, too, a composite discovery arising from bad reasoning on the side of the other party. An instance of it is in *Ulysses the False Messenger:* he said he should know the bow, which he had not seen; but to suppose from that that he would know it again (as though he had once seen it) was bad reasoning. (6) The best of all discoveries, however, is that arising from the incidents themselves, when the great surprise comes about through a probable incident, like that in the *Oedipus* of Sophocles, and also in *Iphigenia*, for it was not improbable that she should wish to have a letter taken home. These last are the only discoveries independent of the artifice of signs and necklaces. Next after them come discoveries through reasoning.

XVII.

At the time when he is constructing his plots and engaged on the diction in which they are worked out, the poet should remember (1) to put the actual scenes as far as possible before his eyes. In this way, seeing everything with the vividness of an eye-witness as it were, he will devise what is appropriate, and be least likely to overlook incongruities. This is shown by what was censured in Carcinus, the return of Amphiaraus from the sanctuary. It would have passed unnoticed if it had not been actually seen by the audience; but on the stage his play failed, the incongruity of the incident offending the spectators. (2) As far as may be, too, the poet should even act his story with the very gestures of his personages. Given the same natural qualifications, he who feels the emotions to be described will be the most convincing. Distress and anger, for instance, are portrayed most truthfully by one who is feeling them at the moment. Hence it is that poetry demands a man with a special gift for it, or else one with a touch of madness in him. The former can easily assume the required mood, and the latter may be actually beside himself with emotion. (3) His story, again, whether already made or of his own making, he should first simplify and reduce to a universal form, before proceeding to lengthen it out by the insertion of episodes. The following will show how the universal element in *Iphigenia*, for instance, may be viewed. A certain maiden having been offered in sacrifice, and spirited away from her sacrificers into another land, where the custom was to sacrifice all strangers to the Goddess, she was made there the priestess of this rite. Long after that the brother of the priestess happened to come. The fact, however, of the oracle having for a certain reason bidden him go thither, and his object in going, are outside the plot of the play. On his coming he was arrested, and about to be sacrificed, when he revealed who he was, either as Euripides puts it, or (as suggested by Polyidus) by the not improbable exclamation, 'So I too am doomed to be sacrificed, as my sister was'; and the disclosure led to his salvation. This done, the next thing, after the proper names have been fixed as a basis for the story, is to work in episodes or accessory incidents. One must mind, however, that the episodes are appropriate, like the fit of madness in Orestes, which led to his arrest, and the purifying, which brought about his salvation. In plays, then, the episodes are short; in epic poetry they serve to lengthen out the poem. The argument of the *Odyssey* is not a long one. A certain man has been abroad many years. Poseidon is ever on the watch for him, and he is all alone. Matters at home too have come to this, that his substance is being wasted and his son's death plotted by suitors to his wife. Then he arrives there himself after his grievous sufferings; reveals himself, and falls on his enemies; and the end is his salvation and their death. This being all that is proper to the *Odyssey*, everything else in it is episode.

XVIII.

(4) There is a further point to be borne in mind. Every tragedy is in part complication and in part dénouement; the incidents before the opening scene, and often certain also of those within the play, forming the complication; and the rest the dénouement. By complication I mean all from the beginning of the story to the point just before the change in the hero's fortunes; by dénouement, all from the beginning of the change to the end. In the *Lynceus* of Theodectes, for instance, the complication includes, together with the presupposed incidents, the seizure of the child and that in turn of the parents; and the dénouement all from the indictment for the murder to the end. Now it is right, when one speaks of a tragedy as the same or not the same as another, to do so on the ground before all else of their plot, i.e. as having the same or not the same complication and dénouement. Yet there are many dramatists who, after a good complication, fail in the dénouement. But it is necessary for both points of construction to be always duly mastered. (5) There are four distinct species of tragedy, that being the number of the constituents also that have been mentioned: first, the complex tragedy, which is all peripety and discovery; second, the tragedy of suffering, e.g. the *Ajaxes* and *Ixions;* third, the tragedy of character, e.g. *The Phthiotides* and *Peleus.* The fourth constituent is that of 'spectacle,' exemplified in *The Phorcides*, in *Prometheus*, and in all plays with the scene laid in the nether world. The poet's aim, then, should be to combine every element of interest, if possible, or else the more important and the major part of them. This is now especially necessary owing to the unfair criticism to which the poet is subjected in these days. Just because there have been poets before him strong in the several species of tragedy, the critics now expect the one man to surpass that which was the strong point of each one of his predecessors.

(6) One should also remember what has been said more than once, and not write a tragedy on an epic body of incident (i.e. one with a plurality of stories in it), by attempting to dramatize, for instance, the entire story of the *Iliad.* In the epic, owing to its scale, every part is treated at proper length; with a drama, however, on the same story the result is very disappointing. This is shown by the fact that all who have dramatized the fall of Ilium in its entirety, and not part by part, like Euripides, or the whole of the Niobe story, instead of a portion, like Aeschylus, either fail utterly or have but ill success on the stage; for that and that alone was enough to ruin even a play by Agathon. Yet in their peripeties, as also in their simple plots, the poets I mean

show wonderful skill in aiming at the kind of effect they desire, a tragic situation that arouses the human feeling in one, like the clever villain (e.g. Sisyphus) deceived, or the brave wrongdoer worsted. This is probable, however, only in Agathon's sense, when he speaks of the probability of even improbabilities coming to pass. (7) The chorus too should be regarded as one of the actors; it should be an integral part of the whole, and take a share in the action, that which it has in Sophocles rather than in Euripides. With the later poets, however, the songs in a play of theirs have no more to do with the plot of that than of any other tragedy. Hence it is that they are now singing intercalary pieces, a practice first introduced by Agathon. And yet what real difference is there between singing such intercalary pieces, and attempting to fit in a speech, or even a whole act, from one play into another?

Notes

The best recent editions for English readers are: Ingram Bywater's "Aristotle on the Art of Poetry, a revised text with critical introduction, translation [reprinted here], and commentary," Oxford, 1909; and S. H. Butcher's "Aristotle's Theory of Poetry and Fine Art," text, translation, notes, essays, London, 1895; fourth edition, 1911.

The chapter (VI) in C. S. Baldwin's "Ancient Rhetoric and Poetic" interpreting Aristotle's work contains (pages 135–139) a tabular analysis of its whole course.

1. pity and fear ... to accomplish catharsis. Emotion, that is, is not merely aroused; it is satisfied; it is carried through to a release. Bywater, pages 152–161, has discussed this oftquoted phrase amply, and in an appendix (361–365) has compiled with their dates the successive critical translations.

2. peripeties. The *peripety* is the turning-point, or main crisis, of the play; as, in *Macbeth*, the vision of Banquo's ghost at the banquet; in *Othello*, the first doubt concerning Desdemona; in *The Merchant of Venice*, Portia's "Tarry a little. There is something else."

3. The point of Chapter VII is that plot is a planned sequence of actions. Instead of merely reproducing the crosscurrents of actual living, drama "imitates" life by creative interpretation.

4. propter hoc or post hoc. These terms of logic are used to indicate the fallacy of assuming that what follows in time necessarily follows as result.

5. stage artifice. The point is that the dramatic solution should "arise out of the plot itself," result inevitably from the course of the action, not be foisted on the play by interference from outside. Admirers of the *Medea* will maintain that its solution, though including supernatural intervention, none the less does "arise out of the plot itself," since an essential motive of that plot is Medea's supernatural power.

WILLIAM ARROWSMITH

The Criticism of Greek Tragedy

My purpose here is to do a little superstitious rapping in the hope of persuading into existence something a little different in the kind of criticism we normally bring to bear upon Greek tragedy. If this seems pretentious, blame the subject in part: Greek tragedy requires, I think, a formidable apparition by way of an adequate criticism and certainly a larger one than I can summon up, though also a larger one than presently attends the scene. What I want to do is to outline the nature of the job to be done, as I see it, and to discuss what seems to me inadequate in both the traditional and contemporary ways of writing about Greek tragedy. I think I see—though vaguely—the kind of criticism to which Greek tragedy points, though I recognize that this may turn out to be merely a mirage made up to answer imaginary needs, or an old familiar ghost in a new murk, or even something that concerns no one but students of Greek tragedy. Whatever the results, I am convinced that the need is real; that we have reached some kind of impasse in the study of Greek tragedy in which neither the older nor the newer criticism, nor any compromise between them, is really adequate; and further, that the need is general.

Impasse is perhaps a strong word, and certainly an easy one. Yet the diagnosis should surprise no one. The inadequacies of the older historical and philological criticism are by now notorious, and we can dispense with a parade of slogans that have more than accomplished their purpose. At the

From *The Tulane Drama Review* 3, no. 3 (March 1959). © 1959 by *The Tulane Drama Review*.

moment, the New Criticism enjoys high academic repute; it has, for the most part, been thoroughly institutionalized; it continues to do striking work in the hands of competent critics, and wherever it has allied itself with true scholarship, it has been an instrument of subtlety and depth. But as a method it is liable to the same distortion as any method; and it has everything to fear from the literalness of its zealots. No one who reads much recent criticism can be unaware of the carking restiveness among the pioneers of the New Critics as they see their methods turned into formulae and the crucial tact of the good critic expelled by the needs of schematic order. "I want," says R.P. Blackmur in *The Lion and the Honeycomb*, "to protect the methods [of the New Criticism] from its methodologies." I have the same hope here, and it is a hope which I want as much as possible to put in positive terms. But because the field I have in mind is Greek tragedy and classical studies generally, and because the situation of the New Criticism is different in respect to a dead language than what it is to a modern one, these matters deserve a context.

Roughly since the end of the war the traditional methods of classical scholarship as they affected literary criticism have been under attack in our graduate schools by the advocates of the New Criticism. As compared with studies in modern literatures, the attack on the classical front came late, delayed both by the addiction to cultural lag which is almost a point of pride among classicists, and by the extreme penetration of classical studies by the austere and quasi-scientific methodologies of the German *gymnasium*. Unlike scholars of English who never really wholly renounced criticism, classicists in America came to regard criticism as the perverse imp of the subjective in a field they fondly imagined was objective. This suspicion of criticism, it should be noted, was a peculiarly American thing, just as the reaction against it has been, for the most part, American also. If the stimulus to this dislike of criticism derived from Germany, it is also true that the formidable influence of such great scholars as Wilamowitz countered the current there, while elsewhere in Europe the long tradition of humane scholarship kept the activities of critic and scholar in more or less vital relation. One can point with pride, it is true, to American achievements in classical scholarship in the twentieth century, but the achievements occur in just those fields where the refinement of method, and especially scientific method, is crucial: archaeology, epigraphy, papyrology, numismatics, palaeography. Worse yet, all of these dubious sciences were devoted with an appalling single-mindedness to one end, the discovery of fact, in which fact was arbitrarily and with killing literalness reduced to historical or philological fact. Criticism itself was clearly confounded with the journalism of values and pushed to the fringes where it petered out either in limp impressionistic essays on the value of the classics or in the mellow *obiter dicta* of dying scholars. In short, American classical scholarship for forty years effectively renounced literary criticism as an honorable and rational habit of mind, and the results are apparent in the dreary waste of literary studies during those years; at least I can think of no first-rate, nor even second-rate, critical work on Greek tragedy by an American scholar from 1900 to 1940, though there is God's good plenty of works on the stage, conventions, Attic society, resolved *senarii* and the like. But certainly one finds nothing comparable to the real criticism of such European scholars as Sheppard, Wilamowitz or even the much-maligned Gilbert Murray.

When the attack finally came, it came with the energy that attends any deep habit of mind that has for a long time been rigorously suppressed. It was slowed, not merely by the entrenchment of the Germanic spirit, but by a factor of considerable but neglected importance: unlike English, both Greek and Latin are dead languages, poorly preserved and poorly documented, lacking precisely that richness of information about language which is everywhere the essential condition of the newer criticism. But in the enthusiasm for a method that had the advantage of being at least literary, that honored the work for itself and not for its historical or informational uses, this crucial limitation was brushed aside. Real excesses, however, were prevented by the salutary insistence of the older generation that the fundamental responsibilities of the scholar be observed. This insistence, because defensive, was both surly and grumpy, but it had its effect: at least no classical critic, to my knowledge, has yet proclaimed that the *Oresteia* is a "hierarchy of epiphanies." Moreover, from the first, the impulse to the restoration of criticism to scholarship in America came as much from the humane tradition of European scholarship as from critics like Empson, Brooks, Ransom and Blackmur. Indeed, it was on the whole European scholars who first appreciated the refinement of verbal techniques offered by the New Criticism. Besides, no critic worth his salt, however belligerent, could honestly deny that the extreme poverty of fact which attends classical studies had long ago forced scholars to adopt in desperation something very like the New Criticism: one thinks of Jebb's monumental close-reading of Sophocles, with its susceptibility to shade and texture; Wilamowitz' great edition of the *Heracles*, and now of Fraenkel's *Agamemnon*; on still another level, verging toward the perverse or crankish, are the strange works of Verrall and Norwood on Euripides and such non-classical oddities as Samuel Butler's *The Authoress of the Odyssey*.

But in the last ten years it is abundantly clear that criticism has returned to classical scholarship; if the New Criticism as such is not yet, in classics, the heavy industry it has become in English studies, its pressure is clearly visible and especially among the younger generation. The direct influence of the critics themselves upon classical studies has mostly been oblique, and, more often than not, unfortunate: Francis Fergusson's able but unconvincing piece on the *Oedipus Rex* is some kind of exception, extraordinary in its perceptivity, but crippled in its too great reliance upon theories of the ritual origins of tragedy. And neither Kenneth Burke's strange essay on the *Oresteia* nor Edmund Wilson's perversion of the *Antigone* provides reliable models. But the New Criticism is writ large in Goheen's study of the imagery of the *Antigone*, diffused throughout Kitto's *Greek Tragedy* and Lattimore's superb introduction to his translation of the *Oresteia*, or Owen's fine commentary on the *Iliad*, and everywhere visible in the spate of dissertations which study single plays or single metaphors or the master-tropes of tragedy, and in the insistent emphasis upon the key terms of the New Critics: irony, ambiguity, symbol, tone, image, texture, formal structure and myth. And finally, even the classical journals and the professional societies have shown in the last few years a grudging willingness to admit the newer critics as at least junior partners in the firm.

From the point of view of the past, these are encouraging signs, and all the more so since critical activity has here been accompanied by extraordinary energy in the field of translation—the new translations of Homer, tragedy, Vergil, Ovid, Hesiod, Pindar and Greek lyric. Good translation is, of course, exemplary and creative criticism: to have an *Iliad* or an *Oresteia* as substantial and moving as we have in Lattimore's translations is to have a guarantee of the fresh and right response of feeling without which criticism is an empty exercise. In this sense translations and criticism work hand in hand, each sponsoring the other's vitality: just as criticism is crippled if it neglects scholarship, so the translator's task is vitiated without the act of criticism. In this connection the difference between Lattimore's *Oresteia* and Pound's *Trachiniae* is illuminating; for what makes Pound's translation incomparably the poorer of the two is the way in which, the scholarship suspended almost altogether, the critical sense is so impaired that it can no longer supervise the adjustment of language to the moral and emotional facts of the play. Talent here, tethered to nothing except Pound's extraordinary sense of music, has gone rogue and wild. By which I do not mean, of course, that Lattimore's scholarship makes him an acceptably tame poet; on the contrary, there is an immense turbulence in his translation, but it is a true and Aeschylean turbulence, not an imposed wildness. Good poetry guarantees good turbulence; the work of critic and scholar are required to make that turbulence Aeschylean and true.

Up to now the most conspicuous failure of both the traditional and the new critics in respect to Greek tragedy has been the failure to realize turbulence: turbulence of experience, turbulence of morality in the process of getting made, and the turbulence of ideas under dramatic test. If any one charge can be brought against the older criticism, it would be, I think, that it has seemed to ask too little of Greek tragedy, and asking so little, has rarely discovered much. Its crucial failure has come at the point where all criticism is finally tested: the ability to transfer complex experience from one period or language to another, and to get the substance of that experience—its turbulence as well as its final order—into language. This is, of course, in the end, impossible, but it is the ideal by which we measure the adequacy of any interpretative criticism. Where the older criticism failed was in the deeper skills of the very humanity it professed, the point where passion is used to make the experience from which any great image of humanity, like the Greek one, is made. Intensely obsessed with history and politics, the traditional criticism failed to show how history and politics got into tragedy and what they did there in relation to the humanity of the heroes; concerned with man and his destiny, it could never quite conjure up the complex reality of experience and suffering that in the Greek plays gives human passion its meaning; committed to the task of clarity, it failed on the whole to remove that dense patina of stiffness and strangeness and austerity that makes Greek tragedy so formidable to our first impressions, or translated it into sentimental commonplaces and limp passions.

Who, after all, is really stirred by the standard interpretations of the *Antigone*—that tidy passion of a perfect heroine caught up on the gods' errand and hindered by a brutal Creon, a conforming Ismene, and a dunderheaded chorus with an inexplicable gift of tongues? And who believes the fashionable reverse, with its stubborn and presumptuous Antigone, its tragic Creon and its misunderstood Ismene? These interpretations are, to my mind, not credible because they so clearly violate the emotional experience of the play or reduce its difficulties to the vanishing-point. What has not gotten into them is the play's real turbulence and complexity and what they express is rather the superficial order the play throws up as its terms or its field, not its subject or solution. What is missing is what, to my mind, the play insists upon in both action and character: the way in which Antigone, trying to uphold a principle beyond her own, or human, power to uphold, gradually empties that principle in action, and then, cut off from her humanity by her dreadful heroism, rediscovers herself and love in the loneliness of her death; not the opposition between Antigone and Creon, but the family resemblance which joins them in a common doom; not great heroism justified by great principles, but conduct in the fateful grip of principles, making out of courage and love a deeper principle altogether. And if you look to the *Oedipus Rex* or the *Agamemnon* or the *Bacchae*, it seems to me you find the same impoverishment: what is real or turbulent in the life of those plays is for the most part expelled, either because the critic has let his own principles of order usurp the play, or because his own experience is unequal to it, or because he refuses the act of criticism once it gets near the difficult edge of experience. How many interpretations of the *Oedipus Rex*, for instance, have come to grief on the fruitless quest for a tragic flaw that will justify the hero's suffering simply in order that Aristotle be justified. How commonly the cry of botching is raised against Euripides because his plays refuse to conform to the critic's expectations of proper organic structure. And how little of the full turbulence of the *Orestes* or *Bacchae*—those great pitiless mirrors of the terrible political and social desperation of late fifth-century Hellas—does our criticism get, largely because we ask so much less of tragedy than it requires.

Thanks to the New Criticism, we can hope to see the turbulence of language and rhetoric restored to tragedy, for the New Critics are nothing if not keen-nosed where verbal subtlety and density are concerned. And we have, I think, everything to hope for from the thorough examination of the rhetorical habits of Greek tragedy. But I sometimes wonder whether a keen nose for metaphor, irony or ambiguity is much to the point when the spoor is as old and crossed as that of Greek tragedy. It is, for instance, extremely difficult in fifth-century literature to distinguish between metaphor that is genuinely fresh and metaphor that has hardened into idiom or *cliché*; we simply do not possess the linguistic evidence that might allow us to tell them apart. How fresh, for instance, are those yoke and ship images which run like master-tropes through all three tragedians? Or are these simply the metaphorical idiom of an agricultural and seafaring people? The answer, of course, lies in a desperately difficult tact, but that tact comes far harder in Greek and Latin than it does in a living literature like English where we understand stress and tone as we never can in Greek. And the chances are high, of course, that tact will disappear before the critic's drive for conceptual consistency: I know of at least one treatment of the symbolism of the *Oresteia* where the interpretation derived more from the itch for conceptual rigor in the imagery than from the emotional experience of the play. And this risk seems to me particularly high for the New Criticism in its academic setting, where the old insistence upon methodology and the student's necessary economies with complexity combine to harden method into mere formula.

I would not, of course, like the consciousness of risk to damage the enterprise: we badly need in Greek tragedy just that refinement of rhetoric which has been the success of the New Criticism. We need to know, for instance, just how those *sententiae* with which Greek tragedy is so lavish and which so embarrass modern producers of Greek plays, arise from the action; the structure of *stichomythia*, that brisk staccato exchange of single lines for up to a hundred lines at a time, is badly in need of work; I suspect that the relation between metaphor and dance-figures is crucially important; we know very little about irony in tragedy, so little that the tone of whole scenes and even whole plays is in question; the language itself, with its curious alternation between stiff archaism and colloquial speech, its habits of rhetorical movement, from the big jaw-breaking, piled-up compounds of Aeschylus to the deceptive simpleness of Euripides, is still *terra incognita*; and I suspect that we have barely started to do the work required by the choral lyrics. Beyond these jobs, it is my personal conviction that the study of tragedy would enormously benefit from a shift in perspective; we need to question, that is, our tacit assumption that Greek tragedy is staged in a religious context or represents a kind of collective worship, for the assumption vitally affects interpretation. And it seems to me that nothing but chaos can come from the fashionable notion that because Greek tragedy begins in ritual, its structure is therefore ritual dramatized, its hero a ritual scapegoat, and its action a shadow play of the death of the *Eniautos-daimon* or god of the year. The more I read of Greek tragedy, that is, the more I am impressed with its very distance from its ritual origins and its stubborn refusal to behave as honest ritual should. And there is something violently improbable about an image of the Greek theatre which does the kind of damage done by Gilbert Murray's recanted theory of its ritual elements and more recently by Francis Fergusson in his study of the *Oedipus*.

If we require an idea of the Greek tragic theatre at all, it seems to me that the clue might best be taken from the very charge of rhetoric so persistently brought against tragedy, and against Euripides in particular ever since the time of Schlegel. Over and over again, that is, the late fifth-century tragedy seems to suggest as its informing image a theatre shaped more by the law-court than by the altar. In this theatre, the *agon* is viewed essentially as a trial, and the characters, with all the tricks of sophistic rhetoric, put their cases in opposed speeches—often of identical length, as though timed by the waterclock of the Athenian dikastery. The audience in this theatre sits as jurors, not merely a panel of five hundred jurors, but the full *Heliaea*, the sovereign judicial assembly *(ekklesia)*. No appeal, no matter how emotional, is debarred, and each character in his plea speaks with the formal passion of a man whose life and fortunes hang upon his words. But it is a formal and rhetorical passion, below which we can glimpse, as the jury must, the personal passion and the real motives glozed by the rhetoric and often exposed in action. Such a theatre, of course, is most appropriate to Euripides, but in some degree, I think, to Sophocles also, especially in the later plays. I find tentative confirmation of this not merely in the number of Greek tragedies which openly stage formal trial scenes, but in the very structure of Euripidean drama: its persistent avoidance of the single hero in favor of the *agon* of two chief characters—Pentheus vs. Dionysus, Phaedra vs. Hippolytus, Orestes vs. Menelaus, Ion vs. Creusa—and the corresponding division of so many plays into two almost disparate actions; the flat assertion of the intention to make a formal plea; and, most important, the constant impression of the plays as problem plays in which the judgment is never asserted, but left, as it were, to the audience of jurors. If they understand the play, they make the right decision, or better, understand that no moral decision is relevant because the problems are beyond the reach of moral judgment, i.e. are both tragic and true. If this is correct, it is understandable why the constant imposition upon Euripides of Aristotelian structure and the notion of a religious theatre so regularly distort him. I throw this suggestion out, not as a developed thesis, but merely as a hint. For it seems to me that in the study of tragedy, as in almost any other human study, the discoveries come in that slight shift of perspective which we get when we examine those prejudices and assumptions which are so close to habit that we are almost unaware of them. And both our almost unconscious Aristotelianism and our deep assumption that Greek tragedy is finally religious tragedy are habits which I think need severe scrutiny by any serious critic of Greek drama.

The last charge which I should like to bring against the New Criticism is related to just this refusal to examine one's oldest habits. It is finally full interpretation of the plays and the tragedians that we want, and I find it puzzling that the newer criticism of Greek tragedy so seldom undertakes the full job. This may be modesty, but I suspect it is the old illusion of objectivity in fancy dress; and between *Quellenforschungen* and metaphor-snooping, both uprooted from the values they are intended to discover or reinforce, I can see very little difference. It is not merely that the New Criticis have failed to take up the job of full interpretation, however, that I find distressing, but the fact that their analyses proceed more from the habit of old interpretation than the fresh act. I am not by this proposing that the New Critics should make their fortunes by systematically inverting all traditional criticism, but that

analysis, wherever possible, should free itself from the immense authority of
the standard interpretations. A book I admire, Goheen's analysis of the
imagery of the *Antigone*, originally written as a dissertation and suffering the
handicaps of that impossible genre, ably illustrates just how much the New
Critics have to offer in enriching our criticism of tragedy. But unless I am
mistaken, Goheen's close analysis is subtly hindered by the authority of the
nineteenth-century *Antigone*, whose shape guides the analysis where it needs
to go, but not where it might have gone were its destination a little less
certain. This is not slyness, of course, but the necessarily blinkered gaze of
good conviction: you look where you are going, not askance. But the one
metaphor Mr. Goheen overlooks—the metaphor of alienation, Antigone as
metic or peregrine—a casual sport so far as his theory is concerned, seems to
me the one metaphor that most illuminates the key word of the play—*philia*
or love. Habit is hard to shed, of course, but in the case of Greek tragedy
where critical habit has hardened into cultural habit, I think it is crucial to
any hope of a fresh and exacting criticism.

In this connection one point deserves mention. Greek tragedy is, *par
excellence*, a sacred cow, even more sacred, I suspect, than Shakespeare, since
it is seldom produced or else produced via the atrocious medium of Mr.
Robinson Jeffers and Broadway; and most students get introduced to it in the
killing atmosphere of reverential hush that attends the reading of any classic
in our general humanities courses. Worse, fewer and fewer literary men read
Greek nowadays or read it with sufficient security to challenge the scholars
on their own ground, as Goethe challenged Schlegel and Matthew Arnold
challenged Newman with enormously fruitful results. And in scholarship, as
I suggested earlier, unconscious timidity in the face of the accumulated
judgments of dead scholars is a deep critical habit. In evidence of this attitude
of blind deference to Greek tragedy, let me cite the production not so long
ago on Broadway of two Greek plays by a modern Greek repertory troupe:
night after night, audiences and dramatic critics, unable to understand a
word of the productions, but deeply impressed with the performance of their
cultural duties, willfully applauded on the curious assumption that Greek
tragedy is mostly gesture anyway, and that a modern Greek company, by
virtue of being Greek, somehow must possess the secrets of ancient Greek
tragedy. Against adulation like this, it may be beyond the power of critcism
to help, and the critic himself may be insensibly drawn into the work of
justification rather than criticism. But it needs to be pointed out that we are
in real danger of taking over almost intact the canon of Greek tragedy which
the nineteenth century established. Who, after all, except classical scholars,
now reads any Aeschylus except the *Oresteia* and *Prometheus*, any Sophocles

except the Theban plays, and what Euripides besides the *Alcestis, Medea, Hippolytus* and *Bacchae?* I am not, of course, suggesting that these are not great plays, but that the canonizing of them into a cultural monument damages the chosen eleven as much as the excluded tragedies.

Worse, the difficulty is not merely that we have adopted an old taste, but the habits that accompany that taste as well, and especially the nineteenth century habit of making Sophocles the norm, if not the ideal, of tragedy—a habit which has done great damage to Aeschylus and almost irreparable damage to Euripides. It is no accident, for instance, that the favored plays of Euripides are precisely those which appear to meet the standards of so-called Aristotelian structure, that is, the "organic structure" which critics think they find in Sophocles. Against this tendency, I can only argue that it botches Sophocles as badly as Euripides, and that it cuts off our access to a power in Euripides that meant very little to the nineteenth-century but everything to the twentieth—I mean that part of Euripides that is concerned with political desperation, the corruption of power, and the corrosion of the civilized virtues into a set of specious slogans for demagogic consumption. We need not only the *Bacchae,* but the *Hecuba,* the *Heracles,* the *Orestes, Electra, Supplices* and *Trojan Women*—all plays in which we should sense the full turbulence of one of the very greatest of dramatists in a context that very easily becomes our own. But this means production as well as criticism, since nothing hinders the critic's right perception of a play more than the perpetual unavailability of his material in living form. At the moment, I can think of no greater service to Greek tragedy than the regular production of those plays that lie outside the canon and are so commonly regarded as undramatic, and particularly the plays of Euripides whose structure is censured by critics who have never seen them performed. But such a service needs to be regular, a continuous repertory, production, and not merely those sporadic productions which derive from a duty to the classics; but it is a service I hope some lively academic theatre may be encouraged to perform, since Broadway offers even less to Greek tragedy than it does to the modern playwright.

What, in the meantime, should criticism do? I spoke earlier of the turbulence traditional criticism missed, and, at its most general, the charge I have preferred against the criticism of tragedy is its incompleteness. What was incomplete in the older criticism was that it over-generalized experience and missed whatever was complex and particular in human passion; it took the particular turbulence for granted, that is, and thereby leached its own generalizations of what should have given them life. What the newer criticism missed was meant to be implied by what it got—turbulence of language; but the implications, trapped by the New Criticism's notorious penchant for the autonomy of the work and its deep embarrassment in the face of value, only rarely succeeded; experience got swamped in the generalizing drive of the symbolism or the technique of the dramatist's work. What I want to restore to the criticism of tragedy is a sense, a feel, a look of significantly lived experience, particular before being general, the turbulence of the actual disorder of experience as it moves on to make the dramatist's order. To restore depth and passion to the terms of experience—the notion of a personal fate, responsibility, purpose, the emotions before and after their moralizing, illusion, necessity and reality; to show how values burgeon out of structure and plot; to know again why the plot is the "soul of the play," not its skeleton; to see that any character in a play who lives and uses his passion is prior to anything he may stand for; to refresh the simplicity of reason through the complexity of passion, not the other way around: this is a part of what I mean by turbulence, the turbulence to which both the critic and the producer are responsible. Unless the criticism of tragedy can make itself big enough to talk about experience at the level it proposes, it is doomed to even greater inadequacy than even criticism must normally expect. To talk about literature at the level of experience implies a criticism large enough to contain what is chaotic in experience as well as what is orderly. And it is my conviction that criticism of Greek tragedy, too heavily committed to the criteria of orderly reason and the rhetoric of intelligence, has dehumanized its heroes by cutting them off from the condition in relation to which they win their meaning. The hero, cut off by an inadequate criticism from the actual power and anguish of the condition he can never quite escape without destroying himself, loses the terrible tension and redeeming dignity of his equivocal status.

Nothing comes easier than to ask criticism to become more complete and humane, and nothing is harder to do. Nor can we prescribe methods for doing it without sooner or later ramming our plays into categories which violate them. What we need at this point seems to me not more method, but a refreshment of perspective: and particularly we want perspectives which undercut our old methods as they harden into habit and prevent us from seeing more than they allow. It is by such refreshment of perspective that we are apt to enlarge our criticism. At least this is my hope in the following remarks.

II

I suggested earlier that one refreshment of perspective might be found in a shift in our traditional idea of the Greek theatre, at least as that idea affects Euripides. And I should like to suggest further that we need much more precision in dealing with the hero and a different purchase on that central and elusive concept. What is most urgently needed is some sense of flexibility and variety in the ways heroism is manifested, and more attention to the *dramatic* use of the hero. The difficulty is not merely that we fail to distinguish between generic kinds of heroism or between the heroism of one dramatist and another, but that discussion begs almost all of the questions that affect the *dramatic* status of the hero in relation to his own humanity and also skirts whatever experience is relevant to the earning of heroism. Attempts to meet this problem with a unitary concept, as in Whitman's recent book on Sophocles, have been Procrustean in result: it is, of course, a pleasure to be rid of the view that Sophocles was an enlightened bishop and his heroes Anglicans in trouble, but a Nietzschean Sophocles with a Zarathustrian Antigone hardly helps us much. But most commonly heroism is treated in drastically abrogated moral terms, or made to satisfy the Aristotelian theory of the hero's tragic flaw, or reduced to the protagonist, or hypostatized and used as a critical *deus ex machina*. The crucial questions relevant to heroism, however, seem to me to be the following. First, how is heroism asserted in tragedy and how is it sustained, both morally and dramatically? What skills of experience or reality distinguish the hero from the other characters and from his former self? What is the relation between the achieved dramatic reality of the hero and his symbolic dignity? What is the cost of heroism to the hero in contrast to the values of what his heroism asserts? How does the hero's mortality affect his morality? What are the *legitimate* limits of the hero's responsibility for his nature or his acts? What is the relation between necessity and illusion in the hero's ability to rise to, and even surpass, the meaning of his own experience?

All of these questions are uprooted from the plays that propose them, but they are proposed by the plays at that level where criticism cannot refuse them without really refusing everything. As they affect the *Antigone*, for instance, they seem to me to illuminate the whole moral and experiential fabric of the play. Here if ever, for instance, the tension between the cost of heroism and the values of its assertion is both vivid and crucial. Half of the dynamic horror of Antigone's tragedy is precisely her equivocal status: torn between the cold heroism of her assertion of principle and her humanity, she almost loses her humanity in the fateful grip of her principle. What distinguishes her from Creon? Principle, of course, but look again, and the distinction is replaced by the family resemblance, a stubborn intractable loyalty to principle, and even a resemblance in principle, for both claim to act on behalf of love, *philia*. This principle, it is true, may be translated to another level and replaced by a struggle between family gods and state gods, but both protagonists claim at bottom to be agents of love: Antigone asserts that she was born to love *(sumphilein)* while Creon, in words that have been very strangely neglected, clearly states that he acts on behalf of the state *because philia*, love, can only exist within the context of a stable and orderly society. And this same *philia* is, of course, Ismene's principle too, without Antigone's courage, but *philia* for all that; and when Antigone refuses Ismene the right to die with her, she refuses her sister, her *phil?*, both her own principle and the dignity of a personal fate. If, then, Antigone is the heroine of *philia*, we have to see, in action, what it means to act for *philia* in a conflict of *philiai*; how fate is here set against fate; how the family resemblance between Creon and Antigone is carried out in action up to the moment of heroism, and only then are they separated in a common doom. If we see these things, I think we cannot help seeing and reporting the turbulence also: the real disorder (but also the tragic symmetry) of a world where the living of love involves the denial of love elsewhere; where morality unmakes itself in conflict and is refreshed by significant passion; where heroism in the end means not surpassing one's humanity but discovering and incarnating its dignity at the moment of agony, and where the hero, finding weakness he never suspected, finds also his greatest strength. The hero, says Plato in one of his wonderfully crazy etymologies, "is born of love [that is, *er?s*]"; or, to put it in other terms, the hero is reduced, but also raised, to the human condition. So, at least, it seems to me with Antigone.

What she first accepts as a fate, the principle of love that dooms her to death, is hardened by her desperate plight and her desperate courage and loneliness; and this in turn hardens her—"Great suffering makes a stone of the heart," as Yeats puts it—making her refuse Ismene the same dignity of fate she claims. As she hardens, so does Creon on behalf of the same principle, denying Haemon in order to hurt Antigone, just as Antigone dishonors Ismene in order to honor Polyneices. Still hardened, but increasingly tormented by a loss she does not understand and yet the fate she chose, Antigone is condemned to her symbolic death, walled alive in a tomb, and thus cut off alike from both the living and the dead, the human being still alive, like Niobe, beneath the cold rock of her heroism. And suddenly, as the chorus compares her to a goddess, she knows what has happened, and cries, "I am mocked, I am mocked!" and the rock falls away, leaving that final warm confusion that makes her so human and so lovely. In all this Creon is left far behind, though he suffers perhaps even worse; he never had Antigone's human skills to begin with; he knows only the horror, Antigone knows the horror and the glory. And that knowledge, or better, merely *being* that knowledge, the final knowledge of tragedy, is Antigone's heroism. Until you come to that point, however, the experience is troubled, criss-crossed with paradox, turbulent with lonely passion and isolated meaning; if simplicity supervenes with heroism, that simplicity owes all of its power to the turbulence it tries to resolve.

Alternatively, in dealing with Euripides, we need to observe how the whole context of heroism has altered; that we are dealing with a world where the senselessness of circumstance may deprive the hero of responsibility, or strike at a point where responsibility is no longer relevant, as in the *Hecuba* or *Heracles*. With such an alteration, the nature of heroism is also altered, since its necessities change. Thus in the *Heracles*, the hero declares his triumph over the amoral powers which afflict him by the simple act of enduring in a world which tells him to die. For Euripides preserves the disorder of actual experience, measuring its horror against the unrequited illusion of order which sustains human beings, and the final dignity of Heracles is that he asserts the human cry for order and meaning almost in the very teeth of his own experience of hideous disorder. And the whole motive of the play is to bring the hero to the point where he shares, for the first time, common ground with the other characters. He discovers, that is, his condition and its anguish, an anguish from which his great strength has hitherto exempted him; in the discovery of anguish comes the discovery of community and love in weakness before necessity, Love is the hope which finally permits Heracles to endure a hideous necessity he never made, and from his discovery of love and helplessness flow acceptance and courage, the courage which asserts the human demand for order in a world which annuls all hope of a *moral* order. So much may be immediately obvious, but the point I should like to make is precisely the profound relationship between the hero's progress and the structure of the play, the way in which the created or assumed reality of each part of the play exactly defines, as challenge and disorder, the growth of heroism and order, forcing Heracles steadily back upon his humanity in order to refresh his heroism. Yet the *Heracles* has been savagely censured for its dislocation of plot, its apparent division into two discrete actions bound together by nothing more than sequence. But unless I am mistaken, everything that seems strange about the play's structure can be explained in terms of its intent, the conversion of heroism via the conversion of reality and necessity. At least it seems to me that, far from being botched, the *Heracles* is one of the most wonderfully constructed plays of Greek tragedy, if we mean by good construction a plot exactly designed to force meaning into action. What hinders us here, however, is the deeply Aristotelian bias of our critical habits and especially the habit of imposing the example of the *Oedipus Rex* upon all other Greek plays. We expect unity to be of one kind, and missing it, we misread or condemn the play in order to salvage our own bad habits.

Heroism is, of course, more difficult to comprehend in those plays—far more common than we like to believe—where we have no central dominating hero in the manner of the *Oedipus Rex* and the *Heracles.* Indeed, in the case of Euripides, the single hero is a comparative rarity. We have, for instance, a group of plays on the order of the *Hippolytus* or the *Phoenissae*, in which heroism is diffused over several characters or the whole human cast, and others, like the *Orestes*, the *Hecuba* and—I believe—the *Bacchae*, where there are protagonists but no heroes, and no heroism either. What you get in the *Orestes* is really like what you get in Shakespeare's *Troilus and Cressida:* an image of heroism seen as botched, disfigured and sick, carried along by the slogans and machinery of heroic tragedy and then exposed in action. This is neither a satire of tragedy, however, nor a melodramatic perversion, but tragedy of total turbulence, without a principle of order in sight except that order implied in the observation that heroism has been botched and all order omitted. Consider the *Bacchae* in this respect. Attempts to make heroes out of Pentheus and even Dionysus have not succeeded for obvious reasons: at least I find it hard to see the stuff of heroism in Pentheus' irritable voyeurism and Dionysus has all the heroism of an earthquake. What we have, of course, is not heroic tragedy but a tragic contest between parties who all claim to act on behalf of the same principle—*sophia*, badly translated as "wisdom"—and who all alike deprave their principle in action. What alone can order the play and judge that depravity to which *sophia* is subjected is an understanding of right *sophia;* but it is important to see that the play omits by merely implying the only order appropriate to its instances of heroism failed.

My point, then, is the simple one that heroism is too complex a term to be handled loosely, and that, if mishandled, it generates trouble in other directions. We need a tact with our terms which can distinguish when a particular concept is demanded and when it is superfluous; so far as heroism is concerned, we particularly need precision when we attempt to relate it to *dramatic* movement, plot, genre, and a particular dramatist. Where our definitions tend to be static rather than dynamic, or uprooted from a single type, or abstracted from one dramatist and imposed upon others, we impoverish tragedy in the critical act.

Likewise, in reading Aeschylus, we need to observe how a shifting or evolving cosmology fundamentally conditions the nature and possibilities of heroism. For surely we cannot alter the basic laws of the world in which men live and suffer without thereby deeply affecting the moral quality of their conduct and the judgments relevant to it. And the *Oresteia* is, of course, just such an evolving cosmology: a dramatic image of the gradual evolution, according to the masterplan of Zeus, of the institution of civilized justice. The progress itself hardly needs documentation. No one can read or see the trilogy and miss those wonderful transfigurations that chart the progress of justice from primitive blood-vengeance to civilized trial by jury: the blood-red tapestries on which Agamemnon goes to his death, suddenly revealed as the holy red robes of the transfigured Furies, or the metamorphosis of Persuasion *(Peitho)* from the sinister abstraction that seduces Helen, to Clytemnestra's coiling rhetoric as she lures Agamemnon to his doom, and finally that patient, crucial argument by which Athena persuades the Furies to accept an honored place in the new dispensation of Zeus. We are witnessing nothing less than the conversion of a world *and*, as the Chorus tells us, the reconciliation of Zeus and the Fates. Throughout the trilogy, from murder to murder to murder, we have been promised a fulfillment, a dawn, a delivery out of this intolerable net of contradictory evils, and finally, after so many false dawns and illusory solutions, we are shown the manifest pattern of Zeus the Fulfiller, the silver strand in the tapestry of blood.

A parable, then, of tragic scope, a passion of men and gods struggling from darkness into the light: so much is obvious. But if no one misunderstands the nature of the light, what do we make of the darkness there in the *Agamemnon* where everything is chaos and contradiction, where men are apparently whirled helplessly from evil to worse evil, with no end in sight ever? What, in other words, is the relation of Zeus of the *Eumenides* to the darker Zeus of the *Agamemnon?* Is he an inscrutable god, secretly at work behind all the apparent contradictions, slowly forcing the whole action toward an inevitable conclusion? A kind of Greek Jehovah, that is, tempting men, out of his enormous bewildering mystery, to cramp him in the small boxes of their own petty theodicies? Or is he like the Zeus of the Prometheus-trilogy, an undeveloped god who once again undergoes a progress from callous indifference to a final moral wisdom tempered by compassion? Or is he a gradualist, a reforming Fabian demiurge, hampered by a whole host of discordant powers, the still potent heirs of an older dispensation; and by quarrels on Olympus too?

As I see it, the world of the *Agamemnon* is clearly one in which the possibility of moral action is obscured and prevented by a deep discord in the nature of things. We have a prospect of insuperable moral difficulty, a nightmare of justice in which the assertion of any right involves a further wrong, in which fate is set against fate in an intolerable, necessary sequence of violence. There is Zeus, of course, and Zeus is strong; but if the Chorus, in a famous ode; praises Zeus' power and wisdom, we are meant to read that prayer; I think, not as a factual description of a known Zeus, but as a last desperate act of faith, cried in the very teeth of experience: *sorrow, sorrow, but may good win out in the end*. In other words, the *Agamemnon* presents us with a world which is at all points essentially Homeric; nothing, in fact, in the entire *Agamemnon*, including the choral ode on Zeus, is incompatible with the cosmology of Homer. The life of men on earth, torn this way and that by conflict and irresponsibility in heaven, is a tragic hell; and if men and gods jointly share the responsibility for human actions, the choices are irreparably clouded by inconsistency and discord among the gods. In the *Iliad* and the *Odyssey* there is a double standard: divine adultery, for instance, is comic, but human adultery is terribly punished. So too the *Agamemnon* shows us, in conscious juxtaposition, the same double standard: Agamemnon himself is the fatally chosen instrument of Zeus to punish the adultery of Paris, but Apollo callously and with impunity seduces Cassandra and leads her to her death at Clytemnestra's hands. The contrast could hardly be more glaring. And though in the *Eumenides* Apollo may very well incarnate the ruthlessness of the male in a contest with the female Furies, it is an intentional anomaly in the *Agamemnon* that the same ruthlessness should be visited on a helpless human victim. And what are we to make of the fact that Artemis, "angered at the flying hounds of her father," should openly flout the will of Zeus and demand the sacrifice of Iphigeneia before allowing the Greeks to proceed on the Zeus-enjoined conquest of Troy? The only possible conclusion is surely that there is discord in heaven, just as in the *Iliad* we see god set against god in a perpetual attempt to slow or cross the will of Zeus. Anomaly, contradiction, moral irresponsibility on earth and in heaven: this is the world of the *Agamemnon*, and it is, I think, precisely what we should expect. How else, dramatically speaking, could Aeschylus have shown us his gradual progress toward the light? For the light requires a darkness to dispel, and the darkness of the *Agamemnon* is a deliberately constructed one, not the result of the dramatist's confusion or inconsistency.

A related problem: does Agamemnon enjoy freedom of action or was he compelled to sacrifice Iphigeneia? Once again the answer, I think, is the Homeric one, which is to say that Agamemnon freely chose but he was also compelled to choose. So in the *Iliad* we see Agamemnon freely confiscate Achilles' prize and so bring on the fatal wrath; later, however, he declares that it was not he who did it but Zeus and Ate, which is simply Homer's way of sustaining the crucial doubleness of all his action: Agamemnon chose an act which Zeus also chose him to do. To modern ears this may seem an evasion of difficulty by way of paradox, but the notion, I believe, is firmly classical and also commonsenscial: we all think we act with freedom though upon reflection it frequently seems that we could not possibly have acted otherwise than we did. So in the *Agamemnon* we find the Chorus declaring that Agamemnon put on the yoke of necessity, but before that it asks: "What course without evils?" Which, at least to my ears, suggests choice, however small in fact that choice may have been. In short, Agamemnon chooses his necessity, but equally Zeus' necessity chose him; being the kind of man he is, he chooses as he does. Consider in this connection the famous Aeschylean fragment: "when Zeus wishes to destroy a man's house utterly, he puts an *aitis* [i.e. a cause or responsibility] in the man." What does this mean except that a man acts from the necessity of his nature *and* as god compels him? Similarly we later find Agamemnon asserting that he and the gods are jointly responsible *[metaitioi]* for the destruction of Troy, and Clytemnestra likewise declares to Orestes that she and Destiny are jointly responsible accomplices *[paraitioi]* in the murder of Agamemnon. And surely it is just this joint responsibility that the action everywhere exhibits and requires. Thus in the famous central scene of the red tapestries, we see Agamemnon, reluctant and wary but also deeply tempted and guilty, finally lured into Clytemnestra's net as his fatal vanity once drove him, with the connivance and foreknowledge of heaven, to sacrifice his daughter. So too we can detect in Clytemnestra's action itself both the deep sources of her own motivation *and* the hand of heaven. She too chooses her revenge, but she is also the instrument chosen of heaven to cut down Agamemnon.

Consider also the deliberate parallel with Orestes. At the opening of the *Choephoroe* we find Orestes suffering under almost the same necessity as Agamemnon earlier: just as Artemis ordered Agamemnon to kill his daughter, so Orestes is commanded by Apollo to murder his mother. Hideous punishment is threatened if he disobeys, and yet Orestes, I think, can be said to choose here because he so clearly acts for motives that are properly his own: vengeance for his father and the recovery of his patrimony. He too chooses, that is, the act he is also constrained to commit. But there is this time a crucial difference: the comparative purity of the motive. Unlike Agamemnon and Clytemnestra, Orestes undertakes his murder with the reluctance and misgiving of an innocent heart and also with the determination of justice. Even Electra explicitly questions the wisdom of a god who could command that a mother be murdered by her son. For the first time, that is, in the history of the house of Atreus, a murder is being undertaken in something like purity of heart, for Orestes' act is clouded neither by his father's fatal vanity nor by his mother's jealousy and guilty hatred. It is revenge pure and simple, reluctant and unhappy and uncertain, but the nearest thing to the spirit of true justice that an age of vendetta-justice can offer. For we must be careful to judge the hero by the standards of the age in which he lives, and this is a world whose only justice as yet is the simple and brutal *lex talionis*.

Great consequences flow from this, I think, for innocence in this play is crucial. Not only does it signify to Zeus that the moment is at last ripe for the institution of civilized justice, but it is because Orestes' heart was pure and his action productive of conscience and remorse that he can, without divine inconsistency, be purged and finally acquitted. But there is more to it than that: precisely because Orestes' innocence is deeply his own, the native reaction of his own heart to the callous command of a god who told him to cut down his father's murderers "in their own fashion, to turn to the bull's fury in the loss of his estates," mankind becomes, through Orestes, partner and accessory [*metaitios*] with Zeus in the great act of justice that closes the trilogy. Orestes' act releases Zeus, but because the act was undertaken in free innocence, men share with Zeus the glory of the new justice which we now see has been Zeus' intent from the beginning. But wisdom on earth *must* precede Zeus' revelation: the condition of justice is the free and rightly motivated collaboration of men, and this could only come about when men discovered both innocence and compassion before necessity. Orestes kills but first he hesitates, and the whole world and the fate of mankind hang in that act of hesitation. For the play is about nothing less than the discovery of wisdom [*sophia*] under the yoke of awful necessity. To us, the heirs of Orestes' act, it may seem a small wisdom that a man who must kill should, for pity's sake, hesitate, but this is the wisdom appropriate to the necessity in question. And it marks, I think, in Aeschylus' eyes, a great moment in the fortunes of mankind, since it is the indispensable prerequisite of civilized justice itself. God sends necessity upon man that he may learn, and learning, become the partner of god in the great drama of the making of a civilized world.

Look back now at the *Agamemnon* from this vantage-point. If I am right, what we see is a world of terrible disorder, fate set against fate, god against god, man against man and god, all entangled in the great net of a justiceless, impossible justice. For this confusion, man and god are jointly responsible, but even the mind of Zeus is hampered and restricted by the still potent necessities of an older and more barbaric world-order. In this world, tragedy can only work itself out through time and suffering, and Zeus himself is powerless to act until the heart of man happens on the beginnings of a truer justice. For justice without the wisdom to sustain it would have been a meaningless gift, and wisdom, as the Chorus tells us, is learned in suffering. And so we see Clytemnestra and Agamemnon caught in a necessity which their own natures as well as the conflicting purposes of heaven have made. But we should not judge them too harshly; true, they do what they do and suffer what they suffer because they are what they are, but unless I am mistaken, we can almost hear Aeschylus saying between the lines, how can we expect men to be better than gods? If Agamemnon has murdered Iphigeneia, how much more brutal is the conduct of Apollo towards Cassandra. We must judge, that is, by the standards appropriate to Agamemnon's world, and if we judge him rightly we shall be in a position to understand the true stature of Orestes' heroism, surpassing in moral skills the god who commanded him to kill. Agamemnon, however proud, however guilty of *hybris*, is a man torn between the necessity of his own nature and the necessities imposed upon him by a world of moral disorder. He is not, I think, a true tragic hero—for Orestes is the hero of the *Oresteia*—but the self-involved tragic victim of a world which is as flawed as he is. He is therefore a candidate for compassion as much as judgment, and so are Clytemnestra and her victim, Cassandra. Only a mind unreceptive to the meaning of Athena's justice can refuse to give these casualties of a great cosmology in the making the human justice of pity and compassion. This, it seems to me, is an essential part of the real complexity and enormous moral turbulence of the *Oresteia*.

III

Unless I am mistaken, tragedy is also in deep need of some new perspectives in the matter of its operative moral terms as well as in structure and plot. And particularly, I think, we need to question again the relevance of Aristotle on at least two points—the socalled tragic flaw and the putative Aristotelian theory of tragic structure, the structure that draws its sanction from the *Oedipus Rex* and is reinforced by our modern preference for the organic. Aristotle is, I know, a rough customer: he has of necessity immense authority, and one is never quite sure whether one is talking about Aristotle or about something that has borrowed the authority of his name. But I have never been able to satisfy myself that the *Poetics* is the purely inductive treatise that scholars claim it is: again and again, that is, what is inductive in the *Poetics* seems to me to be directed by what is not, the pervasive notion of a purposive and rational universe and all that such a notion implies for tragedy and for the structure of tragedy. Thus for Aristotle a tragic fall is grounded in a consistent and harmonious sense of a man's responsibility for his nature and his actions: when the hero falls, he falls for his own failure, and behind the rightness of his fall, working both pity and terror by the precise and relentless nature of its operations, stands the order which society and a god-informed world impose upon the individual. What the law requires, the world requires too, and so the Aristotelian play portrays, like an image of human life, the individual torn and suffering between his nature and an objective world-order.

The tragic fall is, of course, in the common reading of Aristotle, based upon the hero's possession of a tragic flaw; and whether as doctrine or habit, the attempt to find a tragic flaw in Greek plays seems to me a persistent stumbling-block. If you really look at the *Oedipus*, for instance, it is immediately clear that Oedipus' tragic flaw is hard to discover: one wants to know—if you begin with the Aristotelian habit—just what in the hero's nature or his acts makes him suffer as hideously as he does, and the obvious answers—his anger, his treatment of Creon and Teiresias, his attempt to avoid his fate—are all unsatisfactory, or if satisfactory, indict the gods that could afflict a man so grievously for such offense. One recent critic of the play, an Aristotelian by conviction as well as habit, recognized his dilemma immediately and proceeded to solve it by the suggestion that Sophocles in this play has generalized *hamartia* into something like original sin: Oedipus has no particular flaws but suffers in the very flaw of his humanity. I suspect that very few classicists, whatever their religious color, will be happy with this theory, and I hope that even Aristotelians might object. But I use it to illustrate the kind of trouble that the expectation of a tragic flaw can create even in the treatment of a play which Aristotle regarded as the paradigm of his theories.

I cannot myself pretend to understand that mysterious play, but I wonder if we are perhaps not the better off for proceeding from the play rather than from Aristotle. Freed from our own *a prioris*, the experience of the play may at least propose itself in different terms. Thus it has always seemed to me that the single most pertinent fact of the *Oedipus* was not the hero's flaw, but his refusal to accept a ready-made fate: he wants his own fate, not the gods', and though his personal fate may be cut short by his doom, Oedipus at the close of the play insists upon distinguishing his own responsibility by blinding himself. It is the magnificence of his own declaration of responsibility that makes him so heroic: his fate is *his* and no one else's. His anger is anger, neither more nor less; it is not the source of his doom, but the irritant that he exhibits on the road to doom; and if he has a *hamartia*, it is not sin or flaw but the ungovernable tragic ignorance of all men: we do not know who we are nor who fathered us but go, blinded by life and hope, toward a wisdom bitter as the gates of hell. The cost of action is suffering, and heroism is the anguished acceptance of our own identities and natures, forged in action and pain in a world we never made. Whatever the final merits of this suggestion, it at least, I think, preserves the dignity of human passion in the play without violating in the name of a crude automatic justice the mysterious destiny that rules the play.

But crude or vulgar Aristotelianism[1] has hurt all three dramatists, and Euripides in particular, and one of the most urgent tasks for the criticism of tragedy is the thorough re-examination of Euripidean structure; once we get Euripides straight, we may be in a position to see just where we have subtly distorted Aeschylus and Sophocles in the name of a misunderstood Aristotle. But here again, I think, criticism might best begin from the obvious—the long insistence of critics that Euripidean plays lack unity, fall into disparate actions or are merely episodes strung together. We start, that is, from the fact of dislocation and attempt to see whether dislocation might not be deliberate method rather than the hit-or-miss *ad hoc* work of a genius who consistently botched. What is immediately apparent if we start from this point is the real co-herence of the plays so far as structure is concerned; what is most obvious in the *Heracles* or *Hecuba* is true also of the *Bacchae*, *Hippolytus* and *Medea:* all lack the kind of unity which the organic theory requires, all exhibit dislocation. If we ask why this is so, I think we find it mirrored by a curious doubleness in the action or in the given and created realities of the plays. Thus the *Heracles* shows two successive plateaus, the first a reality appropriate to legend and old convention, i.e. a world of mythical illusion, the second the full created tragic reality out of which heroism is born. If we look, say, at the *Orestes*, we discover a play which freely invents its own reality and then confronts the action so created with an epiphany of Apollo in which the whole motion of the play up to that point is flatly contradicted. We get a head-on collision, that is, between the action of the play and the traditionalizing impossible *deus ex machina*, and no attempt is made to modulate or explain these incompatible sequences. The same is true of the *Iphigeneia at Aulis*, and also, I think, of the *Medea* and *Electra:* their conclusions are simply at variance, as real events, from the whole tenor of the action. In the *Hippolytus* and *Bacchae* this doubleness is used in a different and less violent way: both plays dramatize the full incredibility of a traditional account of Olympian anthropomorphism—it is incredible that gods, real gods, should act as Dionysus and Aphrodite do. But once the familiar reality has been exposed and displaced, both plays proceed, in a symbolic manner, to hint at a deeper meaning and a different reality for these displaced gods. What I am trying to suggest is that again and again in Euripides, what makes the plays dislocated in structure is a deliberate juxtaposition of antithetical realities—the reality of the material which the play takes from legend and myth, and the new reality which the dramatist forces, as action, from his old material. We get the same kind of jar, that is, that our lives receive when they proceed upon inadequate conviction and are suddenly confronted with difficulty too great for the old conviction. But to my mind our understanding of Euripidean structure rests firmly upon our ability to understand the dramatic experience that bridges the two or even three plateaus of reality that most Euripidean plays exhibit. In the *Heracles*, for instance, we get between the two actions no *propter hoc* connection of the kind Aristotelians insist upon, and yet the connection seems to me, if not quite necessitous, at least valid with whatever validity the conversion of human experience possesses.

If heroism happens to arise from a fortuitous and accidental eruption of the irrational in the nature of things—as in the *Heracles* or the *Hippolytus*—the very fact that it *is* in the nature of things makes the eruption necessary or probable: we tend to disbar it only because our Aristotelian habits predispose us to a dramatic world like that of Sophocles, where the apparent irrationalities of experience are explained by a divine order we cannot comprehend. But as applied to Euripides, these habits and their corollary in a crude notion of the tragic flaw can only complicate chaos further. We need rather a theory of Euripidean structure which starts from dislocation and attempts to show the relation of this form to a world of moral disorder. Unless I am mistaken, such examination must also show the irrelevance of *propter hoc* structure to Euripides, whose sense of necessity in drama derives more from the motion of the human mind under stress and the patterns which men's convictions make when confronted by adventitious realities. A man's character may be his destiny, but for Euripides destiny is often dependent upon and defined by circumstances the hero never made, nor the gods either. Unless we can restore an understanding of the importance of the dramatist's assumed world for his form, Euripides must stand perpetually condemned or be explained with all the willful improbability of Verrall. At least the latest book on Euripidean structure—Gilbert Norwood's *Essays on Euripidean Drama*—makes the implicit claim that these dislocations of plot and internal inconsistencies in the plays are best explained as the work of fourth century redactors. This seems both unfortunate and unnecessary.

One final point. Nothing, I think, more effectively hinders our understanding of the experience of Greek tragedy than the inadequacy and crudity of meaning which critics and translators assign to the operative moral terms of Greek tragedy—*sophia, hybris, anankeē, sōphrosunē, aristeia, timē, authadia* and the like. For in much criticism of tragedy these terms are used as though they possessed simple English equivalents, without, I think, adequate reference to the experience with which they were meant to cope. Alternatively, they are exposed to static definition without regard to the transformations which tragedy may force upon them as the hero moves from a situation of conventional morality and reality to an ordeal for which the traditional wisdom of the Chorus may be utterly inadequate. In such situations it is my conviction that the old moral terms are employed with a meaning so turbulent with fresh or restored experience that they are no longer the same terms, nor the hero to whom they apply the same man. *Timē*, for instance, is normally translated as *honor*, but its root meaning is price, or valuation, and in most tragedies where the concept is important—the *Antigone*, for instance—the word operates very much like the deep sense of our word "respect." Thus when Ismene claims that Antigone has not shown *timē*, to her, and that Creon has not shown *timē*, to Haemon, she means, not that she and Haemon have been dishonored, or insulted, but that they have not been respected: they have been disallowed the dignity of a fate and their dignity as individuals. They have, as it were, been priced all wrong, and this charge is, of course, central to the play, since Antigone claims to act for *philia* because she wishes to give *timē*, to Polyneices. What, the play seems to suggest, is the assertion of *philia* worth without *timē*, too? And what is a *philia* which, in order to respect one person, shows disrespect to another, both equally claiming the rights of *philia?*

Or consider the word *sophia*, which we badly translate as "wisdom," as it gets into the *Bacchae*. Among other things, *sophia* means a knowledge and acceptance of one's nature and therefore of one's place in the scheme of things. It presupposes, that is, self-knowledge, an acceptance of those necessities that compose the limits of human fate. It also means the consequent refinement of feelings by which a man recognizes and respects the sufferings of others before necessity: it issues in compassion.[2] *Sophia* is further contrasted with its opposite, *amathia*, a deep, brutal, unteachable, ungovernable self-ignorance which breaks out in violence and cruelty! If the *sophos* is by definition susceptible to the feelings of civilized humanity, a compassion learned in fellow-suffering, the *amathēs* is callous and merciless, a barbarian by nature. But it is these meanings which crowd into the *Bacchae* and everywhere provide through dramatic action and testing, the play's missing principle of order. For in the course of the action, through the very brutality which they use to support their claims to *sophia*, both Pentheus and Dionysus utterly expose their own *amathia*.

But more than the self-indictment of Pentheus or Dionysus is involved here. For Euripides has taken elaborate pains to show in Pentheus something more than the man who does not know the deep Dionysiac necessity of his own nature: he is also the proud iconoclastic innovator, the rebel at war with tradition, standing outside of the community's *nomos* [custom as law] and as *theomachos*, disdainful of any power above man. Ranged against him are Cadmus, Teiresias and the chorus, who all alike appeal to the massive tyranny of tradition and folk-belief, and constantly invoke as the sanction of society against the rebellious or anti-traditional man the words *sōphrosunē* and *dikē*. Thus in flat opposition to Pentheus' lonely arrogance of the "exceptional" (*perissos*) man, defying the community's *nomos* in the name of his own self-will, is set the chorus' tyrannous tradition: "Beyond the old beliefs, no thought, no act shall go (891–2)." We have, that is, a head-on collision between the forces which represent a brutally depraved conservative tradition and the arrogant exemplar of the ruthlessly anti-traditional mind. Both positions are alike in the cruel and bigoted violence with which they meet opposition, and the *sophia* and *sōphrosunē* and *dikē* which they both claim mock their pretensions and condemn their conduct. If the conduct of the chorus and Dionysus outrage our sympathies and finally enlist them on Pentheus' behalf, it is because, in the nature of things, the *amathia* of a man is less heinous than that of a god. But both are *amatheis*, Pentheus no less than the chorus, and the play as a whole employs them and their struggle as a bitter image of both Athens and Hellas terribly divided between the forces that, in Euripides' mind, more than anything else destroyed them: on the one side, the conservative and aristocratic tradition in its extreme corruption, disguising avarice for wealth and power with the fair professions of the traditional *aretai*, meeting all attempts at change or moderation with the tyranny of popular piety, and disclosing in its actions the callousness and refined cruelty of civilized barbarism; on the other side, the exceptional individual, selfish and egotistical, impatient of public welfare and tradition alike, opportunistic, demagogic and equally brutal in action. In saying this, I do not intend to dispute the obvious religious concerns of the *Bacchae*, but to stress what, to my knowledge, has not been emphasized, that the play is, like the *Heracles*, the *Electra* and the *Orestes*, a composite of discrete conversions, social and political as well as religious. And all of these concerns meet in the term *sophia* and its opposite, *amathia*, which at their widest enclose most of what we mean by "civilized" and "uncivilized," both morally and politically. Thus when Euripides has his chorus assert that to *sophon* is not the same as *sophia*, he means that the pretensions and conventions and habits of civilization are by no means equivalent to civilized practices.

But in my opinion the same widening and deepening of the operative moral terms of Greek culture is to be found everywhere in tragedy—*philia in Antigone, sōphrosunē* in *Hippolytus, eugeneia* in *Heracles, aristeia* in *Orestes,* etc.— and it would be surprising if it were not so. But upon our sense of the play off the traditional or lazy meanings of these words and the definitions which the tragic action makes lies, I think, much of the turbulence now missing from the criticism of tragedy.

Let me close with a brief note on necessity, for necessity seems to me the crucial center of Greek tragedy, just as Greek tragedy seems to me unique in the firmness and sharpness with which it follows necessity into human action. In its basic aspect, necessity *(anankē)* is that set of unalterable, irreducible, unmanageable facts which we call the human condition. Call it destiny, call it fate, call it the gods, it hardly matters. Necessity is, first of all, death; but it is also old age, sleep, the reversal of fortune and the dance of life; it is thereby the fact of suffering as well as pleasure, for if we must dance and sleep, we also suffer, age and die. It is also sex, the great figure of amoral Aphrodite who moves in the sea, land and air and as an undeniable power in the bodies of men, compelling and destroying those who, like Hippolytus, refuse to accept her. Or it is Dionysus, the terrible ambiguous force of the *Bacchae,* "the force that through the green fuse drives the flower," and who destroys Pentheus who lacks the *sophia* that accepts him. It is the great god-sprung trap of the *Oedipus* and also the nature of Oedipus himself, that stubborn human courage of pride that drives him relentlessly into the trap. It is the necessity of political power which, in corruption, destroys Hecuba and Iphigeneia and Cassandra and Polyxena. It is the inherent hostility of blind chance, the incalculable daemonic malice which in the Euripidean *Heracles* calls out to the hero to die and tells him that there is no hope and no moral order in the world at all. Suspend necessity in the form of the play, and you get such charming, romantic plays as *Iphigeneia at Tauris* and the *Helen.* Romantic, that is, because not tragic; and not tragic because necessity, the mainspring of tragedy, has been, for fun, for entertainment and experiment, removed. Where men are freed from the yoke of necessity, their lives cease to be tragic, and with the loss of suffering comes also the loss of dignity and *sophia.*

For it is in the *struggle* with necessity that heroism is born, and even the hero, if he is to retain his humanity, must accept necessity. Ripeness is all. And so we see Orestes discover purity and compassion in the face of a necessity that threatens to deform him as it has already deformed his father and mother and as it inevitably deforms the weak, the flawed, the average human nature. So too Antigone accepts her necessity, the consequence of her own act, humanity pushed to the extreme, and thereby comes again upon her humanity in the very act of acceptance and recognition of loss. So Oedipus by asserting his total utter responsibility for his own fate, wins the victory over a necessity that would have destroyed a lesser man. And so Heracles claims a moral dignity forever out of reach of the amoral powers that persecute him. There is a magnificence here in the power to rise, in the anguished acceptance that must always, in Greek tragedy, precede the winning of dignity. For it is here before necessity that old morality is unmade and then remade into a new thing. Thus Orestes, having discovered at least that compassion that made him hesitate, enables justice to be born. And so too at the close of the *Hippolytus* and *Bacchae* we see the suffering human survivors of the play discover, under the awful yoke of an intolerable necessity, the love and *compassion*, the shared suffering that makes men endure with love in a world which shrieks at them to die. Learn wisdom through suffering, says Aeschylus, and if we are loyal to the turbulence of Greek tragedy, we can see what he means. For, stripped to the bone, the essential *action* of the greatest of the Greek tragedies is an enactment of lives lived out under the double yoke of man's own nature and a world he did not make; the weaker fail or are deformed; the strong survive, and by surviving and enduring, liberate the dignity of significant suffering which gives man the crucial victory over his own fate.

NOTES

1. Much of contemporary dogmatizing about what Aristotle did or did not mean seems to me to rest squarely upon uninformed or unimaginative interpretation of what Aristotle actually said. I am encouraged in this opinion by Professor Gerald F. Else's magisterial *Aristotle's Poetics: The Argument* (Harvard University Press, 1957), surely the most important book on Aristotelian criticism in the twentieth century and one which will inevitably shape and alter the whole tenor of modern explication of Aristotle.

At my request, Professor Else has provided me with a brief statement of his views of what Aristotle actually said, and I quote him verbatim in the conviction of complete agreement. He writes: "There is no doubt that the root and center of Aristotle's theory of tragedy, indeed of all poetry, is the idea of an action (N.B. "*an* action," not simply "action"). It should be easy to say what he means by an action, since he talks about it so much; but there are obscurities and ambiguities. Perhaps the key is that an action is a transaction, the living out of a decisive turn of events by a significant human being. Aristotle seems to say that neither *people* nor *situations*—suffering, hopelessness, demoniacal possession, or whatever—are tragic in themselves. Involvement in action is the signmanual of our human condition and our passport to happiness; it is also the warrant of our possible ruin. Without action a man can be, but he can neither win nor lose; and the winning or losing (not having-lost or being-about-to-lose, or even being-such-as-to-lose) is the tragedy. What is tragic is neither the potentiality nor the actuality of suffering, but its actualization. Tragedy cannot be *displayed*, but only *enacted*. It would seem to follow that the tragic action, though involved with universals—character (type), characteristic acts, pattern of events—is irreducibly a particular. Whether or not Oedipus is a type, the hell into which he enters is his individually, for *only he has entered it through this action*. But it is not clear whether Aristotle is aware of this further corollary. What he does do, beyond any ambiguity, is to insist on the primacy of the action."

2. Cf. *Electra*, 11. 294–5, where Orestes states that pity *(to oiktos)* is never to be found among the *amatheis* but only among the *sophoi*, i.e. compassion is a true component of "wisdom".

JOHN JONES

Sophocles's *Electra*:
The Orestes Myth Rephrased

Sophocles died in 406 or 405, at the age of ninety or ninety-one. Therefore he was born three or four years after 499—the date at which Aeschylus presented his first play. For twenty years or so he will have been an adult spectator of the older poet's work; indeed we know that they competed against each other at the Great Dionysia festival between 468 (when Sophocles won the first prize at his first appearance, aged twenty-eight) and 456, when Aeschylus died. Nobody doubts that Sophocles knew the Aeschylean drama intimately, or that he was influenced by it.

The *Electra* of Sophocles affords a singular opportunity to examine this relationship since nowhere else in the extant literature do we find him dramatising a mythical narrative already treated by Aeschylus.[1] The story of the *Electra* is that of the second play of the Orestes trilogy, the *Libation-Bearers*; Orestes has grown up in exile and now, some years after his father's murder, he returns home to Argos where he makes himself known to his sister and proceeds, with her help, to kill Clytemnestra and Aegisthus. Beneath this surface similarity of plot very substantial differences are perceptible, which must be related at the outset to the fact that Aeschylus was composing the middle section of a trilogy whereas Sophocles intended his *Electra* to stand on its own. The function of the *Libation-Bearers* is transitional; it picks up the story at the stage of inconclusive and uneasy transfer of authority following the king's murder, and it leaves it with

From *On Aristotle and Greek Tragedy.* © 1962 by John Jones.

Clytemnestra newly dead and Orestes's pursuit by the Furies already under way—an entirely open ending. Aeschylus needs more space than a single play provides in order to deploy the resources of his dramatic universe—to realise the *oikos* of Agamemnon and the hazy envelope of guilt surrounding it, to expose the norm in its socio-religious completeness, through rupture to final restitution. But the action of Sophocles's *Electra* is at once distinguished and contained by an entirely new sharpness of definition. Instead of the tissue of family guilt receding into total obscurity we have a single light but firm reference to the original transgression of a famous ancestor, Pelops, as the source of all the trouble that has happened since.[2] And instead of a mother-slaying which is both a desired end and a prolongation of strife ("I grieve for my mother's deed and for my own requital of it and for our whole family",[3] says the Aeschylean Orestes), the killing of Clytemnestra in the *Electra* is understood and accepted as nothing more than the successful execution by Orestes of the god's command to him. Orestes himself rests confidently on the authority of the oracle,[4] and his mother's death, once accomplished, is in the fullest and simplest sense the play's conclusion. By it, so the Chorus declare in the final lines, the family is "made perfect, coming at last, through suffering, to freedom".[5]

Of course, any dramatist who set about rehandling the plot of the *Libation-Bearers* would recognise, if he knew his job, that he must supply the framework which was missing (because not required) in the middle play of a trilogy. We need to show that Sophocles understood the whole mythical situation very differently from Aeschylus, so that the new framework may be seen to grow naturally out of a new conception. A point of departure is provided, as often happens, by the tragic Chorus. The Chorus of the *Electra* are freeborn women of Argos, Electra's friends and advisers; and thus although they are Argives and natives of the city of Mycenae, they do not live in Agamemnon's palace. We recall the Aeschylean Chorus of domestic slave-women who were inmates of—whose entire humanity was contained within—the *oikos*, and who were united with Electra in corporate and passive defiance: "common is the hatred," they tell her, "which we cherish within the house"[6]; and a profusion of imagery presents the *oikos* itself as a sentient creature languishing in subjection. Sophocles now changes all this; and the Chorus's new independence, their altered relationship to those within the royal household, marks a decisive weakening of the family solidarity which dominated Aeschylus's treatment throughout. The *oikos* has lost its sufficiency. There is nothing in the *Electra* to compare with that enormous lyric dirge in which the parts of Orestes, Electra and the Chorus are intertwined in single corporate utterance—the voice of the suffering, the self-restoring house. The Orestes of the *Electra* is in duty bound, as he was in the *Libation-Bearers*, to cleanse the house with purificatory rites and repair its wasted substance; but the main stress (as we shall see in a moment) falls elsewhere: Sophocles does not conceive a stage-figure who stands in urgent and tragic—the word acquires an Aeschylean precision at this point—relation to the larger life which gave him his own life and which is now threatened with extinction; so that Aeschylus denotes him, in majestic and untranslatable phrase, "its hope of saving seed".[7]

The weakening of family solidarity is a much-studied theme of Greek political and social history. This process, a slow one and by no means perfectly understood, was relatively swift during the fifth century, the threshold of which was marked by a set of radical public reforms designed to substitute a new principle of locality for the traditional one of blood—of kinship in the widest sense—as a basis for the ordering of Athenian society. And we may be sure that these public measures would not have proved successful unless a shift in private sensibility had accompanied them. Thus at the close of the same century we find Sophocles, in his *Oedipus at Colonus* with its Chorus of village elders, investing the tiny community of Colonus (which was in fact his own community under the reforms of Cleisthenes) with a keen and very eloquent feeling for the tie of mere neighbourhood. A local Athenian whom the Theban stranger, Oedipus, meets there, concludes his description of the place:

> Colonus has never been honoured in legend, but it has a kind of greatness in the hearts of those who live here.[8]

An earlier poet—Pindar or Aeschylus—could only have rendered the greatness of locality through the mythical heroic ancestor who lived there and through the presence of his blood in living members of the group; but Sophocles in his old age understands local pride, quite simply, and reaches the modern reader to move him.

Local pride is irrelevant, however, to his earlier *Electra*. The weakened *oikos* is not compensated by any very impressive strengthening of locality, which means that our findings in connection with family solidarity do not contribute much to the exposure of active dramatic forces in Sophocles's rephrasing of the Orestes myth.

It should be remarked at the outset that the reader who turns away from Aeschylus disappointed in certain dramatic expectations which are born of his sense of human probability, now finds these expectations fulfilled by

Sophocles. For example, the Aeschylean Orestes's anxiety about his inheritance seems an unsatisfactory reaction to the horrible crime of his father's murder; the apparent gross materialism of his account of himself "turned brute-savage by the loss of my possessions"[9] has shocked some commentators into perverting the text's meaning towards a false modern spirituality; and there is no doubt that inheritance evoked for Aeschylus a complex of family substance and individual status, and also of community in blood and worship, which we cannot recover. Whereas Sophocles gives us an Orestes who is convincingly and almost solely impelled by the desire to avenge his father. The play opens with his return to Argos accompanied by Pylades, his friend, and by an aged retainer of the family. They pause in front of Agamemnon's palace. "Here," says the old man,

> is the house of Pelops's descendants, the deathful house from which, and from your father's killing, I carried you away all those years ago, as your sister charged me. Thus I saved you and brought you up to manhood, to be the avenger of your murdered father.[10]

And in his answering speech Orestes sustains and elaborates the theme of vengeance thus firmly introduced by his companion:

> When I went to the Pythian oracle to learn how I might avenge my father on his murderers, Phoebus answered me the words I tell you now: "Go alone—quite alone—and go unarmed; and secure by stealth the vengeance-killing which is yours by right."[11]

Within forty lines of the play's opening the figure of the solitary avenger (note the requirement that Orestes shall proceed single-handed) has emerged to command the stage. And soon we see that Orestes's avenging role has its counterpart in Electra's waiting and watching for his return; her grief is declared with the same narrow intensity as his retributive anger; intelligibly, with plausible psychological definition, she mourns her dead father.[12] Orestes, she says, has promised to come home[13]; in the meantime she must endure privation and insult. And when her patience fails her, or when she despairs of Orestes's return, her thoughts turn to action and she sounds her brother's note of personal vengeance.[14] Finally, when she receives what seems incontrovertible evidence of his death abroad, she discloses to her sister Chrysothemis a desperate plan (desperate indeed when we recall the enclosed and passive life of women in the Athenian society for which

Sophocles was writing) that the two daughters shall do the job which should have fallen to Agamemnon's son:

> So long as I heard that my brother was alive and well, I went on hoping he would come some day to avenge his father's murder. But I look to you now—now he is dead—not to flinch from helping your sister to kill the man who killed our father— Aegisthus.[15]

The more timid sister will have no part in what she calls "such rash folly",[16] and Electra is left in a calm and bitter solitude which one encounters again and again in the Sophoclean drama: "Well then, I must do this deed with my own hand, and alone."[17]

And so in the place of receding family solidarity we have individuation and (in a vague provisional sense) personalising of consciousness. Revengeful wrath, self-abandonment to grief, an atmosphere of loyalty to Agamemnon's memory—action and sentiment are less remote than in Aeschylus, so that we speak of clearer motive, more realistic emotions, stronger logic. A new apprehension of personal relations is awake, now the dramatic individual no longer bends to an *oikos*-determined life-rhythm and scheme of value. Constancy's and grief's personal nature stands revealed by the touchstone of the Chorus; while the domestic slave-women of the *Libation-Bearers* lament the corporate fortune, the independent friends of the Sophoclean Electra question her thus in the first words they utter:

> Electra, ah Electra, child of a most wretched, most guilty mother, why do I see you all the time wasting away in ceaseless lament for one who died long ago, for Agamemnon ...?[18]

In her *personal* grief, Electra accuses her sister of a *personal* "betrayal"[19] of their dead father, and she leans upon her brother's *personal* promise to come home. Orestes's long delay causes her to lose heart; she fears he has forgotten his duty. He is always sending secret messages of encouragement, but "he never chooses to come".[20] When Orestes returns, alive after all, Electra tells him: "all my joy is a gift from you and not my own"[21]; and we who read these words look inside ourselves and recognise the strange urge towards self-abasement in love, the desire to confess dependence on another human life. This is altogether nearer than the quaint formal talk about "four parts of love"[22] with which the Aeschylean Electra greets her brother. Surely

Sophocles means us to remember that Electra had cried out: "Your death is my death, dearest Orestes",[23] when she felt sure he was dead, and had longed for her own life to be done with; "for when you were alive we shared and shared alike, and now I want to die and share your grave".[24] Her acknowledgment of loving dependence on him has its natural counterpart in this earlier response to the news that he had been killed, and both fall within Sophocles's larger dramatic intention to give the bond between brother and sister all the prominence he can. The Aeschylean nurse who recalls her care of the baby Orestes[25] does not appear in the *Electra*. There, Electra herself is the one who nursed Orestes at that distant time:

> Woe to me for my nursing long ago—my care of you, my loving toil, all gone for nothing. For you were never your mother's darling as much as mine; none but I looked after you in that household, and you always called me "sister".[26]

Personal, too, is the hatred felt towards Agamemnon's murderers. Aeschylus and Sophocles both make Electra express indignation against Clytemnestra and Aegisthus for the way they are treating herself, as well as for what they did to her father long ago; but Aeschylus generalises ("despised, reckoned worthless, shut up like a vicious dog"[27]—the image of the domestic animal is distinctively Aeschylean), while Sophocles specifies the insults and brings them home to the suffering girl:

> like some despised foreign woman, I perform humble tasks about this house which was my father's; shamefully dressed, as you see, and standing to eat my meals at a table miserably stocked with food.[28]

Our response to Electra's degradation, and our broader sense of her, shift with his more circumstantial account of her plight, just as the remote Aeschylean rhetoric investing Orestes ("the man mighty with the spear, come to deliver the house"[29]) gives place to the stage-impression of a young man credibly moved against his father's murderers. And similarly with Sophocles's attitude, and our response, to the guilt of Clytemnestra and Aegisthus; for there is nothing in the *Libation-Bearers* to compare with the enumerative precision of Electra's indictment, declared to the Chorus:

> Then think what my life is like, watching Aegisthus sitting on my father's throne, wearing the robes which he wore, pouring

libations at the hearth where my father was killed by him. And watching that ultimate outrage: my father's murderer in my father's bed, with my mother beside him—if mother is the right word for this mistress of Aegisthus who is so without shame and scruple that she lives with the polluted man and fears no Fury. On the contrary, she appears to exult in her deed. She has noted the day on which my father fell to her treachery long ago, and she celebrates it every month with choral dances and sacrifice of sheep to the gods who have kept her safe.[30]

Thus the Hamlet-oriented sensibility finds consolation at last—though not because the Sophoclean stage-figure is more effectively realised than Aeschylus's in any valid objective sense derivableimmediately from the new precisions and particularities of the *Electra;* for Aeschylus has his own fullness of realisation, achieved through the marriage of his generalising temper to a wonderfully direct feeling for action and the single movement. He gives us scarcely a word of individualised description of Helen or of her states of mind in the entire *Agamemnon,* and yet in such touches as that of the lion cub with its bright eye turned hungrily towards the hand of the man feeding it, the idea of her grows definite. Nor does he attempt to describe Paris and Helen in their adulterous relationship. But no attempt is needed, because when Aeschylus tells of the wife stepping through the rich curtains of her chamber and the Greeks setting out in pursuit of "the vanished track of oars",[31] his art delivers the two lovers within their act of elopement. We encounter the same hushed generic vitality in the scenes of war and fearful imaginings of war in the *Seven against Thebes,* where the statement, "the empty-handed hails the empty-handed, looking for a partner"[32] proves grandly, royally adequate to the horrors of looting in a captured town.

And in the *Libation-Bearers* Aeschylus is content to visualise Aegisthus within Orestes's threat of vengeance: "if I find that man sitting on my father's throne ... before ever he can ask 'Whence this stranger?' I'll make a corpse of him"[33]; the truth here being that a single reference to the throne within the palace is all that Aeschylus needs to point his theme, which is the subversion of the royal household. Therefore we ought not to talk of the Aeschylean massive simplicity as if it were a primitive limitation which he would have escaped had he been born a few decades later than he was: conception and execution are at one. No question of Sophocles's superiority arises, but merely of his difference; we are observing him sharpen and narrow the subversion of the *oikos* into a theme of personal usurpation. Aegisthu's wearing of Agamemnon's clothes, the sleeping in his bed and with his wife, are additions to the older version, and they serve a new idea.

In the course of his rephrasing of the story, Sophocles heightens and isolates its sexual aspect. What Electra calls (in the passage just quoted) Aegisthus's ultimate or crowning "outrage" gains further stress in her long face-to-face arraignment of Clytemnestra during which she tells her mother that living with Aegisthus and bearing children to him are her "foulest deeds of all".[34] The Chorus have already asserted, touchstone fashion, "Lust was Agamemnon's murderer",[35] and the keenest sexual edge is given to the guilt of both partners throughout. Now a modern reader is unlikely to give this the attention it demands because his response to Sophocles's attempt to direct and define his interest has been rendered dull by the assumption that the sexual emphasis he finds in the *Electra* is somehow to be expected. Of course he cannot come to the play as an Athenian would have done, sitting in the bright morning sun while the Chorus danced and sang and the voices from within the tragic masks boomed in his ears. But he can attempt to place it within the ancient dramatic tradition; in particular, he can turn back from Sophocles to the *Oresteia* and see how Aeschylus handles the sexual theme there.

So marked is the subordination of sex in the *Oresteia* that we find ourselves in difficulties when we try to impose a crime-and-punishment logic on the part played by the Furies in the trilogy.[36] The Greek belief was that the Furies exercised a general jurisdiction over wrongdoing within the family—over sexual offences as well as crimes of blood. This is clearly recognised by Sophocles: hence his indicating Clytemnestra's hardened criminality by the fact that she continues to live with Aegisthus "and fears no Fury". Aeschylus is certainly *aware* of the same thing; the wrath of the Furies at the adultery of Thyestes with his brother's wife—an earlier crime in this family's dreadful history—is driven home unsparingly. Which makes us ask why the Furies (who pursue Orestes from the moment he kills his mother) have not been active against Clytemnestra in the long years between Agamemnon's murder and Orestes's return. Again, why does not the god Apollo raise a counter-plea of Clytemnestra's sexual guilt when he speaks in defence of Orestes at the trial? He does urge that Clytemnestra murdered her husband before her son murdered her[37]; but the sexual issue is never mentioned. We also recall that Aeschylus shows no interest in the erotic potentialities of the scene in which Agamemnon and Clytemnestra meet after ten years' separation; and that although we are probably meant to presume a sexual bond between Agamemnon and Cassandra (he calls her "my chosen flower"[38]), nothing is made of it.

Sex is thus subdued in the *Oresteia;* like the revenge motif, it falls within a story of subversion which it is not allowed to distort. (Translations often give Aeschylus's words a limited sexual meaning which he never intended. Thus the sober and accurate Loeb version makes Electra pray: "grant that I may prove in heart more chaste, far more, than my mother",[39] when the Aeschylean *s?phronestrean* conveys a general prudence and moderation which would of course include sexual restraint.) But Aeschylus, as we saw when we examined the upsurge of eroticism in his Clytemnestra, has one very important use for sex. With Clytemnestra the erotic thread in consciousness is brilliantly isolated, and this brings together the Aeschylean and Sophoclean drama for a moment—a moment at which the understanding of both poets requires us to walk delicately. I have tried to bring to life, or at least to drag into the light of criticism, the idea of a socio-religious norm underlying Aeschylus's unitary trilogy, and to interpret Clytemnestra's singular eroticism from the standpoint of the norm which it challenges; and now a nice but vital distinction must be observed between the erotic bias of his Clytemnestra and that of Sophocles's. The Aeschylean Clytemnestra's eroticism is the singularity of aberration, so that the question, aberration from what norm? is always primary. The Sophoclean Clytemnestra, on the other hand, achieves a singularity which directs us not to the norm (there is no norm in Sophocles, in anything like the Aeschylean sense), but to herself; and this is because her lustful disposition does not exhaust itself dramatically in the bare fact of deviation, but is so presented as to make us enquire, and enquire urgently, why she acts as she does.

We are embarking upon a study of motive analogous to the one already undertaken of Orestes's impulsion to avenge his father, and our point of departure is the long dispute between mother and daughter in which Clytemnestra defends her killing of Agamemnon. Her argument, already familiar from the *Oresteia,* is that Agamemnon deserved to die for sacrificing Iphigeneia: "Justice took his life—not I alone",[40] she maintains. Now Sophocles intends (I feel sure) that these words shall send our thoughts back to the earlier choral judgment, "Lust was Agamemnon's murderer", for the question of Clytemnestra's motive is seized on by Electra in her reply. "I'm going to tell you," she says,

> that there was no justice in your killing of him. The truth is you
> were drawn on to it by the seduction of that bad man whose
> mistress you now are.[41]

Clytemnestra's real motive was lust, and her pretext for killing Agamemnon is swept aside. Electra clinches her counter-argument with a single decisive thrust. Will you say, she asks her mother, that living with Aegisthus and bearing children to him—"will you say that this too is retribution for your daughter?"[42]

Sophocles so manages this debate that it becomes inescapably relevant to enquire why Clytemnestra killed her husband. She herself asserts that she was moved to avenge Iphigeneia. Electra challenges this account and advances a different motive as the true one—it all seems simple and obvious, and (as with the erotic emphasis throughout the *Electra*) its importance may easily be missed since some such wrangle as here occurs is vaguely looked for. Again we may redress the critical balance by turning to the *Oresteia*, where Clytemnestra offers the same defence based on Iphigencia's sacrifice, but where no word is said regarding her true motive in killing Agamemnon. Aeschylus can scarcely have been blind to this possible development of the story, for Pindar had also asked whether Clytemnestra was moved by love for Aegisthus when she killed Agamemnon,[43] and the same question was probably raised in other literary sources known to Aeschylus and lost to us. Nor is the silence explained by lack of dramatic opportunity, since Clytemnestra states her case, or has it stated for her, in all three plays of the trilogy. Particularly striking is Orestes's failure to make this point when he is face to face with her and she pleads for her life. Commentators have sometimes made good Aeschylus's omission by urging that while Clytemnestra has a valid claim against Agamemnon on account of the sacrifice, she is in no position to enforce it because her own motives are impure. Thus we resolve the deadlock of conflicting rights in a manner satisfactory to modern expectations, but at the cost of doing violence to the *Oresteia's* own logic. Aeschylus's omission ought not to be made good; his refusal to let the religio-moral office of the Furies crystallise into a distinct guardianship of sex ought to be sufficient warning to us not to try. He says nothing because there is nothing to say: Clytemnestra's eroticism exhausts itself (as I put it) in the fact of deviation, and the entire dramatic energy is bent back upon the ruptured norm.

Sophocles's introduction, through his Chorus and through Electra, of the simple point, "You really killed your husband because of your adulterous love for Aegisthus", is, like Aeschylus's omission of the same point, momentous. It runs to the root of his apprehension of the myth. It explains, for example, why the Sophoclean Furies are preoccupied with sexual wrong-doing to the point of reacting against marital infidelity as the sharpest of provocations.[44] Or better, neither dramatic fact explains the other, but they are neighbours within a single imaginative world whose tone they both communicate, supporting each other in the kind of attention they solicit for the work of art. We are meant to ask why Clytemnestra killed her husband, meant to find the problem interesting; and the ensuing enquiry into motives is part of that general development which I have called, provisionally, the personalising of the dramatic individual in Sophocles. We turn to Clytemnestra and note that her disposition is lustful. We observe a brazen insolence which attends her lust and maintains her in her evil ways, fearing no Fury. It is a characteristic touch, absent in Aeschylus, that she could have instituted monthly celebrations to mark the day on which Agamemnon was murdered. While Aeschylus makes Clytemnestra's irreligion rest mainly on her parody or inversion of ritual forms, her Sophoclean counterpart is distinguished by the pressure of individual will thrusting her along her solitary course against the tide of traditional religious restraints. The tremendous impersonal blasphemies of the one must be contrasted with the outfacing of propriety which makes the defiance of the other so different, so keenly "personal", in its nature.

In fact, the objectivity of Aeschylean villainy is here transformed, and with it the wider objectivity of ritual and language. We remarked the flowing together of the ritual form with the world of fact in Aeschylus, and noted the consequence, at first sight extraordinary, that the working towards a desired end, and also the end's achievement, may be attributed to the ritual form itself. "The victory is the children's", so the *Libation-Bearers* Chorus declare—before the work of retribution has been begun. But in the *Electra*, when at the outset they make a drink-offering to Agamemnon's spirit, a difference is apparent. "Before we do anything else," says the old retainer,

> let us try to carry out Apollo's commands by pouring libations to
> your father. Beginning in this way puts victory within our reach,
> and gives us mastery in everything we do.[45]

Belief in the efficacy of the ritual act is no less firm, but the achievement of the desired end is referred (naturally, we should say) to the human agent. We find a narrower definition of the bounds of selfhood, setting the individual over against his gods and his ritual life. "Why should I take part in the sacred dance," the Sophoclean Chorus ask, "if evil deeds are held in honour?"[46] A question cast in this form would be inconceivable in Aeschylus, in spite of the fact that an anxious, religion-directed probing of the dreadful truths of experience is one of his most characteristic moods. The Aeschylean form of this question is the one adopted by Orestes when he is urging Zeus to support Electra and himself against their enemies: "If you allow us to perish ... where will you find another hand so liberal in making you rich offerings?" I call this Aeschylean because of the single relational stress, now faded in Sophocles for whom the threat to religious wellbeing becomes a placing in jeopardy of the human attitude of piety. Calamity and unpunished wrongdoing lead the Sophoclean Chorus to wonder whether the sacred ritual dance is worth pursuing, or to fear that "reverence for the gods will vanish from the earth";[47] the older reciprocity and preservation of delicate balance is succeeded by a religious drama which stands watch over the flow of human respect towards the gods. The pious individual conceives his ritual activity in a new way, instrumentally. Orestes arms himself with a drink-offering to Agamemnon before he sets out. Electra refuses to cease from formal lamentation because it is her only offensive weapon: that is why her grief and her stubborn loyalty to her father are so closely bound together. In Aeschylus, when Clytemnestra responds to her bad dream by attempting to appease Agamemnon's spirit with offerings, stress falls upon the objective futility of "seeking too late to make amends for a wrong that cannot be put right"[48]; but in Sophocles, when she does the same thing, Electra takes her stand on the certainty that Agamemnon will find these offerings "from the wife who is his enemy"[49] unacceptable; and Electra and her sister substitute tresses of their own hair for Clytemnestra's gifts. The wife's offerings are tainted with the personality directing and permeating the ritual act, and this marks a loss in objectivity which is also a gain in the kind of subjectivity, the collected and limited selfhood, now before us.

This change has an even wider linguistic aspect. Like all men before the Sophistic movement—and many since—Aeschylus and Sophocles believed in the possibility of a substantial connection between a man's name and his nature or fate; and therefore the etymology of proper names (Prometheus= Forethought, and so on) was a serious matter to them, capable of disclosing truths about the world. Sophocles's Ajax cries out: "O misery *(aiai)!* Who could ever have thought that my name *[Aias]* and my fate would fit so perfectly together?"[50] In his commentary, Jebb recalls the second Richard's "Can sick men play so nicely with their names?" in response to Gaunt's "O how that name befits my composition! /Old Gaunt, indeed; and gaunt in being old." And there is justice in the comparison, since Ajax and Gaunt are both wistfully self-conscious in their name-play. But in an Aeschylean context such reference to Shakespeare must always be misleading. Aeschylus deploys his etymologies (which are more numerous than Sophocles's: as well as Prometheus, Polyneices, Clytemnestra, Helen and the god Apollo have their names' "meaning" exposed) with a certain toneless objectivity which divides him from Sophocles and Shakespeare and invites us to apply our initial distinction between objective and instrumental ritual activity within a linguistic frame of reference.[51] Antigone and Oedipus, like the Aeschylean Cassandra, have to sing their own death-dirges, and in their case as in hers a pathetic effect is aimed at and secured; but its plain objective force is deflected in Sophocles by the stage-figure's awareness of *using* the ritual form (which is also the form of words)—in fact by the instrumental sense. Moreover, the instrumental sense distinguishes the Sophoclean poetic sensibility, not merely dramatised consciousness within his plays, and is largely responsible for our impression of his overall sophistication compared with Aeschylus. For Aeschylus is capable, as Sophocles would never be,[52] of seizing upon—probably of coining—a word (*aphertos*) and using it nine times in a single trilogy, and apparently nowhere else. And this is surely because *aphertos* is not a linguistic usage in the Sophoclean or Shakespearean sense so much as a feature of the *Oresteia's* landscape. It belongs there. It is one of the *Oresteia*-words. The practice wears a naïve look, of course, and leaves us puzzled by our feeling that Aeschylus's language can at the same time be more natural and more artificial than Sophocles's. *Aphertos* is at home in the *Oresteia*, and it is utterly factitious.

Again, and with similar bewilderment, when we think about the persistent antithetical fondling of "word" and "deed" in Sophocles (in assertions like "You have shown yourself good in word but bad in deed"), we conclude that his language/action rendering of the appearance/reality tension shared by the tragic literature of the West is at once nearer to ourselves and less immediate than the Aeschylean warrior's bare, direct gesture of determination "not to seem the bravest, but to be".[53]

Our broad contrasting of the *Electra* and the *Libation-Bearers* has revealed the stage-figure in Sophocles appropriating psychic vitality to himself with greatly increased definiteness and consistency. The good and the bad people are equally involved in this development; Orestes's circumspect piety places him in clearcut opposition to his mother, but he and she are at one in their articulate awareness of the distinct attitudes which they maintain in conflict with each other, and which they hold to as their own *vis-à-vis* divinities and other human beings. In fact, we may widen the discussion to include all that the term character has been made to mean.

Sir Richard Jebb was not generalising to very much purpose when he distinguished Sophocles from Aeschylus thus: "With Sophocles the interest depends primarily on the portraiture of human character"[54]; but already enough has been said to make his judgment intelligible. Those contrasts which we have attempted between the two Electras, the two Oresteses, the two Clytemnestras, might understandably (though dangerously) be transposed into a remarking of the growth of human interest in Sophocles, of his introduction of natural touches. Consider the maternal feeling of the Sophoclean Clytemnestra. When she receives apparently reliable news of Orestes's death, a self-division is at once evident between her relief at being finally safe from reprisal and her grief for her child. Conscious of this double response in herself, she broods over the "strange power that rests in motherhood"[55]—power she has already felt and displayed over the death of another of her children, Iphigeneia. Jebb translates (Clytemnestra is engaged in her long debate with Electra):

> this father of thine, whom thou art ever lamenting, was the one man of the Greeks who had the heart to sacrifice thy sister to the gods—he, the father, who had not shared the mother's pangs.[56]

"The one man ... who had the heart"[57] brings out very well the personal bitterness of Clytemnestra's counter-charge, and it recalls the Aeschylean situation in which the mother's claim and the father's duty to lead the Greeks against Troy are opposed with extreme objective baldness. There, Agamemnon's duty being status-determined, the fact that he is king and commander in chief is enough to impress its absolute nature with all necessary force. He has nothing—no physical hindrance—to prevent him disbanding the army and sending the soldiers home; the point is simply that this action is impossible for one in his position (position, we have seen, is inherent in the man; it is not added to the man), and this is the sense in which Iphigeneia's sacrifice is forced on him. But when Sophocles recounts the same incident he manages it differently. Instead of leaving Artemis's anger with Agamemnon unexplained, he prefaces her withholding of a favourable wind with a hunting adventure in which Agamemnon annoys the goddess by shooting a stag in a grove sacred to herself, and then boasting of his marksmanship.[58] This little episode has none of the prominence or splendour of the killing of the pregnant hare by the two eagles—the portent of Artemis's wrath and also, within the Aeschylean dramatic universe, its sufficient cause—but it procures for the independent Tragedy a trimness of effect that was absent before. Secondly, the consequences of Artemis's displeasure are altered by Sophocles.

And so it came about that she was sacrificed, there being no other
means of getting the fleet under way—either homeward or to
Troy. That was why he killed her, entirely against his will, cruelly
constrained....[59]

The detail of the expedition's immovability is most suggestive. It gives
the plight of the commander and his men a wholly new aspect, with the
result that Agamemnon's status is no longer called upon to bear the full
weight of his dilemma. He cannot disband his army, even if he wants to.

I do not conclude from this introduction of a supporting factor that the
status-defined possibilities and impossibilities of conduct are weakly felt in
Sophocles, but rather that the dramatic factor which we provisionally call
personal has grown so importunate (the *Electra* is a late play) that he
acknowledges the need to reinforce the Aeschylean account of Agamemnon's
compulsion to act as he did. A new physical helplessness is called upon to
oppose Clytemnestra's new accusing particularity, her thrusting home of the
issue by way of the assertion that the only Greek who had the heart to go
through with the sacrifice was the human victim's father.

Being aimed at Agamemnon's lack of pity, her challenge has special
force; again and again we shall observe Sophoclean pity transform those cruel
stories which he takes from the common tragic stock, touching them with
healing generosity of vision and an uncanny tonal sweetness, hard to speak of.
Venturing from within the *Electra* a final contrast with Aeschylus's *Libation-
Bearers*, we turn to the scene in which Orestes surprises his mother and she
pleads with him not to kill her. "Have pity" is the rendering given by some
translators for her appeal to Orestes in both plays,[60] and "have pity on your
mother" is precisely what the Sophoclean *oiktire t?n tekousan* means. He is
talking about the human feeling we call pity—the feeling pathetically exposed
when Electra tells her brother whom she has not yet recognised but who has
shown kindness to her, "You are the only one that ever pitied me."[60] But the
Aeschylean Clytemnestra says *aidesai*, which means something like "show
respect for"; so that here the sense of pity is more than a little Pickwickian.
And while the distinction between *oiktire* and *aidesai* is elementary and very
well recognised, most of the further, would-be critical distinctions that are
built upon it, between the religious poet and the poet of humanity, are
altogether too coarse to do more than encourage facile thinking both about
religion and about the dramatic presentation of human beings.

Notes

1. Greek dramatists were constantly rehandling the old stories; thus we know of ten or more poets, apart from Sophocles, who wrote Oedipus tragedies. But only seven plays by Aeschylus survive out of rather less than a hundred, and seven by Sophocles out of considerably more than a hundred. That is why no other examples are at hand. In some cases reliable information is available about the plots of lost plays (thus the *Philoctetes* of Sophocles survives, and we have a fairly detailed account of the lost *Philoctetes* of Aeschylus and the lost *Philoctetes* of Euripides by an essayist of the first century A.D., Dio Chrysostom); but this kind of summary is almost worthless for critical purposes.

2. *Electra*, 11. 505–15.

3. *Libation-Bearers*, 1. 1016.

4. *Electra*, 11. 1424–5.

5. *Ibid.*, 11. 1508–10.

6. *Libation-Bearers*, 1. 101.

7. *Ibid.*, 1. 236.

8. *Oedipus at Colonus*, 11. 62–3. Locality is also emphasised in the respect paid throughout the play to the peculiar religious customs of Colonus. And locality inspires the choral song in praise of Colonus and Attica: 11. 668–719.

9. *Libation-Bearers*, 1. 275.

10. *Electra*, 11. 10–14.

11. *Ibid.*, 11. 32–7.

12. *Ibid.*, 11. 92–5, 129–36, 145–52.

13. *Ibid.*, 1. 319.

14. *Ibid.*, 11. 110–20, 341–50, 399.

15. *Ibid.*, 11. 951–7.

16. *Ibid.*, 1. 995.

17. *Ibid.*, 11. 1019–20.

18. *Ibid.*, 11. 121–5. The Chorus repeat their question at 1. 144.

19. *Ibid.*, 1. 368.

20. *Ibid.*, 1. 172.

21. *Ibid.*, 11. 1302–3.

22. *Libation-Bearers*, 1. 238.

23. *Electra*, 1. 808.

24. *Ibid.*, 11. 1167–9.

25. *Libation-Bearers*, 11. 748–63.

26. *Electra*, 11. 1143–8.

27. *Libation-Bearers*, 11. 445–6.

28. *Electra*. 11. 189–92. "Standing" points to the fact that Electra is being treated as a slave. Free members of the household would eat reclining on couches. See Jebb's note.

29. *Libation-Bearers*, 11. 160–1.

30. *Electra*, 11. 266–81.

31. *Agamemnon*, 11. 687–98.

32. 11. 753–4.

33. 11. 571-6.

34. *Electra*, 1. 586.

35. *Ibid.*, 1. 197.

36. The facts are conveniently summarised by F. Solmsen, *Hesiod and Aeschylus*, p. 182 ff.

37. The Furies meet Apollo with the objection that Clytemnestra's murder of

Agamemnon does not fall within their jurisdiction since husband and wife are not "of the same blood and kin" *(Eumenides,* 1. 212). A number of commentators—not only the old-fashioned modernists—have discussed this point as a mere technicality. I think they are wrong, because while the tone of the arguments on both sides is legalistic (naturally, since Aeschylus is dramatising a trial at law), everybody in the *Oresteia* believes that kinsfolk have the "same" blood in their veins, and that guilt is carried in the blood, simply and inexorably. We must accept the converse of this belief as equally serious and deep-rooted—that where community of blood is lacking, individual guilt is no concern of the guardians of family life.

38. *Agamemnon,* 11. 954–5. The commentator who stresses that Agamemnon is "an unfaithful husband" (Walter Headlam, *Agamemnon,* p. 34) flies in the face of the text and of what little is known about ancient concubinage.

39. *Libation-Bearers,* 11. 140–1.

40. *Electra,* 1. 528.

41. *Ibid.,* 11. 560–2.

42. *Ibid.,* 11. 591–2.

43. *Pythian Odes,* XI, 22-5. The date of this Ode is not known, but it is almost certainly earlier than the *Oresteia.* The sexual motive appears also in the *Odyssey* (I, 35 ff.), where Clytemnestra is not mentioned. However, her name is coupled with the murder elsewhere in the *Odyssey.*

44. *Electra,* 11. 110–14, 489-94.

45. *Ibid.,* 11. 82–5.

46. *Oedipus the King,* 11. 895–6.

47. *Electra,* 1. 250.

48. *Libation-Bearers,* 1. 516.

49. *Electra,* 1. 433.

50. *Ajax,* 11. 430–1.

51. I believe that a study of riddling statements *(griphoi)* in Aeschylus and Sophocles would further substantiate our objective/instrumental distinction.

52. Contrast Sophocles's way of harping on the word *er?mos* in his *Philoctetes,* and on words of wandering in his *Oedipus at Colonus* (noted below on pp. 216–8). This is not entirely unlike such reiterations as "blood" in *Macbeth,* but the Aeschylean practice is.

53. *Seven against Thebes,* 1. 592.

54. *Electra:* Introduction.

55. *Ibid.,* 1. 770. Jebb cites two Aeschylean phrases *(Prometheus Bound,* 1. 39; *Seven against Thebes,* 1. 1031) to illustrate the sense of "a mysterious power" for the Greek *deinon.* It is noteworthy that both are concerned with the generic tie of kinship, not (as here) with a specific relationship such as that of mother and child.

56. *Ibid.,* 11. 530–3.

57. The Greek is a verb form of our old friend *tolma,* and this passage has an exact counterpart in *Agamemnon,* 1. 224, where the same word appears, but where it would be misleading to translate "had the heart"—if my view of Aeschylean *tolma* is correct.

58. *Electra,* 11. 563–72.

59. *Ibid.,* 11. 573–6.

60. *Libation-Bearers,* 1. 896; *Electra,* 1. 1411.

FRIEDRICH NIETZSCHE

The Birth of Tragedy

9.

Whatever rises to the surface in the dialogue of the Apollonian part of Greek tragedy, appears simple, transparent, beautiful. In this sense the dialogue is a copy of the Hellene, whose nature reveals itself in the dance, because in the dance the greatest energy is merely potential, but betrays itself nevertheless in flexible and vivacious movements. The language of the Sophoclean heroes, for instance, surprises us by its Apollonian precision and clearness, so that we at once imagine we see into the innermost recesses of their being, and marvel not a little that the way to these recesses is so short. But if for the moment we disregard the character of the hero which rises to the surface and grows visible—and which at bottom is nothing but the light-picture cast on a dark wall, that is, appearance through and through,—if rather we enter into the myth which projects itself in these bright mirrorings, we shall of a sudden experience a phenomenon which bears a reverse relation to one familiar in optics. When, after a vigorous effort to gaze into the sun, we turn away blinded, we have dark-coloured spots before our eyes as restoratives, so to speak; while, on the contrary, those light-picture phenomena of the Sophoclean hero,—in short, the Apollonian of the mask,—are the necessary productions of a glance into the sacret and terrible things of nature, as it were shining spots to heal the eye which dire night has seared. Only in this sense can we hope to be able to grasp the true meaning of the serious and significant notion of "Greek cheerfulness"; while of course we encounter the

---

From *The Complete Works of Friedrich Nietzche, The Birth of Tragedy*, Vol. 1, edited by Dr. Oscar Levy and translated by William A. Haussman, Ph.D. © 1909–1911, 1964 by Russell & Russell, Inc.

misunderstood notion of this cheerfulness, as resulting from a state of unendangered comfort, on all the ways and paths of the present time.

The most sorrowful figure of the Greek stage, the hapless Œdipus, was understood by Sophocles as the noble man, who in spite of his wisdom was destined to error and misery, but nevertheless through his extraordinary sufferings ultimately exerted a magical, wholesome influence on all around him, which continues effective even after his death. The noble man does not sin; this is what the thoughtful poet wishes to tell us: all laws, all natural order, yea, the moral world itself, may be destroyed through his action, but through this very action a higher magic circle of influences is brought into play, which establish a new world on the ruins of the old that has been overthrown. This is what the poet, in so far as he is at the same time a religious thinker, wishes to tell us: as poet, he shows us first of all a wonderfully complicated legal mystery, which the judge slowly unravels, link by link, to his own destruction. The truly Hellenic delight at this dialectical loosening is so great, that a touch of surpassing cheerfulness is thereby communicated to the entire play, which everywhere blunts the edge of the horrible presuppositions of the procedure. In the "Œdipus at Colonus" we find the same cheerfulness, elevated, however, to an infinite transfiguration: in contrast to the aged king, subjected to an excess of misery, and exposed solely as a *sufferer* to all that befalls him, we have here a supermundane cheerfulness, which descends from a divine sphere and intimates to us that in his purely passive attitude the hero attains his highest activity, the influence of which extends far beyond his life, while his earlier conscious musing and striving led him only to passivity. Thus, then, the legal knot of the fable of Œdipus, which to mortal eyes appears indissolubly entangled, is slowly unravelled—and the profoundest human joy comes upon us in the presence of this divine counterpart of dialectics. If this explanation does justice to the poet, it may still be asked whether the substance of the myth is thereby exhausted; and here it turns out that the entire conception of the poet is nothing but the light-picture which healing nature holds up to us after a glance into the abyss. Œdipus, the murderer of his father, the husband of his mother, Œdipus, the interpreter of the riddle of the Sphinx! What does the mysterious triad of these deeds of destiny tell us? There is a primitive popular belief, especially in Persia, that a wise Magian can be born only of incest: which we have forthwith to interpret to ourselves with reference to the riddle-solving and mother-marrying Œdipus, to the effect that when the boundary of the present and future, the rigid law of individuation and, in general, the intrinsic spell of nature, are broken by prophetic and magical powers, an extraordinary counternaturalness—as, in this case, incest—must have preceded as a cause; for how else could one force nature to surrender her secrets but by victoriously opposing her, *i.e.*, by means of the Unnatural? It is this intuition which I see imprinted in the awful triad of the destiny of Œdipus: the very man who solves the riddle of nature—that double-constituted Sphinx—must also, as the murderer of his father and husband of his mother, break the holiest laws of nature. Indeed, it seems as if the myth sought to whisper into our ears that wisdom, especially Dionysian wisdom, is an unnatural abomination, and that whoever, through his knowledge, plunges nature into an abyss of annihilation, must also experience the dissolution of nature in himself. "The sharpness of wisdom turns round upon the sage: wisdom is a crime against nature": such terrible expressions does the myth call out to us: but the Hellenic poet touches like a sunbeam the sublime and formidable Memnonian statue of the myth, so that it suddenly begins to sound—in Sophoclean melodies.

With the glory of passivity I now contrast the glory of activity which illuminates the *Prometheus* of Æschylus. That which Æschylus the thinker had to tell us here, but which as a poet he only allows us to surmise by his symbolic picture, the youthful Goethe succeeded in disclosing to us in the daring words of his Prometheus:—

"Hier sitz' ich, forme Menschen
Nach meinem Bilde,
Ein Geschlecht, das mir gleich sei,
Zu leiden, zu weinen,
Zu geniessen und zu freuen sich,
Und dein nicht zu achten,
Wie ich!"[1]

Man, elevating himself to the rank of the Titans, acquires his culture by his own efforts, and compels the gods to unite with him, because in his self-sufficient wisdom he has their existence and their limits in his hand. What is most wonderful, however, in this Promethean form, which according to its fundamental conception is the specific hymn of impiety, is the profound Æschylean yearning for *justice*: the untold sorrow of the bold "single-handed being" on the one hand, and the divine need, ay, the foreboding of a twilight of the gods, on the other, the power of these two worlds of suffering constraining to reconciliation, to metaphysical oneness— all this suggests most forcibly the central and main position of the Æschylean view of things, which sees Moira as eternal justice enthroned above gods and men. In view of the astonishing boldness with which Æschulus places the

Olympian world on his scales of justice, it must be remembered that the deep-minded Greek had an immovably firm substratum of metaphysical thought in his mysteries, and that all his sceptical paroxysms could be discharged upon the Olympians. With reference to these deities, the Greek artist, in particular, had an obscure feeling as to mutual dependency: and it is just in the Prometheus of Æschylus that this feeling is symbolised. The Titanic artist found in himself the daring belief that he could create men and at least destroy Olympian deities: namely, by his superior wisdom, for which, to be sure, he had to atone by eternal suffering. The splendid "can-ing" of the great genius, bought too cheaply even at the price of eternal suffering, the stern pride of the *artist*: this is the essence and soul of Æschylean poetry, while Sophocles in his Œdipus preludingly strikes up the victory-song of the *saint*. But even this interpretation which Æschylus has given to the myth does not fathom its astounding depth of terror; the fact is rather that the artist's delight in unfolding, the cheerfulness of artistic creating bidding defiance to all calamity, is but a shining stellar and nebular image reflected in a black sea of sadness. The tale of Prometheus is an original possession of the entire Aryan family of races, and documentary evidence of their capacity for the profoundly tragic; indeed, it is not improbable that this myth has the same characteristic significance for the Aryan race that the myth of the fall of man has for the Semitic, and that there is a relationship between the two myths like that of brother and sister. The presupposition of the Promethean myth is the transcendent value which a naïve humanity attach to *fire* as the true palladium of every ascending culture: that man, however, should dispose at will of this fire, and should not receive it only as a gift from heaven, as the igniting lightning or the warming solar flame, appeared to the contemplative primordial men as crime and robbery of the divine nature. And thus the first philosophical problem at once causes a painful, irreconcilable antagonism between man and God, and puts as it were a mass of rock at the gate of every culture. The best and highest that men can acquire they obtain by a crime, and must now in their turn take upon themselves its consequences, namely the whole flood of sufferings and sorrows with which the offended celestials *must* visit the nobly aspiring race of man: a bitter reflection, which, by the *dignity* it confers on crime, contrasts strangely with the Semitic myth of the fall of man, in which curiosity, beguilement, seducibility, wantonness,—in short, a whole series of pre-eminently feminine passions,—were regarded as the origin of evil. What distinguishes the Aryan representation is the sublime view of *active sin* as the properly Promethean virtue, which suggests at the same time the ethical basis of pessimistic tragedy as the *justification* of human evil—of human guilt as well as of the suffering incurred thereby. The misery in the essence of things—which the contemplative Aryan is not disposed to explain away—the antagonism in the heart of the world, manifests itself to him as a medley of different worlds, for instance, a Divine and a human world, each of which is in the right individually, but as a separate existence alongside of another has to suffer for its individuation. With the heroic effort made by the individual for universality, in his attempt to pass beyond the bounds of individuation and become the *one* universal being, he experiences in himself the primordial contradiction concealed in the essence of things, *i.e.*, he trespasses and suffers. Accordingly crime[2] is understood by the Aryans to be a man, sin[3] by the Semites a woman; as also, the original crime is committed by man, the original sin by woman. Besides, the witches' chorus says:

> "Wir nehmen das nicht so genau:
> Mit tausend Schritten macht's die Frau;
> Doch wie sie auch sich eilen kann
> Mit einem Sprunge macht's der Mann."[4]

He who understands this innermost core of the tale of Prometheus—namely, the necessity of crime imposed on the titanically striving individual—will at once be conscious of the un-Apollonian nature of this pessimistic representation: for Apollo seeks to pacify individual beings precisely by drawing boundary-lines between them, and by again and again calling attention thereto, with his requirements of self-knowledge and due proportion, as the holiest laws of the universe. In order, however, to prevent the form from congealing to Egyptian rigidity and coldness in consequence of this Apollonian tendency, in order to prevent the extinction of the motion of the entire lake in the effort to prescribe to the individual wave its path and compass, the high tide of the Dionysian tendency destroyed from time to time all the little circles in which the one-sided Apollonian "will" sought to confine the Hellenic world. The suddenly swelling tide of the Dionysian then takes the separate little wave-mountains of individuals on its back, just as the brother of Prometheus, the Titan Atlas, does with the earth. This Titanic impulse, to become as it were the Atlas of all individuals, and to carry them on broad shoulders higher and higher, farther and farther, is what the Promethean and the Dionysian have in common. In this respect the Æschylus Prometheus is a Dionysian mask, while, in the aforementioned profound yearning for justice, Æschylus betrays to the intelligent observer his paternal descent from Apollo, the god of individuation and of the boundaries of justice. And so the double-being of the Æschylean

Prometheus, his conjoint Dionysian and Apollonian nature, might be thus expressed in an abstract formula: "Whatever exists is alike just and unjust, and equally justified in both."

Das ist deine Welt! Das heisst eine Welt![5]

10.

It is an indisputable tradition that Greek tragedy in its earliest form had for its theme only the sufferings of Dionysus, and that for some time the only stage-hero therein was simply Dionysus himself. With the same confidence, however, we can maintain that not until Euripides did Dionysus cease to be the tragic hero, and that in fact all the celebrated figures of the Greek stage—Prometheus, Œdipus, etc.—are but masks of this original hero, Dionysus. The presence of a god behind all these masks is the one essential cause of the typical "ideality," so oft exciting wonder, of these celebrated figures. Some one, I know not whom, has maintained that all individuals are comic as individuals and are consequently un-tragic from whence it might be inferred that the Greeks in general *could* not endure individuals on the tragic stage. And they really seem to have had these sentiments: as, in general, it is to be observed that the Platonic discrimination and valuation of the "idea" in contrast to the "eidolon," the image, is deeply rooted in the Hellenic being. Availing ourselves of Plato's terminology, however, we should have to speak of the tragic figures of the Hellenic stage somewhat as follows. The one truly real Dionysus appears in a multiplicity of forms, in the mask of a fighting hero and entangled, as it were, in the net of an individual will. As the visibly appearing god now talks and acts, he resembles an erring, striving, suffering individual: and that, in general, he *appears* with such epic precision and clearness, is due to the dream-reading Apollo, who reads to the chorus its Dionysian state through this symbolic appearance. In reality, however, this hero is the suffering Dionysus of the mysteries, a god experiencing in himself the sufferings of individuation, of whom wonderful myths tell that as a boy he was dismembered by the Titans and has been worshipped in this state as Zagreus:[6] where-by is intimated that this dismemberment, the properly Dionysian *suffering*, is like a transformation into air, water, earth, and fire, that we must therefore regard the state of individuation as the source and primal cause of all suffering, as something objectionable in itself. From the smile of this Dionysus sprang the Olympian gods, from his tears sprang man. In his existence as a dismembered god, Dionysus has the dual nature of a cruel barbarised demon, and a mild pacific ruler. But the hope of the epopts looked for a new birth of Dionysus, which we have now to conceive of in anticipation as the end of individuation: it was for this coming third Dionysus that the stormy jubilation-hymns of the epopts resounded. And it is only this hope that sheds a ray of joy upon the features of a world torn asunder and shattered into individuals: as is symbolised in the myth by Demeter sunk in eternal sadness, who *rejoices* again only when told that she may *once more* give birth to Dionysus. In the views of things here given we already have all the elements of a profound and pessimistic contemplation of the world, and along with these we have the *mystery doctrine of tragedy*: the fundamental knowledge of the oneness of all existing things, the consideration of individuation as the primal cause of evil, and art as the joyous hope that the spell of individuation may be broken, as the augury of a restored oneness.

It has already been intimated that the Homeric epos is the poem of Olympian culture, wherewith this culture has sung its own song of triumph over the terrors of the war of the Titans. Under the predominating influence of tragic poetry, these Homeric myths are now reproduced anew, and show by this metempsychosis that meantime the Olympian culture also has been vanquished by a still deeper view of things. The haughty Titan Prometheus has announced to his Olympian tormentor that the extremest danger will one day menace his rule, unless he ally with him betimes. In Æschylus we perceive the terrified Zeus, apprehensive of his end, in alliance with the Titan. Thus, the former age of the Titans is subsequently brought from Tartarus once more to the light of day. The philosophy of wild and naked nature beholds with the undissembled mien of truth the myths of the Homeric world as they dance past: they turn pale, they tremble before the lightning glance of this goddess—till the powerful fist[7] of the Dionysian artist forces them into the service of the new deity. Dionysian truth takes over the entire domain of myth as symbolism of *its* knowledge, which it makes known partly in the public cult of tragedy and partly in the secret celebration of the dramatic mysteries, always, however, in the old mythical garb. What was the power, which freed Prometheus from his vultures and transformed the myth into a vehicle of Dionysian wisdom? It is the Heracleian power of music: which, having reached its highest manifestness in tragedy, can invest myths with a new and most profound significance, which we have already had occasion to characterise as the most powerful faculty of music. For it is the fate of every myth to insinuate itself into the narrow limits of some alleged historical reality, and to be treated by some later generation as a solitary fact with historical claims: and the Greeks were already fairly on the way to restamp the whole of their mythical juvenile dream sagaciously and arbitrarily into a historico-pragmatical *juvenile history*. For this is the manner in which religions are wont to die out: when of course under the stern, intelligent eyes of an orthodox dogmatism, the mythical presuppositions of a religion are systematised as a completed sum of historical events, and when one begins apprehensively to defend the credibility of the myth, while at the same time opposing all continuation of their natural vitality and luxuriance; when, accordingly, the feeling for myth dies out, and its place is taken by the claim of religion to historical foundations. This dying myth was now seized by the new-born genius of Dionysian music, in whose hands it bloomed once more, with such colours as it had never yet displayed, with a fragrance that awakened a longing anticipation of a metaphysical world. After this final effulgence it collapses, its leaves wither, and soon the scoffing Lucians of antiquity catch at the discoloured and faded flowers which the winds carry off in every direction. Through tragedy the myth attains its profoundest significance, its most expressive form; it rises once more like a wounded hero, and the whole surplus of vitality, together with the philosophical calmness of the Dying, burns in its eyes with a last powerful gleam.

What meantest thou, oh impious Euripides, in seeking once more to enthral this dying one? It died under thy ruthless hands: and then thou madest use of counterfeit, masked myth, which like the ape of Heracles could only trick itself out in the old finery. And as myth died in thy hands, so also died the genius of music; though thou couldst covetously plunder all the gardens of music—thou didst only realise a counterfeit, masked music. And because thou hast forsaken Dionysus, Apollo hath also forsaken thee; rout up all the passions from their haunts and conjure them into thy sphere, sharpen and polish a sophistical dialectics for the speeches of thy heroes—thy very heroes have only counterfeit, masked passions, and speak only counterfeit, masked music.

<h1 style="text-align:center">11.</h1>

Greek tragedy had a fate different from that of all her older sister arts: she died by suicide, in consequence of an irreconcilable conflict; accordingly she died tragically, while they all passed away very calmly and beautifully in ripe old age. For if it be in accordance with a happy state of things to depart this life without a struggle, leaving behind a fair posterity, the closing period of these older arts exhibits such a happy state of things: slowly they sink out of sight, and before their dying eyes already stand their fairer progeny, who impatiently lift up their heads with courageous mien. The death of Greek tragedy, on the other hand, left an immense void, deeply felt everywhere. Even as certain Greek sailors in the time of Tiberius once heard upon a lonesome island the thrilling cry, "great Pan is dead": so now as it were sorrowful wailing sounded through the Hellenic world: "Tragedy is dead !

Poetry itself has perished with her ! Begone, begone, ye stunted, emaciated epigones ! Begone to Hades, that ye may for once eat your fill of the crumbs of your former masters !"

But when after all a new Art blossomed forth which revered tragedy as her ancestress and mistress, it was observed with horror that she did indeed bear the features of her mother, but those very features the latter had exhibited in her long death-struggle. It was *Euripides* who fought this death-struggle of tragedy; the later art is known as the *New Attic Comedy*. In it the degenerate form of tragedy lived on as a monument of the most painful and violent death of tragedy proper.

This connection between the two serves to explain the passionate attachment to Euripides evinced by the poets of the New Comedy, and hence we are no longer surprised at the wish of Philemon, who would have got himself hanged at once, with the sole design of being able to visit Euripides in the lower regions: if only he could be assured generally that the deceased still had his wits. But if we desire, as briefly as possible, and without professing to say aught exhaustive on the subject, to characterise what Euripides has in common with Menander and Philemon, and what appealed to them so strongly as worthy of imitation: it will suffice to say that the *spectator* was brought upon the stage by Euripides. He who has perceived the material of which the Promethean tragic writers prior to Euripides formed their heroes, and how remote from their purpose it was to bring the true mask of reality on the stage, will also know what to make of the wholly divergent tendency of Euripides. Through him the commonplace individual forced his way from the spectators' benches to the stage itself; the mirror in which formerly only great and bold traits found expression now showed the painful exactness that conscientiously reproduces even the abortive lines of nature. Odysseus, the typical Hellene of the Old Art, sank, in the hands of the new poets, to the figure of the Græculus, who, as the good-naturedly cunning domestic slave, stands henceforth in the centre of dramatic interest. What Euripides takes credit for in the Aristophanean "Frogs," namely, that by his household remedies he freed tragic art from its pompous corpulency, is apparent above all in his tragic heroes. The spectator now virtually saw and heard his double on the Euripidean stage, and rejoiced that he could talk so well. But this joy was not all: one even learned of Euripides how to speak: he prides himself upon this in his contest with Æschylus: how the people have learned from him how to observe, debate, and draw conclusions according to the rules of art and with the cleverest sophistications. In general it may be said that through this revolution of the popular language he made the New Comedy possible. For it was henceforth no longer a secret, how—and with what saws—the commonplace could represent and express itself on the stage. Civic mediocrity, on which Euripides built all his political hopes, was now suffered to speak, while heretofore the demigod in tragedy and the drunken satyr, or demiman, in comedy, had determined the character of the language. And so the Aristophanean Euripides prides himself on having portrayed the common, familiar, everyday life and dealings of the people, concerning which all are qualified to pass judgment. If now the entire populace philosophises, manages land and goods with unheard-of circumspection, and conducts law-suits, he takes all the credit to himself, and glories in the splendid results of the wisdom with which he inoculated the rabble.

It was to a populace prepared and enlightened in this manner that the New Comedy could now address itself, of which Euripides had become as it were the chorus-master; only that in this case the chorus of spectators had to be trained. As soon as this chorus was trained to sing in the Euripidean key, there arose that chesslike variety of the drama, the New Comedy, with its perpetual triumphs of cunning and artfulness. But Euripides—the chorus-master—was praised incessantly: indeed, people would have killed themselves in order to learn yet more from him, had they not known that tragic poets were quite as dead as tragedy. But with it the Hellene had surrendered the belief in his immortality; not only the belief in an ideal past, but also the belief in an ideal future. The saying taken from the well-known epitaph, "as an old man, frivolous and capricious," applies also to aged Hellenism. The passing moment, wit, levity, and caprice, are its highest deities; the fifth class, that of the slaves, now attains to power, at least in sentiment: and if we can still speak at all of "Greek cheerfulness," it is the cheerfulness of the slave who has nothing of consequence to answer for, nothing great to strive for, and cannot value anything of the past or future higher than the present. It was this semblance of "Greek cheerfulness" which so revolted the deepminded and formidable natures of the first four centuries of Christianity: this womanish flight from earnestness and terror, this cowardly contentedness with easy pleasure, was not only contemptible to them, but seemed to be a specifically anti-Christian sentiment. And we must ascribe it to its influence that the conception of Greek antiquity, which lived on for centuries, preserved with almost enduring persistency that peculiar hectic colour of cheerfulness—as if there had never been a Sixth Century with its birth of tragedy, its Mysteries, its Pythagoras and Heraclitus, indeed as if the art-works of that great period did not at all exist, which in fact—each by itself—can in no wise be explained as having sprung from the soil of such a decrepit and slavish love of existence and cheerfulness, and point to an altogether different conception of things as their source.

The assertion made a moment ago, that Euripides introduced the spectator on the stage to qualify him the better to pass judgment on the drama, will make it appear as if the old tragic art was always in a false relation to the spectator: and one would be tempted to extol the radical tendency of Euripides to bring about an adequate relation between art-work and public as an advance on Sophocles. But, as things are, "public" is merely a word, and not at all a homogeneous and constant quantity. Why should the artist be under obligations to accommodate himself to a power whose strength is merely in numbers? And if by virtue of his endowments and aspirations he feels himself superior to every one of these spectators, how could he feel greater respect for the collective expression of all these subordinate capacities than for the relatively highest-endowed individual spectator? In truth, if ever a Greek artist treated his public throughout a long life with presumptuousness and self-sufficiency, it was Euripides, who, even when the masses threw themselves at his feet, with sublime defiance made an open assault on his own tendency, the very tendency with which he had triumphed over the masses. If this genius had had the slightest reverence for the pandemonium of the public, he would have broken down long before the middle of his career beneath the weighty blows of his own failures. These considerations here make it obvious that our formula—namely, that Euripides brought the spectator upon the stage in order to make him truly competent to pass judgment—was but a provisional one, and that we must seek for a deeper understanding of his tendency. Conversely, it is undoubtedly well known that Æschylus and Sophocles during all their lives, indeed, far beyond their lives, enjoyed the full favour of the people, and that therefore in the case of these predecessors of Euripides the idea of a false relation between artwork and public was altogether excluded. What was it that thus forcibly diverted this highly gifted artist, so incessantly impelled to production, from the path over which shone the sun of the greatest names in poetry and the cloudless heaven of popular favour? What strange consideration for the spectator led him to defy the spectator? How could he, owing to too much respect for the public—dis-respect the public?

Euripides—and this is the solution of the riddle just propounded—felt himself, as a poet, undoubtedly superior to the masses, but not to two of his spectators: he brought the masses upon the stage; these two spectators he revered as the only competent judges and masters of his art: in compliance with their directions and admonitions, he transferred the entire world of sentiments, passions, and experiences, hitherto present at every festival representation as the invisible chorus on the spectators' benches, into the souls of his stageheroes; he yielded to their demands when he also sought for these new characters the new word and the new tone; in their voices alone he heard the conclusive verdict on his work, as also the cheering promise of triumph when he found himself condemned as usual by the justice of the public.

Of these two spectators the one is—Euripides himself, Euripides *as thinker*, not as poet. It might be said of him, that his unusually large fund of critical ability, as in the case of Lessing, if it did not create, at least constantly fructified a productively artistic collateral impulse. With this faculty, with all the clearness and dexterity of his critical thought, Euripides had sat in the theatre and striven to recognise in the masterpieces of his great predecessors, as in faded paintings, feature and feature, line and line. And here had happened to him what one initiated in the deeper arcana of Æschylean tragedy must needs have expected: he observed something incommensurable in every feature and in every line, a certain deceptive distinctness and at the same time an enigmatic profundity, yea an infinitude, of background. Even the clearest figure had always a comet's tail attached to it, which seemed to suggest the uncertain and the inexplicable. The same twilight shrouded the structure of the drama, especially the significance of the chorus. And how doubtful seemed the solution of the ethical problems to his mind! How questionable the treatment of the myths! How unequal the distribution of happiness and misfortune! Even in the language of the Old Tragedy there was much that was objectionable to him, or at least enigmatical; he found especially too much pomp for simple affairs, too many tropes and immense things for the plainness of the characters. Thus he sat restlessly pondering in the theatre, and as a spectator he acknowledged to himself that he did not understand his great predecessors. If, however, he thought the understanding the root proper of all enjoyment and productivity, he had to inquire and look about to see whether any one else thought as he did, and also acknowledged this incommensurability. But most people, and among them the best individuals, had only a distrustful smile for him, while none could explain why the great masters were still in the right in face of his scruples and objections. And in this painful condition he found *that other spectator*, who did not comprehend, and therefore did not esteem, tragedy. In alliance with him he could venture, from amid his lonesomeness, to begin the prodigious struggle against the art of Æschylus and Sophocles—not with polemic writings, but as a dramatic poet, who opposed *his own* conception of tragedy to the traditional one.

12.

Before we name this other spectator, let us pause here a moment in order to recall our own impression, as previously described, of the discordant and incommensurable elements in the nature of Æschylean tragedy. Let us think of our own astonishment at the *chorus* and the *tragic hero* of that type of tragedy, neither of which we could reconcile with our practices any more than with tradition—till we rediscovered this duplexity itself as the origin and essence of Greek tragedy, as the expression of two interwoven artistic impulses, *the Apollonian and the Dionysian.*

To separate this primitive and all-powerful Dionysian element from tragedy, and to build up a new and purified form of tragedy on the basis of a non-Dionysian art, morality, and conception of things—such is the tendency of Euripides which now reveals itself to us in a clear light.

In a myth composed in the eve of his life, Euripides himself most urgently propounded to his contemporaries the question as to the value and signification of this tendency. Is the Dionysian entitled to exist at all? Should it not be forcibly rooted out of the Hellenic soil? Certainly, the poet tells us, if only it were possible: but the god Dionysus is too powerful; his most intelligent adversary—like Pentheus in the "Bacchæ"—is unwittingly enchanted by him, and in this enchantment meets his fate. The judgment of the two old sages, Cadmus and Tiresias, seems to be also the judgment of the aged poet: that the reflection of the wisest individuals does not overthrow old popular traditions, nor the perpetually propagating worship of Dionysus, that in fact it behoves us to display at least a diplomatically cautious concern in the presence of such strange forces: where however it is always possible that the god may take offence at such lukewarm participation, and finally change the diplomat—in this case Cadmus—into a dragon. This is what a poet tells us, who opposed Dionysus with heroic valour throughout a long life—in order finally to wind up his career with a glorification of his adversary, and with suicide, like one staggering from giddiness, who, in order to escape the horrible vertigo he can no longer endure, casts himself from a tower. This tragedy—the Bacchæ—is a protest against the practicability of his own tendency; alas, and it has already been put into practice! The surprising thing had happened: when the poet recanted, his tendency had already conquered. Dionysus had already been scared from the tragic stage, and in fact by a demonic power which spoke through Euripides. Even Euripides was, in a certain sense, only a mask: the deity that spoke through him was neither Dionysus nor Apollo, but an altogether new-born demon, called *Socrates.* This is the new antithesis: the Dionysian and the Socratic, and the art-work of Greek tragedy was wrecked on it. What if even Euripides now seeks to comfort us by his recantation? It is of no avail: the most magnificent temple lies in ruins. What avails the lamentation of the destroyer, and his confession that it was the most beautiful of all temples?

And even that Euripides has been changed into a dragon as a punishment by the art-critics of all ages—who could be content with this wretched compensation?

Let us now approach this *Socratic* tendency with which Euripides combated and vanquished Æschylean tragedy.

We must now ask ourselves, what could be the ulterior aim of the Euripidean design, which, in the highest ideality of its execution, would found drama exclusively on the non-Dionysian? What other form of drama could there be, if it was not to be born of the womb of music, in the mysterious twilight of the Dionysian? Only *the dramatised epos:* in which Apollonian domain of art the *tragic* effect is of course unattainable. It does not depend on the subject-matter of the events here represented; indeed, I venture to assert that it would have been impossible for Goethe in his projected "Nausikaa" to have rendered tragically effective the suicide of the idyllic being with which he intended to complete the fifth act; so extraordinary is the power of the epic-Apollonian representation, that it charms, before our eyes, the most terrible things by the joy in appearance and in redemption through appearance. The poet of the dramatised epos cannot completely blend with his pictures any more than the epic rhapsodist. He is still just the calm, unmoved embodiment of Contemplation whose wide eyes see the picture *before* them. The actor in this dramatised epos still remains intrinsically rhapsodist: the consecration of inner dreaming is on all his actions, so that he is never wholly an actor.

How, then, is the Euripidean play related to this ideal of the Apollonian drama? Just as the younger rhapsodist is related to the solemn rhapsodist of the old time. The former describes his own character in the Platonic "Ion" as follows: "When I am saying anything sad, my eyes fill with tears; when, however, what I am saying is awful and terrible, then my hair stands on end through fear, and my heart leaps." Here we no longer observe anything of the epic absorption in appearance, or of the unemotional coolness of the true actor, who precisely in his highest activity is wholly appearance and joy in appearance. Euripides is the actor with leaping heart, with hair standing on end; as Socratic thinker he designs the plan, as passionate actor he executes it. Neither in the designing nor in the execution is he an artist pure and simple. And so the Euripidean drama is a thing both cool and fiery, equally capable of freezing and burning; it is impossible for it to attain the Apollonian effect of the epos, while, on the other hand, it has severed itself as much as possible from Dionysian elements, and now, in order to act at all, it requires new stimulants, which can no longer lie within the sphere of the two unique art-impulses, the Apollonian and the Dionysian. The stimulants are cool, paradoxical *thoughts*, in place of Apollonian intuitions—and fiery *passions*—in place of Dionysian ecstasies; and in fact, thoughts and passions very realistically copied, and not at all steeped in the ether of art,

Accordingly, if we have perceived this much, that Euripides did not succeed in establishing the drama exclusively on the Apollonian, but that rather his non-Dionysian inclinations deviated into a naturalistic and inartistic tendency, we shall now be able to approach nearer to the character of *æsthetic Socratism*, the supreme law of which reads about as follows: "to be beautiful everything must be intelligible," as the parallel to the Socratic proposition, "only the knowing one is virtuous." With this canon in his hands Euripides measured all the separate elements of the drama, and rectified them according to his principle: the language, the characters, the dramaturgic structure, and the choric music. The poetic deficiency and retrogression, which we are so often wont to impute to Euripides in comparison with Sophoclean tragedy, is for the most part the product of this penetrating critical process, this daring intelligibility. The Euripidean *prologue* may serve us as an example of the productivity of this rationalistic method. Nothing could be more opposed to the technique of our stage than the prologue in the drama of Euripides. For a single person to appear at the outset of the play telling us who he is, what precedes the action, what has happened thus far, yea, what will happen in the course of the play, would be designated by a modern play wright as a wanton and unpardonable abandonment of the effect of suspense. Everything that is about to happen is known beforehand; who then cares to wait for it actually to happen?—considering, moreover, that here there is not by any means the exciting relation of a predicting dream to a reality taking place later on. Euripides speculated quite differently. The effect of tragedy never depended on epic suspense, on the fascinating uncertainty as to what is to happen now and afterwards: but rather on the great rhetoro-lyric scenes in which the passion and dialectics of the chief hero swelled to a broad and mighty stream. Everything was arranged for pathos, not for action: and whatever was not arranged for pathos was regarded as objectionable. But what interferes most with the hearer's pleasurable satisfaction in such scenes is a missing link, a gap in the texture of the previous history. So long as the spectator has to divine the meaning of this or that person, or the presuppositions of this or that conflict of inclinations and intentions, his complete absorption in the doings and sufferings of the chief persons is impossible, as is likewise breathless fellow-feeling and fellow-fearing. The Æschyleo-Sophoclean tragedy employed the most ingenious devices in the first scenes to place in the hands of the spectator as if by chance all the threads requisite for understanding the whole: a trait in which that noble artistry is approved, which as it were masks the *inevitably* formal, and causes it to appear as something accidental. But nevertheless Euripides thought he observed that during these first scenes the spectator was in a strange state of anxiety to make out the problem of the previous history, so that the poetic beauties and pathos of the exposition were lost to him. Accordingly he placed the prologue even before the exposition, and put it in the mouth of a person who could be trusted: some deity had often as it were to guarantee the particulars of the tragedy to the public and remove every doubt as to the reality of the myth: as in the case of Descartes, who could only prove the reality of the empiric world by an appeal to the truthfulness of God and His inability to utter falsehood. Euripides makes use of the same divine truthfulness once more at the close of his drama, in order to ensure to the public the future of his heroes; this is the task of the notorious *deus ex machina.* Between the preliminary and the additional epic spectacle there is the dramatico-lyric present, the "drama" proper.

Thus Euripides as a poet echoes above all his own conscious knowledge; and it is precisely on this account that he occupies such a notable position in the history of Greek art. With reference to his critico-productive activity, he must often have felt that he ought to actualise in the drama the words at the beginning of the essay of Anaxagoras: "In the beginning all things were mixed together; then came the understanding and created order." And if Anaxagoras with his "νοῦς" seemed like the first sober person among nothing but drunken philosophers, Euripides may also have conceived his relation to the other tragic poets under a similar figure. As long as the sole ruler and disposer of the universe, the νοῦς, was still excluded from artistic activity, things were all mixed together in a chaotic, primitive mess;—it is thus Euripides was obliged to think, it is thus he was obliged to condemn the "drunken" poets as the first "sober" one among them. What Sophocles said of Æschylus, that he did what was right, though unconsciously, was surely not in the mind of Euripides: who would have admitted only thus much, that Æschylus, *because* he wrought unconsciously, did what was wrong. So also the divine Plato speaks for the most part only ironically of the creative faculty of the poet, in so far as it is not conscious insight, and places it on a par with the gift of the soothsayer and dream-interpreter; insinuating that the poet is incapable of composing until he has become unconscious and reason has deserted him. Like Plato, Euripides undertook to show to the world the reverse of the "unintelligent" poet; his æsthetic principle that "to be beautiful everything must be known" is, as I have said, the parallel to the Socratic "to be good everything must be known." Accordingly we may regard Euripides as the poet of æsthetic Socratism. Socrates, however, was that *second spectator* who did not comprehend and therefore did not esteem the Old Tragedy; in alliance with him Euripides ventured to be the herald of a new artistic activity. If, then, the Old Tragedy was here destroyed, it follows that æsthetic Socratism was the murderous principle; but in so far as the struggle is directed against the Dionysian element in the old art, we recognise in Socrates the opponent of Dionysus, the new Orpheus who rebels against Dionysus; and although destined to be torn to pieces by the Mænads of the Athenian court, yet puts to flight the overpowerful god himself, who, when he fled from Lycurgus, the king of Edoni, sought refuge in the depths of the ocean—namely, in the mystical flood of a secret cult which gradually overspread the earth.

NOTES

1. "Here sit I, forming mankind
   In my image,
   A race resembling me,—
   To sorrow and to weep,
   To taste, to hold, to enjoy,
   And not have need of thee,
   As I !"
   (Translation in Hæckel's *History of the Evolution of Man.*)
2. *Der* Frevel. †
3. *Die* Sünde.
4. We do not measure with such care:
   Woman in thousand steps is there,
   But howsoe'er she hasten may,
   Man in one leap has cleared the way.
   Faust, trans, of Bayard Taylor.—TR.
5. This is thy world, and what a world!—*Faust*.
6. See article by Mr. Arthur Symons in *The Academy*, 30th August 1902.
7. Die mächtige Faust.—Cf. *Faust*, Chorus of Spirits.—TR.

R.P. WINNINGTON-INGRAM

Tragedy and Greek Archaic Thought

1

When Dodds describes Sophocles as 'the last great exponent of the archaic world-view',[1] it is a description which most of us would accept, provided we are allowed to write glosses upon it. This essay is, in part, such a gloss.

The Greek archaic world-view was a collection of mental habits which included thought at different degrees of rationality. If it cannot be defined with precision, it can be depicted in its manifold variety; and no one has depicted it more skilfully than Dodds in the book from which I have quoted. Certain aspects particularly relevant to tragedy will be brought into relief in the course of the following discussion. During the second half of the fifth century there was a change in the general climate of thought which is often referred to as the Enlightenment; and it was characterized by the rejection or modification of various modes of archaic thinking. It had its forerunners in Ionia, men like Xenophanes and Heraclitus; the enigmatic Euripides displays its influence; the Sophists spread the ferment of ideas; and finally Plato imposed upon this welter new patterns of thought, the influence of which is still so powerful as to be often unobserved. Indeed I sometimes wonder whether Plato is not largely responsible, along with Christian theology, for the differences of opinion between modern scholars as to the mental competence of such writers as Aeschylus and Sophocles; and whether the

From *Classical Drama and Its Influence*, edited by M.J. Anderson. © 1965 by Methuen.

point at issue is not so much what they actually thought as what a respectable thinker may be allowed to think.

Aeschylus and Sophocles. But are we right to bracket them together as representatives of an earlier mental world? Dodds makes a reservation.[2] 'In his thought Sophocles (save perhaps in his latest plays) still belongs entirely to the older world.... Aeschylus, on the other hand, struggling as he does to interpret and rationalise the legacy of the Archaic Age, is in many ways prophetic of the new time.' To some the very word 'thought' as applied to Sophocles appears inappropriate. They do not of course mean, quite literally, that Sophocles did not think: it would be a remarkable feat to write the *Oedipus Coloneus* without thinking. They mean that, whereas Aeschylus wrestled with fundamental moral and religious problems, Sophocles simply swallowed an existing system of thought and feeling—swallowed it, we might say, steadily and swallowed it whole. They mean that, untroubled morally or intellectually by the old ways, he averted his eyes from the new—and therefore cannot be taken seriously as a thinker. This is not a view that has commended itself to the scholar in whose honour these studies have been collected;[3] and it is not the view which will be maintained in this essay.

2

The *Oedipus Tyrannus* holds a special place in the work of Sophocles. The most powerful of his tragedies, it distils the essence of one aspect of his thought, itself a legacy from the archaic age. I refer to the breach between the divine and human modes of existence, the frailty of man and his dependence upon a god-given destiny. This thought receives its classical statement in the first stanza of the ode which the Chorus sing, when Oedipus leaves the stage having learnt the truth about his life. 'What man wins more of happiness (*eudaimonia*) than just a semblance and, after the semblance, a decline? I call no mortal blessed, for I have the example of your *daimon*, Oedipus, before my eyes.'[4] What do they mean—what did Sophocles mean—by the *daimon* of Oedipus? And by *eudaimonia*? Certainly more by *eudaimonia* than Aristotle meant, when he said that this was the good at which all men aim; and more by *daimon* than we mean, when we speak vaguely of a man's destiny. To quote Dodds again:[5] 'A third type of daemon, who makes his first appearance in the Archaic Age, is attached to a particular individual, usually from birth, and determines, wholly or in part, his individual destiny.... He represents the individual *moira* or "portion" of which Homer speaks, but in the personal form which appealed to the imagination of the time.' The fate of Oedipus, then, is ascribed to a malign superhuman power which had attended him from birth. Surely this provides no evidence of independent thought in Sophocles—or of anything but popular fatalism with superstitious overtones?

The idea of malignity does not indeed occur in the stanza. But let us go back a little in the play. To set the fears of Oedipus at rest, Jocasta has told him about the oracle given to Laius that seemed not to have been fulfilled. But the mention of the place where three highways met rouses a dreadful apprehension in the king's mind, and at last he tells her the story of his encounter at just such a place. If there is any connection (so he puts it, euphemistically) between the old stranger he killed and Laius, who could be more wretched, *of a more hostile daimon* (τίς ἐχθροδαίμων μᾶλλον, 816), than he now is; for he is liable to his own ban pronounced upon the killer of Laius, and he is sleeping with the wife of the man he killed. Not only so, but he is in exile (so he thinks) from his native land for fear of wedding his mother and killing his father. 'Would not a man be right to judge of me that these things come from a cruel *daimon*' (ἀπ ὠμοῦ ... δαίμονος, 828). Oedipus, then, attributes to a cruel and hostile superhuman power the destiny which is so much worse than he yet knows. When it becomes known, when Oedipus, knowing it, has entered the palace, the Chorus argue the nothingness of man from the *daimon* of Oedipus.

Later in the ode they sing (1213 f.): 'All-seeing time has found you out; it brings to justice the monstrous marriage in which the begotten has long been the begetter'. This inadequate translation of the untranslatable omits one word: 'unwilling' or 'unwitting' as the epithet of Oedipus. The conscious criminal seeks to evade detection, which comes upon him against his will. But this does not apply. What, then, was contrary to the will or knowledge of Oedipus? There is perhaps at this point a deliberate ambiguity,[6] which is cleared up, when, a few lines later, a servant comes out of the palace, now polluted (as he says) with new evils which will soon come to light—'evils wrought consciously and not unwittingly' (ἑκόντα κοὐκ ἄκοντα, 1230). A distinction could not more clearly and emphatically be made between the unwilled and the willed deeds of Oedipus; and it is reinforced by the Messenger's general comment, that 'those griefs sting most that are seen to be self-chosen' (αὐθαί-ρετοι, 1231). The distinction is clearly made, and we expect it to be clearly maintained. When he killed his father and wedded his mother, Oedipus was a victim of the gods, but, when he blinded himself, he was a free agent. How attractive to look at matters in this way, and how limited the truth of it may be!

The messenger tells his story of the suicide of Jocasta and the self-blinding of Oedipus. The doors open again, and the blinded Oedipus comes out. The reactions of the Chorus are governed, as those of any audience must be, by this sight, the most dreadful they have ever seen. 'What madness came upon you? Who was the *daimon* that leapt, with a bound exceeding the extreme, upon ...?'[7] Upon what? The whole expression is, once more, essentially untranslatable, but Jebb's translation here seems to miss the point and, above all, the relationship of these lines to the preceding choral ode. I can only conclude with a free expansion: '... upon that *moira* of yours that was already a *daimon*'s evil work.' The evil destiny of Oedipus had seemed to have reached an extreme point and to have provided the perfect paradigm of ill-starred humanity, but there was still a further point of misery to be reached, and that too is ascribed to the assault of a *daimon*. A few lines later, groping in his sightlessness, hearing his voice 'borne from him on the air in a direction over which he has no control',[8] Oedipus exclaims: 'Oh *Daimon*, that you should have sprung so far!' (ἰὼ δαῖμον, ἵν᾽ ἐξήλου, 1311). It is clear from his preceding words and from the response of the Chorus that he is thinking of his blindness. Later again, the Chorus ask: 'How could you bring yourself so to destroy your sight? What *daimon* moved you to it?' (τίς σ᾽ ἐπῆρε δαιμόνων; 1328). Oedipus might have said—and critics sometimes write as though he had said: 'As to my other sufferings[9] they were the work of Apollo, but, when I struck my eyes, the responsibility was mine alone (and you are wrong to ask what *daimon* moved me)'. Actually he replies: 'It was Apollo, my friends, it was Apollo that was bringing these sufferings of mine to completion. But it was none other's hand that struck the blow: it was I.'[10] The reiterated name of Apollo must answer the question: 'What *daimon*?' The expression 'these sufferings of mine' cannot exclude and may primarily denote the visible suffering which dominates the scene. It would be tidy to suppose that, while Apollo was responsible, through his oracle, for the earlier sufferings of Oedipus, the self-blinding was an act of independent will unmotivated by divine power. But that is not how it is seen by either Oedipus or the Chorus.

What then, we may well ask, has now become of the clear distinction between involuntary and voluntary acts with which Sophocles introduced the scene? What, for that matter, has become of the unconsidering Sophocles? Surely here is a mind at work upon a train of thought—working with the formality traditional in Greek literary art in a verbal technique reminiscent of Aeschylus. (Might it not be suggested that, if thought imposes form, equally a poet who works with certain formal methods is almost forced to think?) It was a mind, surely, not unaware of what contemporary minds were thinking. The thought has links with Homer and Aeschylus, but also with Socrates and Euripides. If the play was written in the early 420's (which is as good a guess as any), Socrates may already have been preaching that 'no man errs wittingly'; and, since the self-blinding of Oedipus was the error of a mind clouded by passion, Socrates might have argued that it was not properly a witting or willing act.[11] Euripides, according to Snell,[12] controverted this Socratic doctrine in the *Hippolytus* of 428. This may or may not be true. Euripides, who about this time was writing tragedies of passion, may have been a purely humanistic psychologist or may have believed that irrational passions were external forces of a daemonic character.[13] It is at least clear that the nature and origin of passion was a living issue about the time when the *Oedipus Tyrannus* was written.

When I ask what has become of the clear distinction between involuntary and voluntary acts, I do not wish to imply that it has disappeared, but merely that it has been made to appear in a new light. The distinction has not disappeared, but both kinds of acts have been drawn within the ambit of the operation of *daimones*. What, then, did Sophocles mean, when he represented the 'evils wrought wittingly', the 'self-chosen grief', as the work of a *daimon*, as the work of Apollo? We can perhaps find the answer in two directions. The self-blinding of Oedipus was, as Socrates might have called it, a mistake. The Chorus think that it was the result of an onset of madness. They ask what *daimon* brought him to it; and the word they use (ἐπαίρειν) is appropriate to a transport of emotion. It is true that Oedipus, like a Greek,[14] gives a reason: 'What needed I to see?' But we cannot suppose that he struck his eyes on a purely rational consideration. And the argument progressively breaks down, as it becomes clear that all he has done is to lock himself in a dark prison with the memories of the past.[15] Now, to see in an emotional impulse the work of a *daimon* or god is Homeric; it is Aeschylean; it is a view which may even have left traces in Euripides. But this ascription of the self-blinding to a *daimon* is also part of the whole fabric of the play. By identifying the *daimon* with Apollo, Oedipus links his witting and unwitting acts, so that the self-blinding appears as the culmination of the evil destiny that has attended him since birth. It has often been pointed out—by no one more cogently than by Kitto[16]—that the divinely-appointed destiny of Oedipus comes about largely through actions on his part which spring directly from his character: it was *like* Oedipus that he must leave Corinth to discover the truth about his birth; it was *like* Oedipus to pursue his judicial enquiries with such energy; and so on. ἦθος ἀνθρώπῳ δαίμων: character is destiny. Looked at from this angle, the play might seem to be a commentary on the saying of Heraclitus. Yet, when, still acting characteristically, Oedipus blinds himself, the action is attributed to the influence of a *daimon*—and Heraclitus is turned inside out. There is a kind of symmetry. It needed the unwitting characteristic actions of Oedipus to bring about his fated destiny; it needed the influence of a *daimon* to explain his deliberate act. The divine and human worlds inter-penetrate; and this inter-penetration is Homeric and archaic. It is also Aeschylean.[17]

3

It is clearly beyond the scope of a brief essay to deal adequately with the relationship between the tragic, which means the religious, thought of Aeschylus and Sophocles. There is a similarity and a difference. I shall end by stressing the similarity, which arises out of a similar use of the categories of archaic thought. But, since Sophocles seems to present archaic thought in a purer form than Aeschylus, something should perhaps be said about their differences, though it must necessarily be brief and summary.

Aeschylus dealt with the Theban story in a trilogy of which only the *Septem* remains—a trilogy which Sophocles must have known as well as he clearly knew the *Oresteia*. If we are not in a position to compare the one Oedipus with the other, we can, in one respect, compare Oedipus with Eteocles. Eteocles, in the *Septem*, is confronted with the decision to fight or not to fight his brother in single combat. The human motives and impulses are clearly displayed—his sense of honour, his hatred of his brother. But, along with them, we see—and he sees—divine powers determining the event—the Erinys of his father's curse, a god hastening on the destruction of the hated family of Laius. A *daimon* and a god; and when Eteocles speaks of a family hated by Phoebus and greatly loathed by the gods,[18] we may well compare the ἐχθροδαίμων of the Sophoclean Oedipus, along with all the other passages of the *Tyrannus* which we have been considering. In both plays, divine and human causes run in parallel. The Aeschylean and the Sophoclean character can alike see himself as hated by heaven. Hated by heaven on what grounds?

Believe that events—unpleasant events—are caused by divine powers, and sooner or later you will speculate about the motives by which the divine powers are actuated. And here the tradition which Aeschylus and Sophocles had inherited from the Archaic Age was two-fold: the Inherited Conglomerate (to use a term of Gilbert Murray's) included both the jealousy and the justice of heaven. In the concept of the jealousy of the gods there was a strong element of sheer malignancy. But the longing to find justice in the ordering of the universe—and the fact that justice sometimes seems to be done—had led to another line of thought. Disaster is seen as a punishment, Zeus as the upholder of a moral order, Justice (Dike) as the daughter of Zeus.

This conception is explicitly developed by Hesiod and Solon, through whom the line runs to Aeschylus. In a famous chorus of the *Agamemnon* the old idea is rejected that excessive prosperity alone is sufficient to account for disaster: it is rather the impious deed that produces a disastrous progeny. There must be some likelihood, though of course no certainty, that in the Theban trilogy the disastrous history of the house of Laius was interpreted in terms of justice at every stage and, in particular, that Oedipus was culpable.

We must of course be cautious about inferring the views of a dramatist from views expressed by his characters. Eteocles may not have been gifted with the insight of his creator. By what right do we attribute to Sophocles the interpretations placed upon events by Oedipus and the Chorus? In one circumstance at least we may sometimes be entitled to read the mind of the dramatist; and that is where the words of his characters (or of his chorus) carry, by dramatic irony, implications of which they are unaware. Let us return again to the *Tyrannus*.

Oedipus has been led for the first time to suspect that he may be the killer of Laius; and that to the threat of pollution hanging over him has been added a pollution actually incurred. On either score—and he does not know they are one and the same—he sees himself as the victim of a cruel *daimon*. In the ode which follows (863 ff.), the Chorus reacts to the preceding scene. Few odes of Sophocles have led to more perplexed discussion. For, after a first stanza in which they pray for a destiny—a portion (*moira*)—of purity and piety in accordance with the eternal laws, they appear to shoot off at a tangent. 'It is *hubris* that breeds the tyrant.' Did they think—did Sophocles mean us to think—that Oedipus was, or was becoming, a tyrant? There was indeed enough in his bearing towards Teiresias and Creon to make them uneasy. But could it be said that he was guilty of the conventional catalogue of sins contained in the third stanza? If not, why are they listed? I must limit myself to four observations.[19]

(i) The notions of *daimon* and *moira* are closely linked. When, therefore, the Chorus prays (863 ff.) for a *moira* of purity, we are to think of the destiny of Oedipus which he already feels to be impure as the result of a hostile *daimon*.[20] (ii) The next stanza tells of *hubris* falling headlong from the heights; and once it has begun to fall, the process is inevitable—as inevitable as the force of gravity.[21] So Oedipus falls; and no move he makes can save him. (iii) For such a catastrophe, arrogance—along with the whole catalogue of its manifestations—would provide a possible, a likely, and a religious explanation. Against the arrogant man the Chorus prays: 'May an evil *moira* seize him!' But Oedipus was not guilty of these offences. Nor was he a tyrant, but a ruler that strove for the good of the city. Such an ambition the Chorus prayed the gods to preserve (879 ff.). Yet Oedipus has an evil *moira* from the gods. (iv) The explanation was perhaps not only plausible and religious, but Aeschylean. I suspect, though of course I cannot prove, that the content of the third stanza was prompted by the *Oedipus* of Aeschylus. I cannot prove it, though there are strong hints in the *Septem* that wealth and luxury may have been significant themes in the earlier plays of the trilogy.[22] The explanation may or may not be Aeschylean. If it does not fit, what explanation does? Oedipus may be near the truth.

4

If Sophocles in the *Tyrannus* rejects by implication the idea that the disasters of Oedipus are due to his crimes, in the *Coloneus* Oedipus is made to reject it explicitly.[23] There is no reason to suppose that Sophocles had changed his mind between the one play and the other, though it may well be that he had given further thought to the problem of Oedipus in the light, not perhaps of Aeschylus' Theban trilogy, but of the *Oresteia*. It is through the *Oresteia* alone that we at least are able to grasp how Aeschylus, in the last phase of his thought, envisaged the operations of divinity in the world of men.

It was not the existence, but the character, of the divine justice that created a problem for Aeschylus. 'It was', writes Dodds[24] of the Archaic Age, 'a misfortune that the functions assigned to the moralised Supernatural were predominantly, if not exclusively, penal.' But it is characteristic of Aeschylean tragedy that the penalties are inflicted by human-beings on one another. When Zeus strikes down Capaneus with the thunderbolt, that is a clean end to the affair. But, in the *Oresteia*, Agamemnon is punished by Clytemnestra and Aegisthus, and they by Orestes. The justice of heaven is penal, is retributive, is a matter of *talio*; and it is carried out by human-beings pursuing their own revenges, actuated by a motive basic to the Greek scheme of values, the desire to retaliate. The exception proves the rule. Orestes is pursued by Furies (Erinyes), but human avengers have already been represented in that rôle. The Furies tell us nothing strictly new about the divine justice: they merely bring home in the most vivid and dramatic way its retaliatory penal character. Once again, then, we find that interpenetration of the divine and human worlds, so characteristic of archaic thought, but this time through the inter-locking of divine and human *talio*. The process is as frightful as the Furies look and sound. Evil is perpetuated through its own punishment; and out of the evil past come intolerable constraints which seem to make a mockery of human freedom. This divine penal justice, coercive and violent, horrified Aeschylus, as it horrifies us.

'Aeschylus, struggling as he does to interpret and rationalise the legacy of the Archaic Age, is in many ways prophetic of the new time.' That he interprets and rationalizes is true, but he does not deny the responsibility of the gods for evil or proclaim the autonomy of the human will. If he was able to end the *Oresteia* upon a note of joy, it was not by subtracting anything from the grim vision of divinity that he had inherited, but by adding something to it which was itself rooted in Greek ideas. Persuasion (*peitho*) was the natural antithesis of force (*bia*). So, in the *Eumenides*, the problem cannot be solved by Apollo, who can only abuse and threaten the Furies, but only by Athena, through whose persuasions the Erinyes take on a new—and by all the old ideas paradoxical—character as Eumenides or spirits of good-will. In short, Athena—and behind Athena is her father Zeus (ἐκράτσε Ζεὺς Ἀγοραῖος)[25]—shows the 'moralised Supernatural' acting, not as a coercive, but as a persuasive agency; and this may have been the great contribution of Aeschylus to Greek religious thought.

Sophocles knew and had pondered the *Oresteia*. If I say that he had perhaps re-thought the Oedipus story in terms of this trilogy, my justification is this: that it is unthinkable that he could have placed the end of Oedipus against a background of Eumenides without regard to the poet who had virtually created the tragic significance of Furies.[26] We know how the *Oresteia* ends: it ends with the conversion of Erinyes and with joy. How does the *Oedipus Coloneus* end? We might be tempted to say that it ends with a mysterious solemnity and with a kind of reconciliation between Oedipus and the gods. But this is not quite true, for actually the play ends with Antigone asking Theseus to send her to Thebes: 'to prevent, if we can, the blood-shed that is coming upon our brothers'.[27] The play ends with a window opened upon fresh tragedy directly resulting from the action. By ending with Antigone and her brothers, it takes us back behind the scene of the passing of Oedipus to that in which the father cursed the son he hated and, in doing so, condemned to death the daughter he loved.

That curse has led to some uneasy apologias: such anger, such concentrated malevolence, in the man whom the gods are about to take to themselves! No apologia is needed, no watering-down admissible, if we understand what Oedipus is, what has made him, where he is, and what he is to become. He is a man of wrath (*thumos*), which rises in a crescendo through the play to the cursing of Polynices. His wrath is the product of ancient as well as of recent wrongs—of the sufferings to which he was bred as the son of his father, to which as a father he adds, and of which his blindness is the visible symbol. He now stands close to a grove of the Eumenides, but it was not spirits of good-will that had presided over his own destiny and that he will evoke by his curse. Past this grove he will shortly go to become himself a *heros*, a chthonian power; and it is by his curse that he has well established his claim to be one. By accepting and honouring him, the divine world is, it would seem, ratifying the kind of justice he has administered, which is a vindictive justice, provoked by suffering and issuing in retaliation. He had spoken of the 'ancient Justice that sits with Zeus according to primaeval laws' (1381 f.); and the event bears this out against the rival claim of Polynices (1267 f.) that it is Mercy (Aidos) that shares Zeus' throne. It is justice not mercy that prevails; the violence of Oedipus, not the persuasions of Antigone. At every point Antigone seeks to persuade, and at every point she fails. Her ultimate failure is outside the play, but foreshadowed at the end of the play, and relevant to the play. For the justice of Oedipus destroys the innocent with the guilty.

5

Sophocles shares with Aeschylus a belief that human destiny is influenced by divine powers in a way which involves the very psychological processes of the human-beings themselves. The horror of punitive divine justice is common ground. What Sophocles seems to reject—or to neglect—is the mitigation which we find in Aeschylus, certainly at the end of the *Oresteia* and probably in other trilogies.[28] The gods of Sophocles are pitiless; and against their pitilessness human pity, so pervasive a theme in his tragedies, stands out in a clear, and often an ironical, light.

It is perhaps presumptuous to ask what caused this difference between the two poets, though answers of a kind can be given. One answer might be in terms of technique. It was the trilogy that enabled Aeschylus to range within sight of ultimate solutions. Abandon the trilogy, and you are forced to concentrate upon an irremediable disaster; focus your single tragedy upon a figure of vivid personality, and you must concentrate upon his disastrous destiny. The Aeschylean Orestes passes from Argos to Delphi, from Delphi to Athens, and then leaves the stage to the gods; the Sophoclean Electra remains at the end of the play—and therefore to the end of time—the warped person that tragic events have made of her.[29] This argument, however, is hardly conclusive. Did the form influence the content, or did the tragic concept dictate the form?[30] The horizons of the *Oedipus Coloneus* are wide enough; and yet, when Sophocles does look beyond the confines of his play, he looks out on new tragedy. Certain answers may be rejected: that Sophocles could not or would not think; that Sophocles was pious. Doubtless Sophocles was emotionally attached to the ancient pieties and cults. But there is nothing to prevent a ritualist from making distinguished contributions to theology—nor a believer in miracles or oracles[31] or a plurality of personal gods. We should not fuss too much about these things: the beliefs of twentieth-century man—of all twentieth-century men—will seem one day a very curious Conglomerate.[32] Nor is it clear why conventional piety, as such, should have led Sophocles along these gloomy paths of thought. More, surely, is to be attributed to his trade and to the age in which he lived. His trade he shared with Aeschylus: tragic poets are forced to become connoisseurs of evil and, if they have keen minds capable of general thought, to consider the metaphysics of evil. His age was later. Aeschylus lived through the terrible, but inspiring days of the Persian invasions; he knew the hopes, if also the dangers, of the new Athenian democracy. His optimism (if such a word may be used) was not easy, but it was possible: he could believe in Zeus Agoraios. Sophocles, the urbane friend of Pericles, lived also in the world depicted for us by Thucydides—a world in which the democracy had become an imperialism,[33] arrogant, feared and fearing, based on force and evoking retaliation. He lived to write the majority of his extant plays during the Peloponnesian War. It was not only Thucydides, not only Euripides, that observed that war with an understanding mind. How strange that Sophocles, who had the luck to live to see the Peloponnesian War, should have turned his back, not only on the Enlightenment, but even on the strivings of Aeschylus towards the light!

6

My attempts to define some of the differences between the tragic thought of Aeschylus and Sophocles have, I trust, only emphasized the common legacy that they share from the Archaic Age. Is it to their discredit as thinkers that they thought in archaic terms? The archaic is now fashionable in art, but in the realm of thought the word is still used as a term of disparagement. I would suggest that, under the pervasive influence of centuries of Platonic and Christian thinking, there is a tendency to undervalue the categories of archaic thought as a means of expressing important truths about the universe. There is an implicit criticism which I will put in so extreme and indeed absurd a form that it could not possibly be ascribed to any living scholar. Why, if Aeschylus and Sophocles were thinkers worthy of attention, did they not abandon the Urdummheit of the Archaic Age and become good Platonists before their time? It is true that, if they had enrolled proleptically under Plato's banner, they would not have been allowed to write tragedy, but this would have been no hardship, since, having once given their adherence to Plato, they would have lost both the will and the power to do so.

It is a sad—perhaps even a tragic—fact that advances in human thought tend to be bought at a price, which is the exchange of one set of difficulties for another. We have been concerned in particular with two related features of Greek archaic thought, which may or may not be its most salient characteristics, but are certainly those most relevant to tragedy. One of them might be called the involvement of the mind, the other the responsibility of the gods for evil.

The discovery of the mind (to use Snell's phrase), the disentanglement of the individual human personality, was vital to the development of morals and of civilization. Until the personality has been isolated, it cannot be valued; and it was not for nothing that Whitehead devoted an early chapter of *Adventures of Ideas* to the civilizing influence of the Platonic and Christian conceptions of the soul. Behind Plato is Socrates and the 'tendance of the soul'. But the soul cannot be tended, until it has been recognized; you cannot appeal to conscience except on the basis of the freedom of the will. This would seem pure gain. But then the danger appears. The autonomous will becomes an abstraction; the soul cuts loose from its connections with a body (becoming the ghost in the machine), from its connections with other souls and other bodies and with the totality of the universe. It is characteristic of much modern thought that it stresses the involvement of the human personality in its environment and the consequent limitations upon human freedom. The saying of Heraclitus, already quoted, was, one supposes, a protest against superstition—and a fine one. But one problem it does not solve: it does not tell us where the *ethos* comes from. Syntactically reversible,[34] it yields as good a sense the other way round. It is doubtless a great advantage to be rid of superstitious fears and ideas of mechanical pollution and to get a clear juridical distinction between deliberate and unwitting actions. It may not be so good to forget that our deliberate acts are themselves in large measure the product of innumerable causes in the past over which we have no control. That is something that archaic thought was not tempted to forget—and that tragedy must never forget.

What the Greek poets expressed in terms of a mythology, we may express in psychological terms so little precise and so little understood that they have almost the status of a modern mythology.[35] We argue about free-will and determinism within a philosophical framework unknown to the Greek poets, but the debate is not exclusively a modern one. The Greeks loved liberty above all things and knew what it meant to be deprived of liberty. A slave-owning agricultural society presented obvious paradigms—metaphors which occur again and again in Greek tragedy. The free man follows his own choices; the slave and the yoked animal obey the bidding of a master; they are subject to compulsion *(ananke)*. Feeling their liberty confined not only by external circumstances but even in the realm of their own minds, it was not surprising that the Greeks should ask themselves how far the free man was still free, in what degree he was constrained by the forces they conceived as gods. The question of psychological determination merges into the wider question of the responsibility of the gods for evil, which was such a rock of offence to Plato.

It was an offence that the tragedians—and he cites Aeschylus in particular—made the gods responsible for evil.[36] How far he really understood Aeschylus we cannot tell, but the better he understood him, the more the Plato of the *Republic* was bound to disapprove of him. The gods responsible for evil! But, if the gods are inside nature, as the Greeks' gods so obviously and so firmly were,[37] how can they not be responsible for evil? It was Plato's problem, not the tragedians'. It was Plato's problem how the gods could be made not to be so responsible. To put it rather crudely, the solution involved taking the gods out of nature and then trying to bring them back into it. If we look for the divine in Plato's thought, we find it, primarily, in a perfect world of Forms—and above all in the Form of the Good—to which the soul of man, itself divine, has access. It is, however, the rational soul that is divine and has such access; and we are left with the problem of irrational impulses and desires and the havoc they cause. In the *Timaeus* a divine demiurge is represented as making the world upon the model of the Forms; and, whether he is an external creator god or, as is more probable,[38] a mythical symbol of the Divine Reason working for good ends, we have to account for the manifold imperfections in the world he made. Plato, who on the whole speaks with such confidence and clarity in the *Republic*, was exercised—and, it would appear, increasingly exercised—by these problems. In the *Timaeus* he ascribes the imperfections of the craftsman's work to the imperfect tractability of the material (the metaphysical status of which remains rather obscure): he says[39]—and it is one of the most remarkable sayings in Plato—that 'the generation of this universe was a mixed result of the combination of Necessity *(ananke)* and Reason'. And he goes on: 'Reason overruled Necessity by persuading her to guide the greatest part of the things that become towards what is best; in that way and on that principle this universe was fashioned in the beginning by the victory of reasonable persuasion over Necessity'. Cornford, in an Epilogue to *Plato's Cosmology*, associated this passage with the closing scene of the *Eumenides;* and one would indeed like to think that Plato had taken Aeschylus to heart and that in this his most profound—perhaps his only profound—contribution to the problem of evil he links hands with Aeschylus and Sophocles—with

Aeschylus who was pre-occupied with the successes, with Sophocles who was pre-occupied with the failures, of persuasion in the moral field.

But the *Timaeus* lies between the *Republic* and the *Laws*. It is not the hard sayings of the *Timaeus*, born of metaphysical perplexity, that have influenced subsequent thought and feeling so much as the ardent religious conviction and sheer literary power of the *Republic* and, particularly, the Myth of Er with which it closes. In this eschatological myth, souls are seen to choose their own destinies, but first they are addressed by a Prophetes, or Spokesman of the divine powers. His words are virtually a manifesto against the archaic—and the tragic—worldview. Though he speaks in the name of the Allotting Goddess (Lachesis), daughter of Necessity (Ananke), we find that lot affects only the order in which they choose and necessity only ratifies inflexibly their choice. 'It is not', he says,[40] 'that a *daimon* will get you by lot, but that you will choose a *daimon*.... Virtue owns no master.... The responsibility is the chooser's; God is not responsible.' But in the *Laws* a disillusioned Plato has swung to the opposite extreme. Twice[41] he makes the Athenian speak contemptuously of men as puppets, playthings (perhaps) of the gods, jerked this way and that by their hopes and fears and passions, dancing on a string.

Such disillusionment is perhaps the nemesis that attends upon a too confident idealism. It is, however, no part of my purpose to deny such truth and value as may reside in the words of the Prophetes, but merely to suggest that neither puppets nor human-beings who are in complete control of their destinies can be the subjects of tragedy. The categories of archaic thought, primitive and obstructive though they might be in primitive minds, allowed Aeschylus and Sophocles to write tragedy, because—ascribe it to inferior logic or superior insight—they were able simultaneously to see man as free and as subject to determining powers, and so to produce that tension between freedom and necessity which seems essential to the tragic paradox. At least it can be said that, because of their archaic notions, and the presuppositions on which they were based, they were not tempted, as so many thinkers have been, to fudge the evidence in the interests of the autonomy of the will and the innocence of heaven.

NOTES

1.   E.R. Dodds, *The Greeks and the Irrational*, 49.
2.   Op. cit. 50, n. i.
3.   Cf. H.D.F. Kitto, *Sophocles Dramatist and Philosopher*, passim.
4.   τὸν σόν τοι παράδειγμ' ἔχων,
      τὸν σόν δαίμονα, τὸν σόν, ὦ

τλᾶμον Οἰδιπόδα, βροτῶν
οὐδὲν μακαρίζω. (1193–6)

5. Op. cit. 42. On *daimon* in Sophocles cf. G.M. Kirkwood, *A Study of Sophoclean Drama*, 185 f.

6. 'He had not foreseen the disclosure which was to result from his inquiry into the murder of Laius' (Jebb); he had not known that his actions were crimes. Cf. also *O.C*, 977, 987.

7. τίς σ᾽ ὦ τλᾶμον,
προσέβη μανία; τίς ὁ πηδήσας
μείζονα δαίμων τῶν μακίστων
πρὸς σῇ δυσδαίμονι μοίρᾳ   (1299–1302)

8. Jebb, on 1310.

9. As though it were τὰ μὲν ἄλλα ...

10. Ἀπόλλων τάδ᾽ ἦν, Ἀπόλλων, φίλοι,
ὁ κακὰ κακά τελῶν ἐμὰ τάδ᾽ ἐμὰ πάθεα.
ἔπαισε δ᾽ αὐτόχειρ νιν οὔ-
τις, ἀλλ᾽ ἐλὼ τλάμων. (1329–32)

11. The relationship between action (δράσας, 1327; αὐτόχειρ, 1331) and passion (πάθεα) is a subtle one—and τλήμων can carry both suggestions. In the *Coloneus* Oedipus, looking back, can say (266 f.): τά γ᾽ ἔργα μου πεπονθότ᾽ ἐστὶ μᾶλλον ἢ δεδρακότα.

12. B. Snell, *Philologus*, 97 (1948), 125 ff.

13. This question bulked large in the discussions at the Fondation Hardt in 1958. Cf. *Entretiens*, VI, esp. 73 ff.—the discussion of A. Rivier's paper. I would suggest that Euripides was a poet caught uneasily between two worlds and only at his greatest when he comes closest to the archaic world-view.

14. And a character in a Greek tragedy. R.W. Livingstone, in *Greek Poetry and Life*, 160 f., and B.M.W. Knox, *Oedipus at Thebes*, 185 ff., seem to exaggerate the rationality of his action. 1271 ff. express an instinctive revulsion (upon which he acts with characteristic impetuosity); 1369 ff. are a rationalization, which is then shown to be illusory (see n. 2 below). This criticism does not of course affect the value of Knox's remarks about 'the recovery of Oedipus' (op. cit. 185).

15. The illusion of 1389–90 (τὸ γὰρ τὴν φροντίδ᾽ ἔξω τῶν κακῶν οἰκεῖν γλυκύ) is immediately dispelled, as Oedipus reviews his life, and above all by the vivid picture of 1398 f. Cf. 1401 (ἆρά μου μέμνησθ᾽ ἔτι ...;), but it is Oedipus who must live with this memory (cf. 1318).

16. *Greek Tragedy*[3], 136 f.

17. The best discussions of the relation between divine and human causation in Homer and Aeschylus are among the most recent: for Homer, A. Lesky, *Göttliche und menschliche Motivation im homerischen Epos*, Heidelburg 1961; for Aeschylus, E.R. Dodds, 'Morals and Politics in the Oresteia', *Proceedings of the Cambridge Philological Society*, 186 (1960), 19–31, esp. 25 ff.

18. *Septem*, 691, 653.

19. I owe much to Sir John Sheppard's discussion in the Introduction to his edition of the play: cf. esp. xxxv f.

20. 816 (with 821 f.); 828 f. (with 823). For μοῖρα cf. also 713, 1302, 1458.

21. ἀκρότατα γεῖσ᾽ ἀναβᾶσ᾽
ἀπότομον ὤρουσεν εἰς ἀνάγκαν

ἔνθ' οὐ ποδὶ χρησίμῳ
χρῆται. (876–9)

22.   Cf. *Septem*, 733, 771, 950. I will risk the speculation that, when our Oedipus accuses Jocasta, wrongly, of family pride, a trait has been borrowed from the Aeschylean Jocasta.

23.   Three times; 266 ff., 510 ff., 969 ff.

24.   *The Greeks and the Irrational*, 35.

25.   *Eum.* 973.

26.   I have discussed the relationship of the *O.C.* to the *Oresteia* at greater length in *J.H.S.* 74 (1954), 16–24.

27.   *O.C.* 1769 ff.

28.   Cf. *J.H.S.*, 81 (1961), 151 f.

29.   Cf. *Proceedings of the Cambridge Philological Society*, 183 (1954–55), 20–26.

30.   Cf. C. H. Whitman, *Sophocles, a study in heroic humanism*, 39.

31.   Cf. Kitto, *Sophocles*, 24, 54.

32.   I therefore hesitate to attach much importance to the Holy Snake that lodged temporarily in the house of Sophocles.

33.   Cf. B.M.W. Knox, *Oedipus at Thebes*, 101 ff. (though I cannot agree that the reference to Athens is necessary to explain the relevance of *O.T.* 863 ff.).

34.   As this most oracular philosopher may conceivably have realized.

35.   J. de Romilly (*Crainte et angoisse dans le théâtre d'Eschyle*, 104 f.) has some interesting remarks on the relationship between Aeschylus and modern psychological ideas.

36.   Plato, *Rep.* 379c–380c.

37.   'The Greek gods ... were subordinate metaphysical entities, well within nature.' A. N. Whitehead, *Science and the Modern World*, 202 (Pelican Books edition).

38.   Cf. F.M. Cornford, *Plato's Cosmology*, 34 ff.

39.   47e–48a (translated by Cornford).

40.   617d–e. οὐχ ὑμᾶς δαίμων λήξεται, ἀλλ' ὑμεῖς δαίμονα αἱρήσεσθε ... ἀρετὴ δὲ ἀδέσποτον ... αἰτία ἑλομένου θεὸς ἀναίτιος.

41.   644d–c; cf. 803c–804b.

C.M. BOWRA

The Antidote of Comedy

There is no doubt about the origin of the word 'comedy'. It comes from the Greek *kômôidia*, which means 'song of a band of revellers', but this does not tell very much, since a *kômos* might appear in almost any convivial or exhilarating conditions and was certainly not confined to comedy even in the broadest sense. What emerges is that comedy was connected with revelling bands and must have kept some of their characteristics even when it became an accepted form of poetry. In Athens it received official recognition in 486 BC and was thenceforward, like tragedy, performed annually in the spring. But before this very little is known of it, and it has no pioneer comparable to Thespis. Yet something of the kind seems to have had a long pre-history in several parts of Greece. In Sparta and in Corinth there existed in the sixth century, as we can see from pictures on vases, bands of dancers grotesquely dressed, sometimes as animals, and performing wild antics. Since they are often provided with a phallus, they can be recognized as conducting a fertility-rite and encouraging living things to reproduce after their kind. Their virility is emphasized by padded clothing and salacious gestures. Moreover these dances contained a small element of acting and introduced such obviously comic characters as quack doctors, stealers of food, and robbers of orchards. But, though such performances were lively and popular and played a part in social life, there is no evidence that they did anything for the art of words or, even if they contained songs or interchange of speech,

From *Landmarks in Greek Literature*. © 1966 by C.M. Bowra.

that these were of any lasting interest. Something of the same kind certainly existed in the sixth century at Athens and, though it may have arrived by way of Megara, it was fully established as an Athenian custom when the dancers could be dressed as various kinds of men, birds, insects, animals, fishes, riders on horseback, and the like. The elements of dance and impersonation were already present; what was needed was something to bring them into a wider context and add substance to their performance.

At the same time something quite different was happening in Sicily. Epicharmus of Syracuse (c 530–440 BC) wrote short plays which had some kind of plot. Since they had no chorus and presumably no dancing, they were quite different from the *kômoi* of the mainland, and indeed their titles and the remaining fragments suggest that they were lively farces which dealt with various kinds of subjects. In *Odysseus the Deserter* Odysseus, who has been sent as a spy to Troy, has grave misgivings and wonders how he can get out of it. In *The Marriage of Hebe* Poseidon appears as a fishmonger, and in *Busiris* a main topic was the greed of Heracles. So far Epicharmus must have burlesqued old stories and not been afraid to make fun of gods and heroes. But he seems also to have introduced controversial topics and to have made his plays vehicles for arguments. His *Earth and Sea* discussed which of them gave the more blessings to men; his *Hope and Wealth* forecasts later comedies about money; his *Male and Female Reasons* suggests argumentative possibilities, which unfortunately we cannot unravel; his *Persians* may conceivably be a parody of Aeschylus. He seems also to have introduced stock characters like the parasite and the country bumpkin. Epicharmus catered for an intelligent audience and wrote not in a local dialect but in a literary language. He liked both parodies and philosophical discussions and, if he really was the first to compose plays in this way, he is rightly regarded as the father of comedy. He was certainly known in Athens in the fifth century, and we can hardly doubt that when Attic comedy, as we know it, came into existence, it was the combination of two quite disparate elements, the old *kômos* or ribald and comic dance, and the short, literary farce of Epicharmus. The result is a unique art-form, which has no parallels anywhere in the world. Attic comedy is indeed boisterous and outspoken and reckless, but it is also capable of discussions on politics, literature, and philosophy and is, in its own extraordinary way, a criticism of life. By a strange paradox its primitive side owed something to the cult of Dionysus just as tragedy did, but in the result it is as different as possible from tragedy and looks at life from an antithetical point of view.

There was indeed a third kind of dramatic performance which we might expect to have influenced comedy, but it does not seem to have done so. When tragedies were performed, each triad was followed by a Satyric play, in which the Chorus seems always to have been composed of Satyrs under the leadership of Silenus. This surely would provide ample opportunities for boisterous fun and give a complete contrast to the tragedies which had preceded it. Of such plays one survives, the *Cyclops* of Euripides, and some substantial fragments of the *Trackers* of Sophocles. The first deals with Odysscus' adventure with Polyphemus, the second with the theft of Apollo's cattle by the young Hermes, as it is told in the Homeric Hymn to Hermes, and it gets its title from the Satyrs who set out to find the stolen beasts. In both these plays there is a good deal of humour, and there is nothing that approximates to the tragic spirit. But they are much closer to tragedy than to any Greek comedy known to us. They keep the stately language, the formal interchange of speeches, the choral songs. They are not boisterous or rowdy, and they do not touch on living affairs. Whatever the first Satyric plays may have been, the surviving examples suggest that they have been accommodated to the tone of the tragedies which preceded them and, though they do much to lessen the tragic tension and to provide a contrast with it, they are much too decorous to upset the solemnity of the occasion. Yet the presence of Silenus and his Satyrs indicates that in the beginning such plays could have been developed into an exuberant kind of comedy which might have provided a real antithesis to tragedy. We may guess that they were made to follow tragedies because they also had some relation to the cult of Dionysus and the performance of the dithyramb, but their place was settled for them at an early date and they were kept to it. Authentic comedy grew to maturity quite independently of them and appealed to a much richer range of tastes. The original dances from which Greek drama grew must have been of many kinds. If one was the father of authentic tragedy, another, less dignified and specially concerned with Silenus and his Satyrs, ended up in Satyric drama. Comedy itself was born of a more complex ancestry and contained some remarkable characteristics.

The combination of two quite different elements in *kômos* and farce meant that Attic comedy fortified some sort of plot with a Chorus, which might be clothed in a fantastic manner, and indulged an extraordinary freedom of speech hindered by no laws either of libel or of indecency. The main outlines of this form were settled already by Cratinus (*c* 484–*c* 419 BC), who followed Epicharmus in his burlesques of mythological stories, but also dealt with current matters in a bold, outspoken way. His fragments suggest that he had a remarkable vitality, and Aristophanes compared him with a winter torrent which carries all before it. He made fun in various ways of Odysseus and the Cyclops, of the Golden Age, of the arrival of Perseus as a baby on the island of Seriphos, of the birth of Helen from an egg. In contemporary affairs he ridiculed the Sophists, Pericles, and even himself, presented as a drunkard, whom his true wife, Comedy, tries to persuade to abandon his mistress, Drunkenness. This assertion of his own personality was not so much a novelty as a return to the age of Archilochus, whose work Cratinus knew and who provided him with precedents for ridiculing himself. With him the Greeks coupled Eupolis, whose heyday of creation was from 429 to 410 BC. He was a more elegant and more delicate artist than Cratinus, but his chief interests seem to have been political. He looked back with admiration to the generation of Marathon and compared his own contemporaries unfavourably with it. His chief targets were the demagogues who directed Athenian policy. In 422 BC his *Cities* seems to have been a plea for a more generous treatment of the Athenian allies. His *Maricas* is an attack on Hyperbolus, whom Thucydides calls 'a bad man',[1] and his *Generation of Gold* on Cleon. There is no need to assume with him, any more than with Cratinus, that he looked at politics from any fixed angle or belonged to an established party. His task was to evoke laughter, and this he certainly did. Nor was politics his only theme. He also derided contemporary figures, whether warshirkers in his *Men-women*, whose title explains itself, or his *Friends*, which mocked the cult of a handsome young man called Demos, who was famous for keeping peacocks. In the bursting life of Athens he had much to deride and seems to have done so with confidence and success.

Cratinus and Eupolis are known to us only from fragments, but from Aristophanes (*c* 450–*c* 385 BC) we have eleven complete plays, and to him we may turn with confidence for a full knowledge of Attic comedy. He seems to have done very much what Cratinus and Eupolis did in his choice of subjects, but he reinforced this with his own remarkable genius, a reckless and magnificent fancy, a consummate lyrical gift, and a temper less violent than that of Cratinus and less devastating than that of Eupolis. He outlived the form of the Old Comedy of which he was such a master, but in his hands it took a more or less fixed shape, which at once throws light on its origins and illustrates the Greek talent for giving life to a form which might seem to have few claims except that it was traditional. A character appears with a bold or brilliant idea of putting some large trouble right; a chorus, which needs by no means consist of human beings, comes into conflict with him or is converted to his schemes; much dispute and horse-play follows, which quietens down into a formal debate; the chorus then turns to the audience with addresses combining absurd and serious elements and interspersed with magical hymns to the gods. Behind this must lie the original form of Attic comedy, consisting of a *kômos*, which made a dramatic and voluble entry, incited a struggle or debate, addressed the audience and sang hymns, and ended with a riotous scene such as a marriage or other exuberant celebration. Into this were introduced the old phallic gaieties of the Dorian mime and character-types, who may have started with Epicharmus. Aristophanes picks up all these elements and transforms them into homogeneous works of art by the power of his personality and his poetry. Even at his most earthy and most comic he remains a poet, in his exuberance, his concentration of power, his inimitable fancy. The complex form allowed him many liberties, and he took advantage of them all and, though his plots have seldom a complex coherence, they are undeniably plots, which begin with a striking situation, pass through wonderful adventures, and end in uncontrolled delight. The tone varies with every moment and, though laughter governs the whole design, it is not the only response evoked.

Aristophanes set out to amuse, not sedately and quietly but hilariously and uproariously. The world of his creation lives by its absurdity and, though it is based on actual life, its great strength is that it defies its rules and its limitations. For him laughter is an end in itself, an absolute, which cannot be countered or defied. To the Greeks, who saw themselves severely limited by human nature and divine control, Aristophanes offered an imaginative escape from such restrictions and displayed in action men of unquestionably human capacities and appetites triumphing impossibly over circumstances. There is no limit to what they can do. In the *Acharnians* (425 BC) the chief character succeeds in making peace with Sparta in defiance of generals and public opinion. In the *Peace* (421 BC) Trygaeus ascends to Olympus on a dung-beetle, in a parody of Bellerophon ascending on Pegasus, but meets with no such untimely end. In the *Birds* (414 BC) two adventurers co-operate with the birds in building a city in the air and not only keep out gods and men but end by taking over dominion from the gods. In the *Lysistrata* (411 BC) the women stop the war by refusing to sleep with their husbands. Such conclusions were just what the Greeks knew that they could not have in actual life, and even in other plays, where the themes are less wildly improbable, there is the same assumption that nothing is beyond the power of the gay adventurer. The comedy of Aristophanes is a defiance of the Mean as Greek morality so diligently inculcated it, and it finds its characters in men and women of an abundant, almost overpowering normality. They have a full share of physical instincts and appetites; they respond to events with immediate strong reactions; they have no scruples about getting what they want; they have a vitality which never fails and an ingenuity which surmounts every obstacle. The women, no less than the men, are 'cards', who do the most preposterous things with an instinctive confidence. They fit beautifully into their absurd situations, and we cannot but believe that they are responsible for them. Even in their complaints and quarrels they are delighted to be alive. They are not full characters in the modern sense but in their own world they do all that can be asked of them.

The world of wild fantasy in which Aristophanes moves has close relations with the familiar world of Athens in the last quarter of the fifth century BC. Otherwise it would lack flesh and blood, and these it has in abundance. Aristophanes exploits real circumstances, not only to make his characters convincing, but to provide their talk and their plots with material. Their talk is full of topical references of every kind, to politics, philosophy, literature, war, to recent events, to well known personalities with their mannerisms and foibles and absurdities. It is in turns scurrilous, indecent, imaginative, paradoxical, and always crisp, pointed, and full of zest. It conveys the reality of Athenian life even in a world of fantasy. In all this Aristophanes is not a comedian in the sense that he exaggerates the real; he lifts it into another sphere and gives it a greater degree of reality by his uninhibited invention. But, at the same time, he is concerned with issues which concern his audience very closely and towards which he must define his attitude. This he does, usually through his Chorus, which speaks at length on contemporary matters and often outlines a point of view towards them. This is no doubt his own point of view, and to this extent Aristophanes tempers his comedy with serious reflections. It is true that these reflections are richly interspersed with wit and fancy, but their main purport is usually clear enough. But beyond this it is risky to treat Aristophanes as a man with a message, who uses comic fancy to dress up some serious purpose. Often enough he wishes to be comic and nothing else, and even if he has some more serious purpose in reserve, it is not always easy to extract it. He is not a satirist who writes from an established morality or a comedian of manners whose characters stand for various 'humours' or virtues or vices. In dealing with present issues his first weapon and first aim is laughter, and this after all can be directed with equal justice against what he likes and what he dislikes, and he may not expect us to distinguish between them. It is wrong to assume that Aristophanes uses his art to tilt against persons and causes of which he disapproves. He certainly does so, but it is by no means all that he does.

Aristophanes' most creative years coincided with the Peloponnesian war and, though it did not provide him with all his themes, it was never far from his mind and at times occupied it with nagging insistence. We do not know that he fought on either land or sea, but he knew the war from first-hand because in the first years Attica was annually invaded by the Spartans and Athens itself, crowded with refugees far beyond its ability to contain them, was for parts of the year a beleaguered city. Aristophanes writes about war from the inside, and of course he disliked it, marked its privations and its absurdities, and made riotous fun of its advocates. The *Acharnians* (425 BC) is a play of unflagging brilliance, which mocks the behaviour of many characters, both public and private. The hero, Dicaeopolis, who may have been played by Aristophanes himself, makes a private peace with Sparta, and, having done so, has first to convince his own villagers that he is right, and then to rout the fire-breathing general Lamachus. He is then free to start trading with the enemy, first with a starving Megarian who offers his two small children as sucking-pigs, then with a Boeotian, who offers vast quantities of food and is paid, in the absence of cash, with an Informer, who is stuffed into a bag. The play ends with a riotous feast, the triumph of Dicaeopolis, and a general scene of wild conviviality. The greater part of the play is concerned with the war, with such absurdities as a Persian envoy who is more eager to receive than to give bribes, with Thracians who offer highly improbable help, with generals who look magnificently ferocious but are humiliated by ridiculous accidents, with plain country people who are torn by the issues of the war. Aristophanes has been thought to have written the *Acharnians* as a pacifist tract, and to have been lucky not to have been punished for it. It is certainly true that he makes great fun of the more bellicose patriots, of the causes of the war as presented by Pericles, of the graft and corruption and fat jobs which it bred. But these are just the jokes which men make who really know about war, and in 425 BC all Athenians did, and even if Aristophanes instils a stiff dose of 'commonsense about the war', he would find many to agree with him who would not in the least wish to capitulate to Sparta or shirk their duty to Athens. In the same way anyone involved in war thinks often and eagerly how agreeable it will be when peace comes and how he will enjoy himself. Aristophanes appeals to this feeling and has every right to do so. There is no reason to think that he was regarded as a dangerous pacifist. He was not a pacifist at all, but an ordinary man who released all the complaints and fancies which soldiers on active service indulge. His triumph is that he makes them all hilariously funny, and for that reason alone he must not be treated as a solemn advocate of peace at all costs. His strength is that in the middle of war he can treat it with these high spirits, and the strength of the Athenians was that they could share his feelings and enjoy what he said and yet continue to fight with the same persistence as before.

The *Knights* (424 BC) is less fanciful than the *Acharnians* and reveals a new facet of Aristophanes' genius when he takes prominent men of his time and makes them figures of comedy. He makes their impact more forcible by reducing the plot to fewer and simpler elements and giving to his characters a richer elaboration. He presents two generals, Demosthenes and Nicias, and makes them the slaves of an old man, Demos, who stands for the Athenian people, and the victims of the prominent demogogue Cleon, disliked by Thucydides for his violence. The two generals and Cleon are firmly characterized. Demosthenes is impulsive, pleasure-loving, and not shy of the bottle; Nicias is timid, respectable and careful; Cleon is a loud, boisterous, and offensive bully. No doubt all three are caricatured, but no caricature is worth anything unless it resembles its original in essential points. The *Knights*, even more than the *Acharnians*, shows how far an Athenian comedian was allowed to go in dealing with contemporary personalities. The plot turns on the discomfiture of Cleon by a man who excels him at all his own faults. This Offal-Monger takes Cleon's place in the regard of Demos, but when he is installed becomes a reformed character and promises to clean up Athens. The conclusion of course is a flight of wishful thinking, and adds much to the fun, but it must not be taken as referring to any individual who has won Aristophanes' trust. The *Knights* is, despite its fancy, closer to reality than the *Acharnians*, but it remains a pure comedy because the fun is concentrated on individuals. Both Demosthenes and Nicias are ridiculous, and so is Cleon in a more odious way, but he comes to a comic end, when he is outclassed and humiliated by the Offal-Seller. In dealing with him, Aristophanes allows himself a nice degree of savagery, but that is in accord with Cleon's character and would be accepted as such. Once again the driving power is the absurdity of the situations in which real figures are placed. There is no likelihood that Cleon saw the joke himself or that Nicias and Demosthenes were at all pleased, but the Athenian audience liked the play and saw it for what it was—a vivid mockery of powerful public men and their ways.

In 421 BC Nicias negotiated a peace with Sparta. It was indeed precarious, and did not in fact last long, but just before it was concluded Aristophanes appropriately celebrated it in his *Peace*. Cleon was dead at Amphipolis, and receives only a passing mention, and the plot has again taken a new direction. The hero, Trygaeus, is of the earth earthy, but in his way wise, enterprising, and inventive. He flies to Olympus on a dungbeetle, but when he gets there finds that there is a food-shortage as on earth and that the gods have left and handed things over to War. He has buried the maiden Peace in a deep pit, and is about to pound the cities of Greece in a mortar. Fortunately he has broken his pestle and gone out to get a new one. Trygaeus promptly summons all the Greeks to drag Peace out of her pit, and, when she emerges there follows a scene of revelry and song and Trygaeus is married to her. The *Peace* is the first extant play of Aristophanes which treats gods with the same levity as men, and uses myth to enhance the absurdity. The war is present everywhere, and those who profit from it make brief, laughable appearances, in the forms of an armament-seller, a general, a slave who plans to run away. But the strength of the play is the way in which Aristophanes is able to make vivid, individual poetry out of abstractions and large units such as cities. In pulling Peace out of her hole the Argives are found not to be doing their share—they are too busy selling food to both sides, while the Megarians are too starved to be of any use, and the Athenians are so busy with litigation with each other that they do not really exert themselves. When Peace at last appears, the various cities, wounded and bandaged and disfigured by black eyes, dance around her and laugh for joy. When he wrote the play, Aristophanes knew that peace was near, and into the hope of it he throws a delighted poetry of the good life, but he keeps a wary eye open for opponents and hints at one moment that Cleon, 'the infernal Cerberus', may rise from the dead. The actual peace was signed a few days after the first performance of the play, and Aristophanes could feel for a moment that all was well. He has raised the issues of peace and war beyond local phenomena to a cosmic level, which is none the less comic because it involves gods and peoples, each of whom behaves according to its kind.

In treating the war in these very diverse ways Aristophanes by no means exhausted his creative ingenuity. At the same period he assailed other themes, which might have some relation to politics but were primarily concerned with a different issue—the differences between the older and the younger generation. This is of course a perennial theme for comedy, and usually it is the younger generation which is put in the wrong. Of this we cannot quite acquit Aristophanes, but he sets about his subject with his usual independence. The *Clouds* (423 BC) is concerned with the different attitudes of the father, Strepsiades, and his son, Pheidippides, to what may be called the 'new thought'. Strepsiades is the usual 'card', who stands for no nonsense, while his son is the victim of fashion and takes to new ideas, which are embodied in no less a person than Socrates. For us Socrates has been so sanctified by Plato that we can scarcely believe that Aristophanes presented him as he did, and when Plato, in his *Symposium*, shows Aristophanes and Socrates as being on excellent terms, he clearly wishes it to be thought that they really were. In the *Clouds* Aristophanes gets a lot of fun out of Socrates, to whom he attributes all the absurdities, and more, of the Sophists, but the nub of the play is much simpler than this. Strepsiades is in debt and wants to be taught how to make the worse appear the better reason and so defeat his creditors. This is why he goes to study with Socrates, but he is so inept that he is turned out. He sends his son, Pheidippides, in his place, who goes very unwillingly, but is completely converted to his teacher and shows his new knowledge by beating his father. This is sheer knockabout fun, but the treatment of Socrates is more subtle. He certainly has much in common with his historical self. He and his disciples live in austere poverty, study physics, as Socrates once did, enquire how many of its own feet a flea can jump, how a gnat makes its noise, what causes rain and thunder. These are of course travesties but they are based on solid enough fact. Socrates is made to ascribe spiritual objects to a thin layer of air, and certainly does not respect the usual gods. His mannerism of looking sideways under his brows is marked, as are his habit of walking barefoot, his objection to music at meals, and his theory that the production of thoughts is to be compared with midwifery. This is legitimate fun, and does not fail to amuse. Nor is Socrates accused of anything worse than being dirty. Yet the play is weighted against him in two obvious ways. First, there is an ingenious debate between the Just Cause and the Unjust Cause, of which the latter speaks for Socrates and his works, and the Just triumphs over him. In the debate there is much drollery, but also a strain of seriousness which cannot be quite dismissed. Worse than this, the play ends with the destruction of Socrates' 'Thinking-shop', and cries of triumph over his discomfiture. This is of course a legitimate end to a boisterous comedy, but it is hard on Socrates. It is possible that both these passages come from a later, revised edition of the play, and were put in to catch a public which had begun to distrust him, but even then Aristophanes must have agreed with them. The *Clouds* is not a defence of the older generation, since Strepsiades is a twister and a cheat, nor an attack on the younger generation, but it is certainly an attack on the growth of new beliefs and a new scepticism in Athens. Perhaps this is not to be held against Aristophanes. The war called for great efforts and the spirit which questioned every assumption was full of danger, especially if it was not combined with Socrates' own kind of private religion, of which Aristophanes says and may have known nothing.

In the year after the *Clouds* Aristophanes produced the *Wasps* (422 BC), which also deals with the contrast between two generations. The father, Bdelycleon, is an addict of the law-courts, and likes not only the fees which he receives for being a juror but the sense of power which he gets from taking part in trials; his son is totally opposed to him and keeps him from attending them. Feeling that he must do something to keep the old man busy he stages the trial of a dog, which is accused of stealing some Sicilian cheese. The trial follows the right pattern, and though the dog cannot speak, his accuser can, and Philocleon acts like a bullying judge clamouring for a verdict of 'Guilty', only to find that he has been tricked into acquitting the prisoner. He then tries to follow his son's advice and reform his ways but, after going to a smart party, comes back highly exhilarated with a girl whom he wishes to make his mistress. And so the play ends. Here the main field of comedy is the conduct of the law-courts, in which Aristophanes saw much that was highly laughable but, though there is a difference between father and son, Aristophanes does not take sides between them. He is amused by their different attitudes, just as in depicting the father's old friends as *Wasps* he is amused by their inconsistencies, their mixture of cunning and old-fashioned simplicity. He sees the poetry of this rustic life and treats it handsomely, but that does not mean that he is unreservedly in its favour. The Athenians are litigious because they like money, and, though this is part of their simplicity, he does not pretend that it is admirable. The clash between two generations is equally balanced and what emerges is the comic element in both, but its main function in the play is to make fun of the Athenian passion for litigation and its remarkable effect on the simple countrymen who are engaged in it.

In the spring of 414 BC Aristophanes produced the *Birds* and once again struck in a new direction. Though it may have some slight resemblance to the *Peace* with its adventures on Olympus, the *Birds* sets all its action in the air and maintains its brilliant fantasy throughout. Though it was contemporary with the great expedition to Sicily, it does not mention it, nor need we assume that Aristophanes has it in mind. It is certainly not a consolation for failure, for the expedition had not yet failed; nor need we assume that it reflects the vaulting hopes which inspired and accompanied the sailing of the huge armada. It certainly indulges hopes, but not of an imperial or military kind. It looks rather as if Aristophanes sought to create a work of art which moved of its own right in its own world, and in which even satire is given a subordinate place. The plot of the *Birds* reveals its primary intention, which is to amaze and to amuse. Two enterprising characters, Euelpides and Pisthetaerus, seek a place where they can live more or less in peace, and find it by uniting with the birds to build it in the sky, safe alike from gods and men. But of course both try to enter into it. A rich assortment of dubious human characters try to sell their wares or their talents, and the gods are furious because they are cut off from the sacrifices offered to them on earth. But the two pioneers triumph and bring even Olympus into their dominion. The *Birds* is a flight of fancy, and nothing else. Even when the Chorus talks about human affairs, it draws attention to minor, comic ailments and suggests no policy or bias. The gay vitality of the *Birds* carries it through a series of brief, brilliant situations, each of which is as absurd as the rest, and derives its absurdity from familiar human foibles. If Aristophanes introduces the famous mathematician Meton and the poet Cinesias as well as such low characters as an oracle-monger, a son who attacks his father, and an informer, he is perfectly entitled to treat them all in the same spirit and extract his fun from each. The *Birds* is an imaginary world, free from many human limitations and to be enjoyed because it is free from them. The comic hero has found his full scope and enjoys himself to the utmost in defiance of men and gods.

Though the Athenian expedition to Sicily ended in total disaster, Athens held on for another nine years and not till the very end was it clear that she was beaten. Chances of a good peace were indeed fragile, but a grim determination held her to her task. In this period Aristophanes lost none of his brilliant ebullience, but turned his gifts to new and surprising inventions. In 411 BC he produced the *Lysistrata*. The plot turns on the women of Athens and Sparta refusing to sleep with their husbands until peace is made. They come to this decision with comic reluctance, but, once they have come to it, they are obdurate, and it works. The husbands are in such a state of desire for their wives, who have maliciously and provocatively put on their best clothes and adorned themselves to the utmost, that they cannot go without them and agree to make peace, and the play ends with two choruses, one of Athenian, the other of Spartan women, singing songs of delight and merriment. The play is constructed with considerable care and has a real development, and each scene provides its own hilarious pleasure. Such a subject can be treated only with complete frankness, and of this Aristophanes takes full advantage. The reluctance of his women and the physical agonies of his men are depicted with abundant realism, and the relief of both sides when at last agreement is reached is sheer joy. The *Lysistrata* is one of Aristophanes' boldest flights of fancy, but all its action takes place in a familiar world, and it has the strength that belongs to it. His first aim is to amuse, and this he does throughout, but we feel more in the *Lysistrata* than in the early plays about the war that Aristophanes is really eager to end it. His chief character is a woman, and her predominance gives the lie to any views that the Athenians kept their women locked up at home. Lysistrata conducts the proceedings with skill and eloquence and keeps her more fragile sisters in control but, though we admire her brilliant resource, we cannot fail to be touched by the way in which she speaks of the deprivations of women in war, especially in their separation from their husbands, whom they see only at rare intervals. Aristophanes makes this point with poignancy and pathos, and he means it to be taken seriously. The war strikes at the roots of family life and affection and security. When he makes Lysistrata say that the women would manage things better than men, he does not mean it to be taken literally, but he stresses the harm done by war to what matters most for human beings. Lysistrata is also concerned with the corruption and intrigue bred by war and calls for them to be purified, and among these she classes the harsh treatment of her allies by Athens, which could easily be brought together into an equal and just union. Aristophanes certainly has much to say about the war, and this provides the background of his fantasy, but the fantasy is not damaged or diminished by it. The imaginary situation into which it takes us is all the stronger because of its consciousness of unpleasant facts and its real desire to get rid of them.

The *Lysistrata* is Aristophanes' last full excursion into politics, and for the rest of the war he contented himself with matters less painfully immediate. They may indeed be called plays of escape, but they do not show any abatement in his vigorous interest in all contemporary matters, nor are they an attempt to shirk serious issues. Aristophanes was a poet passionately interested in poetry, and in the last, dark years of the war he turned the minds of his audience to it as a consolation but in no sense as an anodyne. In the same year as the *Lysistrata* he produced the *Thesmophoriazusae*, which is concerned primarily with poetry and incidentally shows how well educated an Athenian audience must have been to take all its allusions. The play turns on the personality and the poetry of Euripides and is both a keen criticism and a farce which makes full use of them. The criticism comes through the farce, since Aristophanes, not only misuses or parodies many lines of Euripides, but makes him appear on the stage to rescue his friend, Mnesilochus, who is being mauled by the women at their special feast, arrive in the role of Perseus rescuing Andromeda, and contrive a getaway by the use of arguments from the *Helen* between Helen and Menelaus. All ends happily, when Euripides escapes with Mnesilochus from the women who wish to punish him for giving them a bad name. Euripides is treated throughout as a figure of fun. His language, his interest in philosophic speculation, his plots, his personal remoteness are all turned to ingenious uses, and the basis of the plot is that women hate him. Here, as in the *Lysistrata*, Aristophanes gives women a prominent place, but for quite different reasons. They provide a stick with which to beat Euripides, and that is good enough. Aristophanes is no champion of women's rights, but women help him here with his unusual plot. His attitude towards Euripides is in some ways ambiguous. For the man he seems to have little liking, and that is perhaps understandable, for Euripides was thought to be a crank and a recluse, and Aristophanes was neither. Moreover, though the Athenians were fascinated by Euripides' poetry, they may by this time have liked him less for his opinions. Soon after this he retired to Macedonia, where he died, and this was surely because he felt himself no longer at home in Athens. The poetry is a different matter. Though Aristophanes makes every kind of fun of it, he knows it incredibly well, and this is at least a kind of admiration. He stresses its more sensational sides—its fallen women, its criminals, its neglect of the gods, its vague metaphysics, its touches of science, but these were novelties which called for attention and were legitimate objects of jest. Aristophanes seems to be both fascinated and shocked by them. In his enormous knowledge of Greek poetry he seems to have felt that Euripides was not quite right, but he could not get him out of his system and plainly enjoyed him hugely. Moreover Euripides provided him with just the right means to create a new world of fantasy. By transferring to actual Athens the devices of Euripidean drama he could achieve a series of unprecedented effects and at the same time make them move at that level between reality and nonsense which parody provides.

A year before Athens surrendered to Sparta, Aristophanes produced his last play in his grand manner. The *Frogs* (405 BC) followed in some respects the precedent of the *Thesmophoriazusae* and dealt mainly with literary topics, and especially with Euripides. Even more than in the earlier play we feel that Aristophanes is trying to cheer his countrymen in a dark time with his most brilliant and enlivening art. But, whereas the *Thesmophoriazusae* mocks Euripides for his plots and his thought, the *Frogs* is concerned with the worth of his poetry. The plot is that Dionysus, the god of the festivals at which comedies and tragedies were performed, goes down to Hades to fetch Euripides, who has just died, back to earth. Athens is short of poets, and Dionysus is convinced that Euripides is his man. The god is himself a comic figure with a comic slave, and tries to make himself impressive in the underworld by dressing himself as Heracles with lion-skin and club. He has little dignity but great resilience and is alike the author and the victim of much knockabout fun. After an adventurous journey under the earth, in which he and his slave are accompanied by Initiates of the Eleusinian mysteries on their way to the afterlife, Dionysus finds a literary crisis in full blast. Euripides has displaced Aeschylus as the enthroned poet of Hades, and there is much dispute about it. This provides the main action of the play. Dionysus is called upon to judge between the two poets, and the struggle, which is the centre of the comedy, is the competition between Aeschylus and Euripides for the throne of poetry. It falls into four stages. In the first the two poets attack one another's subjects, and Dionysus scores off both by his apt comments. In the second their actual lines are set against each other, and, while Euripides accuses Aeschylus of being tautological, Aeschylus accuses Euripides for the flatness of his prologues. In the third their lyrical art is compared, and in the forth selected lines from each are weighed in a scale, and those from Aeschylus always win. In the end Pluto, the god of the dead, confirms Dionysus' judgment that Aeschylus has won, and sends him back to earth. The contest is extraordinarily varied and perceptive. Joke after joke makes an excellent point, and parody and apt quotation on both sides build up perceptive pictures of two different kinds of poetry. Behind the dazzling exterior Aristophanes shows himself to be an excellent critic and, though he couches his criticisms in absurd forms and aims mainly at the faults of the two poets, his shafts go home. In the end Euripides is certainly humiliated and resents it, but that after all is how many comedies end, and we must not take it too seriously. When Aristophanes sends Aeschylus back to earth, it is because he thinks that it is his spirit, more than that of Euripides, which Athens needs in her vast calamities.

With the *Frogs* the great period of Aristophanes' achievement comes to an end, and we can pause to look at some of its more striking qualities. The comic invention is limitless and covers every kind of absurdity, but it is at intervals varied and exalted by outbursts of the purest song. Aristophanes does not often indulge his lyrical gift, but when he does it is in the great Greek tradition and has an effortless ease and melody which are all his own. He much admired Phrynichus, who was an elder contemporary of Aeschylus, and may have learned something from him but the fragments of Phrynichus are too scanty to afford any comparison. Aristophanes puts his finest songs in the *Clouds*, the *Birds*, and the *Frogs*, no doubt because these plays belong to an order of fancy where the lyrical spirit can move at ease. Through it he gives quite a new direction to his themes. The Clouds, who form a Chorus, are chosen because they suit Socrates' new ideas about the Air and what it really means, but, though Aristophanes makes full use of this, he presents them also from another angle in a charming song:

> Clouds, ever drifting in air,
> Rise, O dewy anatomies, shine to the world in splendour.
> Upward from thundering Ocean who fathered us
> rise, make way to the forested pinnacles.
> There let us gaze upon
> summits aerial opening under us;
> Earth, most holy, and fruits of our watering;
> rivers, melodious, rich in divinity;
> sea, deep-throated, of echo reverberant.
> Rise, for his Eye, many-splendoured, unwearying
> burns in the front of Heaven.

Shake as a cloak from our heavenly essences
vapour and rain, and at Earth in our purity
    with far-seeing eye let us wonder.[2]

Here is the authentic genius of song, the rapturous surrender to a moment
of enchanting joy, and the free movement of the spirit in its own world. In
the *Birds*, where the birds themselves are all fierceness and foibles, and join
the human adventurers only after a sharp tussle, Aristophanes shows a
remarkable and intimate knowledge of ornithology, but also creates an airy
poetry suited to these creatures of the air. When the Hoopoe summons the
other birds to join him, he first speaks in bird-notes and then bursts into his
detailed call:

Marshy dyke
leave you now
all who snap
piercing gnats.
    Water-fowl,
leave the moist
meadow-lands;
seek no more
heart's delight
deep in green
    Marathon.
Hither come all,
hither come *you*
speckled and splashed
    francolin,
    francolin.[3]

In the *Frogs* Aristophanes, not only gives the frogs themselves their own
songs of marsh and mere, but makes the Initiates on their way to Hades sing
a Hymn which tells of all that they hope for beyond in the grave, where the
sun shines on roses and sprits dance out the hours. Though Aristophanes
uses song most in these three plays, it belongs to his poetical endowment and
casts sudden lights on even his most boisterous passages. It adds a special
dimension to his plays and accentuates the high imagination which goes to
their making.

Aristophanes was also a master of parody. He applies it to all kinds of
styles, including oracles, laws, physics, philosophy and public speeches. Some

kinds of pomposity may be legitimately punctured by imitation, and Aristophanes has a great gift for it. So in the *Knights* he fashions an oracle to foretell the fall of Cleon, the Paphlagonian, before the Offal-Seller, and it is in the true Delphic tradition of obscurity and bombast:

> Nay, but if once the Eagle, the black-tanned mandible-curver,
> Seize with his beak the Serpent, the dullard, the drinker of life-blood,
> Then shall the sharp sour brine of the Paphlagon-tribe be extinguished,
> Then to the entrail-sellers shall God great glory and honour
> Render, unless they elect to continue the sale of the sausage.[4]

This is of course no more than fun, but parody, aptly and ingeniously applied, can be an authentic form of literary criticism, and this is the use which Aristophanes makes of it in dealing with Aeschylus and Euripides. Though he makes Aeschylus win the contest, he is quite as sharp with him as with Euripides. If he demonstrates how the cleverness of Euripides falls into silliness, he no less demonstrates how the majesty of Aeschylus falls into bombast. His parodies are not merely imitations with a comic purpose; they are based on a clear estimate of the different gifts of the two poets and of the lapses into which each was likely to fall. He could not have done them half so well if he had not been intimately acquainted with their work and in his own way loved it, even for its faults. He was himself so consummate a craftsman in poetry, so at home with its elaborate techniques that even in parody he displays many touches of authentic art.

The fall of Athens in 404 BC brought an end to Old Comedy. Nobody was rich enough to supply the Choruses with the rich dresses which made them so attractive, and, more seriously, the old high independence of spirit, the willingness to hear anything, however outrageous, and the ability to say it, consorted ill with the depressed spirit of Athens. Aristophanes survived for nearly twenty years, and, though we know nothing of his personal fortunes in this time, two plays survive from it, the *Ecclesiazusae*, which means 'Women in Parliament', and the *Plutus*, or *Wealth*. Circumstances forced him to adapt himself to impoverished conditions, and in both plays the Chorus on the old model is missing, with all that it meant in action and song. The *Ecclesiazusae* (391 BC) is based on philosophic ideas of communal ownership of property and wives, such as Plato was to advocate in his *Republic*. From early versions of this, known from talk or from some other philosopher, such as Antisthenes, Aristophanes picked up an idea with great comic potentialities. But, though he has good moments, and in his chief character, Praxagora, creates a successor to Lysistrata in enterprise and ingenuity, the play lacks his old vitality. The plot turns on the establishment of communism by the women and has many possibilities, but the jokes are a little forced and the old gay bawdry has become calculated and cold-blooded, even at times depressing. The *Plutus*, produced in 388 BC, is a new kind of comedy altogether and points forward to what was to come. It has very little fantasy and absurdity, few topical allusions, and no songs. Its theme is that Wealth is blind and helps the wrong people, and in a nice way its chief character, Chremylus, sets out to put this right. Sight is restored to Wealth, and then a series of agreeable results follows. An Honest Man becomes prosperous; a bankrupt Informer is denounced but puts up a good defence for his trade; an Old Woman, who keeps a young lover, is ruined, but manages to keep him all the same; Hermes finds himself almost out of a job and has to be content to be the god of games. Nobody frequents the temples now that money is justly distributed, and the priest of Zeus leaves his master's service, to find that Zeus himself has already departed. The play ends in a great procession and all seems well. The *Plutus* has many good points, some clearly defined characters and some admirable comments on life. But here too something has gone—the enormous zest, the creative drive, the infusion of irresistible song. The play illustrates what has happened to Athens after its collapse, and even hints at what has happened to Aristophanes. It harps on the theme of poverty, and we can hardly doubt that this was appropriate to a hardstricken time, but, more than this, it indicates a decline of confidence, of imaginative vigour, which we can attribute to the collapse of a society which has believed almost too greatly in itself and was able up to its last agonies to temper this belief with laughter.

In the *Plutus* Aristophanes marked out the lines on which comedy was to develop. The New Comedy, of which it is a forerunner, is quite a different art from the Old. Political and literary criticism are out; the observation of manners and types is in. The main interest belongs to a more or less realistic presentation of human situations, which have a humorous but seldom uproarious side. Of this the great master was Menander (342–291 BC), from whose works survive a large number of fragments and one complete play, *The Curmudgeon*. Menander probably owed more to Euripides than to Aristophanes, but avoided mythological subjects in favour of contemporary themes. In general his theme is love, but he manipulated this with endless variety, putting many obstacles in the way of lovers' union and ending sometimes with two or three marriages. He is not a mere creator of types. His miser, swaggering soldier, and slave have other human and engaging characteristics. Menander writes smoothly and easily, more in the manner of Euripides than of Aristophanes and makes the words suit the personalities of those who speak them. He uses comic irony and farcical humour but hardly any verbal display. He much enjoys pithy remarks, and many of them were much quoted in later antiquity, even by St Paul, when he says: 'Evil communications corrupt good manners.'[5] *The Curmudgeon*, which was recently discovered more or less intact, is, it must be admitted, disappointing. It is an early play, and this may account for its short supply in that kind of humanity for which Menander was respected. But it had, like other plays of Menander, an enormous progeny. Adapted into Latin by Plautus and Terence, and taken over from them by masters like Ben Jonson and Molière, the comedy of manners has long been established in our own world. It reflects a civilized, not very adventurous and not very speculative society, curious about its members and fond of improbable situations which illuminate the paradoxes of human character. From it our own idea of comedy is derived, but the boisterous spirits of Aristophanes have no place in its sentimental attractions.

NOTES

1. Thucydides 8.73.3
2. Aristophanes, *Clouds*, 275–90
3. ibid. *Birds*, 244–9
4. ibid. *Knights*, 197–201, translated by B.B. Rogers
5. I Corinthians, 13.23

W. GEOFFREY ARNOTT

From Aristophanes to Menander

At the beginning of 405 B.C., fourteen or fifteen months before the final
catastrophe overtook Athens in the Peloponnesian War, Aristophanes
produced the *Frogs*. It is the last extant play of Old Comedy proper. Its plot
is at times discursive, its subject-matter is passionately tied to the city in
which the play was conceived, and its structure is largely controlled by such
traditional and formal Old Comedy elements as the *agon* and *parabasis*. The
Frogs won first prize. In 316 B.C., just eighty-nine years later, if we accept a
plausible emendation in the Bodmer papyrus, Menander in his turn won the
first prize at the same festival with his *Dyskolos*. The *Dyskolos* is the first extant
play of the New Comedy to which we can give a firm date. Its plot is tightly
knit, its subject-matter is universal, and its structure is largely governed by a
new set of formal elements. Aristophanes' *Frogs* had a chorus of initiates, who
charmed the audience by their nostalgic evocation of the old annual
procession to Eleusis, suspended at the time because of the Spartan
occupation of Decelea. This chorus of initiates sang and danced between the
dialogue scenes a series of specially composed, memorable lyrics which were
relevant to the plot, to the city, and to the period; they and their leader also
delivered the *parabasis*. This vivid, lively, functional chorus is replaced in
Menander by only a dim shadow: a κῶμος of tipsy young men who have no
function whatever in the plot, who serve merely to entertain the audience in
the intervals between the five acts with a song-and-dance routine whose

From *Greece & Rome* 19, no. 1 (April 1972). © 1972 by Oxford University Press.

words are not preserved and possibly were not even specially composed for the play by its author.

What happened in the period between the *Frogs* and the *Dyskolos?* How did it happen that Old Comedy plays like the *Frogs* went like caterpillars into a chrysalis, to emerge eighty or so years later as the butterflies of the New Comedy, so different in form and content? To these questions there is one simple, honest answer: we do not know. We do not know, because out of the 800 plays that were written in the intervening years only two survive complete in their original Greek, Aristophanes' last extant plays, the *Ecclesiazusae* and the *Plutus*, and two or three more perhaps partially survive transmogrified in the Roman adaptations of Plautus. Of the rest, all that we possess is a series of titles and slightly more than a thousand fragments torn bleeding from their contexts by excerptors who wanted to make gastronomic, moral, or lexicographical anthologies. These fragments tell us very little about dramatic contexts. 'How hard it is to get a good idea of a play from a handful of snippets,' Professor Handley himself observed in his inaugural lecture not so long ago, 'one can test very simply by trying one of Shakespeare's plays in a dictionary of quotations, and perhaps adding a few references to him from a large English grammar for good measure.'[1]

If it is so difficult to find out what happened in this transitional period, which it has been convenient since Hellenistic times to call Middle Comedy, what are we to do then? Obviously, we must rely on guesswork. But the guesses need more than inspiration, they need circumspection. We shall press the evidence of the scattered fragments as far as it will safely go, like skaters on thin ice. And we shall try to direct our aim at the right targets, even if sometimes we resemble riflemen shooting at distant rabbits in the dark. What are the right targets? Professor Dover has defined them with his usual precision: 'The attempt to trace, through the fragments of the fourth-century comic poets, the development of elements characteristic of New Comedy constitutes the true study of Middle Comedy.'[2] But one final word of caution. In our way stand some insidious pitfalls that have already trapped a regiment of scholars. One of these is the food fallacy. Writers who allege that Middle Comedy was obsessed with food have forgotten that most of the extant fragments were preserved by one second-sophistic author Athenaeus, whose tastes were gastronomic, not dramatic. Athenaeus' bias leaves a distorted impression of the part that descriptions of food and drink played in Middle Comedy. Secondly, there is the labelling fallacy. It is usual to label certain authors, like Anaxandrides, Antiphanes, Eubulus, Timocles, and Alexis, 'Middle Comedy dramatists'. But several authors straddle more than one period. Alexis, for instance, began writing in the early 350s, right in the middle of the Middle Comedy period, and for this reason he is generally considered a Middle Comedy poet. In fact Alexis went on writing for over seventy years, and he outlived Menander. It would be very surprising if Alexis did not also write a good many plays of the New Comedy type in the New Comedy period. So when we look at the fragments of Alexis, we must expect to find there a mixture of Middle Comedy and New Comedy material.

After taking all these things into consideration, we may then attempt to produce our picture of Middle Comedy. The picture will inevitably be dim and blurred, but we must try to make it as faithful a reflection of the lost truth as the nature of the evidence will allow. In brief, the period of Middle Comedy is most conveniently defined as extending from the end of the Peloponnesian War in 404 B.C. down to the later thirties or the twenties of the fourth century B.C. As Scaliger was the first to observe,[3] it was a period of transition. During these seventy-five years or so Old Comedy died and New Comedy was born. And secondly, it was a period of experiment. Comedies written then had a wide variety of themes, targets, and treatments. Even if different types of play predominated at different times during the period, no one type or genre of play deserves the particular label of 'Middle Comedy' more than any other.

The period begins with the shattering defeat of Athens in 404, when her dreams of imperial power had become a nightmare. The defeat was followed by a decline in political energy which lasted for two decades. Comedy reflected this loss of vitality in its own way. The material of comedy, for example, grew less chauvinistically Athenian and more cosmopolitan. The development may be observed already in Aristophanes' last two extant plays, the *Ecclesiazusae* and *Plutus*, which date to 392–1 and 388 respectively. These two comedies are rightly identified as embryonic products of Middle Comedy. The hero of the *Plutus* is no longer tilting at specifically Athenian bogies, such as corruption in the city, or objectionable leaders. The villain of this piece is Poverty, and the poverty is Hellenic, not merely Athenian. To use Professor R. Cantarella's pungent phrase,[4] the *polis* has been dissolved. There is at the same time an increasing preoccupation in this play and the *Ecclesiazusae* with ordinary people and with certain techniques of characterization which prefigure Menander.[5]

As with content, so also with form. In Aristophanes' earlier comedies the chorus voiced their unashamedly Athenian sentiments in their entrance songs, in the *parabases*, in their lyric stanzas. In the *Ecclesiazusae* and *Plutus*, the *parabasis* has disappeared completely. The magnificent choral songs that characterize Aristophanes' fifth-century comedies have been replaced by ἐμβόλιμα, interpolated lyrics whose words were not considered worthy of

preservation. Their place is denoted in the manuscripts by the laconic note
XOPOY, (a song) of the chorus. By the time of the *Plutus*, the part specially
composed for the chorus is whittled down to their entrance song and a very
few further verses addressed by the chorus-leader to the actors. Here we are
well on the way to the etiolated κῶμος chorus of Menander, which
entertained solely between the acts without being integrated into the plot.
And yet at this point a cautionary note must be sounded. We must again
acknowledge the limited validity of general statements where material is so
fragmentary. The evidence does not allow us to define just when and how the
new type of chorus replaced the old one. Obviously, at some point in the
period of Middle Comedy the Aristophanic type of chorus finally died, and
at some other point the new type of chorus first appeared. The decline of the
old type may have been gradual, but was not necessarily also rectilinear. Both
sorts of chorus could have existed side by side for a spell. Certainly the old
type of chorus was still occasionally flickering in the second half of the fourth
century. The fragments of plays like Eubulus' *Stephanopolides* prove this. This
play, like many in Old Comedy, took its title from its chorus, the garland-
sellers, who appear to have had composed for them by Eubulus an entrance
song remarkably parallel to that of Aristophanes' *Ecclesiazusae*, even though
it was written about fifty years after that play of Aristophanes, and only
twenty years or so before Menander began his career. Two delightful
fragments of this entrance song have been preserved by Athenaeus. The first
(fr. 104 Kock, Edmonds) runs as follows:

> O happy the girl in her bower who wears
> A garland of breeze-borne pinks as she welds
> Her sinuous form to her bridegroom's embrace,
> His breath freshly sweet and his hair softly fine,
> Like ivy that clings to the calamus reed,
> Like ivy that grows in the spring and then fades
> As it pines for the love of a tree-frog.

In another portion of this song, one of the chorus is addressed in exactly the
same way that individual members of the chorus are named in the
corresponding entrance song of Aristophanes' *Ecclesiazusae* (fr. 105):

> Aigidion, now this garland you'll wear,
> Garland all-coloured of myriad flowers,
> Garland so pliant and lovely. O Zeus,
> Surely with this you'll not fail to be kissed.

Thus choral devices of the *Ecclesiazusae* are repeated in a play produced about half a century later. But that is only half the picture. Eubulus' *Stephanopolides* was Janus-headed. Its chorus looks back to Aristophanes and Old Comedy. Its plot, on the other hand, appears to look forward to Menander and New Comedy, for the fragments reveal that its characters included a procuress, a daughter whom she wishes to become a *hetaira*, and two rival lovers. 'The great interest of these fragments', Professor T. B. L. Webster has written, 'is the conjunction of the typical characters of New Comedy ... with a named chorus of the old type.'[6]

A close study of the titles and fragments of Middle Comedy reveals its wide variety of interest and theme. This is all the more remarkable when it is contrasted against the more limited range of plot and milieu in New Comedy. A paper designed to be heard in sixty minutes and read in twenty needs to be relevantly and appropriately selective. Since many previous writers have been misled by the bias of Athenaeus into over-emphasizing the part played by descriptions of food and eating in Middle Comedy, I shall prefer rather to single out three other of its aspects here, equally representative and perhaps more interesting; politics, philosophy, and myth.

Let us begin with politics, that most obsessive theme of extant Old Comedy. Especially in the first half of the fourth century, plays on political themes continued to be produced. Literary forms develop and change, but slowly, gradually. Titles like Eubulus' *Peace* and Anaxandrides' *Cities* remind us, perhaps unjustifiably so, of fifth-century comedy. The most notable political titles in the fourth century, however, are undoubtedly Mnesimachus' *Philip* and Eubulus' *Dionysius*. The latter play was apparently an attack on the tyrant of Syracuse, but the few fragments that remain from it are too scanty for us to be able to identify the main lines of its attack. They include the following description of Dionysius' treatment of flatterers and satirists (fr. 26):

> Towards the pompous he is rather stern
> And flatterers, too. But those who jest at his
> Expense, he tolerates, and what is more,
> He thinks that only they are free, even if
> They're slaves.

Towards the end of the Middle Comedy period political plays seem to have been far fewer, even if one writer who flourished in the last thirty years of the fourth century, Timocles, may have tried to revive something of the old fierce bitterness and political commitment. But political references can be introduced into comedies with a non-political theme, and here, although our evidence is perhaps unrepresentative, witty political comment on non-Athenians and Athenians alike must have entertained audiences throughout the period, without any notable diminution in the second half of the fourth century. Thus all the important Athenian politicians of the time came in for their share of ridicule, even if their political beliefs were rarely criticized directly, and the brunt of the ridicule fell on incidentals and accidentals.

Demosthenes, for instance, gave contemporary comedians an easy opportunity for humorous disparagement by his notorious quibbling antithesis in the dispute between Athens and Macedon over the ownership of the barren island of Halonnesos in the Aegean Sea just north of Euboea. In the year 343 Philip offered this island to the Athenians, but Demosthenes then countered with the claim that as the island was *de jure* Athenian and not Macedonian, Philip had no right *to give*, but only *to restore*, the island to the Athenians. This antithesis became the popular catch-phrase of the time, and contemporary dramatists made all the comic capital they could out of it by spatch-cocking echoes of this ridiculous quibble into the most alien contexts. Athenaeus collects a sample of these jokes, and one of the most interesting examples comes in a play by Alexis, the *Soldier* (fr. 209). Two unidentified characters are speaking:

> *A:* Here, take it back.
> *B:* What is it? *A:* Here, the baby I took from you,
> I've come back with it again. *B:* How do you mean?
> Don't you want to bring it up? *A:* It isn't ours.
> *B:* Nor ours, neither. *A:* You gave it us.
> *B:* No we didn't, we didn't *give* it to you.
> *A:* What? *B:* No, we *restored* it to you!
> *A:* But I'd no *right* to take it ...

It is a tantalizing fragment for several reasons, of which two are here especially relevant. First, there is not much wit in this exchange; the joke about *giving* and *restoring* depends entirely on the political echo that has been foisted into a comically irrelevant context. Political jokes of this kind quickly grow stale, and I dare say that Alexis' *Soldier* paraded on the stage a very short time after the Halonnesos incident. Secondly, the year 343 is twenty-two years before Menander began writing, and writing about babies who had been found abandoned and whose ownership was disputed by the finders. Once again a fragment of Middle Comedy turns out to be Janus-headed, looking backwards with its political echo and implicit joke against

Demosthenes, but looking forward to Menander and New Comedy with its pre-echo of a situation in the *Epitrepontes*.

Old Comedy, on the evidence of Aristophanes' *Clouds*, sometimes posed as the anti-intellectual opponent of philosophy. Here Aristophanes' victims were Socrates and the sophists. The evidence for a comparable stance in Middle Comedy is inevitably far more limited, but several fragments show parallel ridicule of fourth-century sects like Platonism and the Pythagoreans. The most interesting of these victims of comic misrepresentation and abuse is obviously Plato himself, particularly because the picture we receive through the admittedly distorting lenses of the comic poets is rather different from the one we get from Plato's written works. Here is a little snippet preserved from a play by Alexis (fr. 1):

> You don't know what you're talking about. Run off
> And get together with Plato, then you'll learn
> All about soap (λίτρον, in fact) and onions ...

The precise point of this sneer is obscure now. Was it directed at the Academy's interest in definition and classification towards the end of Plato's life? Was there a dig at the elegant and fastidious cleanliness that is said to have distinguished the members of the Academy from the scruffier Pythagorean ascetics, those fourth-century hippies? Do those onions purposely recall the vegetarian diet proposed by Plato for his simplest ideal state in the second book of the *Republic*? Or is the comic poet here indiscriminately labelling all philosophers as vegetarians just because some of them (the Pythagoreans, for instance) were?

Other digs at Plato and Platonism are sometimes less obscure. Epicrates' long anapaestic sneer (fr. II) at the allegedly Platonic fondness for definitions and identifications, and Ephippus' elaborate description (fr. 14) of a Platonist from the Academy addressing the Athenian assembly, are too well known to need quotation here. Less familiar is this fragment from Alexis' *Meropis* (fr. 147), which seems to offer a man-in-the-street's—or more precisely a woman-in-the-street's—view of the philosopher:

> You've come just in time, I'd almost given up hope.
> I've been walking up and down, just like Plato,
> But I haven't made any clever discoveries,
> I've just worn out my feet.

Elegant philosophers like Plato, scruffy vegetarians like the

Pythagoreans: both sorts were grist to the mill of Middle Comedy. But not only politics and philosophy. The themes were even more varied, as I have said, than the time and space at my disposal allow me to illustrate. For example, sometime during the fourth century the theme of mistaken identity seems first to have been exploited. It became very popular. Modern scholars have posited with a great deal of plausibility Middle Comedy Greek originals for the *Amphitruo* and *Menaechmi* of Plautus.

To me, however, the most interesting type of play during the period of Middle Comedy was mythological burlesque. It was a type that flourished particularly well in the earlier part of the period, here doubtless continuing and developing the technique of Old Comedy once again. It is an unfortunate accident that no play of Aristophanes survives structured entirely as a myth travesty, despite the valuable glimpses offered by scenes of parody in plays like the *Acharnians* and *Thesmophoriazusae*. Nevertheless, the popularity of myth travesty as a genre in the period of Old Comedy too is indicated by a wealth of titles of lost plays, supplemented in a few cases by informative fragments or descriptive material of other kinds. Of these Old Comedy burlesques the best known is Cratinus' *Dionysalexandros*, whose complicated plot is preserved on a scrap of papyrus. It was an elaborate burlesque of the story of the rape of Helen, incorporating political innuendoes relevant to the time of the play's production about the beginning of the Peloponnesian War.

In the period of Middle Comedy, two related types of mythological burlesque seem to have coexisted. The first would be a direct travesty of a myth, with the heroes and heroines of the story redrawn as contemporary, rather vulgar Greeks and barbarians. How much the process of vulgarization here owes to previous comedy, and how much to the influence of Euripides, with his modernized and deglamorized views of ancient legend, we do not now know. In these Middle Comedy direct travesties Aphrodite, for example, becomes a bawd, advertising the fee she charges for the services of her boy-friend Phaon (Plato's *Phaon*, fr. 174); Pelops complains of the meagre meals he receives in Greece, after he has been used in Persia to his large portions of roast camel (Antiphanes' *Oenomaus or Pelops*, fr. 172); and Orestes and Aegisthus leave the stage at the end of their dispute together, the best of friends (an unknown play, referred to by Aristotle in the *Poetics*).[7] Here is what remains of an amusing exchange between Heracles and his teacher in Alexis' *Linus* (fr. 135); Heracles and Linus are in the library:

> *Linus:* Go and get a book out. Any you like.
> Then read it. I've got Orpheus, Hesiod,
> Greek tragedy, Epicharmus, Homer, Choerilus,

All sorts of stuff. That way you're sure to reveal
Your own true self, what you go for most.
Heracles: I'll take this. *Lin.:* First, just show me what it is.
Her.: A cookery book, that's the title. *Lin.:* You are
A cultured fellow, clearly, passing over
Such great literature, and choosing this,
Simus' manual. *Her.:* This Simus, who was he?
Lin.: A very talented man. He's just gone in
For tragedy, and according to the connoisseurs
He's now by far the best cook among actors
And the best actor among cooks.

Alexis here does not miss a trick. The joke at the end, which incidentally marks the first appearance in literature of one of the modern world's favourite joke formulas, is a good one. The hackneyed vulgarization of Heracles' gluttony is given a new twist which enables the writer concomitantly to poke fun at a fashionable cookery-book of the time. And the presence of Heracles and Linus in a fourth-century Athenian library produces a delightful gallery of literary anachronisms; could Linus perhaps have owned a text of Sophocles' *Trachiniae* or Euripides' *Heracles*?

Exploitation of a myth by comic vulgarization forms one kind of burlesque apparently practised in Middle Comedy. The second kind would subsume the parody of currently popular tragedies, and particularly those of Euripides. Both kinds of burlesque might sometimes occur in the one comedy. It is true that there is no direct, incontrovertible evidence that tragic scenes or even whole tragedies were ever guyed by the dramatists of Middle Comedy, but a number of hints do exist, all pointing in the one direction. Euripidean melodramas such as the *Orestes* were extremely popular in fourth-century Athens. They were remounted on the stage frequently enough, and some of their lines became familiar enough for them to be inserted into alien comic scenes for parodic purposes. It is interesting to observe how many titles of Middle Comedy plays are identical with titles from tragedy, especially Euripidean ones. The playwright Eubulus, for instance, has fifty-eight titles of Middle Comedy extant. About half of them are mythological in implication. Eleven titles are here shared with Euripides, and eight with other tragedians. Is it then unlikely that, at least in some of the plays with shared titles, Eubulus would have parodied some of the more celebrated Euripidean scenes? Aristophanes after all had parodied scenes from the *Helen* and *Andromeda* of Euripides already in his *Thesmophoriazusae*, a comedy not predominantly devoted to the burlesque of myth. Eubulus and other fourth-century comedians could hardly have done less in plays whose titles so often reflected the tragic treatments of myth: two *Seven against Thebes* titles, for example, at least two *Helens*, at least one *Bacchae, Antiope, Orestes* ...

In fact, if the sands of Egypt were ever to restore to us large sections of just one play of Middle Comedy, I hope and pray it would turn out to be a mythological burlesque partly at least devoted to the parody of extant scenes of Euripides. The total loss of plays of this type makes us pose so many questions, none of them at the moment remotely answerable. The most interesting of these questions is one that I would gladly give my eye teeth and what remains of my hair to know its answer. Was there any connection between these postulated Middle Comedy parodies of Euripidean tragedy, and the later New Comedy games played by Menander with a Hellenistically intellectual cunning in some of his plays, where a well-known situation is taken from a Euripidean play, everted, and then modernized in non-mythological, contemporary Athenian terms with an occasional quotation from the Euripidean original tossed in to point the connection?

The most familiar example of this technique comes in Menander's *Sicyonians*, where one scene exploits the messenger speech from Euripides' ever-popular *Orestes*.[8] In Euripides the messenger enters with the news that Electra and Orestes have been condemned to death by the popular assembly of Argos. He begins his narrative (866 ff.):

> I'd just come into town from the country,
> Thinking to get some news of how things stood
> With you and Orestes ...
> I may be poor, but I'm loyal to my friends.
> I saw a crowd going to take their seats on the hill ...
> Seeing the crowd, I asked a citizen
> 'What's new in Argos? Has rumour of war
> Excited the city of Argos?' He said
> 'Don't you see Orestes there,
> On his way to stand trial for his life?'

The messenger vividly paints his picture of the debate in the assembly. The fourth speaker is lovingly described by the far from impartial messenger (917 ff.):

> Another man stood up to take the other side,
> Not handsome in appearance, but a real man,
> Not the sort one sees loafing about the market
> And the public places, but a small farmer,

One of that class on which our land depends,
An honest, decent man untouched by scandal.

The failure of this Dandie Dinmont's plea need not concern us here.
Menander, like a goodly number of his audience, must have known this fine
speech very well. In his *Sicyonians* he exploited it with considerable subtlety,
by imagining a modern, bourgeois, Athenian parallel to Euripides' tragic
situation. Occasional reminiscences of Euripides' own words pointed the
connection. The Menandrean situation was an informal debate before a
popular audience at Eleusis. The heroic figures from the past are replaced by
ordinary, unimportant Greeks: a young girl and her loyal attendant slave.
The heroic situation, which culminated for Orestes and Electra in sentences
of death, is trivialized into a dispute merely about the girl's legal connections.
Like Euripides, Menander introduces a messenger to describe his debate,
and although his long and vivid speech is only partially preserved by the
Sorbonne papyrus, enough remains to prove the intentional parallelisms.
Menander's messenger, for instance, begins his speech with an echo of the
Euripidean opening (176 Kassel), 'I'd just come ...', and a few lines later that
reference to 'that class on which our land depends' reappears in Menander
too (182). Like Orestes, the girl in Menander has a stalwart supporter in the
debate, and he also is described as a man '[...] in appearance, but a real man'
(215). And in general, the Menandrean debate also develops into a series of
vividly presented speeches for and against the victim of the situation.

Was Menander the inventor of this sophisticated type of exploitation—
parody and burlesque here would be inappropriate terms—of a Euripidean
situation? Or was he merely adding an extra dimension to the cruder devices
of Middle Comedy? As I've said before, I'd give much to know, but such
questions are as futile as they are fascinating. We do not possess the material
for the answers. There is, however, another important question which has
been aired thoroughly in recent years, particularly in those two books which
are indispensable to all students of later Greek comedy and its development:
Professor F. Wehrli's *Motivstudien zur griechischen Komödie* (Zürich and
Leipzig) and Professor Webster's *Studies in Later Greek Comedy*.[9] Let me
phrase this question in the way that Wehrli also does at the beginning of his
book.[10] How did the New Comedy pattern of plot, with fixed character
types, frequently repeated motifs, and an emphasis on intrigue, develop out
of the Old Comedy pattern of play, apparently so different in plot and
structure? In presenting his answer to this riddle, Wehrli claims that most of
the seeds of New Comedy intrigue and characterization had already
germinated in fifth-century Old Comedy. The braggart soldier, for example,

was the natural son of Aristophanes' Lamachus. The typical κῶμος endings
of New Comedy were foreshadowed in plays like the *Birds* and the *Peace* of
Aristophanes. *Hetairai* were already a common subject in the plays of Crates
and Pherecrates, playwrights contemporary with Aristophanes. Wehrli's
thesis is a welcome corrective to those scholars who err by flying to the other
extreme and assuming that New Comedy's main debt was owed to the plays
of Euripides. If we had more information, we could be more certain of the
truth; but I believe that in this case that truth would prove to be far more
complex than most scholars are prepared to concede. The seeds of New
Comedy grew in many fields: Old Comedy and Euripidean tragedy certainly,
the characterological studies of Peripatetic philosophy very probably,
possibly also mime and Sicilian comedy. But one important source is too
often curiously neglected: the inventions of the Middle Comedy dramatists
themselves. Their contribution was all-important. The first identifiable New
Comedy type of play was hatched out of its egg during the period of Middle
Comedy, perhaps shortly before the middle of the fourth century. The play
and its hatcher cannot now be safely identified, although here it is perhaps
appropriate to recall that the *Suda* maintains it was a Middle Comedy writer
named Anaxandrides who invented 'love affairs and the rapes of maidens'.[11]
Of course Anaxandrides was not the first writer to incorporate such things in
his plays, but in the *Suda* note there may be a garbled memory of a tradition
that Anaxandrides was the first comic writer to use love affairs and rapes as
incidents of ordinary life in a non-mythological plot. In that case he would
have some right to be called the inventor of New Comedy.

Anaxandrides' career can be dated on inscriptional evidence from at
least the early 370s to 349 B.C. or later. Shortly after the end of his career we
get glimpses of a very early example of a new-comedy type of plot from the
fragments of a play by Alexis entitled *Agonis*. This play of Alexis may be dated
with some confidence to the year 340 or thereabouts. Its fragments reveal
that the play's characters included a young man in love, a *hetaira* (the Agonis
of the title), and a ξένος, a non-Athenian described as a 'fiery man'. In the
play there was a confidence trick involving the display of some strangely
small silver vessels. Was the fiery foreigner intended to be the dupe? Let me
quote the most informative fragment, in which the setting up of the trick is
described (fr. 2); the speakers are the young man in love and his girl friend,
who may have been the *hetaira* Agonis.

> *Young man:* I met the foreigner
> And brought him to the lodging. He was a fiery man!

I told the slaves—I'd just brought two from home—
To put the cleaned cups in full view. There was
A silver ladle ...
And a bowl that weighed perhaps four drachmas, and
A small cooler, weighing ten obols, skinnier than
Philippides. *Girl:* Not bad at all, the idea
Was splendidly devised for a confidence trick.

Here we see clearly the ingredients of a typical New Comedy pattern of intrigue: young man in love, girl, a fiery foreigner, a confidence trick. We must not of course press the evidence too far. We cannot be certain that the fiery man was the victim of the trick, and perhaps we ought not even to speculate whether he might have been a soldier and a rival for Agonis' favours, whether the young man had no money and used the borrowed silverware to secure some by means of the confidence trick. What is certain, however, is that this play was produced about twenty years before Menander embarked upon his career.[12]

If some at least of the ingredients of typical New Comedy plots were being used already in the period of Middle Comedy, at about the same time also some of the fixed character types were being standardized. A good example is the cook, or (to be more precise) the μάγειρος, which means something more than mere cook. The μάγειρος was the professional butcher and meat cook who could be hired to officiate at special dinners. We see no traces of this role, in any form recognizably analogous to that of its familiar presentation in New Comedy, much before the middle of the fourth century, as Dr. Dohm's recent book conclusively shows.[13] It was in the twenty years between 370 and 350 B.C., at the heart of the period of Middle Comedy, that the figure of the μάγειρος was developed by the dramatists, and provided with the typical attributes that we see exemplified in dozens of cook speeches or cook scenes from the period of Middle Comedy up to the New Comedy of Menander and the Latin adapters. These typical attributes are partly formal, partly material. The μάγειρος often enters alone, to deliver an impressive monologue to the audience. In it he will habitually dilate upon some particular aspect of the art of cookery, and the tone is one of conceit and contempt for all his inferiors. Let me illustrate these typical attributes by quoting part of one such speech, full of fustian and braggadocio, from an obscure Middle Comedy writer by the name of Dionysius (fr. 2). Although this particular speech is ostensibly addressed to another character on the stage, it has most of the qualities that we instinctively label monologic:

(5) If a chef considers only one single question, viz.
How the dish is to be prepared in style,
And ignores or fails to provide for other questions, viz.
How and when to serve it, how to dress it,
That man is no chef, but merely a cook.
The two jobs aren't the same, but very different.
Not everyone who takes a post is truly called
'General', but only the man who can see
Clearly in a crisis and rally his men—
He's a general, the rest are merely officers.
So too with us chefs. It's in our competence
To dress dishes, carve, cook sauces, blow the fire;
But anyone can do that, for example cooks.
The chef, however, is something very different.
Ordinary people don't have the necessary knowledge,
Of locale, season, host, guest, when and what
(20) Fish to buy ...
(36)   ... This man you mentioned, Simias,
Just now, you called him a connoisseur
Of rich banquets. I'll make him forget them all
Once I show him my *omelette aux feuilles de figuier*,
And serve him a meal all redolent of Attic breezes.

This amusingly garrulous passage was written in the middle of the fourth century, but all those typical cook attributes are there—the gasconading conceit, contempt for inferior practitioners like ὀψοποιοί, the arrogant assumption that cooking is an art analogous to and on the level of such highly valued skills as military strategy. Such attributes continue into New Comedy and later, in all their variety.

Dionysius' cook is typical. Such standardized roles were developed during the period of Middle Comedy, just as some at least of the typical motifs of the New Comedy type of intrigue also were. By examining a motif here and a character type there in the extant fragments of Middle Comedy, we begin to get a dim, blurred picture of how comedy developed in the period between Aristophanes and Menander. The general proportions of this picture will always, in the nature of things, remain dull and blurred. But several significant details may yet be painted into this picture with preciser definition. The tailpiece of this paper is concerned with one of those details. How far it is significant, and how far insignificant, I leave to your own judgement.

In that brilliantly shrewd analysis of ancient comedy published in *Fifty Years of Classical Scholarship*,[14] Professor Dover discusses and illustrates in different ways what he rightly calls 'the essential continuity of comedy'. For example, in the period of Old Comedy Eupolis produced his *Parasites*, in whose *parabasis* the chorus of parasites described at length their way of life (fr. 159). In subject-matter this *parabasis* is directly comparable to certain monologues of New Comedy, like that of the parasite Gnatho in Terence's *Eunuchus*, adapted from Menandrean sources. Such parallels from Old and New Comedy point to a progressive continuity of motif. New Comedy is not so much repeating older material as developing it further in an interesting way and adapting it to different conditions of production after the decline of the Old Comedy type of integrated chorus.

Accordingly, Dover's comparison between the Eupolis choral *parabasis* and the Terence monologue has a special significance, which can be additionally examined in the light of the discovery of Menander's *Dyskolos* not so long ago. In this play of Menander, the metre changes suddenly during the fourth act from iambic trimeters to trochaic tetrameters. The change comes at the point when Knemon launches into his great speech of self-justification (708 ff.). This speech turns relevantly into a sermon on human behaviour, and in it the play's hero, as Professor Handley's commentary notes, to a certain extent 'transcends his ordinary dramatic role' and speaks with the poet's voice. The listener or reader here realizes with a sudden shock of recognition that in this speech of Knemon's there is a metamorphosis of the *epirrhemata* of Old Comedy *parabases*, which incidentally were delivered in the same metre of trochaic tetrameters, dealt with the same subjects of social concern, and even occasionally were structured in the same way. Thus the *antepirrhema* of Aristophanes' *Birds* goes (786 ff.):

> So if each spectator of you'd got himself a pair of wings,
> Then been bored and hungry as he heard the *tragic* songs,
> Why, he could have gone and flown away off home to lunch,
> Flying back to watch *our* actors afterwards when he was full ...

And so on, with a series of unfulfilled conditions. Knemon's speech similarly closes with a list of unfulfilled conditions addressed as much to the audience as to the other actors (743 ff.):

> If all men had been like that, there'd be no need of courts of law,
> Or of putting men in prison, or of war ...

The decline of the chorus and the death of its *parabasis* did not mean the end of general social comment in comedy. Such comment was instead transferred from the chorus to solo speeches in the course of the plot, speeches which might sometimes be delivered at moments of unusual solemnity in the epirrhematic metre of trochaic tetrameters. Here we have an attractive example of continuity and metamorphosis at the same time, the caterpillar and the butterfly. But how and when was the change initiated? Where is the chrysalis, the connecting link? The answer clearly is Middle Comedy. Several fragments of this period are extant,[15] written in trochaic tetrameters and containing social comment of a type analogous to that in Old Comedy *parabases* and Knemon's great speech. A fragment of Alexis provides the most entertaining example of its kind, portraying with an almost Aristophanic vigour the manners of *hetairai*, their cosmetics, high heels, false bosoms (fr. 98):

> First of all, compared with profits and plundering the neighbours,
> Other things come second, for *hetairai*. Machinations
> They must weave 'gainst all the world, and once that they've got wealthy,
> Then new girls are introduced, trainees for the profession.
> These they mould from scratch—their manners, looks, and figures
> Don't stay the same for very long. Suppose a girl's too tiny,
> They stitch high heels on to her shoes. Suppose the girl's too tall, she'll
> Wear thin soles and walk about with head cocked on her shoulder;
> That removes some height. Or if she's got no hips, she wears then
> Artificial padding, so her enthusiastic audience
> Swoons at her posterior. But if they're flat in front here,
> She will wear false bosoms like the ones on comic actors ...
> Eyebrows just a shade too light, perhaps? Paint them with mascara.
> Eyebrows just too black? Well then, you plaster on some powder.
> If she's got a white complexion, rub on rouge for ever ...

This fragment is cited by its excerptors without context or any indication of its speaker. Despite these deficiencies, it affords a further clue to the linking function of Middle Comedy, which, like Janus, looks both ways, backwards here to the epirrhematic tetrameters of Old Comedy *parabases*, and forwards to speeches of social comment in New Comedy such as that of Knemon in the fourth act of the *Dyskolos*.

Continuity, metamorphosis, variety, inventive development: these are the keywords which help to unlock a few of the mysterious doors of Middle Comedy. Over eight hundred plays were written during the period, and all except two have plunged into oblivion. Accordingly, many of the riddles and mysteries are likely to remain dark for ever. This the interested scholar must necessarily regret, although I dare say that his tears of grief will not be shared by ordinary readers of the ancient classics. Perhaps Middle Comedy, after the death of Aristophanes, created no deathless masterpieces. It may have been a literary interregnum between Aristophanes and Menander. In that case, the loss of its plays will be, in the words of Scott, 'a lamentable proof of the great truth, that in the fine arts mediocrity is not permitted'.[16] But if none of the Middle Comedy writers had ever put his foot upon the ladder, how would Menander have been able to ascend to the very top of it?[17]

NOTES

1. *Menander and Plautus: A Study in Comparison* (London, 1968), I. Over a century before Otto Ribbeck had said something very similar in his Berne lecture *Über die mittlere und neuere Attische Komödie* (Leipzig, 1857), 3: 'It is as if one of our descendants wished to make up Goethe's or Schiller's works from the German dictionary of the Grimm brothers and occasional references in bellettrists.'

2. In his essay on Greek Comedy in *Fifty Years of Classical Scholarship* (edited by M. Platnauer, Oxford, 1954), 118.

3. J.C. Scaliger, *Poetices Libri Septem* (Lyons, 1561), i. 7, p. 12.

4. *Dioniso* xl (1966), 41.

5. Cf. particularly G. Maurach, *Acta Classica* xi (1968), 1 ff.

6. *Studies in Later Greek Comedy* (Manchester, 1950[1], 1970[2]), 62. On the chorus in Middle Comedy see especially K.J. Maidment, *CQ* xxix (1935), 1 ff.

7. 1453 [a] 36–9.

8. Cf. E.W. Handley, *BICS* xii (1965), 47 ff.; R. Kassel, *Eranos* lxiii (1965), 8 f.

9. Footnotes in this paper have been reduced to the minimum. If bibliographical references had been produced for every unsupported, dogmatic, or anticipated statement and instance, the small print would have luxuriated and swamped the large. The largest number of these references would undoubtedly have been to Webster's seminal book, as all experts in this subject will be well aware. Let this footnote, therefore, testify, however inadequately, to my own indebtedness to this book and to its author's stimulating discussions. I play the page to his Wenceslas.

10. p. 12.

11. S.v. Ἀναξανδρίδης.

12. Cf. *Proc. Cambridge Phil. Soc.* cxcvi (1970), 9 ff.

13. H. Dohm, *Mageiros* (Munich, 1964).

14. p. 119

15. Cf. Handley's edition of Menander's *Dyskolos* (London, 1965), commentary pp. 252 f.

16. The quotation comes from the first chapter of *The Bride of Lammermoor*.

17. This is the written form of a lecture delivered variously in Leeds, Manchester, Edinburgh, and elsewhere; its author has profited greatly from suggestions made by members of its audiences.

E.T. KIRBY

Greece: The Forms of Dionysus

Ancient Greek tragedy and a certain type of comedy called the satyr play made their first "official" appearance together, or nearly so, at the Athenian festival of the City Dionysia in 534 B.C., founded in honor of Dionysus Melanaegis (Dionysus of the Black Aegis, a shield, perhaps a goatskin), also called Dionysus Eleuthereus. A statue of the god had been brought to Athens from the city of Eleutherai to commemorate an episode in which the daughters of the eponymous Eleuther had been driven mad by the god. Performances of another type of comedy, identified with Aristophanes and the "old comedy," made their first appearance at the City Dionysia almost fifty years later, in 486 B.C. The question of the origins of these three forms of drama has provided scholarship with a source of apparently endless and inconclusive debate.

A basic hypothesis, to be developed in the following pages, would be that the three forms of drama originated in the dithyramb as circular choruses danced and sung to the music characteristic of Dionysianism. Tragedy, we know, began, as Aristotle tells us, with "the leaders of the dithyramb." Thespis, it is said, added a prologue and a set speech, but there was only a chorus and a single actor for the some sixty-two years of performances of tragedy until Aeschylus added a second actor about 472 B.C. This fact is of paramount importance; in its origin and for more than sixty-two years, tragedy was a choral performance of the dithyramb-plus-actor, not drama as interaction between persons. There is reason to believe that the

From *Ur-Drama: The Origins of Theatre.* © 1975 by New York University.

169

supposed originator of tragedy, Thespis, was a mythologized personage, his name derived from the adjective *thespis* meaning "inspired," as combined with "song" or "singer" in passages of the *Odyssey* (Pickard-Cambridge, 72). The word itself suggests the ecstatic or Dionysian nature of tragedy. In regard to Thespis, it is not of much use to speculate on how long tragedy as dithyramb-plus-actor antedated 534 B.C. However, something curiously like it occurred some sixty-five years earlier, about 600 B.C. At that time, the Suda lexicon says that Arion of Methymna, a lyric poet, "invented the tragic mode and first composed a stationary chorus and sung a dithyramb and named what the chorus sang and introduced satyrs speaking verses," and other scholia support the attribution to him of tragedy arrived at through innovation in the dithyramb (Pickard-Cambridge, 97–98).

It is to this point in time that our current problems in regard to the origins of tragedy and its relationship to comedy seem most clearly to return. They stem from Aristotle's observation that tragedy derived from comedy. Because tragedy "changed from *satyric* [comedy's] small plots and laughable diction were solemnized late" to become tragedy (Pickard-Cambridge, 89); or, said in another way, "short incidents and the language of ridicule developed in length and dignity as the satyrplay changed into tragedy" (Grube, 9). This is difficult to accept literally. The basic dithyramb, as will be considered, was an ecstatic trance-dance. There is no reason to believe that it had to pass through comedy, in the form of a satyr play, before it again became serious. Literally, the satyr play didn't change into anything; it continued to exist in its own mode. Since we then must be considering influence, there are two important ways in which comedy, as a dithyramb performed by satyrs, appears to have influenced the serious, lyric, and ecstatic dithyramb. The first, cited by Aristotle, was a change in meter from tetrameter to iambic, "when speech came in." We note that Arion introduced satyrs speaking verses, not singing them, and the satyrs might previously also have been comic performers. The second, stated by Aristotle simply as "the number of scenes," would seem to relate directly to introduction of the second and third actors in the tragic dithyramb, clearly a means of facilitating the playing of a number of scenes. It seems most likely, considering the nature of comedy, that the satyr play moved from the strictly choral form sooner, and that it had three actors throughout the some sixty-seven years of Dionysia performance that it took to add the second and third actors to the tragic dithyramb. The only extant satyr play, Euripides' *Cyclops*, dated about 423 B.C., shows that its form was then like that of tragedy, with three actors and a similar use of the chorus. In this sense, tragedy as dramatic action was "solemnized late," though it is a regrettable phrase.

For a long time, scholars attempted to associate tragedy with a satyr chorus by deriving the word *tragoidia* from *tragos*, meaning "goat." But the satyrs were horse-men, not goat-men. It is now observed that a meaning of "song of goats" is linguistically impossible (Else, 25) and that any derivation from "singers dressed in goat-skins" can be safely discarded (Pickard-Cambridge, 124). Webster thinks it might mean "singer at the goat-sacrifice" or "singer for the goat-prize" (Pickard-Cambridge, 123). Jane Ellen Harrison suggested that the word derived from the name for a cereal, a type of spelt, known as "the goat" (Harrison [P], 420). She later retracted this, although it continued to please Robert Graves, apparently because of the affinity with vegetation theory. The point is that such variants are possible, to the extent that they no longer mean "goat."

The word *komos* or *komus* from which the designation for comedy derives, sounded like the word for "village," so early commentators said comedy came from the village, just as they said tragedy meant dancing around a goat or for a goat prize. The actual meaning of the word *komus* is unknown, and it may not be of Hellenic origin. The meaning of dithyramb is not known, but the word is not of Hellenic origin. Perhaps it would be best not to overtax the abilities of philology in attempting to associate "tragedy" with "goat." If the satyrs, who were horse-men not goat-men, were instrumental in the creation of tragedy, as they most probably were, they soon went their own way into satire. More importantly, they were trance dancers, as we shall see.

The Kuretes and Korybantes represented basic types of the trancedance complex which was characteristic of Dionysianism. From them, or from the modes which evolved from them, such as the ecstatic dithyramb, we may trace the origins of tragic drama. In mythological terms, the Kuretes and Korybantes were thought of not only as the etiological foundation of the trance-dance complex but of the Greek religion itself. The chorus of maenads in Euripides' *Bacchae* speaks of this as follows:

And I praise the holies of Crete,
the caves of the dancing Curetes,
there where Zeus was born,
where helmed in triple tier
around the primal drum
the Corybantes danced. They,
they were the first of all
whose whirling feet kept time
to the strict beat of the taut hide

and the squeal of the wailing flute.
Then from them to Rhea's hands
the holy drum was handed down;
but, stolen by the raving Satyrs,
fell at last to me and now
accompanies the dance
which every other year
celebrates your name:
Dionysus!
(120–34, Arrowsmith; trans., Grene and Lattimore, 166)

The passage describes an etiological sequence in which the "primal drum" was passed from one trance-dance group to another. The satyrs are one of these. The Korybantes (or Corybantes), however, were not Cretan, but were of Thraco-Phrygian origin. Their name meant "whirlers" (Rose, 171), which would associate them with a well-known means of inducing trance, both shamanistic and Middle Eastern. Guthrie observes that "to 'korybant' served as a verb in Greek, meaning to be in a state of ecstasy or divine madness in which hallucinations were possible" (Guthrie, 118). There seems to have been a "Korybantic malady," common in Phrygia and apparently similar to maenadism.

> Those affected by such fevers saw strange figures that corresponded to no objective reality, and heard the sound of invisible flutes, until at last they were excited to the highest pitch of frenzy and were seized with a violent desire to dance.
>
> (Rohde, 286)

Mythologically, the Korybantes were the "attendants" of Kybele, the Phrygian goddess identified with the rites of Dionysus in the *Bacchae* (78ff.). We will show that the rites of Attis, associated with Kybele, were shamanistic, and this basis is further indicated in H. J. Rose's summary of the nature and function of the Korybantes.

> ... they are constantly associated with ritual dancing, with mysteries and magical cures; the latter it seems were taught only to women. Here again it seems not impossible that behind all lie the figures of very old medicine-men, dancers, like the Roman Salii, of sacred dances and performers of magic, and deified in process of time.
>
> (Rose, 171)

The Korybantes and the Kuretes were apparently so much alike that the names came to be used interchangeably. The best known information in regard to the latter is the Song of the Kuretes preserved in fragments found on Crete. The type of inscription used places it quite late, in the third century A.D., but attempts have been made to date it earlier. The vegetation concept of Harrison's *Themis* was based upon Gilbert Murray's translation of this song, which reads as follows:

> Io, Kouros most Great, I give thee hail, Kronian, Lord of all that is wet and gleaming, thou art come at the head of thy Daimones. To Dikte for the Year, Oh, march, and rejoice in the dance and song,
> That we make to thee with harps and pipes mingled together, and sing as we come to a stand at thy well-fenced altar.
> Io, etc.
> For here the shielded Nurturers took thee, a child immortal, from Rhea, and with noise of beating feet hid thee away.
> Io, etc....
>
> And the Horai began to be fruitful year by year (?) and Dike to possess mankind, and all wild living things were held about by wealth-loving Peace.
> Io, etc....
>
> To us also leap for full jars, and leap for fleecy flocks, and leap for fields of fruit, and for hives to bring increase.
> Io, etc....
>
> Leap for our Cities, and leap for our sea-borne ships, and leap for our young citizens and for goodly Themis.
> (Harrison [T], 7–8)

The intention was to consider the dance a fertility ritual, and the translation appears to have been forced and misinterpreted for that purpose. Nilsson pointed out in 1927 that the operative words should be read literally, as they stand, with the meaning leap *into*, not supplied with meaning from a derived, secondary form signifying leap *on behalf of* (Nilsson, 478). Joseph Fontenrose's 1966 critique of ritual theory supplemented the text with other fragments that have been discovered, and he arrived at the same conclusion in regard to translation. The meaning of the words in question must be read as "into"; "'To us' must be stricken, the 'full jars' become herds of cattle, the 'hives' become houses, and Themis is renowned rather than goodly" (Fontenrose, 29). To support belief in fertility ritual, interpretation as well as text had been forced, since the verses were thought to call upon the god to leap as the dancers did, thus representing the "sympathetic magic" involved in vegetation ritual as the Frazerian school understood the basic principle to be. This is far from a satisfactory concept of ritual practices. The significant point, however, is that the verses originate in the mode of the trance dance. They call upon the spirit of the god to leap *into* the cattle, the houses, the ships, etc., into all the forms of the surrounding world, as into the dancers. They call down illumination; they do not invoke procreation.

In etiological myth, the Kuretes and the Korybantes were associated with the origins of the religion as such. The Kuretes were said to have protected the infant Zeus, while the Korybantes were sometimes said to have performed the same function in regard to the infant Dionysus. These are clearly metaphors of origin. The trance dances guarded and "nourished" the infancy of the concepts that found configuration in the worship of Zeus and Dionysus. It was sometimes said that the "infant Zeus" was guarded by the Kuretes with a clashing of shields, and sometimes, as in the Song of the Kuretes, that his cries were disguised and hidden by the sounds of the dancers' beating feet. The first image suggests an exorcism, with arms taken up against supernatural powers. But the Korybantes were women, or principally women. The image of shields seems to be based on metaphor. That is, the trance and the trance-dance itself were the "shield" that protected the "infant deity," and "his" cries were those of the dancers themselves in participation in the phenomenon from which the religion was born and around which its conceptual religious structure formed.

One function of trance dance in the ancient world was exorcistic, as represented by the troupe of dancers imported into Rome in 361 B.C. to alleviate a pestilence. That Gilbert Murray referred to their function as "a sort of Fertility Charm," epitomizes the devious logic and doubtful conclusions that have characterized ritual theory (Murray [R], 46). Apotropaic dances against disease are certainly "a sort of magic." Dances to exorcise forces harmful to crops, if they were practiced at all, and of which we have no evidence concerning ancient Greece, were also "a sort of magic," but they were not the basis of the function.

Contrary to general belief, Dionysus was not a vegetation or fertility god, and there is virtually nothing in any of Greek mythology that suggests that he was. The earliest reference to him, found in Homer, calls him "mad

Dionysus" (*Iliad*, 13.143). Other myths say that he was driven mad by Hera and that he himself drove others mad—Pentheus; Agave and her sisters; Lycurgus; Boutes; the daughters of Minyas; the daughters of Proetus; the daughters of Eleuther; the pirates who captured him; and so on. The name of his women followers, the maenads, meant "madwomen." He was associated with the *effect* of wine, as a means of producing religious ecstasy, and with the *effect* of ivy, which was an intoxicant and was chewed by the maenads to induce an ecstatic state. Dionysus was the god of insanity and of catharsis. This may be observed as the basic function of "maenadism," and studied in terms of the uses and symbolism of ivy which characterized Dionysianism.

> For women possessed by Bacchic frenzies rush straightway for ivy and tear it to pieces, clutching it in their hands and biting it with their teeth; so that not altogether without plausibility are they who assert that ivy, possessing as it does an exciting and distracting breath of madness, deranges persons and agitates them, and in general brings on a wineless drunkenness and joyousness in those that are precariously disposed toward spiritual exaltation.
>
>   Wherefore it is excluded from the ritual of the Olympian gods, nor can any ivy be seen in the temple of Hera at Athens, or in the temple of Aphrodite at Thebes; but it has its place in the Agrionia and the Nyctelia, the rites of which are for the most part performed at night.
>
>   (Plutarch, *The Roman Questions*, 291 A,B)

This observation pertaining to an age of syncretistic religion would be of less value if ivy were not a basic symbolism in Dionysian myth. From there its funtion in the behavior of the maenads can be reconstructed.

First, the origin of ivy, according to myth, was that it appeared simultaneously with the birth of Dionysus in order to shield him from the lightning that destroyed his mother, Semele. In the *Bacchae*, the still-smoking tomb of Semele is covered with vines that are most probably ivy, and it was Dionysus who thus "screened her grave" with the vines. An Orphic Hymn describes the role of ivy in the prevention of the destruction of the palace of Pentheus when it was struck by earthquake and lightning, as in the *Bacchae*. Ivy "is supposed to have wrapped itself around everything and to have checked the shocks of the earthquakes which accompanied the lightning bolts" (Otto, 153). This can only mean, quite literally, that ivy was supposed to have sustained, preserved, or held integrated the "ground" of the mind, and to have checked the shock to the structure of personality in an episode of insanity.

Identification of the lightning bolt with the tree and pillar as representations of the vertical axis associated with Dionysus was the reason why an ivy-twined column was held sacred to this god by the Thebans, and why he was known as "the one who is entwined around pillars" (Otto, 153). Ivy was also twined about the thyrsus, the staff used in Dionysian worship, indicating it to have been thought of in an identical sense, as a "conductor" of "illumination" in religious experience. Dionysus as ivy protected the Power; he could cause insanity or cure it.

Symbolizing the spirit of Dionysus, ivy was essentially an image of the "entangling growth" of delusion and hallucination that creates around one its own particular darkness, the enclosed dark space that phenomenology calls the "tomb world" of psychosis. Thus, and with this meaning, ivy sprang up in the apartments of the daughters of Eleuther to represent their madness when they saw a "vision" of Dionysus, a hallucinatory image of the god they had refused to worship. In a similar manner, when Dionysus had been kidnapped by pirates, it was said that he caused ivy to grow up suddenly about them, entangling and enshrouding the operations of the ship, and that he then changed the culprits into dolphins. The maenads described by Plutarch, then, were attempting to break out of the enclosing "dark space" of the "tomb world" of insanity by rending the ivy as if it were the enclosure. Amok, one of the fugue states similar to maenadism, is characterized by a sudden, unmotivated murder spree, and those who have "gone amok" and survived have described "a feeling of blackening of eyesight from which they tried to slash their way out" (Arieti, 557). The breaking out of an enclosing darkness represented by the ivy seems to have been an ecstatic ritual devised as a symbolic surrogate, as a "release," and as a cathartic protection of sanity. Irwin Rohde noted in general terms the development of the concept of catharsis that was central to Dionysianism.

> We hear of a "Bakis" who "purified" and delivered the women of Sparta from an attack of madness that has spread like an epidemic among them. The prophetic age of Greece must have seen the origin of what later became part of the regular duties of the "seer": the cure of diseases, especially those of the mind; the averting of evil of every kind by various strange means, and particularly the supply of help and counsel by "purifications" of a religious nature. The gift or art of prophecy, the purification of

"the unclean," the healing of disease, all seem to be derived from one source. Nor can we be long in doubt as to what the single source of this threefold capacity must have been. The world of invisible spirits surrounding man, which ordinary folk know only by its effects, is familiar and accessible to the ecstatic prophet, the *Mantis*, the spirit-seer. As exorcist he undertakes to heal disease; the *Kathartic* process is also essentially and originally an exorcism of the baleful influences of the spirit world.

(Rohde, 294)

These are the functions and heritage of shamanism as it was manifest in ancient Greece. Dionysus Eleuthereus, the god of the City Dionysia, was associated with apotropaic and curative functions, and the introduction of his image also caused disease. "In Athens, as in some other places in Greece, the god was not well received, and the men of Athens were smitten with a disease from which (it was said) they only freed themselves (on the advice of an oracle) by manufacturing *phalloi* in honor of the god" (Pickard-Cambridge [F], 57). We will have reason to consider the apotropaic function of the phallus later. For the moment, let us consider the postulate that the function of catharsis in ritual trance dances led directly to the understanding of the function of tragedy as expressed in Aristotle's famous definition that "through pity and fear it achieves the purgation (catharsis) of such emotions" (*Poetics*, 1449C).

Gerald Else has shaped a theory which has met with some attention in which he holds that the dithyramb performed at the City Dionysia was "the literary dithyramb as Arion had shaped it" and that tragedy had some other source than the ecstatic dithyramb, since it was characterized by *logos*, which "is not only un-dithyrambic and un-Dionysiac, it is anti-Dionysiac" (Else, 74, 69). I will later sketch how Orphism, an "anti-Dionysiac" movement within Dionysianism, did indeed bring *logos* to bear in a transformation of the ecstatic dithyramb. But it cannot be shown that Arion's "literary" dithyramb was an "unecstatic," for Pindar's certainly was not, nor can the origin of the "literary" modes of performance in ancient Greece be neatly separated from the ecstatic. Plato (*Ion* 534 AB) made this observation in regard to lyric poets:

Just as the Korybantian worshippers do not dance when in their senses, so the lyric poets do not compose those beautiful songs in their senses, but when they have started on the melody and rhythm they begin to be frantic; and it is under possession, as the Bacchants are possessed and not in their senses when they draw honey and milk from the rivers, that the soul of the lyric poet does the same thing, by their own report.

To Else's view that Arion's dithyramb was somehow suddenly "un-Dionysian" because it was "literary," we may oppose the concept of Werner Jaeger, based on an extensive knowledge of ancient literary modes, who judged that the choral dithyramb had originated "when a poet realized that dithyrambic ecstasy provided a spiritual tension which could be translated into art" (Jaeger, 249–50). He associated this spiritual tension with the effect upon an audience, with the reason for the condensation of tragedy into "one fateful moment," and with the characteristic of lofty, imaginative language,

> ... which reached its highest emotional tension when supported by the rhythm of dance and music in the dithyrambic ecstasy of the choruses. By deliberately avoiding the vocabulary and syntax of ordinary language, it transported the audience to a world of higher reality.   (Jaeger, 248–49)

The choral dithyramb-plus-actor of early tragedy achieved its effect by a fusion of elevated, literary images (*logos*, if you will) and ecstasy. The tragic aesthetic must have been achieved, as it was in later tragedy, by choice of those moments in which the chorus, composed of fifty members, was gripped in turn by a series of powerful emotions: fear, pity, hope, pathos.

> It was naturally impossible, then, for early tragedy to represent a realistic series of events with lifelike details. The chorus was entirely unfitted for such a task. All that it could attempt was to become a perfect instrument of the varied emotions called out by the plot, and to express them in song and dance. The poet could make full use of the limited possibilities of this instrument only by introducing several violent and sudden changes in the course of the events described by the plot, so as to draw from the chorus a wide range of contrasting types of expression.
>
> (Jaeger, 250)

Having avoided considering the chorus by labeling it "literary," Else observes that "the actor's speeches, as we first glimpse them in Aeschylus, are not spoken as if by one possessed, but on the contrary in a sober, rational, even pedantic style, without a trace of frenzy" (Else, 69). A single example can serve to remind us of another view, another "hearing" of the plays.

An echo of such daimonic possession, and of the horrible reality and terror that it had for the possessed, can still be heard in the cries and convulsions which Aeschylus in the *Agamemnon* gives to his Kassandra—a true picture of the primitive Sibyl, and a type that the poets of that prophetic generation had reflected backwards into the earlier past of legend.

(Rohde, 293)

How many other examples of tone and character could we cite to support a rather traditional view that Greek tragedy was not "un-Dionysiac"? It strove through a representation of pity and terror for a catharsis that was in fact based upon ritual concepts and practices still present in the Dionysian worship to which the performances were dedicated.

An understanding of the origins of ancient Greek theatre, of tragedy, comedy, and satyr play, cannot be arrived at without an understanding of Dionysus and of Dionysian worship. Dionysus was the god of an ancient shamanism, and his rituals were essentially cathartic and apotropaic. To establish this concept in detail, it is necessary to examine the myths of Dionysus and, quite literally, to disentangle them from interpretation which would see them as representations of "vegetation rituals" which are alleged to have formed the basis of comedy and tragedy. This seems particularly necessary in view of the fact that Professor T. B. L. Webster has chosen to present vegetation theory concepts as a basis for drama in his updating and revision of the standard text on the ancient theatre, the 1927 edition of *Dithyramb Tragedy and Comedy* by Arthur Pickard-Cambridge, which has been called "the classic treatment of the subject not only in English but in any language, in the sense of a truly critical review of the evidence and judgment of what it is worth and what it indicates" (Else, 108). Pickard-Cambridge had found neither evidence for the existence of the so-called *eniautos daimon* vegetation rituals of death-and-resurrection alleged to have been practiced in ancient Greece nor significant traces of these rituals as they were supposed to have been preserved in tragedy, according to the theory of Gilbert Murray, or in comedy, as proposed by Francis Macdonald Cornford. Professor Webster chose to abridge the careful analyses of these topics and to present vegetation theory again in a more general way that would almost seem to bypass any need for direct evidence. He agreed that Cornford's theory of comedy "clearly does not work when applied in detail to the plays of Aristophanes," but it was still "suggestive and valuable," since Dionysus was "a god of vegetation and all his festivals were therefore vegetation festivals," so that "comedy certainly was vegetation ritual." Murray's theory of tragedy, although lacking any proof, was likewise "tenable and valuable." Both comedy and tragedy derived from a "rhythm" which had been established by vegetation ritual of the *eniautos daimon* type in the Mycenaean age (1580–1120 B.C.). The opponents of Dionysus in the myths about him were based on personified forces that were the opponents of the vegetation exorcists, as we might call them, in the ritual.

> The ritual is designed to overcome the forces of nature which resist the new growth of vegetation, but in story this resistance is translated into the resistance of human kings to the worship of Dionysus and his maenads, such as the Pentheus story in Thebes, the Proitos story and the Perseus story in Argos, the Erigone story in Attica, and other stories located in Orchomenos and Eleutherai.   (Pickard-Cambridge, 128–29)

To the contrary, it can be shown that these stories were based upon a symbolism derived from shamanism. First, however, I would like to review the evidence that has been used to support the belief that Dionysus was a vegetation god and a god of the year-cycle. The standard, often-cited references are found in two passages in Plutarch dating from the first century A.D. and four lines of poetry by the Christian Rhetor, Himerius, dating from the fourth century A.D. There is little else, if anything. In one passage, Plutarch cites two lines purportedly from Pindar that run:

> May gladsome Dionysus swell the fruit upon the trees,
> The hallowed splendour of harvest-time.
>
> (*Isis and Osiris*, 35)

I believe that Plutarch's comment upon these lines elsewhere (*Moralia*, 348) is sufficient and apt criticism in regard to relevance that should be attached to them.

> He showed [this poem] to Corinna, but she laughed and said that one should sow with the hand, not with the whole sack. For in truth Pindar had confused and jumbled together a seed-mixture, as it were, of myths, and poured them into his poem.

The second passage from Plutarch (*Isis and Osiris*, 69) is famous as evidence for the belief that Dionysus was a god of the year-cycle.

The Phrygians, believing that the god is asleep in the winter and awake in the summer, sing lullabies for him in the winter and in the summer chants to arose him, after the manner of Bacchic worshippers. The Paphlagonians assert that in the winter he is bound fast and imprisoned, but that in the spring he bestirs himself and sets himself free again.

Harrison apparently did not feel that "lullabies" were appropriate to the Bacchic worshipers, and translated the key phrase as "they celebrate to him Bacchic revels, which in winter are Goings to Sleep, and in summer Wakings-up" (Harrison [T], 179). The worth of these folk tales as reflection of what more the gods might represent or mean is inadequate. Religion in this period had lost awareness of earlier beliefs and practices and was extremely syncretistic and confused. Plutarch, for example, identified Dionysus with Osiris; with Serapis, the Egyptian god of healing; and with Pluto, the Roman god of the underworld. Osiris, he believed, was a Greek god. Pans and satyrs, he said, had given the warning that Typhon had shut Osiris in the chest, but he drew the line at the people who said that Typhon had fled from battle for seven days mounted on the back of an ass and then fathered two sons named Hierosolymus and Judaeus. Such people, he said, "are manifestly, as the very names show, attempting to drag Jewish traditions into the legend" (*Isis and Osiris*, 31).

Martin Nilsson, who wanted to believe in Dionysus as a god of the year-cycle, observed in 1927 in regard to the Plutarch passages that:

> ... the authenticity of this information may be questioned, since it occurs in an Egyptianized discussion of the identity of Dionysus and Osiris.... In this age of syncretism, which very seriously affected the mysteries, we have always to reckon with an introduction of foreign elements and ideas.   (Nilsson, 493)

Rather than abandon the idea of Dionysus as a vegetation god, Nilsson postulated two separate types of Dionysian worship. One had an origin in Thrace, and since its observances were restricted to the winter it worshiped a Dionysus who "cannot be a representative of vegetation." Another cult, he said, had its origin in Asia Minor and worshiped a "spirit of vegetation" that "vanishes during winter and revives in spring" (Nilsson, 498). The only evidence to support belief in this second cult was a few lines of extremely flowery poetry from Himerius (A.D. 310–390) that appear to cite Lydian practices of some kind. They mention bacchantes and the spring. They are later than Plutarch, as poetic as Pindar, and I doubt that they are at all meaningful.

Let us consider another fiction, a fabrication of vegetation theory, that Professor Webster suggests should still be taken seriously. This involves Lewis Farnell's interpretation of a legend from Eleutherae concerned with Dionysus of the Black Aegis, in which, according to Webster, "he finds evidence of a ritual duel between Xanthos and Melanthos, 'fair man and black man,' which (following Usener) he interprets with great probability as 'a special form of the old-world ritual fight between winter and summer or spring'" (Pickard-Cambridge, 120). Webster goes on to cite Farnell's description of how the play might have spread through the villages of Greece. Usener's study, published in the *Archiv Für Religionswissenschaft* of 1904, was cited by Murray and by Cornford as evidence of the combat or *agon* that served as an element in their hypothetical ritual series. Since it had been pointed out that this "ritual" had no chorus, George Thomson agreed that it must lie off the direct line of descent to tragedy, but felt both that it was "the stuff of which tragedy was made" and that it "would lend itself to boisterous treatment," and could have been the origin of comedy (Thomson, 169). Even H.D.F. Kitto, in a paper of 1960 in which he referred to ritual theory as "modern moonshine," assumed that there is a record of a "ritual and mimetic fight" at Eleutherae and that "it is likely enough that this represents the triumph of a winter-spirit over the summer-spirit" (Kitto, 6, 18).

The account on which this fabrication has been based is given by the Scholiast on Aristophanes. This has been translated by William Ridgeway.

> War broke out between the Athenians and the Boeotians for the possession of Celaenae, a place on their borders. Xanthus, the Boeotian, challenged the Athenian king Thymoetes. When the latter declined the challenge, Melanthus, a Messenian (of the race of Periclymenus, the son of Neleus), then living at Athens, took up the challenge with an eye to obtaining the kingdom. When they met in single combat Melanthus saw someone behind Xanthus clad in the skin of a he-goat, that is, a black goatskin (*aegis*), and he cried out that it was not fair for him to bring a second. The other looked behind, and Melanthus at once struck him and slew him. In consequence of this the festival of the Apaturia and of Dionysus Melanaegis was established.
>
> (Ridgeway [O], 75–76)

This is all we have. It is apparent that it is a legend based on an event that happened once or was supposed to have happened and that it does not represent a "mimetic" combat. There is not the slightest scrap of evidence to suggest that this combat was then repeated as a ritual or "mumming," so it makes little sense to talk about whether it had three actors or two, etc. The trick or ruse appears to be just that, but it relates to other "apparitions" of Dionysus, most of which cause insanity, as we shall see. There is nothing in the legend to suggest that the situation or the names of the characters relate in any way to a "battle between the seasons." Even in those terms, we note that Melanthos (black man) is the victor, which runs counter to the theory, since he would supposedly represent evil and the "old year."

In order to establish a relationship to the ritual pattern, it was necessary for Usener, who had originally introduced the theory, to (1) associate the legendary figures with gods and (2) indicate some connection between the hypothetical ritual and the vegetation cycle.

This was done as follows. Suidas, an encyclopaedist of the tenth century A.D. referencing Polybius of the second century B.C., had preserved, according to Usener, "a few words that are worth their weight in gold" (Usener, 302). These few words of Polybius told of a mockbattle or tournament of armored cavalry held by the Macedonian army in the month of Xandikos, in the spring. In the same month, an important civic festival or feast, called the Xandika, was known to have been held. It is far from clear that there was any connection between the mock-battle staged as a "purification" of the army and the civic festival, although Usener assures us they were "closely connected" (Usener: 302). It is clear, however, that there is no connection between the mock-combat engaged in by armored Macedonian horsemen and the alleged ritual inferred from the Greek legend. It has been assumed that they had a name, Xanthos, in common. The necessary connection between the festival Xandica, the cavalry tournament and the month named Xandikos was made by Usener by (1) supposing that "the great festival ... has given its name to the Macedonian month Xandikos," and (2) that "back of the feast of Xandika and the similarly derived month-name stands a god, but a god downgraded to a hero, and he is named Xanthos" (Usener, 303). It would be more reasonable, and even more likely, to suppose that the month was named "fair" because it was in spring, that the name of the festival derived from the name of the month in which it was celebrated, and that no god or hero was involved at all.

The names Xanthos and Melanthos and their cognates, as associated with the meanings "fair" and "dark" or "blond" and "brunet," were common enough, and were applied as names for rivers and localities, among their varied uses. No Melanthos is mentioned in the Macedonian material, and it seems apparent that no one named Xanthos was either. The mock cavalry combat was not a manifestation of the alleged battle between the seasons, and it had no association, direct or otherwise, with the combat in the legend. There is nothing to support the belief that the figures in the legend were once gods who had been downgraded to the status of heroes. To sustain this view Usener suggested, in effect, that the whole of the Greek pantheon of gods had been marked by a dualism between dark and light, offering Poseidon, Hades and Dionysus as "three candidates for the role of Brunet," and observing that "no one of classical Greek times could think of Apollo as other than 'golden-haired' or blond" (Usener, 303). This simplistic view is similar, both in ease of application and in lack of further definitive context, to the allegation that identities such as "dark" and "fair" were once actually representative of the participants in a seasonal, year-cycle combat ritual. If we can accept Webster's contention that "there can really be no doubt that Dr. Farnell has correctly interpreted the Melanaigis story in itself" (Pickard-Cambridge, 120), we can accept any amount of preposterous fiction passing as scholarship.

Of far more interest is the vegetation theory view that certain of the myths concerning Dionysus were based on rituals of human sacrifice. It has often been said that the myth that prefigured Euripides' *Bacchae* was based on such a ritual. A. G. Bather's "The Problem of the *Bacchae*" of 1894 antedated the Harrison-Murray view of the ritual origins of tragedy by eighteen years and has continued to sustain interest. Bather proposed that the various stages of a ceremony from which the *Bacchae* derived could be reconstructed from folk customs illustrating the following stages: (1) the dressing up of a constructed figure as a woman; (2) leading it through the town so that all could see it; (3) setting it on a tree; (4) pelting it with sticks and stones; (5) tearing the figure to pieces and scrambling for the parts; (6) carrying the head of the figure back at racing pace; (7) attaching the head to the house. This pattern was thought to prefigure the death of Pentheus. Not all of these stages could be successfully illustrated, but several of the parallels are of interest.

Most significant, because of their diffusion and unusual character, are folk customs from Estonia, Austria, Russia, and elsewhere in which a tree is dressed like a woman, as Pentheus was, or a figure is carried affixed to a long pole, then suspended on a tree or torn apart. The folk customs seemed to Bather to be survivals of a ritual of human sacrifice, just as Frazer said of the fate of Pentheus that "the description suggests that the human victim was tied or hung to a pine-tree before being torn to pieces" (Dodds, 209).

The manner of his death links the dismemberment of Pentheus with the dismemberment of Zagreus, the Orphic version of Dionysus. A common view of both myths then is that they were based on a ritual that associated rending of a victim *(sparagmos)* with cannibalism *(omophagia)*. Zagreus was the infant Dionysus, He was given certain toys to play with by the Titans who then whitened their faces with gypsum and attacked him while his attention was occupied. In order to escape them, the myth said, Zagreus went through a series of changes of shape, finally becoming a bull, in which form he was slain. The Titans dismembered Zagreus, cooked him in a cauldron, and ate him. For this they were destroyed, and the race of man was created from their ashes, while Zagreus-Dionysus was born again from his heart, which had been saved (Cook, II, 1029f.). The whitening of the faces, and perhaps even the toys, suggest a ritual. It has been thought that it was similar to that which had prefigured the *Bacchae*. George Thomson, for example, wrote that:

> It cannot, of course, be doubted that behind the myth of Pentheus there lies a real death. The totemic sacrament of the primitive clan has been transformed from a simple act of magical communion into the bloody sacrifice of a secret society. Pentheus was torn to pieces by the Bacchantes as an embodiment of Dionysus, who was torn to pieces by the Titans; or, rather, the death of Dionysus was a mythical projection of the actual death reflected in the myth of Pentheus. In the myth of Dionysus, the death is followed by a resurrection; but in the ritual itself, after the substitution of a human victim, this element was necessarily eliminated, except in so far as the victim's death conferred newness of life on all in contact with his flesh and blood.
>
> (Thomson, 131–32)

As we have noted, reconstructions of totemistic human sacrifice by vegetation theorists invariably suggest Christian communion. Farnell, speculating on the Thracian origins of Dionysianism, used the same, standard vocabulary.

> ... we may suppose that the incarnation was more often an animal or an effigy ... devoured sacramentally by the Thracian votary, so that he or she might enjoy communion with the divinity by drinking divine blood and eating the flesh on which his spirit resided. At times of great religious exaltation or public

excitement they may have eaten the priest himself in this solemn
way.   (Farnell, V, 106)

There is no need to argue the invalidity of this view in regard to actual
totemic practices. In the two myths and the folk customs we have a pattern
and conjunction of symbols, the dressing in women's clothes, the
dismemberment, and the tree, which clearly show shamanistic antecedents.
The centrality of the tree in Dionysian concepts is shown by the fact that the
god was worshiped throughout Greece as a "tree-Dionysus," as a "god of the
tree," or as "the Power in the tree." The myths show that the tree associated
with Dionysus was the tree as "vertical axis" in shamanist ritual, the source
of the shaman's "power."

The two following facts are of primary significance in regard to the
association of Dionysus both with insanity and with the tree, and in regard
to the dismemberment of Pentheus that was associated with the tree: (1) The
shaman is driven mad by the spirits of his ancestors who live in the tree, and
recovers some degree of sanity only by shamanizing. (2) In the course of the
"initiation" that transforms insanity into shamanic practice, the person
undergoing the experience is taken to the sky-world or to the underworld,
dismembered by the spirits, often cooked in a pot or oven, eaten by them,
and then "resurrected" as a shaman. As Eliade emphasizes, *"It is only this
initiatory death and resurrection that consecrates a shaman"* (Eliade, 76).

During the insanity, the period of "initiation," which often lasts several
years, the person afflicted frequently acts out in a compulsive fashion the
ritual, imaginary ascent that is characteristic of the shaman's trance. In
Sumatra, for example, the candidate undergoing the nervous breakdown
often disappears from the village, and, if he does not return,

> ...a search is made for him and he is usually found in the top of a
> tree, conversing with spirits. He seems to have lost his mind, and
> sacrifices must be offered to restore him to sanity.   (Eliade, 140)

Much the same thing occurs among the Yakut, where insanity and the
initiation are thought of as dismemberment by spirits.

> Before men become shamans they are ill for a long time. They
> grow thin, are nothing but skin and bone. They go out of their
> minds, talk meaningless nonsense, keep on climbing up into the
> tops of larch trees. All the time they talk rubbish, as though their
> eyes were being put out, their bodies being cut up, as though they

were being taken to pieces and eaten, as though new blood were
being poured into them and so on.   (Lommel, 59)

The death of Pentheus by placement on the tree and dismemberment was
not intended as an image of death at all, or at least did not derive from actual
death, having been prefigured by the initiatory "death and dismemberment"
of shamanism. As noted, Dionysus appears again and again in mythology as
a force or supernatural power that drives persons insane. We have a direct
association in this context of Dionysus as "the Power in the tree," and as
"render of men," "hunter of men," "the raging one," and "the mad one"
(Otto, 109ff.).

The myths of Attis and Kybele show the shamanistic origins of
Dionysianism. When the maenads in the *Bacchae* "raise the old, old hymn to
Dionysus," Dionysianism is associated with "they who keep the rite of
Cybele the Mother," and the god is spoken of as being brought "home" from
Phrygia. Cybele (or Kybele) was associated, as a cult partner, with the
worship of Attis in Phrygia (Syria). It seems most probable that
Dionysianism had its origins there in archaic times, and the worship of
Kybele-Attis was later encompassed by the worship of Zeus. The various folk
customs that Bather felt had prefigured the *Bacchae* are, in fact, more or less
identical with a custom associated with the worship of Attis in Roman times.
There was a ritual in which a pine tree was cut down in the woods, decorated
with ribbons and flowers, and brought to the sanctuary of Kybele. This tree
was identified with Attis, specifically as the tree beneath which he had
emasculated himself, and an effigy of a young man. "doubtless that of Attis
himself," was fastened to the middle of the tree (Frazer, 370).

In a similar manner, young people in Bohemia cut down a small tree,
fasten to it a doll dressed to look like a woman, and parade with it, collecting
gifts (Frazer, 119). Russian villagers do much the same thing, dressing a
young birch tree in women's clothing and decorating it with ribbons (Frazer,
117). In Silesia, a straw figure dressed in women's clothes is carried about on
a long pole, then taken to a field and torn apart; and in Estonia, about A.D.
1500, a figure that might be either a man or a woman was carried about on
a long pole and then finally set up in a tree in the woods (Bather, 250–51).

The fact that the figures associated with the trees in these folk customs
are dressed as women is a significant point; the shaman is most often
identified, at least in popular awareness, with the sex change that is a
worldwide phenomenon in shamanistic culture and derives from the essential
derangement or from a customary ritualization of identity. This is
symbolized in the emasculation of Attis and was undoubtedly the basis for

the dressing of Pentheus in women's clothes in the *Bacchae*. The two examples of figures raised high on poles identify them as representations of the shaman's ascent by means of the ritual pole as "tree." The ribbons that may decorate the trees are like those in a Buryat shaman's ritual (Eliade, 117–18).

There is good reason to believe, as Bogoras has suggested, that Kybele, the strange progenitor and cult partner of Attis, was the archetypal "mother" in shamanistic cosmology, the animal ancestor that controlled the animal souls and the souls of the clan. Kybele was also identified with Agdistis, who seems to have been an alternate identity of her (Rose, 170). Agdistis-Kybele was a bisexual being that had sprung from the ground and then had its male genitals shorn by the gods. We find in this representation the metaphysical belief in superior being as a synthesis and resolution of sexual polarity arrived at, or symbolized by, a sex change like that associated with shamanism. The severed genitals of Agdistis produced a tree that grew up from them, clearly the world-tree or vertical axis of shamanism. Attis was then born from a nymph that had been impregnated by a leaf or blossom from this tree. Kybele, however, drove Attis insane, just as shamans are driven insane by their ancestor spirits, and he then emasculated himself beneath a pine tree, again repeating the same hieratic symbolism of the shamanistic attempt at achieving neuter being.

While the *Bacchae* contained an ancient memory of "dismemberment" in shamanic initiation, the Orphic myth of Dionysus (Zagreus) used a similar schema of images for didactic purposes. Zagreus was hacked into pieces, cooked in a kettle, and eaten by the Titans, who were the "ancestors" in the sense that mankind was composed from their ashes. The Orphic movement, which appeared late in the seventh century or early sixth century B.C., drew upon previous myths for their material, but consciously, even intellectually, modified them. "All the evidence points to [Orphism] having been in its origin the product of a few individual minds active over a limited period of time" (Guthrie, 120).

Zagreus was identified with, and was meant to be, Dionysus, but this distinct name was apparently given so as not to conflict with existing tradition. The myth pictured Zagreus-Dionysus as an infant so as to make the statement that he represented the "childhood" or "early age" of Dionysianism. It was an etiological myth, and the events it portrays show clearly that the early age from which Dionysianism evolved was intended to be understood as identified with shamanism. The boiling and eating of Zagreus-Dionysus corresponds in detail with the initiation experience of the shaman.

The insanity that compels the victim to become a shaman is directly associated with distortions of the body image. These are not only delusionary beliefs that the person has been taken to the sky-world or to the underworld and is being cut up and dismembered by spirits; among the Yakut, white froth flows from the mouth of the victim and his joints trickle blood (Lommel, 56). High fever and other somatic changes accompanying the psychosis have caused the traditional images of shamanistic dismemberment to be described as baking in an oven or boiling in a cauldron.

> When the souls of the dead shamanistic ancestors have instructed the Buryat novice, whom they are forcing to become a shaman, in heaven, they boil him so that he shall become ready (mature, properly cooked). In antiquity all shamans were boiled, so that they should learn the shamanistic knowledge. While this is going on he lies for seven days as though dead.   (Lommel, 56)

The myth of Zagreus-Dionysus cooked and eaten by the Titans seems clearly to have derived from this traditional representation of shamanic insanity and dismemberment. The whitening of their faces by the Titans, the toys given to Zagreus, and the shape changes he goes through when attacked place the myth in the context of ritual in general and of the shamanistic seance in particular.

The Altai and Goldi shamans cover their faces with suet so as not to be recognized by the spirits; that is, they use this device as a disguise, just as the Titans did (Eliade, 166). The "toys" given to Zagreus were the ritual instruments of the shamanistic seance. Of these, the most significant is the mirror into which Zagreus was gazing, his attention occupied when the Titans surprised him. The shaman uses such a mirror in order to "see the world" and to "place the spirits"; that is, to concentrate his attention so that he can go into trance (Eliade, 154). The other "toys" have not been identified with any precision. An Orphic fragment speaks of them only in vague general terms as "tops of different sorts, and jointed dolls, and fair golden apples from the clear-voiced Hesperides." Clement of Alexandria, writing about A.D. 200, adds that they were actually "a knuckle-bone, a ball, tops, apples, a mirror, a lump of wool" (Guthrie, 121). Clement's words for "tops" seem to have been *konos* and *rhombos*, which Guthrie translates as "pine-cone" and "bull-roarer," clearly associating them with Dionysianism. A rhomb, however, is listed among the equipment of a North American shaman (Eliade, 178), and the objects, spoken of with intentional euphemism, were most likely not tops but similar shapes suspended at the end of a thread for

purposes of divination (Eliade, 257). They had been "brought back" from the
"Hesperides" visited in trance.

Perhaps the most significant representation in the myth of Zagreus-
Dionysus is that of the shape changing. It is a key to the meaning of other
myths in which Dionysus employs this technique to drive persons insane,
and to the *Bacchae* in which he twice appears to Pentheus as transformed into
a bull. According to Cook's account, which includes the Orphic fragments,
Zagreus-Dionysus became a young Zeus, an ancient Kronos, a baby, a young
man, a lion, a horse, a horned snake, a tiger, and then finally a bull, in which
form he was slain (Cook, II, 1029f.). In the seance, mesmerization induced
by the songs, drumming, and acts of magic causes the shaman's series of
transformations to become apparent reality.

> ... this strange figure, with its wild and frenzied appearance, its
> ventriloquistic cries and its unearthly falsetto gabble ... is no
> longer a human being, but the thing it personifies.... If the
> shaman ejaculates that he is ... a bear, forthwith it is a bear that
> they behold ... if he says that the dance-house is full of spirits they
> will see them in every corner.   (Charles, 119)

The moment of death in the myth is a dramatic one. As Zagreus-Dionysus,
in his transformations, arrived at the form of a bull, "A bellowing in mid-air
from the throat of Hera was the signal for his fate" (Cook, II, 1029). This
striking image seems to have been suggested by the ventriloquism of the
shaman that projected sounds and voices so that they were heard to originate
in space.

Among the Yakut, the bull was the supreme shamanic identity.

> The music swells and rises to the highest pitch ... Then sombrely
> the voice of the shaman chants the following obscure fragments:
> Mighty bull of the earth ... Horse of the steppes!
> I, the mighty bull, bellow!
> I, the horse of the steppes, neigh!
> I, the man set above all other beings!
>   (Lommel, 69)

The shaman's identification with the bull and with the horse, the vehicle in
trance flight, is understood as the manifestation of an animal soul that has
made the shaman supernatural, unique, and thus set apart from others in
society. The association of Dionysus with the bull and other animals is

derived from a similar world view, and his transformations in mythology are particularly significant. Dionysus in *Bacchae* appears twice to Pentheus as a bull (618f., 920f.). The key to this image is that he so *appears* and that he has (or has not) changed from what he was. These are episodes of delusion in which the world or persons appear to have changed. When Dionysus drove the daughters of Minyas insane, he did so by appearing to them in he form of a young girl and then suddenly transformed himself into a bull, a lion, and then a panther (Otto, 110). The schema of this shape changing, as a technique, motif, or standardized image in myth, derived from the shamanistic seance but was used to refer directly to insanity as such, the "change of world" experienced in its occurrence.

The myth of Pentheus on which *Bacchae* is based is one of four in which we can perceive a similar pattern of adaptation from shamanism. They pertain to four different cities and present, as E. R. Dodds says, "an odd fixity of outline": (1) The myth from Orchomenus tells of the three daughters of the king, Minyas, who became insane, were taken with a craving for human flesh, and chose by lots the child of one of them to be torn to pieces and eaten. (2) The myth from Argos tells of the three daughters of King Proetus who went mad, induced the women of the city to kill their children and eat them and to go as bacchantes to the mountains. (3) The myth from Thebes tells of the three daughters of King Cadmus who were driven mad by Dionysus, made to lead the women of the city as bacchantes to the mountains, and destroyed the son of one of them, the king, Pentheus. (4) The myth from Eleutherae tells of the three daughters of the king, Eleuther, who were driven insane for refusing to worship Dionysus when the god appeared to them in a "vision."

Dodds writes:

> ... always it is the king's daughters who go mad; always there are three of them (corresponding to the three *thiasoi* of maenads which existed at Thebes and elsewhere in historical times); regularly they murder their children, or the child of one of them.
>
> (Dodds [B], xxvi)

Dodds suggests that these were historical events, murders of children by royalty, that had been given a triadic structure by ritual. "History no doubt repeats itself, but it is only ritual that repeats itself exactly" (Dodds [B], xxvii). But there is no reason to suppose that these myths relate to history at all or that they reveal the nature of actual events. The pattern of the king with three daughters is a convention of structure that can be inherent in myth itself, and the myth can pertain neither to history nor to ritual.

Plutarch records that triadic allusions in common speech were conventional references to greater numbers, to multiplicity. He observed that "we have a habit" of using triadic expressions to mean a great many, as in using "thrice" in the expression "thrice happy" to mean "many times" (*Isis and Osiris*, 89). The three daughters in the myth pattern then signify "many daughters." The myths themselves indicate why the king, by means of this symbolic expression, was said to have many daughters. The "king's three daughters" linked the mythologized royal house with the women of the city, who were his "many daughters."

The people of Orchomenus, for example, spoke of the Oleiae ("Murderesses") as the women descended from the family of Minyas; that is, as the "daughters" who figured in the myth. This must certainly have been a figurative allusion, not a literal truth. In two other of the myths, the three daughters of the kings of Argos and Thebes lead all the women of their cities to the mountains to become bacchantes, again identifying the "three" with the "many."

In this pattern, the city as an entity identified with royal personifications seems to have developed from the shamanistic clan pattern in which all were members of a group identified with important ancestor souls or spirits. If we begin with the correlation between the myths of Zagreus-Dionysus and Pentheus as based upon shamanistic "dismembering," the key to the grouping of the four very similar myths becomes apparent. The children destroyed by the women are like the shaman driven mad and dismembered by the ancestor spirits, the souls of the clan. These souls are conceived of in a generalized way as feminine and as created by a mother-beast, all living at the base of the clan tree (Anisimov [S], 97, [C] 168–69). This would seem to be a reasonable source for the transposition onto the women in the myths, as the "mother-beasts" who eat their children, of the *sparagmos* and *omophagia* of the shamanistic initiatory insanity.

The myth of the daughters of Minyas, who choose a child by lot, seems to be saying that insanity will make its "selections" by the methods of chance. In general, one judgment made by the myths is that the women who turn to maenadism "kill" or "sacrifice" their children by involvement with a mode that has no concern with the bearing and rearing of children, thus breaking off the lineal descent of the clan (the city as symbolic entity) and sacrificing the future of the line. The murder of children, in these purely symbolic terms, means the sacrifice of the future both as individual experience, to madness, and as perpetuity of the "family" in time. The myths from Argos and from Orchomenus relate that the madness was cured by Dionysian priests or dances (Thomson, 136). But we may be reasonably sure that no ritual murder of children by insane daughters of kings gave symbolic configuration to the myths of Dionysianism in the four cities represented. Behind the myth of Pentheus lay not a "ghastly ritual in which a man is torn to pieces" (Otto, 109) and eaten as a human sacrifice, but another ritual, with its own horror, in which the mind was lost.

The "apparitions" of Dionysus to those he drives insane relate indirectly to the practices of shamanistic illusionism that characterized the cult of Dionysus. In the festivals of Dionysus, miraculous streams of wine gushed forth in phenomena that must have been based on mass delusion. In Elis, a carefully sealed room containing three empty basins was opened the next day to show them filled with wine (Otto, 97). The trick is similar to that of a Chinese "doctor" leaving a sword in a sealed room and next day showing there the blood of the specters it had slain (de Groot, 993); both probably used secret entrances to the sealed room. Chinese pseudo-shamanism also practiced changing water into wine (van Gulik, 149). Walter Otto cites a fragment of Sophocles that spoke of so-called one-day vines and refers to another example of the miraculous growth of plants.

> Euphorion knew of a festival of Dionysus in Achaean Aigai in which the sacred vines bloomed and ripened during the cult dances of the chorus so that already by evening considerable quantities of wine could be pressed.   (Otto, 99)

In a similar manner, Chinese magicians "planted dates and melons and after a few moments one could eat their ripe fruit" (van Gulik, 120). If the Eleusinian mysteries did show grain that ripened magically like this, the trick was also those of North American shamans who "are credited with the power to make a grain of wheat germinate and sprout before the eyes of the audience" (Eliade, 315). Something like this appears to have been practiced in the Liknophoria festival and in secret Orphic initiations for Dionysus Liknites, centering on use of the *liknon*, a shovel-shaped winnowing fan. Illustrations show the initiate masked with a cloth (Harrison [P], 519–20), and there is a striking parallel with Munda shaman initiation in India, in which the initiate in trance stirs rice in a winnowing fan and both he and the *guru* are covered with a cloth (Rahmann, 684).

With this awareness of the shamanistic basis of Dionysianism, the origins of the satyr play and of old comedy can be reconstructed. Both evolved from trance dances in which animal costume, or thereomorphic identity, signifies the nature of trance possession. There has been reason enough for the confusion that has designated the satyrs as "a wild and gross cult" (Ridgeway [O], 15), as representations of an alien people, the Satrai (Harrison [P], 379), or as personifications of "spirits of the wild life of woods and hills" (Rose, 156). Even as shown in pottery designs engaged in cult activities, satyrs are often already mythologized, not shown realistically, being pictured with pointed ears, horses' tails that grow directly from their bodies, and sometimes horses' hooves instead of feet. The merger of man with horse most probably derives from identification with the horse ridden on the shaman's trance flight and with the spiritual horse-identity assumed by the shaman. The Buryat or Muria shaman appears to represent trance flight, as well as practice it, by riding a "horse stave," a rod decorated with the carved head of a horse. But there is an even more fundamental meaning of the horse-rider relationship as based on the nature and dynamics of the trance state as such. In the dissociation of consciousness, the body becomes a "horse" for the possessing god as "rider." In voodoo practices, the trancers are known as the "horses" of the *loa*, the gods who seize and "mount" them (Métraux, 24). Trancers of the *bori* spirits of the Hausas of West and North Africa are similar, "a male being a *doki* (horse), and a woman a *godiya* (mare) because the bori mount their heads or upon the backs of their necks, and ride them" (Tremearne, 275). In North Thailand, "mediums are called *maa khii*, that is, 'horses ridden' by spirits" (Tambiah, 283). Likewise, "the Greek oracle at Delphi was mounted by the God Apollo who rode on the nape of her neck" (Lewis, 58).

The horse-man satyrs represent a complete merger of the horse-rider configuration. But they are very like another trance dance merger of horse and rider into a single image, commonly known as the "hobby horse," in which the trancer wears about his body a framework representation of a horse or rides upon such a representation. In Bali, as observed by Jane Belo, the hobby horse that is ridden is made of rattan with a head and tail of leaves or fibers.

> The player would start out riding the hobby horse, being so to speak, the horseman. But in his trance activity he would soon clearly become identified with the horse—he would prance, gallop about, stamp and kick as a horse—or perhaps it would be fairer to say that he would be horse and rider in one. For though he would sit on the hobby horse, his legs would serve from the beginning as the legs of the beast.   (Belo [T], 213)

There are many survivals of such hobby-horse dances in the folk performances of Europe, and evidence for them can be found from virtually all over the world, in diverse and unrelated cultures.

And now there is no end to it. We are drawn from dance to dance, from country to country, from the Basque *Zamalzain* and the German *Schimmelreitermaske* (mask of the man on the white horse) to the ecstatic hobby-horse dance of the Javanese.... From ancient China in the north comes another horse dance, the characteristics of which are not known.... Is not the dance of Mallorca that same hobby-horse dance which is performed to the point of extreme ecstasy by the Rumanians and Bulgarians ... ?

(Sachs, 338)

The type of representation is not known, but in the ecstatic dances of the Himalayas in honor of the god Airi, the truly possessed are called the god's "slaves" or "horses" (Wood, 44). The rider-horse relationship is everywhere that of god-trancer or consciousness-body. Again, this is shown by the description of trance mediums as observed by Verrier Elwin in India.

At Metawand I watched for several hours the antics of a medium who was carrying on his shoulders the wooden horse of his clan god and at Bandopal a medium carrying an imaginary horse on his shoulders "ambled, caracoled, pranced and plunged" for two miles before my slow-moving car as we made our way into the jungle.... "The god rides upon him," they told me, "and he cannot stop dancing for days at a time."   (Elwin, 21)

It makes no difference that these trancers both *carry* their horses rather than riding them or that one horse is invisible. The reversed relationship between horse and rider indicates the *burden* of trance possession, just as does the god who "rides" the medium. It is this relationship which shows the chorus of Greek old comedy to have evolved from thereomorphic trance possession. It is generally agreed that old comedy was based on the parabasis of a thereomorphic chorus, representing and enacting animal identities, such as those illustrated on certain pieces of pottery. Theories differ concerning the form of the parabasis (Sifakis, 16–17), but it may be defined in general terms as the entrance dance song, presentation, and exit dance song of the chorus. At any rate, the importance of these choruses seems established. "In the whole prehistory of drama there is perhaps no other point of more general agreement than the importance of the thereomorphic choruses (i.e. choruses of men dressed up as animals, or riding on animals), represented on Attic vases of the sixth and early fifth century, as evidence for the origins of comedy" (Sifakis, 3).

One vase, thought to represent or prefigure the chorus in Aristophanes' *Knights*, shows men wearing masks mounted on other men who represent horses dancing upright, hands on their knees. The "horses" have tails and their faces look out from beneath horse-head masks worn on top of the head. At least three vases show helmeted riders on dolphins, and two of these (perhaps the third) picture the flute player who clearly shows them to be dance choruses. This is significant, because the artist in each case has rather curiously chosen to show the riders seated upon actual dolphins, rather than upon performers costumed as dolphins. In a similar manner, another vase pictures a chorus seated upon huge ostriches, rather than upon humans costumed as ostriches. Granting the degree of artistic license evidenced in Greek art, the representation of actual animals as "vehicles" for the chorus is most probably based on the heightened identification of the performers with such animals in trance. That which shows the "horses" as disguised humans would be an enactment of the basic trance rider-horse relationship. Mythology tells how Dionysus transformed the pirates who had captured him into dolphins. Essentially, this image represents the complete metamorphosis of consciousness that occurs when persons become insane, but it may have been suggested by a common type of Dionysian trance performance in which the transformation was only temporary. Arion was said to have traveled to Tainaron on the back of a dolphin, which was probably legend's way of saying that he brought there a "supernatural" possession-dithyramb of this type.

Other choruses in old comedy seem not to have used persons mounted on dancers, although the choruses were still thereomorphic, representing a given type of animal. As versions of *Birds* by Aristophanes, Crates, and Magnes suggest, this representation was popular. It is pictured in a pottery design which shows a chorus of men with beards wearing winglike constructions fastened to their arms and with feathered bodies. A flute player and vines in the background show them to be Dionysiac dancers. The image of bird flight relates them to dances of the maenads, who are so often depicted on vases precisely as Lawler has said, "having their hands twisted into their garments in such a way as to suggest birds' wings when their hands are lifted" (Lawler, 76). Euripides' *Bacchae* (748) describes how the maenads who had run mad flew like birds across the fields. The three daughters of Minyas, driven mad by Dionysus, ran the fields in this way until Hermes changed them into birds. Pindar commented with wonder upon Arion's creation of the choral dithyramb:

Whence were revealed the new charms of Dionysus, with the accompaniment of the ox-driving dithyramb? Who made new

means of guidance in the harness of steeds, or set the twin king of
birds on the temples of the gods?   (Ridgeway [O], 5)

The reference seems to be to the new dithyramb as artistic control of
the satyrs as trance horses and perhaps of the maenads as "birds." The bird-
identity relates not only to flight but to trance flight, and this concept and
costume are among the oldest associated with shamanism. Weston La Barre
relates drawings found at Lascaux and other prehistoric sites to other
evidence of this symbolism.

> Thus, however variously interpreted, the majority of students
> would agree that the bird-headed man with the bird staff is a bird
> shaman, perhaps like the bird-headed men at the Roc de Sers
> cognate with the bison-masked shamans, the chamois shamans,
> the dancing shaman of Trois Frères, etc. Not only ancient context
> but also contemporary ethnology support this view. According to
> the recent Levin-Potapov anthology on Siberia, the Altai and
> Kachin shaman's garb symbolizes a bird, and birds are associated
> with shamanic spirit travels.   (La Barre, 419)

The shaman's costume has fringes in back and hanging from the arms,
representing feathers and wings. "The Mongolian shaman has wings on his
shoulders and feels himself changing into a bird on donning his costume. A
Tungus shaman declared, 'A bird costume is necessary for flight into another
world'" (Lindsay, 248).

The animal choruses are most usually taken to be thereomorphic
demons (Sifakis, 79). This doesn't mean much, since any kind of Greek
demons would be so ancient that nothing is known about them. The
primordial type of shamanistic animal dance would be that of a hunting
culture in which the dancers represented the animal spirits, the "boss spirits"
of animal species, with whom the shaman could establish contact, as among
the Bacairi of western Brazil. Among tribes in Bolivia, these same spirits are
demons, hostile to mankind (Zerries, 266). The "demon" hypothesis, of
which there is actually no suggestion in the choruses, is an aspect of other
"totemic" interpretations, but the choruses are apparently late developments,
so speculation in regard to their origin is difficult. However, a comparison
with similar forms found elsewhere can be useful.

If we consider the choruses represented by the titles of such plays as
Gall-Flies, *Ants*, *Wasps*, and *Bees*, we might feel that thereomorphic enactment
in general, and particularly that based on trance possession, would be

impossible or unlikely. Reich felt that primitive peoples didn't have dances such as these, and that even as a solo a fish or ant dance would be unthinkable (Sifakis, 83). In principle, this is incorrect. It is the unusual nature of the dancer's identification, not the difficulty in representation, that suggests that these are trance dances. Possession dances of the Tonga of Zambia include animals, such as the elephant, jackal, and crane, but also possession by the spirits of modern vehicles, such as the train, motor boat, and airplane (Colson, 86–87). In Bali, *sanghyang* trance enactments include the white horse, toad, snake, and turtle, but also objects, such as the broom and the potlid. The potlid trancer has bells and the potlid tied to his hand, and he goes about striking things rhythmically. The broom trancer has a small broom tied to his hand and sweeps in small circles (Belo [T], 201). These enactments and dances suggest that the choruses of *Wasps, Frogs*, and even *Clouds* could have developed from trance dances within the Dionysian cult. Innovation was certainly a factor in regard to the choruses of old comedy, as it has been in the introduction of new types of possession in the Tonga dances. The *sanghyang* performers are insulted for comic purposes, and there is much playfulness connected with them. The festival background of the thereomorphic choruses would seem to have much in common with African masquerades, where much comedy is associated with masked trance performances. It is said that a chorus of stilt walkers shown on an Attic vase may "anticipate a chorus of Attic comedy" (Trendall and Webster, 21), and stilt walkers identified with possession by water spirits dance in African masquerades.

The hypothesis of an origin in trance enactment would also seem to explain another type of old comedy chorus which otherwise seems quite bizarre and inexplicable. Titles such as *Dionysoi* and *Odysses*, which are plurals of proper names, must have had choruses which multiplied individual identity into choruses of Dionysuses and Odyseuses (Sifakis, 90). Multiple possession by a single identity, which can result in comic encounters, could have suggested this type of chorus.

It seems most probable that the thereomorphic chorus that served as the basis for old comedy did not derive from ancient animal dances, but rather that it was an epiphenomenon suggested by the more serious trance involvement of the basic Dionysian trance dance complex. The thereomorphic chorus is often thought of as the *komus*, from which he word "comedy" comes, but the actual origin and meaning of the word are unknown, and it may not be of Attic origin. Philology is not a game, but the following correspondences in shamanistic cultures are of interest in this context. "The Soiot call [the jews' harp] *komus* (the Yakut, *homus* or *hamys),* but the Altaians (using the term in the narrowest sense), who also have the word *komus*, use it to designate the stringed instrument resembling the Russian *balalaika*, which only shamans play" (Czaplicka, 216).

The satyrs, as shown in vase paintings, have three distinct identities: (1) they are trance horses practicing cathartic and shamanistic ritual; (2) they are performers in comic situations, dances, and dramas; (3) they appear in scenes from historical mythology which represent in symbolic terms the shamanistic origins of Dionysianism. From the relationship between these three distinct identities, and from the reasons for them, we can reconstruct the origins of the satyr play. For the satyrs were neither originally nor essentially creatures of comedy and satire. We forget this because, misrepresented by others, they came to misrepresent themselves. But Pollux's account of their dances on Malea leaves us a single vivid image: "There were Silens and with them satyrs dancing in terror" (Pickard-Cambridge, 116). And we know that these were the "raving satyrs" who had stolen the "primal drum" of the trance dance from the Korybantes and Kuretes. Caricature and suppression of the satyrs, the traditional followers of Dionysus, was due to their identification with shamanistic origins and to their association with dithyrambic music and with an archaic, ritual phallicism.

Two pictures on a bowl dating from the mid-sixth century B.C. show a "fat man" and a satyr each riding a platform conveyed by numerous bearers and supporting a huge phallus pole that they seem to "ride" (Pickard-Cambridge, Plate 15). In the background of each are the vines of Dionysus that symbolize the trance. Each of the phallus poles has a prominent eye at the end, with other eyelike designs down the shaft. One of the poles also has what appear to be animal ears rising above the eye. A basic function of representations of the phallus in the ancient world was to ward off the "evil eye," but the eye of the phallus pole reminds one of the eye on the prow of seagoing vessels, which might have been apotropaic but was also a "seeing" or "opening of the way"; and this association, coupled with the horselike ears on the pole, indicates that the poles were vehicles of the trance flight.

The phallus poles are set at an angle of about forty-five degrees and appear to have derived from a tradition of somewhat similar poles in shamanistic culture. The well-known horse sacrifice of the Altai, for example, suspends the dead horse on a pole set at just this angle. It is run through the horse from the rear so that it points it upward at an angle, aimed, as it were, toward the place where its soul will go, and the function of the shaman in the ceremony is to accompany the soul there in trance flight. The *obo* poles characteristic of Siberia are also angled in this way and seem to have served a similar function; they are erected at the sites of past disasters and seem to have served to point the direction of flight the soul has taken (Diozegi, 327). These are variants of the shamanic tree as the vertical axis of trance flight. A fragment which shows satyrs riding on a ship carried by "komasts" (Pickard-Cambridge, Fig. 4) probably represents an enactment of trance flight. It would then have been similar to that of the Salish Indians in which "the journey to the underworld in a boat is made graphically visible to the onlookers by a crew of ten shamans in rows of four carrying out paddling movements in front of the community, while the chief shaman plays the part of steersman.... Spirits that fall upon him during his journey are played by boys carrying torches" (Lommel, 137–38).

It can be shown that Dionysian ritual phallicism, like the processional phallus poles, was directly associated with trance flight. It has been thought, of course, that Dionysian phallicism relates to vegetation magic. Frazer proposed, on the basis of a few scattered examples, that the copulation of married couples, representing the order of nature, was a primitive, archetypal method of inducing the growth of vegetation with sympathetic magic by miming in this way the "marriage of trees and plants." The apparent anarchic lasciviousness of the satyrs could not have been a representation of this necessary order. The tribes of the northwest Amazon associate the fertility of the fields with male potency and perform a masked dance in which males masturbate large phalluses and then carry and scatter the invisible semen everywhere for magical purposes (Zerries, 280). There would seem to be a possible analogy here with Dionysian practices, but the fact is that the association of fertility magic with Dionysian phallicism has been a theoretical attribution incorrectly arrived at, as can be seen when the basic evidence is considered.

In many pottery designs, satyrs appear either completely naked or with their genitals exposed by brief trunks to which the horsetail is attached. The renderings are often very realistic, and the trunks seem to represent the costume in satyr plays and dances. Several of these designs show the satyr's penis erect and/or thrown about by the movement of the dance (Pickard-Cambridge [F], Figs. 38–40, 49). The trunks emphasize the phallicism, but nudity in performance was not exceptional. Pyrrhic dancers at the Panathenaia "were naked save for a light helmet and a shield on the left arm" (Lindsay, 107), and by rough count seventy-five of the one hundred and five pottery designs purported to illustrate the performances of tragedy in the Trendall and Webster volume show some or all naked figures, though these are sometimes women, which would be impossible, and much must be due to artistic license. At any rate, the phallicism of the satyrs, not to be confused with the use of an artificial phallus in old comedy and in mimes, derives from the phallic Dionysus.

Dionysus in ritual was characteristically worshiped in the form of a post or column running from floor to ceiling, costumed, with a mask representing his face, and from which branches often sprang. Maenads and satyrs dance and make offerings to this image. As noted, it is Dionysus as the the shamanistic vertical axis. Related to this is a statue-like post, apparently often life-sized, topped by the bearded head of Dionysus and with an erect phallus (Trendall and Webster, 26–27). This is known as a herm because similar phallic posts have been identified as associated with Hermes. One picture shows in the foreground a Dionysus herm with an erect phallus, while in the background are the sillhouettes of another such phallic pedestal-with-bust and of a dancing satyr, crouched, also with an erection (Goldman).

Analysis of the mythological symbolism of Dionysus and Hermes shows that both gods were identified with shamanic trance flight represented in terms of the copulation of two snakes and strongly suggests that the phallicism of the herms, and hence of the satyrs, derives from this source. Orphic myth tells us that Zagreus-Dionysus was born from the union of Zeus and his own daughter (Persephone or Kore) when they copulated in the form of snakes. The daughter had been born when Zeus copulated with his own mother (Rhea or Demeter) when both were in the form of snakes. The daughter, mother of Dionysus, had horns and four eyes, two located in the normal position and two in her forehead, and also had another face on the back of her head. I take this to be an "iconization" of shamanic shape changing which Orphism did not find overly attractive, and which figures also in the death of Zagreus-Dionysus. The symbolism of the *caduceus* staff of Hermes, with two snakes twined into the so-called Heraclean knot, derives from the intercourse in the form of snakes told of in this myth (Cook, I, 398). Hermes, a very ancient god, as conductor of souls and as a messenger between gods and men, is very clearly a personification and deification of the shamanic function. The shaman often wore wings on his hat, just as Hermes did (Eliade, 155,157). The caduceus staff is again the vertical axis of trance flight. "The prime function of the caduceus is to be the instrument of Hermes as conductor of souls. In Homer it puts men to sleep, a property which makes Raingeard ask whether behind this tradition of its qualities lies an association with hypnotism or cataleptic trance" (Butterworth, 154). The snakes on the caduceus are schematized into an abstraction that is like a figure eight open at the top, probably to suggest the world of reality that opens into the world of the gods in the trance flight.

The association of the copulation of snakes with trance flight is found in a very ancient level or stratum of shamanism. The copulation is represented in the Naga (snake) worship of South India (Devi, 129), and detailed information derives from Australia. There, the shaman lying in trance dreams of flying and "the shaman's power 'rises' in his body and causes his penis to become erect." The soul of the shaman then rides on a snake that thus rises, but remains linked to his body by a thin thread that comes from the penis or navel.

> Before the beginning of a dream-flight the dreamer has the feeling that he is climbing a tree, from which he rises up into the air. Often the shaman—in his dream—has to lean a woman against the trunk of this tree and climb over her up the tree. In the air, during the flight, the shaman rides on a snake. Often he copulates with this snake during the flight. Often, too he believes that he is lying between two snakes which copulate during the flight: (Lommel, 99)

Zagreus-Dionysus was "born" of such copulation, and it is represented as the instrument of Hermes' travels. This leads to a logical conclusion similar to that which has been arrived at on the basis of other evidence. "The Caduceus-god was, therefore, the predecessor of the Priapic herm-god. The two-sex snakes conveyed the same idea as the phallus" (Frothingham, 211). Scholarship has already disentangled Hermes from vegetation theory. Jacqueline Chittenden has observed that "the views are all inconclusive," but "Hermes has almost nothing to do with the fertility of the earth." Norman Brown in four brilliant pages does the same. "Phallic symbols of the cult of Hermes were placed on mountaintops, rural waysides, state boundaries, city streets, in the doorways and courtyards of houses, in gymnasia and libraries, in sacred precincts, and on graves; which of these is an appropriate place for a fertility symbol?" (Brown, 35–36). These are the herms with which Dionysus was also identified. Their use is clearly apotropaic, and they almost certainly derive from the small wooden figures called *darisal*, *terke*, and *daragun* in Siberian shamanism that are posted to guard the actual as well as the mythological boundaries of the clan and the "road" of the shaman's tree.

The copulation of snakes as trance flight is one element in an interlocking pattern of shamanistic symbolism that allows interpretation of other myths associated with Dionysianism. The Thraco-Phrygian god Sabazios, "a sort of savage un-Hellenized Dionysus" (Dodds, 194), is associated with the worship of Attis (Cook, I, 399). Copulations with mother and daughter, as in the myth of Zagreus-Dionysus, are done in the form of snakes and then of bulls. The second is achieved only after Sabazios shows the genitals of a newly gelded ram, pretending they are his own. The reference, as in the cult of Attis, is to the sex change of the shaman, and intercourse can still be accomplished in trance flight. A relief from the Roman period shows Sabazios surrounded by the shamanistic symbols (Cook, I, 392–93). His foot is on a ram's head, the symbol of his castration, and in his right hand he holds a pine cone, such as topped the thyrsus staff of the maenads. A snake twines upward around a post, the vertical axis, on which a bird is perched, symbol of the trance flight, and from which a tree grows, rather as if it grows from the bird. Next to the bird-tree-post is a caduceus. Flanking the head of Sabazios, between his own and the heads of the women that figure in the myth-copulations, are what appear to be head-sized eyeless masks with horns. The shaman is often blindfolded or wears an eyeless mask to concentrate on inner vision. Initiates in the rites for Sabazios were reported to have participated in a practice of "passing a golden adder through their bosoms and out below" (Cook, I, 394), apparently identifying the snake with the soul and with the penis and miming its trance flight.

The coupling snakes of trance flight also provide the key to the myths of Teiresias and Melampus, figures associated with Dionysianism. Teiresias was blinded, obtaining inner vision, and turned into a woman, again the shamanic sex change, when he saw two snakes coupling and killed the female. Melampus was a famous seer who gained his powers when his servants killed two snakes they saw coupling, but he burned the bodies, cared for the young, and they licked his ears so that he could understand the speech of all creatures. It was he who then cured the daughters of Proëtus and the women of Argos of their insanity by means of Dionysian cathartic dances. His myth suggests that he had been given the healing power of a shamanism that had been "killed" by the culture. In both cases the myths symbolize a manner of gaining the power of a "seer" which is essentially identical with that of the Australian shaman.

> The soul of the man who is becoming a shaman leaves him. His body lies asleep. It is a deep sleep and no one dares to wake the sleeper, even if this sleep lasts for days. During the sleep the soul goes to the water-hole from which it originally came. It does not remain in this water-hole, however, but dives down from there into the innermost part of the earth. There, after a long journey through dark water, it suddenly comes to a brightly lit cave in which two snakes, a male and a female, are mating. From the union of these two snakes there continually spring "child

seeds"—many of which enter into the shaman's soul, so that henceforth he bears more soul-strength than an ordinary person.

(Lommel, 50–51).

Asclepius, the god of healing who received his power from a centaur, Chiron, would "actually" seem to have received it in this way. He is identified with a single snake climbing a tree or up his polelike staff, and he was the son of the mantic Apollo. To this we may add the myth of the fate of Cadmus and Harmonia, described in the *Bacchae*, who are transformed into a pair of snakes for defiance of Dionysus. Cadmus and Harmonia are transformed back into the animal ancestors, progenitors of the clan, sentenced to live again the archaic Dionysianism, a shamanism, that "dismembered" Pentheus. The sentence has the effect of a déjà vu. It is said that as snakes they will lead a great barbarian horde, incommensurable in numbers, that will plunder Greece and be turned back only when it has desecrated the shrine of Apollo itself (*Bacchae*, 1333ff.). Worship of Dionysus in Athens had been placed within the temple of Apollo, apparently to resolve a tension of polarized opposites, of ecstasy and logos. In a sense, Dionysianism remained a perpetual desecration of the Apollonian. In sentencing Harmonia and Cadmus to the barbarism of his own archaic origins, Dionysus draws again the rational limits of his worship, as he does throughout the drama.

The *agalma* drawn in a cart at the City Dionysia was a winged, birdlike phallus, again the identification with trance flight. One of the fragments of phalli found around the temple of Dionysus on Delos is birdlike (Sifakis [S], 7). These may be from monuments commemorating the victories of *choregoi*, so we may say that at a late date the phallus was identified with the ego. Its basic function was clearly apotropaic. The exaggerated phallus worn in mimes and in old comedy needs no other justification than comedy.

A satyr with a huge erection is shown chasing a maenad, but this is clearly a caricature (Pickard-Cambridge, IIb). It is possible that satyr rituals were licentious. Shamanistic rituals sometimes used trance for the arousal of sexual passion, as that in which the shaman as horse causes the women as mares to leap upon him in erotic ecstasy (Lommel, 74). But there is good reason to believe that this was not actually the case in regard to the satyrs as cultists. It is necessary to separate their ritual identity from that attributed to them by popular mythology. Their satyr plays represented silens and satyrs as debauched, drunken, and lascivious. But these were caricatures, just as were the characters of the gods and heroes to whom the satyr chorus devoted its satiric attention in these plays. It is probable that the popular caricature of the satyrs as drunken and licentious was as slanderous and "delusionary" as

Pentheus's belief about the maenads. It can be shown that popular mythology about the satyrs subjected them to parody and satire for conceptual and didactic reasons. Made ludicrous by the society and world view in which they found themselves, the satyrs turned the weapon of the comic back upon their accusers in the satyr play. In considering how this situation came about, we may best proceed by tracing the history of the centaurs.

The most ancient man-horse or trance horse was the centaur. The earliest pictures of them show figures of men with the body and rear legs of horses appended, as if crudely attached. In time, this composite being becomes more harmonious, the body of the horse is merged more completely with the torso of a man that rises from it, although the forelegs are sometimes pictured as human. A Greek design from about 410 B.C. shows four centaurs pulling a chariot in what is apparently a comic performance, black-bearded heads above torsos that take the place of the heads of horses (Pickard-Cambridge [F], Fig. 77 a,b,c). They have their hands behind their backs and appear to be captives of Herakles who drives the chariot. Perhaps in a performance each creature was played by two men, like the Balinese lion-*barong*, but the artist might only have "mythologized" single dancers. In art and mythology that preserves their history, it is apparent not only that the centaurs are representations of an alien people (Harrison [P], 384; Rose, 257), but of a shamanistic culture.

Centaurs are not known in Peloponesian art of the Mycenaean period (1580–1120 B.C.). They first appear, it seems, among the Babylonian Cassites and Hittites about 1350 B.C. (Baur, 2–3). The Hittite and Cassite centaurs often have small wings growing from their backs, a symbolism identifying them with the flight of the shaman's horse as trance vehicle. They have panther and leopard skins draped about them and use bows and arrows, indications that they are of a hunting people, perhaps alien in origin.

The centaur appears in Greek art itself early in the geometric period, possibly in the ninth century B.C., being figured in a style associated with the Hittites. These early vases show variations on a repeated stylized motif of a centaur with an upraised tree in his hand confronting a man armed with a double ax or a sword (Cook, II, 614–17). It is difficult to decide whether these designs represent a conflict between cultures or within a culture. Sometimes it seems as if the confrontation is amicably resolved and essentially symbolic, as in a design in which a centaur and a man both grasp a tree. What is certain, however, is that the tree the centaurs extend toward the men, or the tree they wield as a weapon, is their distinct "religion," the shamanistic world view itself, identified with the tree as vertical axis of the shaman's trance flight.

As the designs become more sophisticated, the tree theme remains; a centaur is shown about to uproot a tree or with a tree slung over his shoulder or wielding it as a weapon. Here, the centaurs are often shown battling among themselves. It is an image that derives, I believe, from the well-known practice of shamans fighting each other during, and by means of, their trances. The centaurs are also shown fighting naked men, the Lapiths or the followers of Herakles, on vases that picture the myths of cultural contact and change.

In the course of the development of these designs, an interesting transformation in the conventions of style may be observed. The trees that are at first shown uprooted and whole often become huge branches, more realistic as weapons than entire trees, and then they frequently become replaced with vines used as weapons. The vines are drawn in the same way as those that wind sinuously in the background of other satyr and centaur designs, and they are precisely the conventionalized vines of Dionysus. We have noted that the vines of Dionysianism are representations of trance and hallucination. Their use by the centaurs as weapons is a natural extension of this image. Figuratively, the trance is shown to have been the weapon of the centaurs, just as it was literally the weapon of the shaman. Vase pictures associate the centaurs directly with the full range of Dionysian subjects. One centaur is pictured as having torn a fawn to pieces like a maenad or like Dionysus. Centaurs are often shown together with satyrs, and one vase shows both "hairy" and "smooth" centaurs, just as there were also these two types of satyrs.

Mythology tells us that the centaurs were a race of beings that was born of a delusion. Their etiology was traced from Ixion's attempt to possess Hera. Zeus replaced her with a cloud shaped in her likeness, with which Ixion copulated, and the cloud (Nephele) gave birth to the being, part horse, part man, from which the race of centaurs sprang (Cook, I, 198). The cloud was an illusion as hallucination, like the figure of Dionysus formed of the "ether that surrounds the world" shown to Hera to deceive her, or like the figure of "gleaming air" that appears to Pentheus, or like the figure behind Xanthos, and so on. Ixion's act was also like the delusionary copulations of the trance flight. The deception of Ixion was metaphysical—and sociological. The myths state that the shamanists (Ixion) had desired divinity, but had never reached it nor participated in it, and had experienced only illusion. They were rash to desire one of the Olympian pantheon.

In punishment for his presumption, Ixion was bound to a winged and flaming wheel and set to spin forever in the sky (or later, in the underworld); an image that reproduced in perpetuity the spinning dance of the shaman and the terrible price of insanity associated with his trances. It was the price paid for "reaching the sky." In one vase picture, Athena (the wisdom of rational thought) is shown bringing the wheel to which Ixion will be bound, while two other gods hold him. He was, in fact, bound there by the whole Olympian pantheon (Cook, I, 200). Ixion's progeny, the centaurs, representing the shamanists, are shown in further conflict with the Olympians in myths that detail both their suppression and their influence.

Cheiron, the wisest of the centaurs and their leader, he who had taught the art of medicine to Asclepius, received from Herakles a wound that could not be healed. This was, perhaps, the psychic wound that already characterized shamanistic practice, and Cheiron gladly gave up his immortality to Prometheus, who would himself suffer, but in a new way, under the bonds of rationalism. Cheiron's wound was an accident; Herakles had aimed at one of the unruly centaurs, not at their wisdom. This seems to have been intended to indicate that the new gods and their world order had, in effect, superseded shamanism unintentionally, outmoded it; that it was, abstractly speaking, immortal; that it had, in part, contributed to the culture; but that it could not, and should not, sustain itself at the price of the psychic suffering it was paying for its practices. Herakles, opponent of the shamanistic centaurs, had long since disposed of the serpents of trance flight, having strangled a pair of them while still in his cradle.

The licentiousness of the centaurs was a necessary postulation of didacticism. The battles with the centaurs were caused by their interruption of two weddings, that of Herakles and that of the Lapith god, Kaineus. In both cases the bride, whom the centaurs tried to abduct, was named Hippodameia, "female tamer of horses." She represented the ethos of the society that would tame *these* horses, the horses of the trance. Kaineus seems to have been a deified leader in Thessaly, and was clearly a shaman—or shamaness. He had been a woman, was raped by Poseidon, chose to be transformed into a man and then worshiped only his spear, which he set up in the ground like the vertical axis. Also descended from Ixion, Kaineus was invulnerable to weapons, but the centaurs won the battle against the Lapiths and hammered him into the earth with the shamanistic fir tree.

The characteristic of drunkenness attributed to the centaurs and to the satyrs derived from a specific didactic symbolism. Wine was represented as the cause of the battle between Herakles and the centaurs at Pholus's cave. Pholus refused to break the seal on an ancient amphora of wine just so that his guest, Herakles, might be served, saying that the wine was the common property of all the centaurs. Herakles insisted, observing that Zeus had wanted it saved for this particular occasion, and when the wine was poured its aroma immediately attracted all the other centaurs, who stormed the cave in a fury.

It is apparent that the wine symbolizes the ancient religion, the shamanistic wisdom and world view, that the centaurs wanted to keep for themselves. The battle occurs when Herakles, the representative of the Olympian world view, gets it opened to him. We know that wine as intoxication was a symbol of the ecstatic Dionysianism of which the centaurs were ancient creatures. The centaurs fought to save their religious experience, not their wine, but popular mythologizers attributed drunkenness to them on this account. In a similar manner, Silenus was made drunk on wine to learn the secrets of his ancient wisdom, probably a reference to its ecstatic nature. He was the eponym of the silens, a type of trance horse shown as aged, and the leader of the satyrs in the satyr plays, in which he then came to be represented as drunken.

The rapes and abductions attributed to satyrs and centaurs by myth were therefore didactic metaphor, representations of the forced seductions of a particular world view seen from the perspective of a specific attitude toward it. The drunkenness of their world view was clearly a disparagement of trance, based on wine as a symbol of religious experience, as was the licentiousness of the satyrs, and their unruly nature derived from the internecine warfare of the shamans pictured as centaurs battling among themselves.

The satyrs and centaurs represented the archaic, shamanistic level of Dionysianism. The attitude toward them expressed in their mythology was not actually overly biased. It was, in a sense, an accurate history. But it had an inherent aspect of humor, even of ridicule. Thus, in the process of time, the satyrs became mythologized by parody. When they came to be performers in satyr plays, it was natural that they should turn this same satire and parody back upon the Olympian pantheon in general and upon its particular emissary, Herakles, the antagonist of the horse-man in the mythology that had, in effect, slandered them. The myths of Herakles, subordinator of the primitive, already contained humor, and he was also frequently parodied by Dorian farce. This type of blasphemous metaphysical farce is maintained by socioreligious sanction and represents an archetypal level in the development of comedy. The satyrs became "trapped" in this mode, as it were.

Satire and parody were not the only weapons in society's reformation of archaic Dionysianism. The battle between Apollonian and Dionysian was symbolized as a war of musical modes. Conclusions were presented didactically and unambiguously. Athena had given up the double flute of her ancient origins on becoming the image of rational thought, but it was picked up by the satyr, Marsyas, who continued to play this Dionysian instrument, much to her displeasure. Marsyas was then defeated by Apollo in a famous contest of musical modes. As a consequence, he was flayed alive, and his skin was hung on a pine tree, the world-tree of his shamanistic origins. The goat-satyr Pan was also defeated by Apollo in a similar musical contest.

One of the major myths in the revision of Dionysianism was that concerning Orpheus and his dismemberment by the maenads. Significantly enough, the Orphic movement originated around 600 B.C., contemporaneous with Arion's reform of the dithyrambic trance dance. The Orphics worshiped Dionysus, and Orpheus was said to have been a follower or priest of Dionysus (Guthrie, 82). But the musical instrument he played so well was the lyre of Apollo, not the pipes and cymbals of Dionysianism. Orphism sought to mediate the polarity between the Dionysian and the Apollonian.

The descent of Orpheus to the underworld to bring back his wife, Eurydice, has been observed to derive from a shamanistic pattern (Eliade, 392). That is, it relates to the trance marriage in another world to a spirit wife. The Orphic variation of this pattern as an apparently purposeful negation of it is interesting. Eurydice dies from stepping on a snake, again the snake of trance flight. Orpheus fails to bring her back; he cannot keep his spirit wife. He seems, therefore, to have founded the institution of homosexuality (Rose, 255). The sex change of the shaman clearly provided a precedent.

Orpheus, it was said, went to Thrace for the purpose of suppressing sacrificial murder there. As noted, Thrace was an area of shamanistic influence upon Dionysianism. The sacrificial murder Orpheus intended to suppress was undoubtedly the dismemberment and boiling associated with shamanic initiation. But this representative of Dionysus met an analogous, and distinctly incongruous, fate; he was hacked to pieces by the maenads, who were also followers of Dionysus. This was unlike the fate of Pentheus, as Guthrie observed, since the women used various weapons, thus making "it clear that he is not taking the part of a victim in a Bacchic orgy" (Guthrie, 49). The murder of Orpheus by the maenads, relating indirectly to dismemberment of Zagreus-Dionysus by the Titans, seems to have been an intentional symbolism in a conscious, conceptual revision of Dionysianism.

Orpheus, in fact, seems to have been torn apart only so that his severed head might continue to sing and prophesy. What it sang was the music of Apollo, "music regulated and chaste," as Plutarch called it, composed of rational, mathematical harmonies. It was the music of the mode of the mind—even of the head severed from its body—not music of the mode of the body, of the god born from the thigh of Zeus, nor of "the dithyrambic strains laden with emotion." The myth of Orpheus presents him as a martyr to the Dionysian mode, and it opposes to Bacchic violence a style personified by a figure with a "calm and civilized air" who was "always on the side of civilization and the arts of peace" (Guthrie, 42, 40). The rending or *sparagmos* of Orpheus was purely a didactic invention.

It is ironic, in this regard, to note that by 425 B.C. the satyrs singing in contests of dithyrambs at the Panathenea were accompanying themselves on the lyre, the instrument of Apollo and Orpheus (Pickard-Cambridge, Ia).

FRANCES MUECKE

'I Know You—By Your Rags'[1]
Costume and Disguise in Fifth-Century Drama.

To the memory of Colin Macleod

In Euripides' *Bacchae*, first produced in the last five years of the fifth century, that is, after the tragedian's death, there is a remarkable sequence of scenes which constitutes the turning point of the play. In the first of these scenes (787–861), making the last section of the great central epeisodion, the god Dionysus, masquerading as a mortal, tries to persuade Pentheus that in order to spy on the maenads on Mt. Cithaeron, he must put on woman's dress, or rather, allow himself to be dressed in female garb by Dionysus himself (827). The elements of the θῆλς στολή are detailed in advance at 830 ff.—long flowing locks, skirts down to the feet, a μίτρα for his head, and as the special equipment of the bacchant, a thyrsus and a dappled fawnskin. Pentheus strongly rejects the stranger's suggestion, though fascinated by it, and when he goes indoors at the end of the scene he has not yet committed himself to the plan. However, it is clear to the audience from Dionysus' speech to the chorus after Pentheus has left the stage that Pentheus, in his last attempt to exercise control and freedom of action, will not be able to withstand the power of the god. In order to fulfil the god's plan of vengeance Pentheus must be driven out of his right mind, since only then will he accept the female disguise. When the two main characters return after the third stasimon all this has happened. Dionysus calls Pentheus out of the palace to display himself as a bacchant, and Pentheus looks to Dionysus for approval of his costume. As adjustments are made to it each element of the disguise is

---

From *Antichthon* 16 (1982). © 1982 by the Australian Society for Classical Studies.

spotlighted—the curls and the μίτρα (928–9), the girdle and the long dress (936–7) and the thyrsus (941–2). In keeping with his costume Pentheus must learn to play the part of the bacchant, and Dionysus instructs him in the correct wielding of the thyrsus (943–4) before the two set out for Mt. Cithaeron.

In Aristophanes' *Thesmophoriazusae*, produced in 411, Euripides, in danger of condemnation by the women of Athens at their festival the Thesmophoria, expounds his μηχανή (87) to his relative at the beginning of the play. He plans to persuade Agathon, a tragic poet noted for his effeminacy, to go among the women secretly, dressed in female costume (στολὴν γυναικός 92), to speak on his behalf. Agathon in fact refuses to lend himself to the plan and the relative volunteers to go instead. After shaving and singeing he is dressed, *on stage*, in female clothes supplied by Agathon— a κροκωτός (the yellow dress worn by Athenian women on festive occasions), a belt, a στρόφιον, a hair-net and μίτρα, and a mantle and shoes. With final instructions from Euripides on adopting a female voice he is left to play his role among the women at the Thesmophoria (249–65).

The similarities of the two 'toilet' scenes have been noted by commentators on Euripides rather than commentators on Aristophanes. It is certainly remarkable that Euripides' comic role as 'dresser' and 'producer' is taken over by Dionysus in the tragedy, but whether Euripides was bold enough to use or allude to Aristophanes' scene in his tragedy is a question I leave open for the moment.[2] The *Bacchae* scenes have raised a number of questions of interpretation: what is the meaning of the disguise in relation to the themes of the play as a whole? What is its dramatic function? Is it an element of ritual, comedy or satyr play?[3] In this paper I am primarily concerned with the dramatic function of disguise and will work towards an interpretation of the *Bacchae* scenes from that perspective.

In a recent treatment of the *Bacchae* Seidensticker argues that the dressing of Pentheus in woman's clothes is what he calls a 'comedy element' or 'motif'.[4] While accepting his distinction between comic elements and comic treatment, and entertaining his argument that the disguising may be exploited by Euripides for some kind of comic effect, I question his assumption that the dressing of Pentheus is to be situated entirely in relation to comic use of disguise. It cannot be denied, of course, that disguise, and especially transvestite disguise, becomes a 'comedy element' in New Comedy and its derivative, Renaissance Comedy, in fact one of the most persistent of all comedy elements, but, all the same, disguise continues to be used by the writers of tragedy, and not necessarily for comic effect.[5]

What Seidensticker does not take into account is, on the one hand, the history of the disguise motif, and, on the other, its dramatic and theatrical potency, which makes it attractive to writers of tragedy and comedy alike. It is only by comparison with the conventions and functions of disguise in tragedy that the comic elements (if any) of the dressing scene in the *Bacchae* can be identified. Equally the distinction between 'dressing up' on stage[6] and disguise as a stratagem needs to be taken into consideration, as well as the role of the disguise in the plots in which it occurs. Therefore the aim of this paper is, within a historical framework, to give a synoptic view of the use of costume and disguise in fifth-century tragedy and comedy, analysing the differences in the generic conventions and exploring the possibility that comic treatment may modify tragic practice.

In order to provide an interpretative perspective I begin (out of chronological order) with a discussion of Aristophanes' famous parody of the use of disguise in Euripides' *Telephus*, for not only does the explicit connexion of the two plays allow us to clarify the different interests of the tragic and comic poets, but also Aristophanes' self-conscious exploitation of costume and disguise points up the special relation of these elements of play and plot to the dramatic transaction as a whole.

Aristophanes' interest in Euripides' use of disguise began early in his career. His parody of the *Telephus* (438) in the *Acharnians* (425) produced the 'costume' scene of that play, a scene which was later remodelled for the Agathon scene of the *Thesmophoriazusae*, and the plot of the *Telephus* was exploited in both these comedies.[7] Aristotle included Telephus in his list of those families whose vicissitudes provide 'the best tragedies' (*Poetics* 1453 a 19 ff.) and this opinion is borne out by the number of Telephus tragedies attested.[8] We should note, however, that the notorious disguise as a beggar, which Telephus assumes primarily to avoid detection in Argos, the seat of his enemies, seems to have been introduced into the story by Euripides, after whom it became obligatory.[9] In disguise Telephus infiltrates the palace of Agamemnon, and still in disguise defends himself and the Mysian support of the Trojan cause in the assembly of the Greek warlords. In the course of the assembly he falls under suspicion and is exposed, probably by Odysseus. The exposure leads to the famous hostage episode, which, it has been argued, took place off-stage and was related in a messenger speech.[10] This fund of events is largely reconstructed from the two Aristophanes plays and assumes that Aristophanes changed the order of some of the happenings for his own purposes. But since we are concerned with the use of disguise in plot, it is important to realize that the moment to which everything leads in the first half of the *Acharnians* is the speech 'in the assembly', where the 'disguised' hero is to say things that will offend his hearers. As Telephus defended the

Mysians in the assembly of the Greeks, so Dicaeopolis defends the Spartans before the Acharnians, and the Old Man in the *Thesmophoriazusae* defends Euripides in answer to the attacks already made on him by the two women speakers, thus betraying his own 'female' cause.[11]

Two questions might be raised here: what did Euripides gain by introducing disguise into his tragedy? and what aspects of the disguise were parodied by Aristophanes?

Aeschylus and Sophocles dealt with the healing of Telephus in Argos, but nothing is known of the details of their treatment. For Euripides' play there is enough information from various sources to attempt a reconstruction of the course of events. The fragments of the prologue are particularly valuable, in that they show Euripides using the story pattern of the 'nostos'.[12] In an opening monologue Telephus presents himself as returning home (Handley and Rea point out the parallel with Orestes in the *Choephoroe*). Though king in a barbarian land, he is in reality a Greek, born in Arcadia. The Greeks of the Trojan expedition, however, know him only as 'Mysian Telephus',[13] and a barbarian enemy, and so, in order to win their sympathy and the healing he is in quest of, he takes on the identity of a Greek and a beggar. The disguise is therefore part true and part false—a kind of doubling of the theme of identity that is crucial to the plot, in the way that Handley and Rea put it: 'To fulfil his mission, Telephus had not only to be recognized, but to be recognized as a Greek.'[14] Thus the disguise is constitutive in the plot, preparing for the reversal, the crisis created by Odysseus' exposure of the beggar as Telephus, which is itself a false recognition requiring the further recognition of Telephus as the Greek referred to by the oracle. At the same time the disguise is the basis of the ironies of the first assembly in which Telephus, in the character of a Greek speaking to fellow Greeks about a barbarian, defends Telephus and the Mysians and causes a rift between Agamemnon and Menelaus. It also facilitated a typically Euripidean contrast between the beggar Telephus' appearance and behaviour (*Ach.* 440 ff., 497, *P. Oxy.* fr. 6.1 in Handley and Rea).

Aristophanes used Telephus' disguise both as a plot element and as an object of parody in its own right. As I mentioned above, Aristophanes wanted to recreate the assembly scene, and this was not only so that Dicaeopolis could plead for peace before a hostile chorus, but also so that Aristophanes could defend himself as a poet before the actual Athenian audience of the play (366–84).[15] The overlap between situations is foregrounded at the beginning of Dicaeopolis's long speech, where tragic parody is adapted for the theatrical situation and Dicaeopolis says (496–9):

Μή μοι φθονήσητ᾽, ἄνδρες οἱ θεώμενοι,
ει πτωχὸς ὢν ἔπειτ᾽ ἐν Ἀθηναιοις λέγειν
μέλλω περί τερὶ τῆς πόλεως, τρυγῳδίαν ποιῶν.

The 'costume' scene is an interlude between the announcement of Dicaeopolis' intention to speak in favour of the Spartans and the ῥῆσις μακρά itself (416). For this speech he requires a pitiable costume (384, 436),[17] and taking advantage of the function of the tragedian as both producer and stage manager,[18] Dicaeopolis approaches Euripides for a suitable costume. The rags of a series of unfortunate heroes are rejected in favour of those of Telephus, which are chosen for the hero's terrible power with words (429) as well as for their deceptive nature, which is linked to Telephus' rhetorical ability (440 ff.). With the rags Dicaeopolis assumes the character of Telephus, becoming not only endowed with Telephus' powers of persuasion, but also a persistent beggar, pestering Euripides for the rest of his gear, until Euripides has to cry φροῦδά μοι τὰ δράματα (470).[19]

On the surface the main object of satire is Euripides' realism, which is criticized in a similar way by Aeschylus in *Frogs* 1060–4:

ΑΙ. Κἄλλως εἰκὸς τοὺς ἡμιθέους τοῖς ῥήμασι μείζοσι χρῆσθαι·
   καὶ γὰρ τοῖς ἱματίοις ἡμῶν χρῶνται πολὺ σεμνοτέροισιν.
   Ἀμοῦ χρηστῶς καταδείξαντος διελυμήνω σύ.
ΕΥ.   Τί δράσας;
ΑΙ. Πρῶτον μὲν τοὺς βασιλεύοντας ῥάκι᾽ ἀμπισχών, ἵν᾽ ἐλεινοὶ
   τοῖς ἀνθρώποις φαίνοιντ᾽ εἶναι.

I also suspect that Aristophanes is accusing Euripides of turning an effective theatrical device into cliché by overdoing the scene in which a hero enters in rags after a catastrophe.[20] Such scenes would have occurred in the *Phoenix* and *Bellerophon* at least, and there may have been comments on the rag costumes of Philoctetes[21] and Oeneus at their first entrances linking their appearances with their misfortunes.

But in Aristophanes' scene[22] the costumes do not simply evoke the heroes, or stand for the plays, but they are the plays themselves, by an extension of the images of weaving and sewing often used for poetic composition, as C.W. Macleod showed. 'Euripides "creates" beggars and Dicaeopolis asks him for "a tatter of that old play", because the texts of his work, the very material it is made of, are nothing but rags.'[23] Costume here is the link between the poet and character, and it stands for the metamorphosis of actor into character effected by the dramatist.[24] Disguise, being a doubling of the costume, calls attention to that transformation, which Aristophanes shows happening before our eyes as Dicaeopolis puts on the rags and acquires the other props for his performance of Euripides' *Telephus*. Aristophanes presents the assumption of disguise as an image of the actor's dressing in a costume and taking on a new character, or rather, he comically confuses the two transformations. His awareness of costume as costume easily leads him into the realm of the meta-theatrical.[25]

This is because costume, or what it can easily stand for, impersonation—the actor's pretending to be a fictional character—is the most basic element of theatre.[26] As Aristotle says, tragedy is a *mim?sis*, which, while not primarily of people *per se* (*Poetics* 1450 a 16), is produced by people doing things (1449 b 36 ff.). And this basic fact of drama, which is a matter of both personal identity and physical disguise, is 'internalized' in countless plays by further impersonations, most obviously by disguise and the taking on of false identities, by twins and confusion of identities and by plays-within-plays, as part of the general tendency of drama to incorporate the conditions of its theatrical performance into its own form and thematic content. The same phenomenon may be recognized in the less obvious impersonations in plays concerned with hypocrisy, real and apparent character and searches for psychological identity.[27]

With this in mind let us turn to an examination of the history and function of disguise in Greek tragedy.

At *Wasps* 351 the chorus urge Philocleon to escape from his son's house ῥάκεσιν κρυφθεὶς ὥσπερ πολύμητις Ὀδυσσεύς. Πολύμητις Odysseus is indeed the 'master of disguises' in Greek literature.[28] At first Concealment of his identity (as with the Cyclops), and then various assumptions of false identities, culminating in the divinely worked disguise of the last act in Ithaca, are the stratagems by which his famed resourcefulness enables him to protect himself from others, to manipulate them to his own purposes, to test their loyalty and finally to execute his revenge. The handling of the disguise from the moment of Odysseus' return to Ithaca with the opportunities it provides for ironic effects both comic and pathetic, with a recognition which in the style of New Comedy makes all right at the end, but has been anticipated by the possibility of a dangerously premature disclosure of Odysseus' identity by the nurse—all this could have provided playwrights with an influential model for the exploitation of disguise in plots of revenge and escape.[29] Is it accidental that rags are the means of disguise Euripides chooses in the two disguise episodes that he has added to the traditional stories—those of Telephus, and of Menelaus in the *Helen*?[30] And could this be a result of the general similarity of situation between Odysseus, Telephus and Menelaus as infiltrators in palaces controlled by their enemies? Similarly the situation of Telephus speaking as a beggar at the assembly of princes recalls Odysseus among the suitors.

Surviving tragedies yield relatively few examples of disguise proper—defined as a change of costume bringing about 'a change of personal appearance which leads to mistaken identity'[31]—but it would be a mistake to isolate these cases from the more commonly found theme of mistaken identity with its concomitant plot element—recognition. Disguise in tragedy is usually part of a plot of intrigue.[32] The stratagem of concealing true identity, or assuming a false identity, is undertaken in the characters' intrigues for the sake of the end aimed at (e.g. revenge or escape), but in the plot of the dramatist himself it is for the sake of the complications and ironic situations it can generate. Revenge is the chief aim which calls for intrigue in its dramatic realization, as Lattimore has pointed out: 'Since a mere crushing of the unrighteous by force of arms gives no suspense, complication, or scope for story telling, the treachery is dramatically essential, and the corpus of lost tragedy is full of stories of revenge on usurpers whose guilt offers (apparently) no problems of morals, but whose strength of position poses elaborate problems of means for the avengers.'[33]

In the archetypal revenge story of Greek tragedy, the intrigue springs naturally from another basic story pattern of Lattimore's—the pattern of the missing person.[34] I refer, of course, to the revenge of Orestes.[35] Sent from home as a child Orestes returns as a young man. He exploits his 'lost' status to pose as a stranger bringing the news of the death of Orestes. Similarly the disguise of Odysseus as a beggar in Ithaca is furnished as 'the stratagem of revenge' (μῆτις, *Od.* 13.386) Odysseus requests from Athena.[36] Orestes' revenge is already an *exemplum* in the *Odyssey*, and the similarities and differences between the two situations are recalled at significant moments in the epic. Right at the beginning Zeus' mind is 'full of Lord Aegisthus, slain by renowned Orestes, the child of Agamemnon' (*Od.* 1.29–30),[37] and later in Book 1 Athena holds up Orestes as a model for Telemachus, a lesson the young man has absorbed-by the time he speaks to Nestor in Book 3. In the *Nekyia* Odysseus meets the soul of Agamemnon, who tells the story of his death and contrasts his misfortune with the advantages of Odysseus who has a faithful wife and son at home. This contrast is recalled when Athena tells Odysseus about the suitors and he immediately invokes the parallel with Agamemnon: 'This is evil news. I see I might well have perished in my own halls by the same ill doom as Agamemnon' (*Od.* 13.383–4).[38]

The parallels could perhaps be taken further if we knew how Orestes executed his revenge in the pre-Aeschylean myth, but we do not know if

concealment of his identity was always part of the Orestes story.[39] There are
indications of a version in which Orestes surprised Aegisthus sitting on his
father's throne and killed him instantly (cf. *Choe.* 571–6).[40] This may be what
Odysseus is thinking of when he alludes to a battle with the suitors in the
speech I have just quoted from.

The question of Orestes' identity is handled simply but powerfully in
the *Choephoroe.* The recognition of Orestes by Electra occurs early in the play
as a prelude to the revenge.[41] The pattern 'arrival-of-stranger/recognition'
is used twice over in the play, the first time with the emphasis on the
recognition of Orestes by Electra, the second with it on the deception that is
built upon the stranger's arrival. Orestes' identity is made clear to the
audience in his opening speech, which stresses the 'nostos' theme,[42] and he
soon identifies Electra among the women bringing libations. Electra is
prepared for his appearance by the lock and footprints and her suspicion of
a trick (220) is only a momentary barrier to her acceptance of the stranger as
her brother. It is only after the great conjuration scene that Orestes outlines
his plan of deception, explicitly following the instructions of Apollo (556–7).
The motif of deceit emphasizes the irony in the situation, for Orestes, like
Oedipus, is in fact a stranger to his mother. Clytemnestra herself recognizes
the appropriateness of the retribution: δόλις ὀλούμεθ᾽, ὥσπερ οὖν
ἐκτείναμεν, (888) is her answer to the slave's riddling explanation of the
uproar caused by the killing of Aegisthus, τὸν ζῶντα καίνειν τοὺς
τεθνηκότας λέγω (886). After this no words need be wasted on 'recognition'
when Orestes, sword in hand, stands before his mother the second time.

The stratagem of Orestes announcing his own death *was* used, with a
difference (the disguised Paedagogus announces the death [42 ff., 660 ff.],
while Orestes appears later disguised as an urn-bearer [1098 ff.]) in
Sophocles' *Electra* but not in Euripides'.[43] In the latter play, in fact, Orestes
is singularly devoid of μηχαναί and it is the Old Man who suggests the two
young men should get themselves invited to Aegisthus' sacrifice as strangers.
In the *Electra* of Sophocles the problem of identity hangs over the whole play,
for after almost occurring in the Aeschylean position, the recognition is
postponed for a thousand lines, so that Electra herself is deceived by, and
suffers from, the stratagem. As Reinhardt says: 'The deception spreads
beyond all bounds and even overshadows its own aim, vengeance.'[44] Since
the disguise stratagem has not brought about its paradoxical result,
recognition, in the early part of the play, this element of the pattern is
repeated to trigger the Orestes/Electra recognition later on.

If Euripides dropped disguise from its central place in the Orestes
story, he introduced it into myths in which it had previously not been found.

Telephus we have already noticed. A second example is *Philoctetes*. Thanks to Dio Chrysostom's comparison of the three plays (*Or.* 52) we can set the surviving tragedy of Sophocles against the earlier lost versions of Aeschylus and Euripides. In Aeschylus' play Odysseus dealt directly with Philoctetes. He was not recognized by him (a possible implausibility defended by Dio) and practised on him with a false story of the misfortunes of the Greeks. Euripides raised the problem of recognition and solved it by having Athena transform Odysseus' appearance—as in Homer, says Dio.[45] He is still a Greek and again he tells Philoctetes a false story about his identity and purpose. Sophocles kept Odysseus behind the scenes for the first part of the play, managing his practice through Neoptolemus, and thus eliminated the need for disguise. But it is interesting that he invented a way of reintroducing it into the plot.

The new role of Odysseus, analogous in his relation to his creatures to the playwright with his characters, far from weakening the intrigue, only strengthens its hold upon the play. Reinhardt, describing the *Philoctetes* as 'the most exquisite and profound Attic play of intrigue, the poetic justification for the whole genre'[46] shows how Sophocles restores intrigue from a mere theatrical cliché to the realm of art. It is in this light that we should consider the merchant scene (542–627). In this scene a messenger from Odysseus, disguised as a merchant on his way home from Troy, outlines a menacing intrigue being practised against Philoctetes by his enemy Odysseus. This ironically true and false tale, mirroring the real intentions of Odysseus and the plot of the whole play, is terribly effective. In turning away from it the victim is to entrust himself to Neoptolemus and lay himself open to a more profound deception.[47] The motif of disguise matches the 'staging' of the stratagem by Odysseus. Its outward simplicity contrasts with the inner struggles of Neoptolemus trapped in his ambiguous position.

Leaving the *Bacchae* till last, we must notice Euripides' use of disguise in an intrigue in one more play. In the *Helen* the disguise is part of the stratagem of escape from Egypt, but the self-conscious use of costume is not confined to this moment of the play. Though 'recognition' precedes 'intrigue' in this plot, the element of mistaken identity must play its part in the recognition scene between Helen and Menelaus. In this play Menelaus arrives on the scene from his shipwreck already in disguise, as it were. Clad in rags he is mistaken by Helen for a ruffian, and later tells her how he had been driven away from the palace door as a beggar. Clothes makyth man and he had beaten an ignominious retreat. Having lost his heroic role by virtue of his rag costume (unlike Odysseus who is simply a hero in disguise), Menelaus cannot rise to it again until he is dressed as a hero, the costume dictating the character as it does in Aristophanes' parody of *Telephus* in the *Acharnians*.[48] Helen's stratagem, which draws inspiration from the fortuitous arrival of Teucer at the beginning of the play,[49] involves turning Menelaus costume of rags into a deliberate disguise. Using the trick of the *Choephoroe*[50] Menelaus is to come to Theoclymenus with the story of his own death by shipwreck.

Anne Burnett has shown how the self-conscious handling of costume meshes with the theme of contrast between appearance and reality which pervades the whole play, and more importantly for my theme, has also identified the Aristophanic character of the equally self-conscious handling of the intrigue. When Helen has outlined her scheme Menelaus' comment is: 'This plan of yours is a bit old hat' (1056) and, told that he must act the part of the sole survivor of his own crew, he replies: 'Yes, and the rags I have round me, survivors of the wreck, will confirm my story' (1079–80).[51] To my mind Burnett's earlier perception of these moments as Aristophanic is more convincing than her later derivation of them from satyr play.[52]

We may find this confirmed by the alacrity with which Aristophanes took up the challenge in the *Thesmophoriazusae*.[53] We left the Old Man among the women at the Thesmophoria in his female disguise. At the end of the assembly scene, his hostage ploy with the wine skin disguised as the baby having failed, he is put under guard and awaits the promised rescue by Euripides (270–1, 765).[54] The series of rescue attempts is based on μηχαναὶ σωτηρίας from three recent plays of Euripides, *Palamedes*, *Helen* and *Andromeda*, all of which in some way backfire on their author. The first major parody is that of the *Helen*, introduced by the Old Man as follows (849–51):

Τῷ δῆτ᾽ ἂν αὐτὸν προσαγαγοίμην δράματι;
Ἐγῶδα· τὴν καινὴν Ἑλένην μιμήσομαι.
Πάντως ὑπάρχει μοι γυναικεία στολή.

In the hilarious sequence which follows in which Euripides, in rags,[55] plays the part of Menelaus, comic force is derived not so much from specific parody of Euripides, as from the persistent contrast of reality and illusion introduced by the woman who is guarding the Old Man. Not recognizing the parody of the *Helen* as a play, she interprets it simply as an attempt to deceive, which it is as well. She constantly asserts the reality of the comic fiction, refusing to accept her role as Theonoe in the tragedy (897–9), and suspecting Euripides-Menelaus, because of his disreputable attire, of being a thief come to steal the jewellery of the women (892–4, cf. *Hel.* 553–4). The total effect is, on a more massive scale, that of the self-consciousness of

Euripides' play. To quote Burnett on the *Helen:* 'By keeping the spectator always conscious of the theatrical illusion, Euripides has made the play itself into his largest conceit on the theme of appearance and reality.'[56] The difference lies in the reversal of the importance of the two elements, for in Euripides play with the theatrical illusion is for the sake of the play with ideas in the drama, while in Aristophanes contrast between reality and illusion is used for the sake of reflecting upon theatrical illusion itself.

In our survey so far we have found that disguise in tragedy is primarily a device of an intrigue and involves a character known to the audience taking on a second role in order to deceive another character or other characters.[57] Care is taken to keep the spectators in the know, for otherwise the opportunity for exploitation of irony and pathos offered by such gaps in knowledge between the audience and some of the characters would be lost.[58] It is difficult now to gauge the extent to which such tragic disguises involved change or modification of costume. For example, Orestes in *Choephoroe* (560) says that he will arrive at the palace door 'like a stranger, with all kinds of baggage' and that he and Pylades will 'imitate Phocian speech', and accordingly at line 674 he uses a false name (Daulieus from Phocis) to introduce himself to Clytemnestra, but the text gives us no further details of the disguise.[59]

In Sophocles' *Electra* the plan of the intrigue is fully disclosed at lines 39–76. The Paedagogus (whose changed appearance precludes the need for any further disguise) is to present himself as a messenger from Phanoteus of Phocis (45, 670), and Orestes and Pylades are similarly to arrive later as messengers from Phocis bringing the urn (53 ff., 757–60, 1106 ff., 1110 ff., 1442). The care taken to ensure that the audience will know that the urn-bearers are Orestes and Pylades (knowledge that is essential for the recognition scene with Electra) allows for some measure of physical disguise, even if it does not prove it.[60] Similar care is taken to establish the identity of the man used as scout (45, 126–9) before he is sent back in disguise in the *Philoctetes*.[61]

Of the other tragic instances we have discussed, Telephus arrives in disguise, but immediately discloses his true identity to the audience, as does Menelaus in *Helen,* explaining the absence of his royal robes (421–4). Another situation worth noting, even if it is not strictly assumption of a second role, is Helen's own change of costume, for it is she who has to convince Theoclymenus of the death of Menelaus, and her most impressive weapon of persuasion is the mourning she puts on (1087–9, 1186–90).[62]

In comedy, on the other hand, the relative importance of these features of the use of disguise is reversed. While comedy does employ change of costume and assumption of another role for the purposes of deceit practised by some characters on others (e.g. *Frogs* 498–589), disguise is chiefly treated as costume. When an actor playing a part takes on another part from another fiction and becomes that character (for this point to be made Dicaeopolis temporarily *becomes* Telephus) the gap between the actor and his role is collapsed, in order, paradoxically, to foreground the actor's own 'deceit' of the audience (cf. *Ach.* 440 ff.). This meta-theatrical exploitation reaches its climax in the *Thesmophoriazusae*, as we have seen, with the internalization of the tragedian himself, he who constructs the plots of plays becoming the intriguer within the plot of a play. The degree of self-consciousness Euripides had displayed in *Helen* may have prompted Aristophanes to stage him in this role.

In the *Bacchae* we meet the fullest demonstration in extant Greek tragedy of the theatrical and dramatic potential of disguise and change of costume. Without aspiring to give an exhaustive interpretation of the two scenes concerned[63] I will approach them by way of three main perspectives—dress and disguise in the *fabula* or basic story of the play, dress and disguise in the constructed plot of the play, and dress and disguise in relation to tragic and comic conventions.

Whether or not the female dress of Pentheus is an echo of a primitive sacrifice ritual in which the victim must be consecrated to the god by being decked in apparel symbolic of the god, as Dodds suggested,[64] the transvestism of Pentheus *is* intimately connected with the religious theme of the tragedy, androgyny being a central aspect of the deities of vegetation and fertility and transvestism in primitive times an essential part of their worship.[65] There seems to be no good evidence, however, for conceiving of the god Dionysus himself as androgynous,[66] though the sexuality of the figure Dionysus takes on—that of one of his own followers—is ambiguous (Pentheus calls him τὸν θηλύμορφον ξένον, 353). Seaford has seen the correct explanation of 'Dionysus'' effeminacy: 'In fact of course the effeminacy and transvestism of the god derives from the transvestism of his adherents.'[67] In this context the god's transformation of Pentheus to a man-woman who is a grotesque imitation of his own divine and perfect androgyny may still be seen as a tellingly ironic punishment for a refuser of his worship.[68]

I do not find such a view of the symbolic/ritual meaning of the female disguise incompatible with interpretation of it as a plot device, and as such it is motivated by the logic of the plot as a whole, even if the motivation in the story is fleeting and inconsistent.[69] Without wishing to deny the presence of traditional material drawn from the mysteries and the shaping influence of ritual on the plot (both explored in detail by Seaford), I would like to revive the idea that these archaic elements are also shaped and made assimilable by a modern plot, by the familiar structures of the revenge and intrigue plays.

The advent of Dionysus in Thebes is a 'nostos'—the return of the unrecognized native—and the aim of the god is to achieve recognition of his true status, as Odysseus' aim was to achieve restoration of his.[70] Like many other avenging protagonists Dionysus works through deceit and disguise, and his intrigue has already begun when the play opens. Therefore Pentheus's intrigue against the Maenads, which comes at the same point in the play as many other Euripidean μηχαναί, is not the central action as in other intrigue plays, but it is decentered and reversed in meaning. Though Pentheus does not know it, it is in fact the climax of a larger intrigue also involving disguise, the intrigue by which Dionysus works his revenge. While Dionysus' deception of Pentheus is shown on stage, the result of Pentheus's mission is recounted in a messenger speech. Likewise, the off-stage recognition-manqué, when Pentheus tears off his disguise in a vain attempt to save his life, is superseded by the recognition of her son by Agaue which takes place on stage, culminating in the aweful recognition of the god Διόνυσος ἡμᾶς ὤλεσ᾽, ἄρτι μανθάνω (1296). Within the larger circle of disguise and recognition completed by Dionysus is the parallel action of Pentheus, which fails.

One of the functions of the change of dress is to stress this parallel. As well as being an echo of ritual it is a theatrical device, integrated into the plot. I agree with those who see Pentheus's change of dress as an ironic counterpart, not only to the Cadmus/Teiresias scene, but also to Pentheus's own threats to take from the stranger his Bacchic thyrsus and to cut off his 'delicate locks' (434 ff.).[71] The change of dress also works like the emblematic changes of costume in tragedy that we have already noticed.[72] Just as in the *Persae* the entrance of Xerxes conveys to us visually the full significance of the defeat of the Persians, so the appearance of Pentheus in his disguise as a maenad, coaxed out by Dionysus, dramatically conveys Pentheus's loss of autonomy and defeat by the god.[73] Besides the symbolic meaning of the transvestism (Pentheus is transformed into a worshipper of Dionysus), there are other aspects of the two scenes which confirm this interpretation. At lines 857 ff. Dionysus explicitly associates the dress with the death to which it will lead:

ἀλλ᾽ εἶμι κόσμον ὄνπερ εἰς Ἅιδου λαβὼς,
ἄπεισι μητρὸς ἐκ χεροῖν κατασφαγείς,
Πενθεῖ προσάψων·[75]

Equally significant is the conflict between the two strategies of open attack under arms and spy mission in disguise on which the first of the two scenes turns. In the middle of this scene Pentheus calls for his weapons to be brought (809), as the gear appropriate for his sex and status as king and protector of the social and moral order. Dingel in fact identifies this scene as the arming scene of tragedy and believes that the weapons were actually brought onto the stage into the sight of the audience, thus making the conflict visually explicit.[75]

Therefore, to my mind, the fact that Pentheus is disguised in female dress is not enough to identify the basis of the second 'toilet' scene as a comedy element.[76] The change of dress is handled in a way consonant with tragedy, which rarely shows a change of costume taking place on stage, but does allow a return to the stage in a new or modified costume.[77] There is still a superficial similarity between the scenes of the *Bacchae* and *Thesmophoriazusae* which needs to be accounted for. The very explicit comments made as Dionysus adjusts Pentheus's dress are most unusual in tragedy, and could be taken as the closest tragedy could come to showing a disguising on stage. Yet for the meaning of the scene it is important that they represent a repetition of the dressing not shown on stage, and a correction by Dionysus of the disorder into which Pentheus has fallen in his new enthusiasm.[78] Seaford shows that the adjustments also have meaning as part of the initiatory ritual.[79] But they are still stage-actions and it is to them that the 'disturbing effect' of the scene is largely to be attributed.[80] Those who find humour in the scene are led to do so, I think, by the 'comic' handling of the action, for the realism with which the disguise is treated points up its incongruity. Dionysus himself anticipates a perception of the ridiculous in Pentheus's female dress (854).

What kind of humour is this? Words that come up in descriptions of the scene include 'gruesome', 'macabre',[81] 'grotesque'[82] and 'tragicomic'.[83] Of these I would regard 'grotesque' as the most appropriate, for it suits best the indissoluble tension between the tragic and comic which Seidensticker rightly discerns in the scene.[84] The grotesque arises from 'the confusion between a sense of the comic and something—revulsion, horror, fear—which is incompatible with the comic.'[85] What makes this scene grotesque is the element of incongruity or incompatibility in the transformation, which involves a systematic juxtaposition of opposites,[86] as well as the realistic presentation and the element of the physically abnormal.[87] The fact that the ironic gap in awareness between Dionysus and his victim is at its widest here also adds to the horror.

To conclude, the use of disguise in the *Bacchae* is to be set within the tragic tradition in which disguise is a plot device, and an element of intrigue. The change of costume entailed also functions independently as a dramatic device of tragedy. The play as a whole shows a further aspect of intrigue and disguise that we have found to be implicit in tragedy and explicit in comedy, and which finds its climax in our scenes, with the sense of Dionysus as the master plotter, manipulating and staging Pentheus's intrigue in a manner analogous to that of the tragedian as producer and stager of his characters in a performance of a play,[88] for the role of Dionysus in these scenes of the *Bacchae* is equivalent to that of 'Euripides' in Aristophanes' play, and as Seidensticker reminds us, Dionysus was the god of tragedy and comedy and presided over the dramatic festivals of Athens.[89]

NOTES

1. H. Grégoire (*Byzantion* 13 [1938], 396–9) proposed the emendation ἀφύων for the unmetrical ἀφύων of R and against the less immediately relevant ἰφύων of the Scholia and the Suda at *Thesm.* 910. The whole of this paper could be taken as an essay in support of the appropriateness of this emendation.

2. The parallel between the plots, as I have sketched them, may result from their possible common derivation from Aeschylus' *Pentheus*. Aeschylus wrote a series of Dionysus plays, and in the Agathon scene of *Thesm.* Aristophanes explicitly draws attention to the *Lycurgeia*, quoting from Lycurgus' reaction to the effeminate Dionysus in the first play of the tetralogy, the *Edonoi (Thesm.* 134 ff.). We are also told by the hypothesis of Aristophanes of Byzantium that the plot of Euripides' *Bacchae* was dependent on Aeschylus' *Pentheus*, according to Dodds (xxx ff.) the third play in Aeschylus' Theban Dionysus tetralogy. (See H.J. Mette, *Der verlorene Aischylos* [Berlin 1963], 141–8.) If then Dodds is right in suggesting that the disguise of Pentheus is a traditional element of the myth which did not originate with Euripides (xxviii, and on lines 854–5), what we may have is a comic version of Pentheus' disguise in Aristophanes and a tragic version in Euripides, with (in *Thesm.*) Agathon as the Dionysus figure and the Old Man as Pentheus. However, the disguise in *Thesm.* might be seen as parody of ritual transvestism. See further F.I. Zeitlin, 'Travesties of gender and genre in Aristophanes' *Thesmophoriazusae*' in *Reflections of Women in Antiquity*, ed. H. Foley (London and New York 1982), 194–7.

3. E.R. Dodds, *Euripides: Bacchae*[2] (Oxford 1963), xxvii–viii, and on lines 854–5, 912–76; G.S. Kirk, *The Bacchae of Euripides* (Cambridge 1979), 14–15, 93 ff. (on lines 857–60); B. Seidensticker, 'Comic Elements in Euripides' *Bacchae*', *AJP* 99 (1978), 303–20 (with bibliography in note 1); D. Sansone, 'The *Bacchae* as Satyr-Play?', *ICS* 3 (1978), 40–6; R. Seaford, 'Dionysiac Drama and the Dionysiac Mysteries', *CQ* 31 (1981), 252–75.

4. Op. cit. 305. 'Comedy elements' are defined as 'structural forms, characters, dramatic situations, motifs, themes, and story patterns which were already or soon to become typical elements of comedy'.

5. Cf. M.C. Bradbrook, 'Shakespeare and the Use of Disguise in Elizabethan Drama', *Essays in Criticism* 2 (1952), 167. For the later history of disguise see V.O. Freeburg, *Disguise Plots in Elizabethan Drama* (New York 1915); P.V. Kreider, 'The Mechanics of Disguise in Shakespeare's Plays', *The Shakespeare Association Bulletin* 9 (1934), 167–80; J.V. Curry, *Deception in Elizabethan Comedy* (Chicago 1955); K.A. Newman, *Mistaken Identity and the Structure of Comedy* (diss. Berkeley 1978).

6. For example, major changes of costume probably did not occur on stage in tragedy. See J. Dingel, *Das Requisit in der griechischen Tragödie* (diss. Tübingen 1967), 141–4 and O. Taplin, *The Stagecraft of Aeschylus* (Oxford 1977), 158 ff. on the arming of Eteocles in the *Seven*. Taplin is doubtful about whether the chorus don red robes at Aesch. *Eum.* 1028, and makes the point that it is not a *change* of costume (412 ff.), but see C.W. Macleod ('Clothing in the *Oresteia*', *Maia* 27 [1975], 201–3) for a discussion of the symbolic and emblematic use of dress in the trilogy.

7. E.W. Handley and J. Rea, *The Telephus of Euripides*, BICS Suppl. 5 (1957); P. Rau, *Paratragodia* (München 1967 = *Zetemata* 45), 19–50; T.B.L. Webster, *The Tragedies of Euripides* (London 1967), 43–8.

8. Roscher, *Lexikon* 5. 274 ff.; L. Séchan, *Etudes sur la tragédie grecque*[2] (Paris 1967), 121 ff., 503 ff.; H.D. Jocelyn, *The Tragedies of Ennius* (Cambridge 1969), 404 ff.

9. Jocelyn 408.

10. In contrast, Aristophanes shows both the 'disguising' and the taking of the hostage on stage (Handley and Rea 24; cf. Taplin 118 n. 1).

11. Cf. the role of the 'disguised' Odysseus in the debate with the Trojans in Eur. *Philoct.* (T.B.L. Webster, *Sophocles: Philoctetes* [Cambridge 1970], 4).

12. Fr. 17 Page GLP[3] (1950). The idea of an entry evoking the story pattern of the 'nostos' is Taplin's (124).

13. Fr. 704N.

14. Op. cit. 32–3.

15. That Aristophanes uses disguise here to convey the idea that he himself, as poet, is speaking through the actor's mouth, was pointed out to me by Dr. A.C. Cassio. Cf. W. Süss, 'Zur Komposition der altattischen Komödie', *RhM* 63 (1908), 12–38 = *Wege der Forsch.* 265, ed. H.-J. Newiger (Darmstadt 1975), 1–29, esp. 13.

16. τρυγῳδίαν ποιῶν refers ambiguously to the situations of both actor and poet.

17. These lines are parodic (Rau 29 n. 31).

18. Taplin 14.

19. For detailed analysis of this scene see Rau 29 ff., C.F. Russo, *Aristofane, autore di teatro* (Florence 1962), 59–60, 85–92 and Dingel (above, n. 6), 206 ff. For L. Biffi ('Elementi comici nella tragedia greca', *Dioniso* 35 [1961], 89–102) Euripides himself had already transformed Telephus into 'una specie ... di Ulisse della commedia' (97).

20. The earliest example would be Xerxes at *Pers.* 909 (Taplin 123 ff.).

21. Odysseus wonders at Philoctetes' dishevelled appearance: ἡ τε στολὴ ἀήθης· δοραὶ θηρίων καλύπτουσιν αὐτόν (Dio Chrys. *Or.* 59.5). Cf. Soph. *Philoct.* 226, 274.

22. My discussion of this scene assumes that both in Euripides and in Aristophanes the rags were represented by ragged costumes. This has often been doubted—in the case of Euripides, e.g. A. Pickard-Cambridge, *The Dramatic Festivals of Athens*[2] (Oxford 1968), 202 n. 14; Handley and Rea 29. C.W. Dearden (*The Stage of Aristophanes* [London 1976], 118 n. 14) also extends this scepticism to Aristophanes—but recently Taplin (36, 121 n. 1, 122) has questioned the necessity of maintaining that costumes had no naturalistic features. Dearden is influenced by a problem of staging in *Ach.* When did Dicaeopolis remove his rags? Russo (87) has suggested that it was in the course of his 'recognition' by Lamachus (593 ff.): Lamachus describes Dicaeopolis as πτωχός (593), and Dicaeopolis casts off his costume with the imputation (595). Line 593 is *Telephus* parody: Cf. line 578 with Rau 41.

23. 'Euripides' Rags'. *ZPE* 15 (1974), 221 ff. Do the rags which are emblematic of misery in Euripides' tragedies become symbolic of the writer's poverty of invention in Aristophanes' mockery of the poet himself?

24. L. Salingar (*Shakespeare and the Traditions of Comedy* [Cambridge 1974], 102–3) expounds similar ideas in relation to this scene: 'A metaphor, in brief, is one meaning impersonating another; an actor is a living metaphor. This, at least, seems to correspond to Aristophanes' view, though he is also aware of the logical gulf bridged by analogy in metaphor and, equally, of the actor's 'deceit' in assuming a role.' In spite of the similarity of approach and idea my work was substantially complete when I discovered his. I do not use the word 'impersonation' with the specialized sense he gives it.

25. A special feature of Aristophanes' exploitation of these ideas is the internalization of the playwright, whose relation to his own characters is seen as mimetic. See my article 'A Portrait of the Artist as a Young Woman'. *CQ* 32 (1982), 41–55 and Zeitlin (above, n.2), 171–81.

26. See R.B. Sharpe (*Irony in the Drama: An Essay on Impersonation, Shock and Catharsis* [Chapel Hill 1959], 4 ff., 12) on the functional primacy of impersonation in drama.

27. My discussion here owes much to the work on irony and drama of my father, Dr. D. C. Muecke, most recently in *Irony and the Ironic* (London and New York 1982), 66–85.

28. For suggestive discussions of the role of disguise in the *Odyssey* see F. Ferrucci, *The Poetics of Disguise*, transl. A. Dunnigan (Ithaca and London 1980), 34 ff. and D.J. Stewart, *The Disguised Guest. Rank, Role and Identity in the Odyssey* (Lewisburg, Pa. 1976). For Stewart the theme of the disguised guest is the 'chief organising idea' of the poem; he treats it through the perspectives of personal identity and the heroic code To both authors the use of deceit and disguise in the *Odyssey* suggests the meta-literary theme of artistic illusion and deceit (Ferrucci 52–3, Stewart 163–4). Stewart even compares the role of the poet in the *Odyssey* to that of the 'author' in Old Comedy (170)!

29. Cf. Taplin (124) on the *Odyssey* as archetype. As archetype of comedy, Euanthius 1.5, B. Knox, 'Euripidean Comedy' in *The Rarer Action*, ed. A. Cheuse and R. Koffler (New Brunswick, N.J. 1970), 89.

30. The parallel of Odysseus and Menelaus is provided by the *Odyssey*.

31. The definition is that of Freeburg (above, n. 5), 2. I take disguise as a change in personal appearance assumed or exploited in order deceptively and deliberately to conceal identity and maintain two roles. This would allow the Paedagogus's exploitation of his old age, and assumption of a false name (in Soph. *El.*) to count as disguise, but not the change in dress and appearance that makes Electra unrecognizable in Euripides' play.

32. F. Solmsen, 'Zur Gestaltung des Intriguenmotivs in den Tragödien des Sophokles und Euripides', *Philologus* 87 (1932), 1–17 = *Wege der Forsch.* 89, ed. E.-R. Schwinge (Darmstadt 1968), 326–44; H. Diller, 'Erwartung, Enttäuschung und Erfüllung in der griechischen Tragödie', *Serta philologica Aenipontana*, Innsbrucker Beitr. zur Kulturwiss., Bd. 7/8 (1962), 93–115. On recognition in relation to these themes see S. Dworacki, 'Anagnorismos in Greek Drama', *Eos* 66 (1978), 41–54.

33. *Story Patterns in Greek Tragedy* (London 1964), 50–1.

34. Op. cit. 52–3.

35. For Orestes as 'a type of principal in vengeance plot' see A.P. Burnett, *Catastrophe Survived* (Oxford 1971), 11, 12, 81.

36. W.B. Stanford (*The Ulysses Theme*[2] [Oxford 1963], 84 n. 9) points out that this disguise was anticipated by his beggar's disguise in Troy (*Od.* 4. 241 ff.). H. Lloyd-Jones (*GRBS* 12 [1971], 192 n. 40) suggests that the example of Odysseus (believed to be dead) may be a precedent for the pretended death of Orestes in the tragedies (cf. Soph. *El.* 62 ff.). Diller (96) suspects that the trick in *Choe.* derives from epic.

37. Translations of the *Odyssey* are from W. Shewring, *The Odyssey* (Oxford 1980).

38. At *Od.* 11. 455–6 Agamemnon tells Odysseus to come home secretly. See Ferrucci 48 and Stewart 58–60 on the forward references of this episode.

39. See Roscher, *Lexikon* 3. 955 ff. There is no explicit mention in the *Odyssey* of his killing Clytemnestra. See J.C. Kamerbeek, *The Plays of Sophocles, Part V, The Electra* (Leiden 1974), 1.

40. H. Lloyd-Jones, *Aeschylus: Oresteia, The Choephoroe* (London 1979), on line 571.

41. *Choe,* is the archetype of the plot in which recognition is followed by intrigue. On this pattern in Eur. *Cres.* see Webster (above, n. 7), 14 and Burnett (above, n. 35), Appendix on *Cresphontes,* 18 ff.

42. Cf. *Frogs* 1163–5.

43. On the relation of the δόλος to the revenge see G.H.R. Horsley, 'Apollo in Sophokles' *Electra*', *Antichthon* 14(1980), 20–1. No certainty has been reached in the dating of the two plays, though Euripides' *Electra* is generally thought to be prior to Sophocles'. See Kamerbeek, *Electra*, 5 ff. and H. Lloyd-Jones, Introduction to Karl Reinhardt, *Sophocles*, transl. H. Harvey and D. Harvey (Oxford 1979), xxii–iii.

44. Op. cit. 136–7.

45. When gods are associated with disguise it takes the form of a magical transformation (cf. Taplin 428, on Hera in the *Semele*). Dingel (above, n. 6), (140) points out that gods arrive in disguise (as frequently in the epics): Hera and Athena in the *Rhesus*, Dionysus in the *Bacchae*.

46. Op. cit. 163.

47. See Reinhardt op. cit. 175 ff.

48. I owe these points to Professor C.W. Dearden.

49. A.N. Pippin, 'Euripides' *Helen*: A Comedy of Ideas', *CP* 55 (1960), 151–63: on Teucer (154), on the role of clothes (151, 154).

50. A.M. Dale (*Euripides: Helen* [Oxford 1967] on lines 1050 ff.) points out that Menelaus's comment (παλαιότης … τῶλόγῳ) refers to the whole idea, the λόγς and θρῆνος. Taplin, however, (133 n. 2) favours Hermann's emendation ἀπαιόλη γὰρ….

51. See R. Kannicht (*Euripides: Helena* [Heidelberg 1969]) on these lines. Both he and Dale compare Eur. fr. 697N *(Telephus)*.

52. *CP* 55 (1960), 154–5; *Catastrophe* 82, 92 n. 10.

53. Cf. the suggestion that *Frogs* is a reply to the *Bacchae* (H. Jeanmaire, *Dionysos* [Paris 1970], 270).

54. Cf. *Thesm.* 867, 1012; Salingar (above, n. 24), 103–4, Muecke, 'Playing with the Play: Theatrical Self-consciousness in Aristophanes', *Antichthon* 11 (1977), 64 ff.; P. Rau, 'Das Tragödienspiel in den "Thesmophoriazusen"' in *Wege der Forsch.* 265 (above, n. 15), 339 ff.; Zeitlin (above, n. 2), 186–9.

55. Cf. *Thesm.* 910 with note 1 above, and line 935 ἰστιορράφος: L. Stone, *Costume in Aristophanic Comedy* (diss. Chapel Hill 1977), 333–5.

56. *CP* 55 (1960), 154. See also Kannicht 1. 53–73.

57. See Dingel 139 ff.: 'Requisit und Mechanema'.

58. Cf. Kreider (above, n. 5), 167–8. Kreider's observation that this is Shakespeare's practice should be supplemented by the extended study of Shakespeare's exploitation of 'discrepant awareness' in B. Evans, *Shakespeare's Comedies* (Oxford 1960).

59. Dingel (68) mistakenly, to my mind, accepts the view of Verrall and Tucker that 'Orest und Pylades erscheinen nach v. 651 verkleidet als Kaufleute' (but see his note 4):

60. Dingel (131–3, 152 ff.) does not consider the possibility of disguise.

61. Dingel 141 and n. 2.

62. Dingel 37 ff., 140.

63. Add to Seidensticker's bibliography (above, n. 3): Dingel 156 ff.; O. Taplin, *Greek Tragedy in Action* (London 1978), 76; R. Seaford, op. cit. (above, n. 3).

64. Dodds on lines 854–5. Kirk ([above, n. 3] on lines 857–60) expresses scepticism. To him the disguise suggests 'a variant of an old and widespread theme of death by mistaken identity.' See also C. Gallini, 'Il travestimento rituale di Penteo', *SMSR* 34 (1963), 211–28, esp. 215.

65. P. Ackroyd, *Dressing up, Transvestism and Drag* (Thames and Hudson 1979), 39. Seaford (258–9) interprets the disguise in relation to initiatory ritual.

66. The evidence adduced by Gallini (217) is very weak, but see Dodds on lines 453–9. Add now Aesch. *Theoroi* 58 and 69: γύννις ... ἄναλκις (of Dionysus).

67. Op. cit 258.

68. R.P. Winnington-Ingram, *Euripides and Dionysus* (reprinted Amsterdam 1969), 53.

69. Seaford 258 and n. 57. I agree with Dingel (157 n. 2) against H. Strohm (review of Dodds in *Gnomon* 33 [1961], 520–1), though I accept the emphasis the latter puts on deceit and trickery.

70. Dingel (142) underplays the thematic importance that the question of recognition retains. See also H. Strohm, 'Trug und Täuschung in der euripideischen Dramatik', *WJA* 4 (1949/50), 140–56 = *Wege der Forsch.* 89 (above, n. 32), esp. 362 n. 32.

71. Dodds, 191 ff. Kirk (101–2) doubts that lines 932 ff. are a deliberate reversal of lines 493–6. Cf. H. Diller, 'Die Bakchen und ihre Stellung im Spätwerk des Euripides', *Abhand d. Akad. d. Wiss. und. d. Lit.* (Mainz 1955) phil.-hist. klasse 5 = *Wege der Forsch.* 89, 469 ff., esp. 491. Already at lines 341–2 Cadmus has attempted to dress Pentheus as a worshipper of Dionysus.

72. See notes 6 and 20 above and Seidensticker 318. T.G. Rosenmeyer (*The Masks of Tragedy* [Austin 1963], 147–8) compares the red carpet scene of Aesch. *Ag.*, but does not make the connexion with the visual role of the costume in *Bacch.* On the emblematic use of costume see Dingel 142.

73. Rosenmeyer 147–9; Schmid-Stählin 1.3.676; Dingel 143–4: 'lediglich ... ist das Mechanema-Requisit zugleich Pathos-Requisit'.

74. Cf. the change of costume in Eur. *H.F.*, where Amphitryon, Megara and the children go indoors before the first stasimon to put on κόσμον ... νεκρῶν (329 ff., 442 ff.).

75. Op. cit. 156 ff.

76. Cf. Biffi (above, n. 19), 97.

77. Dingel 158.

78. An ironic reversal of Pentheus' earlier attempts to correct the 'disorder' of the Bacchants, as Dr. A.C. Cassio has pointed out to me.

79. Op. cit. 259.

80. Taplin, *Greek Tragedy* (above, n. 63), 76.

81. Taplin, loc. cit.

82. G.M.A. Grube, *The Drama of Euripides* (repr. London 1961), 9; Dingel 159; A. Lesky, *Die tragische Dichtung der Hellenen*[3] (Göttingen 1972), 494; Gallini 213.

83. Seidensticker 319. His view of tragi-comedy is that it synthesizes tragic and comic, whereas according to P. Thomson (*The Grotesque* [London 1972], 63) tragi-comedy in the normal sense involves a clear distinction between the comic and the tragic, the grotesque a fusion of the two. Cf. G. Wilson Knight, 'King Lear and the Comedy of the Grotesque' in *The Wheel of Fire*[4] (London 1977), 160–76.

84. Loc. cit.

85. Thomson 7.

86. Taplin, *Greek Tragedy* 76. Thomson 37: 'the macabre, if one understands it as the horrifying tinged with the comic, is a sub-form of the grotesque.'

87. Thomson 7–9.

88. Dingel (158) talks of Dionysus as 'Regisseur'. Cf. Salingar (above, n. 24), 111 ff. on the special connexion of theatrical metamorphoses with Dionysus, and H. Jeanmaire (above, n. 53), 301–12. See further H. Foley, 'The Masque of Dionysus', *TAPhA* 110 (1980), 107–33 and C. Segal, 'Metatragedy: Art, Illusion and Imitation', in *Dionysiac Poetics and the Bacchae* (Princeton 1982). The last two references are from Zeitlin (above, n. 2), n. 29.

89. An earlier version of this paper was read at the 21st AULLA Congress held from 27 January to 3 February 1982 in Palmerston North, New Zealand. I would like to thank Professors C.W. Dearden and K.H. Lee, and Dr. A.C. Cassio for help towards its revision.

JACQUELINE DE ROMILLY

Fear and Suffering in Aeschylus and Euripides

It would be a long but not difficult task to demonstrate the importance of these two emotions in the entire works of these tragic authors.[1] But the results would only be conclusive, however, if they were drawn from direct comparisons. After all, it is undeniable that there is as much 'suffering' in Aeschylus as there is 'fear' in Euripides. Our concern is rather to establish which of these two emotions each author emphasizes. We should therefore compare specific descriptions of these sentiments. But what instances should we choose? Indeed, there is scarcely anything in common between the terror which seizes Orestes at the end of the *Choephoroi* and Electra's pained anxiety at the prospect of someone unforeseen possibily arriving. Both these instances can be subsumed under the term 'fear', and yet one would hardly want to use them to demonstrate a difference of psychology, inasmuch as they are particular reactions to different stimuli. For this reason it seemed more valuable and significant to deal only with cases that are truly parallel. And since both Aeschylus and Euripides have many themes, dramatic techniques and even actual scenes in common, it would seem wisest to examine the relative emphasis each author places on fear and suffering in moments that are truly similar.

Under these circumstances we would inevitably see how on each occasion there is a kind of emotional symmetry between the two authors, one using fear as a mode of expression, the other employing suffering for the

From *Greek Tragedy*, edited by Erich Segal. © 1983 by Erich Segal.

same purpose, one author using 'anxiety' before the event, the other 'suffering' after the event.

Perhaps the paramount tragic theme common to both authors is the effects of war. Both men knew it first hand, and both evoked its cruelty. Each of them described the anguish and confusion of cities taken by assault and sacked. Yet how different are the natures of their descriptions. On the one hand we have Aeschylus' *Seven Against Thebes*, a play completely pervaded with descriptions of war. Granted, the city is not captured and will not be. And yet from their first entrance until the great scene of the shields, the women of the chorus never cease for an instant to imagine and discuss the imminent disaster. And they persist despite Eteocles' remonstrances. Their capture is anticipated in their imagination, the images unfold in a kind of great chaotic disorder. These are the women who are dragged along as 'widows of the defenders, alas, young and old together—dragged by their hair like horses, their clothes in tatters.' Thus there is chaos everywhere. 'When a city falls, alas, numberless are its sufferings. One conqueror may take prisoners, the other may kill them, still another may set the city on fire. Smoke will stain the entire city. The furious breath of Ares beats down the men and desecrates all they revere.'[2] But all these evocations by the Theban women have their impetus in anxiety: 'What will become of me?' they cry (297).[3]

Euripides, on the other hand, prefers to dwell on disasters which have already occurred. He loves to have them evoked after the fact by the women who have had to suffer them. Through the medium of their suffering he has them gasp out their memories. In this case we should examine the *Hecuba* or the *Trojan Women*, for—by a rather remarkable coincidence—both plays take place among captive women after the fall of Troy. It would be difficult to say with certainty which of these plays should be considered the earlier, because the facts in both plays are not consistent. And if the *Trojan Women seems* to be the earlier, it is perhaps only because its action takes place before the very walls of Troy.[4] And yet in each play the capture of the city has already occurred, an event one would logically expect to inspire mourning, but not anxiety. We find here the same themes repeated by Aeschylus now presented in a completely different tone.

The chorus in *The Septem* merely evokes an imagined scene of women being dragged along against their will with wild and brutal violence. But in the *Trojan Women* they actually appear before us. Here in a series of successive episodes we see one weeping woman after another each bemoaning all that they are leaving behind. Cassandra is but one example. After Talthybius says (419): 'Follow me to the ships,' she leaves the stage, enraged but still proud, on her way to captivity. The next episode shows us Andromache, entering on a Greek chariot (617: *agometha*). She has already prepared for departure and laments her destiny in the long scene at the end of which they begin to take her son away from her (774: *agete*). Finally in the *Hecuba* it is merely a memory, as the chorus of captive Trojan women sing 'I was dragged away, having seen my husband dead, dragged across the vast expanse of waves' (937: *agomai*). The violence has diminished somewhat; and fear gives way to sadness.

It is the same with the smoke of burning cities. Although the *Trojan Women* does conclude with the flames that will be the ultimate destruction of the city,[5] nonetheless in both Euripidean plays what is evoked is rather the morrow of a conflagration, with its somber traces of smoke. The Trojan women speak of it in the present (586–588): 'The sad end of my city where the ashes are still smoking.' The chorus of the *Hecuba* also says it,[6] but in the perfect (911–912): 'Everywhere smoke has blackened you with its sorrowful stain.'

It would now follow that the descriptions of that infamous night have also changed in tone. What causes sadness now is the contrast between the joys of a normal life and the mourning which replaces it. In the *Hecuba*, the women remember how they were seated before the mirror arranging their hair when they first heard the shouts of the Greeks. In the *Trojan Women*, they recall the songs and festivity with which they welcomed the notorious wooden horse. Neither of these scenes is at all violent,[7] but rather sad, immediate and natural. And their laments are mixed with an evocation: 'I have been ruined, sad captive that I am'; 'I am damned! Never more will I walk upon your soil'; 'But stricken by sadness I have succumbed to grief'.[8] A favourite Euripidean word, *talaina* [wretched, long-suffering] has a bitter echo which permeates the play from beginning to end.

If we add to this the fact that in the *Andromache*, the characters also hark back to the misfortunes following the capture of Troy, and its chorus devotes yet another stasimon to this recollection,[9] we will understand that this is a theme and an attitude dear to Euripides' heart. One might say that in his tragedies he loved to echo and re-echo the sobs of women in mourning, as wretched in one camp as in the other,[10] and a bitterness for a happiness forever lost.

The comparison between these different texts would be extremely characteristic if it did not give rise to a possible objection, which at first glance would seem quite serious. After all, Aeschylus also evokes those same tears of women in mourning. Indeed, he devoted an entire play to comment on defeat and massacre: *The Persians*. Here Aeschylus has also chosen to situate the action after the events, using the pain of those who were present to evoke memories of the battle, and to take as his protagonist the King's mother with all her sorrow. Aeschylus even makes the entire second part of the tragedy (with the exception of the scene with Darius), into a huge fresco of despair. And this play lacks the austerity and anonymous piety with which the *Septem* concludes. Here the dead are named in a long terribly real series, and the individuals play a role along with the conquered King and his mother. Aeschylus' decision to commemorate the Athenian victory in this particular form would seem to deviate sharply from the difference of dramatic emphases we have just established.[11] And yet all one has to do is re-examine the *Trojan Women* after reading the *Persians* to see how very different the tone is. Now and then in the *Troades* we do find an expression of grief or a lament for a dead person which might recall Aeschylus.[12] Yet the atmosphere of the two plays is quite different. For one might say that Aeschylus has done everything possible to inform his tragedy with a great sweeping forward motion which, every time it comes to a halt, brings back moments of anxious waiting, and with this waiting, fear.[13] The first 248 verses of the play—before the arrival of the messenger—is but one long cry of anguish. Then suddenly the messenger appears and announces the disaster. The chorus responds to his words with cries and sobs. For the moment at least, is not the period of anxiety completed? Not at all. For now the queen expresses her dread at the possibility of learning of Xerxes' death. Moreover, even after giving his first bit of news, the messenger has not said all. The long speech, deftly divided into successive phases (keeping the end to be the object of Darius' predictions), causes a certain amount of anxiety to remain, an anxiety which gradually emerges, with each successive revelation. Indeed, how could it be otherwise? The unending anxiety in the *Persians* is no accident, and it cannot be explained simply as a product of a playwright's clever technique. There are reasons far more profound: in the world of Aeschylus every misfortune becomes a sign of divine anger—with the fear of more to come. Consequently, even after the messenger has said everything he knows, a mood of fear still pervades the scene. And while the chorus agonises over what will henceforth become of the Persian imperial power (584 ff.), the queen, on the other hand, seeks to appease these gods, for their wrath still terrifies her about what yet may come:[14] 'Friends, whoever has known misfortune knows that from the very day a wave of evil has fallen upon them, men incessantly fear everything, whereas those who have a happy life believe that fate will bring them only joy. For me today everything is ridden with fear; all that appears before my eyes is the hostility of the gods, and all that touches my ears is the sound of catastrophe, saying that my pain will never cease—so great is the terror that grips my heart!' (598 ff.). Both she and the chorus want to know, to know when all this evil will at last come to an end (632).[15]

Thus the final threnody is really the only part of the tragedy devoted to grief pure and simple. Again we should note that even then, five out of the eight pairs of strophes are matched questions and responses, and contain a new bolt of pain which gives rise to yet another anxiety.

Therefore the apparent exception to the rule which the *Persians* supposedly represents, is in fact a confirmation: even when dealing with a real historic event, when Aeschylus wanted to describe a people stricken by a disaster, he still endowed his description with a force that made it a regular succession of grief followed by dread. In this sense, Aeschylus' tragedy stands in stark contrast to the futile laments which punctuate the entire *Trojan Women* turning it into a long series of misfortunes which come without having been feared. There is no remedy for these ills, and the only emotions they can evoke are suffering and resignation.

We can also compare the *Trojan Women* to another Aeschylean play. Both playwrights share a penchant for great scenic effects which are intended to create a moving and forceful impression. The *Trojan Women* concludes with just such a grandiose effect: Talthybius comes to announce that the time has come to depart; the captive women must go to the ships while what is left of Troy will be put to the torch, so that only ruins will remain. At first Hecuba wants to hurl herself into the fire of her burning city; but then she watches the fire, 'Ilium is but a flame; it scorches the roofs of Pergamum' (1295–1296). She and the chorus now throw themselves to the ground, beating the earth with their hands as a sort of farewell to the dead, just as the city itself is collapsing:

Hecuba	Did you see, did you hear?
Chorus	The crash of the citadel.
Hecuba	The earth shook, riven
Chorus	to engulf the city
	(1325–1326 Lattimore).

This spectacular ending inevitably evokes another: that of Aeschylus' *Prometheus Bound*. There the scenic effects, whatever they might have been, were destined to suggest the catastrophe which the Titan himself describes just as he is about to disappear, swallowed with his rock by the earth: 'But now there is action and no more words. The very earth shakes while, in its depths, the voice of thunder is roaring. Brilliant lightning bursts and burns;

a cyclone stirs the dust, the winds blow wildly at war against each other; the sky and the sea commingle' (1080 ff.). But if the action is similar, we must nonetheless bear in mind this end of *Prometheus* is not the end of the entire trilogy. Even during his downfall there remain threats and calls for revenge. Indeed the last words of the hero are not complaints at his misfortune but mighty proclamations against the iniquity of his suffering: 'O my majestic mother, and you, O sky, who makes the sun circle the world with its light, you see the injustices I must endure?' (1091 ff.). The crash which hurls Prometheus down with his apocalyptic roars, marks only one phase in a greater struggle, whereas when Pergamum falls at the end of the *Trojan Women*, the play (and the trilogy) ends on a note of irremediable misery.

Thus the facts are consistent. Unless a god makes a surprise visit to interrupt the course of events, human beings in Euripides must surrender. And thus in Euripidean drama the only ending is suffering.[16]

The difference in orientation which characterises the scenes we have studied may also be found in the plays as a whole. In a study written long ago, F. M. Cornford made the following observation: whereas in Aeschylus half of the so-called *kommoi* are lamentations, two-thirds of the *kommoi* in Sophocles are in this category, and eighteen of the twenty-one Euripidean *kommoi* are lamentations.[17] A nice proportion, but hardly surprising. For in the world of Euripides no one waits, no one stays on guard, men simply bend before a catastrophe which is already inevitable.

NOTES

1. I have pointed out the significance of 'fear' in Aeschylus in *La Crainte et l'angoisse dans le théâtre d'Eschyle* (Paris, 1958). B. Snell underscores the importance of this emotion in *Aischylos und das Handeln im Drama, Philologus* Suppl. (1928), 164 n. 8.

2. *Seven Against Thebes* 325–9; 338–44. I cite only a small passage from a much longer description.

3. In Aeschylus there is but a single description of the sacking of a city which does not take place *before* the event—and not inspired by fear. At least it is imagined before it is actually announced: Clytemnestra's evocation of what the sack of Troy may have been like (*Agamemnon* 320 ff.). Moreover, she concludes by expressing the fear that the conquerors will be in danger if their actions are excessively brutal. There is more of this same sentiment expressed in the two succeeding *stasima*.

4. In principle, *Hecuba* is regarded as the earlier: Cassandra is still present (88), and Polyxena—who is dead in the *Trojan Women* (621)—is still alive. But on the other hand the army is no longer at Troy (8).

5. See below p. 394.

6. We have the present at 477.

7. The most general—and chaotic—description is at *Trojan Women* 557–65, where it concentrates—yet again in Euripides—on the image of 'tender infants', clutching with frightened fingers at their mothers' clothing.

8. *Trojan Women* 518 (translation slightly altered); *Hecuba* 913; 942.

9. 1010 ff. (cf. 293 ff.). Here it is Troy itself that is *talainan talainan* (miserable). Moreover, the laments do not come from the victims. The instance is somewhat akin to that in *Agamemnon*. (See above, n. 3.)

10. *Androm.* 1037 ff.; cf. also, *inter alia*, *Helen* 1107 ff., *Hec.* 1107 ff., *Tro.* 1084 ff.

11. On the other hand, we will not dwell here on the notion that the *Agamemnon* deplores the misfortunes of the Trojan war. Aeschylus emphasizes this theme, but in the commentary of the chorus. He never makes an explicit statement of the sorrows and suffering caused by the war (the weariness is mentioned at 551 ff.). His descriptions of mourning are very strong, but always from a distant viewpoint, and as part of a great chain of crime and retribution.

12. The mournful perfect *bebasi* ('they are gone') repeated at *Persians* 1002 and 1003 is also repeated at a significant moment in *Andromache* (1023 and 1027) as well as twice in line 582 of the *Trojan Women*. We find it again in the *Suppliant Women* (1139) and *Orestes* (971).

13. Cf. Snell, (above n. 1), p. 67.

14. Yet even when she speaks of sacrificing to the gods, she must, in some way, excuse her behaviour and constant anxiety about what may come (525–6): 'I know it is for what has already happened, but perhaps we may henceforth have a happier future.'

15. This is the meaning of the scene with the ghost of Darius. This has a curious aspect, for though he comes from the dead he expresses disquiet about the future of his family—as if he did not know it.

16. One might even say that in other scenic effects we find the same disparity: the winged chariot that flies Medea off at the end of the play which bears her name recalls the winged chariot—or chariots—of the Oceanids in *Prometheus Bound*. But the latter is merely an aspect of the Oceanids' divinity, and merely calls attention to a concern with which their fear was not all bound up. On the other hand, Medea's chariot seems to have but one purpose: to situate husband and wife for a moment both out of reach yet within earshot, so their enmity can be welded into final and indissoluble suffering. The *Triptolemus* of Sophocles is too little known for us to make any judgments about the wingèd chariot used therein.

17. *Class. Rev.* 27 (1913), 41 ff. This was called to my attention by Professor J. C. Kamerbeek, who was kind enough to read an earlier draft in which most of the ideas were first put forth.

MALCOLM HEATH

Aristophanes and His Rivals

Just as there was a canon of three tragic dramatists, so the ancient world
recognized a canon of three dramatists of Athenian Old Comedy:
Aristophanes, of course, but also Cratinus and Eupolis.[2] This article is
chiefly concerned with Cratinus and Eupolis—a frustrating and
unsatisfactory subject. Their plays are lost, and we have to rely on meagre
fragments, preserved in quotations or on papyrus, and on various kinds of
indirect evidence about their work. There is therefore very little that can be
said about them, and even less that can be said with confidence.
Nevertheless, the attempt to say something is worthwhile, in part because of
the light that it may shed on Aristophanes' surviving works if we can discern
something of the context in which he was working, but also because these
men were evidently masters of their craft. One word of warning is in order:
despite their mastery of the comic craft, uproarious entertainment is not to
be expected from a paper on Cratinus and Eupolis; if jokes that have to be
explained are notoriously unamusing, what can we expect of jokes that have
to be reconstructed conjecturally before they are explained?

I shall begin with a playwright who was not, strictly speaking, a rival of
Aristophanes: Crates, whose career is thought to have ended before
Aristophanes' first play was performed in 427. Crates' output was small—
seven or eight plays over a period of perhaps 20-odd years; but three of them
took first prize at the Dionysia, so that he was proportionately very

From *Greece & Rome* 37, no. 2 (October 1990). © 1990 by Oxford University Press.

successful. If we can believe Aristotle, Crates made a crucial contribution to
the development of comic drama; he was the first (or possibly the first
Athenian) comic dramatist to compose 'universal' plots (*Poet.* 1449b5–9): 'As
for plotconstruction, originally it came from Sicily; of those at Athens,
Crates was the first to abandon the iambic form and construct universalized
stories and plots.' This is usually taken to mean that he abstained from
abusing individuals, an interpretation at first sight recommended by the
reference to iambic poetry (i.e., lampoons); so far as we can tell Crates did
abstain from abusing individuals. But that cannot be what Aristotle means.
'Universal', in the *Poetics*, is a technical term concerned with plot-structure:
a plot is 'universal' if the events which constitute it are connected with each
other 'in accordance with necessity or probability' (1451b8–9, cf. 54a33–6);
the opposite is the 'episodic' plot in which things happen one after another,
but not because of each other (1451b34–5). So the implication of Aristotle's
remark must be that earlier comedy had consisted of a series of essentially
independent incidents, and that it was Crates who began to tie them together
into a causally consequential plot, such as we find in Aristophanes.[3]

    This, if true, tells us something interesting about Cratinus. Cratinus'
career overlapped Crates' at both ends: he won his first victory in the late
450s, at least two years before Crates' first victory (as we know from an
inscribed list of victors), and survived to compete against Aristophanes in the
late 420s. So the implication of Aristotle's claim about Crates is that
Cratinus' earliest plays will have been episodic in structure, without a
causally coherent development of plot.

    There is something to support this judgement in the remnants of later
ancient scholarship on comedy. One anonymous source (test. 19) says that
the earliest Attic comic poets introduced their characters in a disorderly way
(ἀτάκτως)—a fair description of what Aristotle would call episodic structure.
Cratinus (it is said) checked this disorder, but without escaping from it
completely (which was left to Aristophanes). Platonius praises Cratinus'
inventiveness, but says that the development of his plots was incoherent and
inconsequential. So we may imagine a dramatist who is imposing some
structural coherence on his plots, perhaps under the influence of his
contemporary Crates, but whose plot-construction is even so less developed
than we observe in Aristophanes.

    It nicely reflects the limitations of our knowledge that the one case in
which we can gain some idea of Cratinus' handling of plot lends no support
to this hypothesis. Our knowledge of the *Dionysalexandros* ('Dionysus playing
the role of Alexander'—or, to use his other and to us more familiar name, of
Paris) depends largely on a plot-summary partially preserved on a papyrus

published at the beginning of this century.[4] Unfortunately the first part of the papyrus is lost, and the summary does not begin to make connected sense until the parabasis. Before the parabasis we know or can guess that there was a search of some kind; that Hermes appeared—he made an exit immediately before the parabasis, having made some arrangement about the judgement of the three goddesses; and that it has been arranged that Dionysus will take the place of Paris in judging the goddesses surreptitiously, in disguise. We do not know why this has been arranged, or on whose initiative. Given the devious Dionysus of *Frogs*, and the Hermes of *Peace*, easily flattered and bribed, I would guess that Dionysus took the initiative, lecherously wanting to see the goddesses naked.[5] But that is a guess; and with comedy, in which so much depends on bizarre and unexpected invention, guesses are more than usually precarious.

However that may be, after an encounter of some kind with the Chorus (which consists of satyrs accompanying Dionysus) Hermes goes to fetch the goddesses, and the Chorus are left to address the audience 'about the poets'. (There is a problem here to which I will return; for now just think of the parabases in which Aristophanes talks about himself and other comic poets.) Paris at this stage of his career is living as a shepherd on Mt Ida, so when Dionysus returns he is disguised as a shepherd; the Chorus make fun of him, perhaps because of his disguise. Then Hermes returns with the goddesses, each of whom offers Dionysus (Paris, as they suppose) an inducement. It is inevitable in comedy that a sexual inducement will be preferred; Dionysus awards the prize to Aphrodite.

There is a problem about the staging of this scene. If each of the goddesses spoke, as well as Dionysus and Hermes, we would have five speaking actors on stage at once; the evidence suggests that this was not possible.[6] So either the goddesses were put on show one after another, with lyric interludes between the scenelets, or else they were played by mutes and made their offers through Hermes, just as in Aristophanes' *Peace* Peace herself is a mute and communicates only through Hermes.[7] I prefer the latter reconstruction; having the goddesses visible together seems a better way to run a beauty contest. One other consideration favours their keeping silent: since the contest is properly one of beauty, the inducements are bribes, which can hardly be offered publicly; the offers should be made in secret. Hermes is an appropriate intermediary, not only as the divine herald, but also as god of trickery.[8]

Having awarded the prize to Aphrodite, Dionysus goes off to Sparta to fetch his reward; presumably a choral song covered the interval. He returns with Helen; but then things begin to go wrong. First he hears that the

Greeks have invaded and are looking for Paris (that is, for him). We know from *Frogs* that Dionysus is not a brave god, and now he panics. He hides Helen in a basket (the first attested use of this classic bit of slapstick, so far as I am aware), and disguises himself as a sheep; this gives us a context for a striking fragment, preserved by quotation: 'The idiot's going round saying, "baa, baa" like a sheep' (ὁ δ᾽ ἠλίθιος ὥσπερ πρόβατον ᾽βῆ βῆ᾽ λέγων βαδίζει, fr. 45). But then the real Paris intervenes; he discovers the miscreants, and gives orders to have them handed over to the Greeks. Helen, presumably and understandably anxious about her reception, is reluctant to go; Paris takes pity on her, and decides to keep her as his own wife (at least, pity is the only feeling the papyrus mentions: other emotions may have come into play in the original). So Paris keeps Helen, which neatly reconnects the plot of the comedy to the traditional story of the Trojan War. But Dionysus is still to be given back. The play ends with his being taken away, accompanied by the satyrs, who offer encouragement and promise never to desert him.

The play thus ends with a question-mark hanging over Dionysus' fate; this might be seen as a weakness in the plot-structure. But otherwise the handling of plot (in so far as we can discern it) seems admirable.

I must now admit much is uncertain even in the sparse account I have given. For example, I said that the parabasis is 'about the poets'; in fact the papyrus has not *TWN* but *YWN*, 'of pigs' or 'of sons', while 'poets' renders an abbreviation that has been interpreted in other ways. There are some scholars who think that something can be made of 'about making sons'; I am confident that Körte's emendation is right, but it remains a conjecture.[9] Again, I said that Hermes accompanies the goddesses; the papyrus does not mention him at this point, but this may be an accident, since it is clear on other grounds that some words have dropped out here through miscopying. His presence is a reasonable inference from the traditional story, but is, again, conjectural. This is not the only miscopying: in particular, Aphrodite's bribe has been garbled, although it is clear from what follows that Cratinus is adhering to the conventional story, and Helen was what was on offer.[10] Most irritating of all, between the title and the name of the author is another line with an eta, a space, and a gap in the papyrus. The eta almost certainly means 'or', introducing an alternative title (we have more titles for Cratinus than the attested number of plays); but what was the title? Of those known, *Idaioi* ('people from Mt Ida') has been suggested. In its favour are the locale and the fact, known from a scholion on *Thesmophoriazusae*, that the play contained a scene of disguise, in which (as in *Thesmo.*) someone was shaved (fr. 90)[11] There is also the possibility that 'divine forms' appeared in this play, although little weight can be attached to a possibility which depends on two emendations in a desperately corrupt scholion on *Ecclesiazusae* (fr. 91). However, the title implies a Chorus of people, presumably shepherds, from Mt Ida, and we already have a Chorus of satyrs. A second Chorus is conceivable, as in *Frogs*; I see no plausible role for them in the second part of the play, but since we know so little about what happened before the parabasis, a subsidiary Chorus cannot be ruled out.[12]

Another possibility is perhaps *Dionysoi* ('Dionysus and his companions', a use of the plural found in several of Cratinus' titles). Of that play we know only that the Chorus sang the line 'May he who speaks best for the city win' (fr. 52), which would fit a parabasis about the poets—unless the parabasis was about pigs or sons instead. This illustrates the kind of compound uncertainty that hinders any enquiry into lost comedies.

One other thing the summary tells us: the play attacked Pericles by innuendo for bringing the war on Athens. (On this basis the play is conjecturally dated to 430, early in the Peloponnesian War.) Although we cannot hope to trace the innuendo in detail,[13] the idea is plausible in principle. An obvious parallel is Dicaeopolis' speech in *Acharnians* (496–556), where likewise the Peloponnesian War is assimilated to the Trojan War, Pericles is blamed for it, and scurrilous motives are alleged. The Greek invasion and Dionysus' cowardly reaction to it could make an excellent satire on Pericles' defensive strategy in the face of Peloponnesian invasions, a policy we know to have been derided in comedy (Hermippus fr. 74); Athene's offer of 'courage in war' would then be an ironical allusion to this alleged cowardice of Pericles. A complication is that, while Athene offers (and Dionysus declines) something which Pericles did not have, Hera's offer of 'unshakeable tyranny' (also declined) alludes to something which Cratinus elsewhere claims Pericles did have (a theme we will return to shortly). So we can see various possibilities of political innuendo, but cannot tell how exactly Cratinus exploited them.

It is worth mentioning in passing that Cratinus' mythological burlesques did not always have a political target. According to Platonius, his *Odysses* ('Odysseus and his companions') was a straightforward burlesque of the Polyphemus episode in the *Odyssey*. This play began with Odysseus and his crew putting into land to avoid a storm; it seems that their ship was portrayed by some piece of stage-machinery, and one fragment suggests that steering was troublesome (fr. 143b)—there is obvious scope here for comic business. The fragments give us many of the elements of the story familiar from Homer, but without revealing how they were turned into comedy. Polyphemus was perhaps more cautious than in Homer: in one fragment he enquires about Odysseus' whereabouts; he is told—curiously enough—that he was last seen on Paros 'buying a huge ripe cucumber' (fr. 147). Certainly, Cratinus' Polyphemus was on a higher level of civilization than Homer's; instead of eating his victims raw, he took a lively interest in how to prepare them: 'for that I'll take all you "trusty comrades", and roast and boil and toast and broil you; I'll dip you in brine, and in vinegar-brine, and in garlic-brine; and whichever one of you seems most nicely done—I'll swallow him up, o soldiers' (fr. 150). 'Trusty companions' is a Homeric phrase, and the whole passage is written in hexameters.

Platonius, who tells us that the play was pure burlesque, also tells us that it was a forerunner of Middle Comedy, in that it had no choral lyrics and no parabasis. This is absurd. The play certainly had a Chorus—we have some of its recitative lines (fr. 151), as well as one fragment of glyconics (fr. 153); and you cannot have a Chorus that does not sing. It is possible that the play was preserved only in an incomplete text, without the lyrics. We know that some of Cratinus' plays did not survive at all; and the lyric portions of dramatic texts were sometimes omitted in copies.[14]

To return to the use of mythology in political satire: in a number of fragments Cratinus casts Pericles in the role of Zeus; again, *Acharnians* provides a parallel, which Dicaeopolis calls Pericles 'the Olympian' (530, cf. Telecleides fr. 17 Kock). Some of these turn on a joke about Pericles' head, which was oddly-shaped (this is why he is always portrayed wearing a helmet). In *Cheirones* ('Chiron—the centaur—and his companions'), the Chorus (presumably of centaurs) sang a mock-theogony. Cronos mates with Stasis (Civil-strife), and begets 'a great tyrant, whom the gods call ...': and then the Homeric epithet for Zeus, 'cloud-gatherer' is slightly altered, so that 'cloud' becomes 'head': κεφαληγερέτης (fr.258; another fragment of the same song casts Pericles' mistress Aspasia as 'bitch-faced' Hera—Homer says 'cow-faced'—offspring of Cronos and καταπυγοσύνη, shameless sexual misconduct: fr. 259).

This theogony combines the motif of Pericles as Zeus with that of Pericles as tyrant. The same combination is found in a fragment of *Ploutoi* ('gods of wealth'). The Chorus of this play consisted of Titans who, in the Golden Age when Cronos ruled, had been in charge of wealth; when Zeus overthrew Cronos, he had imprisoned them along with the other Titans. But now that the tyranny is overthrown and the δῆμος rules (δῆμος δὲ κρατεῖ, fr. 171.23) they have come back to visit their relative (αὐτοκασίγνητον, fr. 171.25); it is not certain what relative they are referring to: perhaps Plutus, the god of wealth, himself, anticipating Aristophanes' play. The overthrow of the tyranny and the restoration of democracy (the latter detail making it clear that a contemporary reference underlies the mythological joke) is generally taken as a reference to the impeachment and temporary ousting from office of Pericles in 430;[15] the play would then date from 429.

Not much of the action of this play can be discerned, but we know that an enquiry is instigated into the affairs of those who have been enriched, perhaps improperly, in the Chorus's absence. We have some lines from a scene in which the politician Hagnon is under investigation; his defence counsel denies that he is a dishonest *nouveau riche*: on the contrary (fr. 171.70) he is ἀρχαιόπλουτος (that is, he is from a traditionally wealthy family), since he has all his property ἐξ ἀρχῆς 'from the beginning'—but also 'from public office'.[16] This pun puts us in territory familiar from Aristophanes, with the automatic assumption that politicians are corrupt profiteers.

We do not know how *Dionysalexandros* and *Ploutoi* fared in competition. But there is no doubt that Cratinus was the most distinguished comic poet at work in Athens in 430–29, the years to which these plays are conjecturally assigned. But 429 was also the year in which Eupolis made his début; and Aristophanes' first play, *Banqueters*, was produced two years later, in 427. A challenge to Cratinus' supremacy was afoot.

Aristophanes' plays were at first produced on his behalf by others; it was not until 424, with the *Knights*, that he produced a play himself. In the parabasis of *Knights* (507–50) he explains his earlier reticence, and characteristically takes the opportunity to insult the audience: you are untrustworthy and treated earlier poets most unfairly. As examples of this unfairness he mentions Magnes (one of the great names from the earliest generation of Athenian comedy) and Crates (discussed already), but also, sandwiched between them, Cratinus. The placing of Cratinus between two poets whose careers were already over is not an accident. Aristophanes is full of praise for the talent Cratinus *used* to display; but he is scathing about his present drivellings. The audience's unkindness lies precisely in the way they make him go on spouting nonsense, even now he is incapacitated by old age and alcoholic indulgence; they ought to let him go into retirement and give him a seat of honour in the audience (*Kts* 526–36).

It cannot be emphasized too strongly that there is nothing to substantiate the picture of Cratinus which Aristophanes draws in this passage; it should be treated instead as an abusive and tendentious caricature of a still-vigorous rival. It is true that Cratinus was elderly (although if he began competing in the 450s he could still have been under sixty in 424); and there are enough jokes about his heavy drinking in the comic fragments to suggest that he was far from abstinent. But there is no reason at all to believe that he was incapacitated by age or by drink. Consider these facts. In the previous year, at the Lenaea of 425, Cratinus had been beaten into second place by Aristophanes' *Acharnians;* at the Lenaea of 424, he came second to *Knights* itself. The previous year's success obviously gave Aristophanes an opening for deriding his senior rival as past it, but it does not justify the claim; after all, Cratinus came second, not third. In fact, in 425 third place had gone to Eupolis, who was presumably no push-over, since he had won first prize at the Lenaea in 426, and was to win first prize at the Dionysia of 424. Cratinus was hardly, on this evidence, washed out.

In the following year, Cratinus got his revenge. At the Dionysia of 423 Aristophanes' *Clouds* failed (if there were only three comedies, it came third out of three, but that is now uncertain);[17] the first prize was awarded to Cratinus for his play *Putine* ('Wine-flask'), a play ingeniously founded on Aristophanes' slanders. We know something about its content from a scholion to *Knights.*

The chief character in the play was Cratinus himself, along with his 'wife', Comedy. The play began with Comedy explaining to the audience that she was going to leave Cratinus and sue for divorce on the grounds of neglect and ill treatment. But friends of Cratinus arrive and urge her not to act in haste; I take it that this is the entry of the Chorus. There followed a debate in which Comedy set out her complaints and Cratinus defended himself. The fragments indicate that this exchange was in iambic trimeters, rather than the recitative metres we generally associate with a comic agon (although there is always a margin of uncertainty about the assignment of fragments to any particular scene).

The details of Comedy's complaint are uncertain. Clearly, Cratinus was unfaithful; she speaks of him running after every pretty little bottle (οἰνίσκον a paradoxical substitute for νεάνισκον 'youth', in fr. 195). Some have thought of a mistress called Drink; unfortunately, when our source describes Comedy as complaining that 'he no longer writes comedy but devotes himself to drink', we cannot tell whether μέθη is to be construed as a personification, parallel to Comedy herself. But the sum of her complaint is clear: 'I used to be his wife, but am so no longer' (fr. 194; it is possible that another ground of complaint was poverty—at least, at some point in the play a character said 'I can't see even a cabbage-leaf or a bone any more': fr. 204). Of Cratinus' reply we have the first line, parodying a cliché of legal oratory: 'you are aware, perhaps, of the preparations [sc., of my opponent]' (fr. 197);[18] and the memorable epigram 'if you drink water you'll never get a good idea' probably belongs here (fr. 203). A fragment which praises the forcefulness of his expression may perhaps be a reaction to his speech (though since it refers to 'poems' this is doubtful); a nice touch is the way it echoes Aristophanes' double-edged compliments from the year before, exploiting the same metaphor of a torrent (fr. 198, cf. *Kts* 526–8).

As often in comedy, it seems that the debate did not resolve the issue.[19] In another fragment an unidentifiable speaker (not Comedy, since the speaker is masculine) wonders how to stop Cratinus' excessive drinking, and has the idea of smashing all his wine-jars (fr. 199). We also find Cratinus lamenting over an empty container: 'is your belly truly full of cobwebs?' (fr. 202). But at some stage Cratinus acknowledged the error of his ways (fr. 200), and there must have been a reconciliation between him and Comedy. There are traces of a scene in which two characters are consulting about the writing of a comedy. 'Don't talk nonsense,' one of them says, 'put him in an episode; Cleisthenes will be a laugh playing dice ...' (fr. 208); and 'rub out "Hyperbolus" and write "in the lamps"' (fr. 209)—a reference to the standard comic portrayal of the politician Hyperbolus as a lamp-maker, just as Cleon was represented as a tanner. This scene surely follows the reconciliation; for it must be Cratinus who is writing the comedy, and who better to offer advice than Comedy herself? The conception is stunning: the comedian is being advised by Comedy on writing a comedy in a comedy. Of all lost comedies, this is the one I would most like to read.

We also know a little about the play's parabasis. The epirrhematic section criticized the citizens for neglecting the navy (fr. 211); this passage included a personification of triremes (fr. 210), in which one can detect an echo of the personified triremes of the second parabasis of *Knights* (1300–15). That is cheeky: for the 'parabasis proper' contained a counter-attack on Aristophanes, and accused him of being a plagiarist (fr. 213), a point to which we shall return.

Putine is the last play that we know Cratinus to have produced, although given the gaps in our knowledge that does not prove that it was in fact his last play. We do not know the programme of the Dionysia of 422 or the Lenaea of 421. At the Dionysia in 421, in *Peace*, Aristophanes refers to Cratinus' death: he could not stand the sight of a wine-jar being smashed by the Peloponnesian invaders (700–3). Since there had been no invasion between the production of *Putine* in 423 and the *Peace* in 421, this cannot be taken very literally; and the joke would be just as good if Cratinus were sitting in the audience, so we cannot be sure that he really was dead by 421. Just as I disbelieve the portrait of Cratinus offered in *Knights*, so I think we should be cautious of the sentimental image some have constructed of the burnt-out old poet pulling himself together for one last heroic effort before he died. In reality, we know nothing about the end of Cratinus' career.

I mentioned that in *Putine* Cratinus accused Aristophanes of plagiarism, specifically of plagiarizing Eupolis. Eupolis himself took up this charge in a later play, claiming to have 'made a gift' of the *Knights* to 'baldy' (τῷ φαλακρῷ, fr. 89).[20] This was itself a reaction to the charge (which we find in the revised parabasis of *Clouds*, 553–6) that Eupolis had copied *Knights*, and made a characteristically bad job of it (κακὸς κακῶς).[21] What are we to make of these charges and counter-charges?

Reading through the comic fragments in bulk gives the impression that there was a common pool or repertoire of comic material: anything put on stage in a comedy would become public property and be absorbed into the repertoire, so that all comic poets contributed to it; and all drew on it, although each would aim to give a new and original twist to the material which he borrowed, so that the repertoire constantly evolved. If this was so, then any poet could lay claim to originality (since he gave the pooled material a novel twist); and any rival could make a counter-claim of plagiarism (since the material was in part drawn from the pool). Both claims have to be evaluated (and discounted) in the light of this constant process of exchange and evolution of material. The charges of plagiarism are part of a system of ritualized insults; they are not meant to be believed, but to make the other party lose face. There is a close parallel in Athenian political practice, where (as we know from Demosthenes and Aeschines) rival politicians swapped extravagant claims about each other's origins and morals.[22]

Invective based on a claim of foreign descent is a feature of the treatment of politicians by comic poets, as well as by other politicians; it was also a feature of comic poets' treatment of each other. Phrynichus, a contemporary of Eupolis and Aristophanes, was accused by his rivals of being a foreigner, as well as a rotten poet, a plagiarist and bad at metre. (These charges are recorded by a scholion to the prologue of *Frogs*, where Phrynichus is one of the rivals Aristophanes mocks. The note adds, rather touchingly, that there is nothing like this in Phrynichus' surviving plays, 'but presumably there was something of the kind in his lost works'; this commentator had clearly not grasped the ritualized character of such invective.)

Recall here the doubts about Aristophanes' origins that surface in the biographical tradition. If he were associated only with Aegina, we would obviously regard this as an inference from the parabasis of *Acharnians*, where Aristophanes associates himself with Aegina. But the sources also link him with Rhodes and with Naucratis in Egypt. This suggests the possibility that the charges are rooted in comic insults.[23] A fragment from one of Eupolis' parabases rebukes the audience for admiring 'foreign poets' and looking down on native ones 'at least as clever' (μηδὲ ἓν χεῖρον φρονῶν, fr. 392), which surely attests to the mutual, insults of comic dramatists; whether or not Aristophanes is one of the 'foreigners' specifically in view.

But let us now look more closely at Eupolis himself. The play which was, according to Aristophanes, plagiarized from *Knights* was Eupolis' *Maricas*, presented probably at the Lenaea of 421, that is, after Cleon's death, when Hyperbolus had come to political prominence. Hyperbolus (whom we have already met as a lamp-maker) was the play's target, disguised as the barbarian slave Maricas, in a household, with a master.[24] The basis for the charge of plagiarism is obvious. We can also trace some correspondences of detail in the fragments; like the Sausage-seller, Maricas had acquired only the rudiments of literacy (fr. 208; his education was informal, mostly picked up through eavesdropping in barbers' shops, which were centres of gossip: fr.194). In spite of these resemblances, *Maricas* was certainly not a mindless reproduction of *Knights*; even the scanty fragments, eked out now by the discovery of a few bits of commentary on papyrus (fr. 192), suffice to prove that Eupolis innovated while borrowing.

One addition that Aristophanes disparagingly attests to was Hyperbolus' mother (*Clouds* 552). There was a stock joke about Hyperbolus' mother being a bread-seller (just as Euripides' mother was supposed to sell vegetables): Hermippus, another contemporary, wrote a play about Hyperbolus which had a Chorus of bread-sellers, the *Artopolides*. The comic potential of the female bread-seller can be deduced from Aristophanes. In *Frogs*, Dionysus refers to Aeschylus and Euripides abusing each other like bread-sellers (857–8); and when Lysistrata summons the market-women as allies to beat off the policemen, it is the bread-sellers who provide the climax: ὦ σπερμαγοραιο-λεκιθο-λαχανοπώλιδες, ὦ σκοροδο-πανδοκευτρι-αρτοπώλιδες (*Lys.* 457–8). These allies are summoned specifically for their violence, abusiveness, and shamelessness (459–60). The bread-seller deprived of her wares appears in the *Wasps* (1388–1414; cf. 238), and also in one of Aristophanes' lost plays (*Geras*, fr. 129). Although he is not above exploiting bread-sellers himself, Aristophanes naturally puts an unfavourable gloss on the introduction of Hyperbolus' mother into *Maricas*, calling her 'the drunken old woman who danced the *kordax*' (*Clouds* 555; the *kordax* was a vulgar dance). Even that, he says, was plagiarized; Phrynichus had done it years ago (apparently in a burlesque treatment of the Andromeda story: fr. 71 Kock).

Another innovation in Eupolis' play, confirmed by the papyrus, was the division of the Chorus into two groups: rich opponents of Maricas, and poor supporters. One may compare the division of the Chorus in *Lysistrata*. It is easy to see how this division, with the added dimension of conflict it makes possible, could have been a distinct improvement on the uniformly partisan Chorus of *Knights*. But the fragments do not give much away about how Eupolis exploited this potential. We have one fragment (fr. 193) in which a politically naive common man is being questioned by Maricas in an attempt to frame Nicias on a charge of treason: ' "How long have you been associated with Nicias?" "I've never seen him—except just now, standing in the agora." "He admits it! He's seen Nicias! And why would he have seen him, if he wasn't a traitor?" ' The semichorus of poor men exclaims that Nicias has been caught red-handed; the rich semichorus dismisses the charge with contempt.

How the plot developed, we have no idea. The Chorus presumably united for the parabasis, in which Eupolis called on his audience to 'wake up' and to 'rub the drivel of ephemeral poets' out of their eyes (fr. 205), and which referred to a god angrily inflicting disease on an army—a denunciation of the folly of the Athenians and/or their leaders (fr. 206). But the Chorus seems still to be divided after the para-basis.

One other joke we can discern is a parody of Aeschylus' *Persians;* the beginning of the lyric part of the parodos, where the Persian elders sing 'the city-destroying royal army has crossed over', is emended, the royal army being replaced by the 'city-destroying Maricas' (πεπέρακεν μὲν ὁ περσέπτολις ἤδη Μαρικᾶς, fr. 207). This alludes simultaneously to Hyperbolus' alleged barbarian birth, and to the grandiose imperialist ambitions which are mocked also in the second parabasis of *Knights* (1303–4), where Hyperbolus is said to be planning to send a hundred triremes against Carthage.

The impossibility of reconstructing the plot of *Maricas*, even to the limited extent that we were able to reconstruct the plots of Cratinus' *Dionysalexandros* and *Putine*, is a problem that plagues us wherever we turn in Eupolis. But in a couple of other plays we can at least glimpse the comic idea on which the irrecoverable plot was based. Probably the most famous of Eupolis' plays in antiquity was the *Demes*, produced (it is thought) in 412. In it, four statesmen from the good old days—Solon, Aristides, Miltiades, and Pericles—were brought back from the dead to put Athens to rights.

The man who brought them back was called Pyronides. It has generally been believed that this Pyronides was identical with Myronides, the famous Athenian general active in the 450s. This identification gives rise to reconstructions like that of Page, in his *Literary Papyri*, in which the recently dead (this is a guess) Myronides reports the degenerate state of Athens to the other dead, who thereupon decide to send a deputation to the upper world to sort things out.[25] But the identification of Pyronides and Myronides rests solely on a corrupt variant reading in a single manuscript of Plutarch. I can see no reason why Eupolis should have changed the name nor why, if five dead men returned, Aelius Aristides, our main source, mentions only four. The identification is untenable, therefore, and Myronides should be left out of account entirely; Pyronides was an ordinary Athenian exasperated by the state of affairs in contemporary Athens (a man like, say, Dicaeopolis), who has the idea of retrieving someone from the dead to solve his problem (as does Dionysus in the *Frogs*)[26]

The discovery of a papyrus (fr. 99) with the end of the parabasis and parts of the following scenes gives us one fixed point in the plot to work with. After the parabasis, which contains attacks on various prominent contemporaries, Aristides arrives in Athens in company with Pyronides and greets his native land (fr. 99.35–6); they meet some unidentifiable interlocutor, and are welcomed by the Chorus, which also questions Pyronides about—something: his identity, journey, whatever (fr. 99.68ff.). What has become of the other statesmen? They cannot have arrived before Aristides, because the Chorus seems to be greeting Pyronides for the first time; but not more than sixty lines into this scene a plurality of visitors from the dead are seated together (with Pyronides alone remaining standing, and talking to the Chorus: fr. 99.64–5). So the other statesmen must have arrived with Aristides, and must have been played by mutes; at any rate, if we have Aristides, Pyronides, and the unidentified interlocutor as speaking parts, we clearly cannot have all the other statesmen speaking as well. (The constraints are the same as with the goddesses in *Dionysalexandros*.)

The papyrus also contains fragments of a subsequent scene in which a sycophant tries to justify his activities, describing an incident in which he had tried to blackmail a foreigner on a trumped-up charge of profaning the Eleusinian Mysteries: he had barley in his beard, and a barley-drink was used in the Mysteries, so clearly he must have been involved in a parody of them (fr. 99.81–2). Aristides the Just has him carted off to summary punishment, and lectures the Athenians on the importance of justice (fr. 99.112ff.).

Although the other statesmen were probably played by mutes after the parabasis, with Aristides as their spokesman, the others did speak at some point in the play; we have fragments in which Miltiades and Pericles speak (fr. 106, 110). Furthermore, although the four apparently arrive in Athens together, there is also evidence that at some point in the play they were introduced on stage one after another (if they are all to speak, this procedure is inevitable). The last in the series was Pericles, and Eupolis revives the old joke about his head: Pericles is the 'summing up' of those from below, κεφάλαιον (fr. 115). Pericles then asked about his sons (fr. 110, 111, 112; the dead are interested in news from up here, as in the *Odyssey*, 11.492–3) and perhaps about the state of oratory—at any rate, there is discussion at some point about contemporary oratory (fr. 103, 116). Since sons and oratory are both treated as degenerate, Eupolis is here engineering an opportunity to insult living individuals.

This serial introduction of the statesmen must have occurred before the parabasis. Presumably it was Pyronides who gave them news about the living; there are also traces of someone who introduced the dead to him—a guide or assistant, whose identity is unknown (fr. 102). Given the parallel in *Frogs*, it is natural to assume that Pyronides went down to the underworld to get his statesmen; and the Chorus do speak of him as having 'come' from somewhere (fr. 99.70). But this is not the only way to raise the dead—we have seen already that Eupolis had read Aeschylus' *Persians*. So perhaps we should remain agnostic on this point, as on many others; in particular, one would like to know how the continuity of the Chorus before and after the parabasis was handled.[27]

The comparison of Pyronides with Dicaeopolis and Dionysus in the *Frogs* should recall the point made earlier about the shared repertoire of comic material, drawn on by the poets, but constantly varied and reworked. The buffoonish Dionysus of *Frogs* was a more common and stereotyped element in comedy than the surviving works of Aristophanes suggest. He appeared in our first example, *Dionysalexandros*, and also in Aristophanes' lost *Babylonians*; he also appeared in my last play, Eupolis' *Taxiarchs* (the taxiarchs were the elected commanders of the infantry contingent of each of the ten Athenian tribes).[28]

Apart from Dionysus himself, the leading character in this play was Phormio, the great Athenian general, active since 440, but best known for the naval victories described in the second book of Thucydides. Phormio is mentioned in *Lysistrata* as an example of the rugged, manly soldier type (*Lys.*801–4); and clearly he fitted the same mould in Eupolis' play: 'don't you know my name is Ares?', he asks in one fragment (fr. 268.13). The contrast with the soft, effeminate, and cowardly Dionysus has obvious comic potential, which Eupolis tapped by making Dionysus a new recruit who Phormio has to train in military ways; for example, he was instructed in how to hold his shield (fr. 276), and in how to row: 'Stop spraying us, you in the prow ... stretch out your leg ...' (fr. 268.50–3). The parallel with Dionysus' rowing-lesson in *Frogs* (197ff.) leaps to mind here, and illustrates again how foolish it would be to take seriously Aristophanes' charges of plagiarism.

Presumably Dionysus made a complete mess of his training. Certainly, he was unpromising raw material: he came to the camp equipped (as

Phormio contemptuously remarks) with a bath-tub and a cauldron, like a female camp-follower from Ionia (fr. 272, the Ionians being regarded as notoriously soft); he may even have had a parasol (fr. 481). He is confronted with the grim facts of military rations: a peeled onion and three salted olives (fr. 275); but he retains a longing for a better way of life, 'Naxian almonds to eat and wine to drink from Naxian vines' (fr. 271; the god Dionysus had a particular association with Naxos). But how this potentially rich situation was developed (to what extent, for example, Phormio was deflated by his inept pupils, as Aristophanes deflates Lamachus)—once more, we do not know. The information we have in this case is so sparse that the limits of responsible speculation are encountered even sooner than with the other plays I have discussed. The greatest wisdom in the study of lost plays is the knowledge of when to fall silent.

Notes

1. This paper was given to the Oxford Branch of the Classical Association on 17 May 1989. References to comic fragments and testimonia are to R. Kassel and C. Austin, *Poetae Comici Graeci* (Berlin & New York, 1983–), unless otherwise specified.

2. 'Plures eius [sc., antiquae comoediae] auctores, Aristophanes tamen et Eupolis Cratinusque praecipui,' Quint. 10.1.66; cf. Hor. *Sat.* 1.4.1.

3. I have argued for the coherence of Aristophanes' plots in *Political Comedy in Aristophanes* (*Hypomnemata* 87, Göttingen, 1987), pp. 43–54; for a more detailed discussion of Aristotle's notice of Crates see *CQ* 39 (1989), 348–52.

4. For a translation see F. H. Sandbach, *The Comic Theatre of Greece and Rome* (London, 1977), p. 49; some severely damaged scraps are omitted, and the text of Aphrodite's offer translated is probably corrupt (see n. 10 below).

5. For this portrayal of Hermes see my paper in *PLLS* 9 (1990).

6. See K. J. Dover, *Aristophanic Comedy* (Berkeley, 1972), pp. 26–8; the strongest evidence is provided by *Clouds* 887, where Socrates has to make an unmotivated exit to release an actor for the confrontation of Right and Wrong.

7. The former solution is preferred by E. W. Handley, *BICS* 29 (1982), 113; the latter by W. Luppe, *Philologus* 110 (1966), 173–4.

8. On Hermes *dolios* in Aristophanes see Heath (n. 5).

9. The most recent discussion supports the conjecture: W. Luppe, *ZPE* 72 (1988), 37–8.

10. See W. Luppe, *GGA* 227 (1975), 187–90, *Philologus* 124(1980), 154–8. (The summary was copied onto the beginning of the roll by its owner, who was evidently careless; cf. Handley (n. 7), 114.)

11. The youthful Paris would naturally be portrayed beardless. Since Dionysus himself was usually portrayed as beardless in the late fifth century, it could be argued that he would not need shaving; but the bearded Dionysus is also found.

12. Luppe (n.7), 184–91 argues for *Idaioi* as the alternative title, taking the shepherds as the main chorus and the satyrs as subsidiary; Handley (n. 7), 115 is rightly cautious of this proposal.

13. For a notably flat-footed attempt see J. Schwarze, *Die Beurteilung des Perikles durch die attische Komödie* (Zetemata 51, Munich, 1971), pp. 6–24.

14. For the omission of lyrics see W. S. Barrett, *Euripides, Hippolytus* (Oxford, 1964), p. 438 n. 2 (Taplin's sceptical discussion, *LCM* 1 (1976), 47–50, infers from the use of the formula χόρου μέλος where no lyrics had originally been composed that it was not used where the original lyrics had been omitted; this does not follow). Platonius' notice is discussed by M. Bertan, *Atene e Roma* 29 (1984), 171–8.

15. This interpretation is impossible if Pericles was restored to office before the following year's elections (thus, e.g., Gomme on Thuc. 2.65.4). For the contrary view see C. W. Fornara, *The Athenian Board of Generals from 501 to 404* (Historia Einzelschriften 16, Wiesbaden, 1971), p. 55; D. Kagan, *The Archidamian War* (Ithaca, 1974), p. 93 and n. 69.

16. Some scholars are sceptical about this pun. W. Luppe, *WZHalle* 16.1 (1976), 79–80 and n. 105, followed by Schwarze (n. 13), p. 47 n. 105, distinguishes ἐξ ἀρχῆς from ἐκ τῆς ἀρχῆς; but many Aristophanic puns put a greater strain on 'common usage'. J.C. Carrière, *Le carnaval et la politique* (Paris, 1979), p. 280, objects that the speaker is supposed to be defending Hagnon, but see K.J. Dover (n. 6), pp. 59–65, on 'discontinuity of characterisation'.

17. For the assumption that the number of comedies performed was reduced from five to three during the Peloponnesian War, cf. A.W. Pickard-Cambridge, *The Dramatic Festivals of Athens*² (Oxford 1968), p. 83; *contra* W. Luppe, *Philologus* 116 (1972), 53–75.

18. Cf. Andocides 1.1, Lysias 19.2, L. Radermacher, *Artium Scriptores* (SB Vienna 227.3, 1951), C29; παρασκευή often implies corrupt machinations, e.g. Lys. 13.12 δικαστήριον παρασκευάσαντες, of a 'packed' jury, cf. 13.26, 28, Dem. 43.38.

19. Cf. T. Long, *TAPA* 103 (1972), 285–99.

20. For Aristophanes' 'baldness' cf. *Knights* 560, *Peace* 767–74; the Eupolis fragment is discussed by A.H. Sommerstein, *CQ* 30 (1980), 51–3.

21. It is not safe to assume that Aristophanes attacked Eupolis for plagiarism only in the revised parabasis of *Clouds* (for another possible case see fr. 58, with the note in Kassel-Austen; others may simply have been lost). Hence D.P. Fowler's claim that Eupolis 'can rely on the audience knowing the revised *Clouds*' (*CQ* 39 (1989), 258) is groundless, and no inference can be drawn concerning *Buchpoesie* in fifth-century Athens.

22. On the use of humour in political invective see P. Harding, *Phoenix* 41 (1987), 29–32.

23. Cf. M.R. Lefkowitz, *The Lives of the Greek Poets* (London, 1981), pp. 112–13.

24. On the derivation of the name Maricas from Old Persian ('male child', whence 'slave' and 'rogue') see A. C. Cassio, *CQ* 35 (1985), 38–42, with J.D. Morgan, *CQ* 36 (1986), 529–51. Morgan cites the comic and rhetorical invective against Hyperbolus based on his alleged servile or foreign birth; it is, of course, nonsense: H. Wankel, *ZPE* 15 (1974), 88–9.

25. D.L. Page (ed.), *Select Papyri, 3: Literary Papyri, Poetry* (London, 1941), 202–4. Since the text is outdated, the translations in this volume should also be used with caution.

26. For the source of the 'Myronides' confusion, see Kassel-Austin's apparatus to fr. 110, with that to fr. 100 for the correct form; they retain the identification, but cannot solve the problems it entails ('cur hoc nomine Myronides comice appellaverit ... poeta non liquet'). The contrary arguments in K. Plepelits, *Die Fragmente der Demen des Eupolis* (Vienna, 1970), pp. 116–32, are convincing.

27. For an unconvincing discussion see Plepelits (n. 26), pp. 69–75.

28. Other appearances of Dionysus in Old Comedy are known: Aristophanes wrote a *Dionysus nauagos*, Aristomenes a *Dionysus asketes*; two plays entitled *Dionysus* are attributed

to Magnes; Dionysus appeared in Ameipsias' *Apokottabizontes* and a play of Hermippus (fr. 77, spoken by Dionysus according to Athenaeus).

JON D. MIKALSON

The Tragedians and Popular Religion

Previous chapters have frequently noted similarities and differences of religion in tragedy and in fifth-century Athenian life. Here I summarize these similarities and differences, first as they consistently appear in all three tragedians, then turning attention to Aeschylus, Sophocles, and Euripides individually and pointing to ways in which each idiosyncratically presents elements of popular religion. Here we must keep in mind the components of religion in tragedy described in the Preface: (1) the anthropomorphic deities of the Homeric epics; (2) beliefs and deities once part of popular religion but in the classical period virtually extinct; (3) deities, beliefs, practices, and cults of contemporary society; (4) a concern with the morality and justice of the gods; and (5) contemporary or recent philosophical conceptions of deity. The similarities of tragedy and life are obviously to be explained by the third element: that the tragedians employed deities, beliefs, practices, and cults of contemporary society. When the tragedians consistently share a difference from practised religion, we might reasonably speak of a tragic convention. For understanding these tragic conventions and for the differences between the individual dramatists we must look to the other components of the hybrid of religion in Greek tragedy.

Conclusions on the similarities and differences between religion in tragedy and in life and between poets are necessarily general in nature, subject to exceptions. Differences between the poets are largely a matter of

From *Honor Thy Gods*. © 1992 by the University of North Carolina Press.

frequency and tone, not of single occurrence. Almost any idea expressed about religion or gods in Aeschylus can be paralleled by a line from a play or fragment of Euripides. The significant differences are those which occur frequently and appear to be emphasized.[1] Against such differences the isolated counter-example cannot be given much weight. Hence in the following pages I stress persistent similarities and differences. The details have been assembled in chapters 2–5. Here I draw from them the general outlines.

The Olympian gods of tragedy are often abstracted from cult limitations of time, place, and function. Whereas Athenians worshiped at different altars, with different rites, on different occasions, and for different purposes Zeus Boulaios ("Of the Boule"), Zeus Phratrios ("Of the Phratries"), Zeus Herkeios ("Of Fences") and Zeus Ktesios ("Of the Stores") in family cult, Zeus Olympios, Zeus Soter ("Savior"), Zeus Horios ("Of Boundaries"), Zeus Teleios ("Of Marriage"), Zeus Naios of Dodona, and so forth, the tragedians, like Homer, tend to represent one generalized Zeus, the Zeus of the epic cycle who is married to Hera, rules on Mount Olympus, and wields the thunderbolt. The worship and the tragic representation of other Olympian deities are analogous to that of Zeus.[2] There are, of course, exceptions, such as the Athena and Apollo of Euripides' *Ion* and the Athena of Aeschylus' *Eumenides*, where the poets have established some ties to Athenian cult.

   Once abstracted from cult these same deities may be refashioned. Aeschylus' reshaping of the Homeric Zeus is discussed at some length later in this chapter. Euripides on occasion made Olympian deities into, at least in part, representatives of psychological forces, like the Artemis and Aphrodite of the *Hippolytus* and the Dionysus of the *Bacchae*. In most plays, however, he like Sophocles follows the Homeric model of composite Panhellenic deities living as a family on Olympus and not closely tied to local cults. The Homeric deities and divine machinery are the standard in tragedy, and variations from it reflect personal or dramatic interests of the individual poets.

The tragic poets give to their characters a closer relationship to, more direct contact with, and a better knowledge of their gods than average Athenians enjoyed. Some characters, like Theseus, Heracles, Ion, and Helen, are sons or daughters of gods; others, like Cassandra, Creusa, and Io, are their lovers. In Sophocles' *Ajax* Odysseus and Ajax are intimates with Athena in the Homeric model of the *Iliad* and *Odyssey*.[3] Other tragic figures—men such as Orestes, Hippolytus, and Pentheus—for good or ill, also have close encounters with gods. Numerous other characters and choruses see their gods, usually as *dei ex machina*, and learn directly from them their wishes, plans, and purposes.[4] Real-life Athenians when awake never saw, or even claimed to have seen, Olympian gods.[5] Oracles and seers in tragedy also explain, much more so than their counterparts in real life, the ways and purposes of the gods,[6] so that tragic characters are, by and large, much better informed of what the gods do and why they do it. This degree of intimacy with and knowledge about the gods is thus, compared to popular religion, a tragic convention. It is also a Greek literary convention, found in nearly identical form as early as the *Iliad* and *Odyssey*. Like Homer the tragic poets adopt a pose of omniscience and know which god intervened in each situation and why.[7] Homer, as narrator, may provide this information himself, but tragic poets convey it, if they wish, through seers or the gods themselves. As a result the religion of tragedy has, compared to that of everyday life, far greater specificity. The audience and often the characters know in detail what the gods do and how and why they do it. This is the order that poets, from their superdivine, omniscient posture, can impose on situations which would have been, to ordinary people, often bewildering and inexplicable.

The gods of tragedy provide many of the benefits that their real life counterparts did. Individual gods have special areas of expertise and activity, but, taken together, individual gods and "the gods" as a collective give fertility and health of human beings and their crops and animals. They offer protection against the greatest hazards of Greek life: disease, sea travel, and war. To individuals and states they give economic prosperity. These three major areas of divine intervention—fertility and health, protection, and prosperity—are found throughout Greek tragedy and life. In these matters there are differences between life and tragedy, but they are of detail, not substance.[8]

The gods of tragedy, more than those of life, are blamed for evils.[9] This goes beyond Aphrodite's causing the deaths of Phaedra and Hippolytus or Dionysus' causing that of Pentheus. Throughout tragedy many misfortunes of life, including death, which in popular religion are attributed to fate, fortune, or a *daimon*, are attributed to the collective of the gods. As a result tragic characters—themselves, of course, often in perilous situations—are fearful of what the gods may bring and distrustful of the beneficence of their gods. This fear arises in part because the poets make their characters more aware than ordinary people of the plans and purposes of the gods. But in general terms, the gods of literature are more hostile, less beneficent, and less forgiving than those of popular religion. The sins of tragedy are more heinous than those commonly committed in everyday life, and the gods are more harsh and more feared. In the distilled world of Greek tragedy sins, punishments, and divine emotions are all more potent.

In both life and tragedy the gods were concerned with oaths taken in their name and with the rights of parents, *xenoi*, those having asylum,[10] and the dead. It was the consensus of popular belief that violators in these matters were deserving of punishment. In all the plays of Aeschylus, Sophocles, and Euripides all such violators suffer, and it seems indisputable that the tragedians were thus lending support to these core popular beliefs about piety and impiety.[11] In both tragedy and life those who planned but did not accomplish the violation escaped punishment. What mattered was the action, not the frame of mind.[12]

Tragedy, as distinct from life, frequently presents individuals who directly and frontally assault the τιμή of a god: the *theomachoi*.[13] Although not unknown to epic,[14] the human *theomachos* is particularly a topic of tragedy. Because the *theomachos* overvalues his own prowess, whether of mind or body, he demeans the τιμή (as function, honor, and cult) of the god. Unlike more ordinary sinners in life and tragedy, he may suffer for his boasts alone. His punishment, when it comes, as it always does, is severe. Every *theomachos* dies, and by his defeat and death the τιμή of the god is reasserted.

Because impiety was a form of injustice, the gods who in life and tragedy punish sinners also punish certain forms of injustice. But a wide area of injustice lay outside the realm of impiety, and both tragedy and popular religion, though by different means, attempted to involve their gods in these. Through promissory oaths by new citizens, by jurors, by public officials, by signatories to treaties, and by parties to a contract, and through assertory oaths in legal proceedings, the Athenians attempted to motivate divine interest in and concern for profane matters which otherwise were alien to the gods' functions.[15] The tragedians, as we have seen, rarely use oaths for such purposes and tend rather to make their gods personally interested in justice.[16] That the gods, Zeus in particular, be just is a preoccupation of Aeschylus', but we find also in Sophocles and Euripides characters who assert that the gods are, or should be, just. They invoke the gods to help them in their just causes and often complain bitterly when the gods fail them. In such cases the justice attributed to the gods or demanded of them is identical or similar to that expected in dealings between men.

There is little evidence that the personal justice or morality of the gods was a concern in popular religion. In literature they are first unmistakably an issue in the *Odyssey* and become a focus of attention in Hesiod and Xenophanes.[17] It was from this literary and theological tradition, not from cult, that they found their way into tragedy. After the fifth century they were developed in the philosophical tradition, especially by Plato. Throughout the classical period the justice and morality of the gods remained matters for theological and philosophical speculation, not for cult and worship.

The heroes of tragedy and cult also differ.[18] Some heroes who received cult in real Athenian life, especially Theseus and the eponyms of the ten tribes, were regarded as beneficent, as providing valuable services to their fellow Athenians, and apparently had nothing fearful about their sanctuaries or rituals. But most heroes of tragedy, such as Oedipus and Eurystheus, are hostile, malignant forces who must be appeased and whose cult is pervaded by fear. Their hostility to their own people, left behind in other countries, may benefit the Athenians, but that benefit is primarily a by-product. Here tragedy may reflect the character of older hero cults, whereas the beneficent heroes may be largely the result of politically motivated innovations of the sixth and fifth centuries. In any case the heroes of tragedy are much grimmer and more fearful than those of real life. It is also noteworthy that in tragedy the funeral cults of deceased kings, like Agamemnon and Darius, are presented in the guise of hero cult. As such the dead kings could be invoked and expected to aid the living, beleaguered members of their families.

As their audiences did, tragic characters consult oracles on colonization, plague, infertility of land and humans, marriage, disease, and identity of parents. They question seers about war, voyages, health, omens, dreams, and religious needs. But the conventions of divination in tragedy contribute to a religious atmosphere significantly different from that of practised religion. The responses tragic characters receive, whether they believe them or not, are virtually all accurate and true.[19] This is a convention also found in Homer, a convention of "high" literature but not of comedy.[20] Real oracles were mostly directed to changes in religious cult or to the success of foreign enterprises such as colonization, and real seers tested for their clients the likely success of private and public ventures. Tragic oracles, seers, and *dei ex machina* explain the deeds, plans, and purposes of the gods and offer detailed predictions of the fortunes of individuals and families.[21] Tragic characters are thus better informed of the divine world about them, but as a result characters such as Oedipus and Orestes seem subject, to some degree, to the inevitability of the events predicted about them. Because, unlike in life, the fates predicted by tragic seers and oracles are usually bad, the characters often appear to be functioning in a world of malignant divine forces. The same can obviously be said of Hippolytus, Phaedra, Ajax, and the Trojans, whose misfortunes are all planned and directly predicted by gods themselves, speaking in the prologues.

It is another tragic convention that prophetic dreams prove true and that they are "nightmares" sent from the chthonic world.[22] Athenians of the classical period received their dreams from the Olympian gods, and most of their dreams pointed to good fortune or ways of achieving one's purpose. The oracles, seers, dreams, and predictions of gods in tragedy cast forth a dark cloud under which characters live their lives. Gloom and uncertainty are sometimes increased by riddling or misleading oracles, themselves a literary convention. By contrast, to the ordinary Athenian divination was a positive factor in daily life, a practice that clarified life and was sought out for signs of encouragement in the face of uncertainty. Thus the divination of tragedy, like its conception of the gods and heroes, was more frightening and malevolent than that found in real life.

Both tragedy and popular belief had Olympian gods withdraw at the approach of death, but the tragedians often make individual gods or "the gods" as a group responsible for an individual's death. In popular belief death was attributed to fate, fortune, or a *daimon*. In cult, gods were not involved with death and the afterlife. But the tragedians, who introduce such literary figures as Thanatos and Hades, had available, as their dramatic purposes might require, four quite distinct concepts of the afterlife: that the dead were virtually nothing, with no consciousness and no awareness of the doings of the upper world; that the dead in Hades were alert, talkative, and enjoying activities and a society much like that of the upper world; that the ψυχή of the deceased went to the *aether*; and that in Hades sinners were punished for crimes committed while living. The Agamemnon and Darius of tragedy are *sui generis*, both probably of Aeschylus' creation, with a status between that of hero and the cognizant dead. They retain their royal status in Hades but, unlike the other social dead, can be summoned by prayers and offerings to help members of their families in the upper world.

That sinners were punished in Hades for their crimes is a particularly Aeschylean conception, one that he drew from Homer and Pindar. That at death the soul might go to the *aether* is particularly Euripidean, a concept probably taken from contemporary philosophy. The notion that the dead mill about in Hades as if at a remote resort is based, in good part, on the scene of the *Nekyia* in *Odyssey* II, where Odysseus observes and chats with dead men and women of the past. The first-mentioned conception, that the dead are virtually nothing, at best ψυχαί lacking perception, thought, and strength, is to be found in all three dramatists and is, I have argued above, most like what ordinary Athenians expected the afterlife to be.[23] Death is not thus to be desired, except as an escape from life's miseries, but it is also not to be feared. The many suicides of Greek tragedy lament the loss of the delights of this life; they do not look to pleasures or sufferings expected in the afterlife.[24]

Piety was a form of justice and a product of "sound thinking." It was a reasoned attitude of "honor" towards the gods, their functions, sanctuaries, cults, and ritual. This honor resulted from a proper understanding of humans' inferiority to and dependence on the gods. Piety also included honor of parents, *xenoi*, those having asylum, oaths, and certain unwritten traditions governing human social, sexual, and religious behavior. To "dishonor" any of these was sin, folly, and injustice, and the malefactor could expect to be punished. Thus far tragedy and popular religion seem to be in agreement. In popular religion one revealed his impiety by action. In tragedy impious and blasphemous words alone are sufficient to bring retribution. In neither case do plans for impious deeds, if not executed, result in punishment.

   In tragedy the gods themselves, but often through human agents, punish the impious. For Aeschylus these punishments may take place even in the afterlife. The punishments, when they come, are always severe: death, or suffering worse than death. In real life punishments for impiety were often imposed by human judicial processes, in Athens especially through criminal trials for ἀσέδεια.[25] Even so, in comparison to those for profane crimes, Athenian legal punishments for ἀσέδεια were severe: usually death or exile.

   In both popular religion and tragedy the rewards of piety were success in those areas particularly under the gods' control: fertility and health of human beings and their crops and animals, protection in sea travel and war, and prosperity for individuals and states. Hence the consternation and crisis of faith which Athenians experienced when they saw the pious and impious perishing equally in the plague of 430–426 and when the exceptionally pious general Nicias failed, suffered, and died at Syracuse.[26] Life is not as simple as literature. In tragedy the impious eventually suffer, the pious are eventually rewarded. In life the pious occasionally suffered in those areas where they were confident of divine assistance.

AESCHYLUS

Zeus is the most distinctive feature of religion in Aeschylus' plays. My interest here is not so much Aeschylus' particular conception of Zeus and its literary, particularly Hesiodic antecedents as in how his "Diocentrism" led him to reformulate and distort certain popular beliefs.[27] Fundamental is his assignment to Zeus of functions and responsibilities which, in popular religion, were not his or were not solely his. Simply put, Aeschylus' Zeus grew in stature at the expense of other deities or of different religious concepts. We have seen how, in the *Suppliants*, Aeschylus shifted responsibility for protecting the Danaids to Zeus and from the gods in whose sanctuary they took asylum.[28] For this purpose he employed a Zeus Hikesios—a literary figure, not a deity of Athenian cult—and placed under his protection suppliants throughout the world, regardless of place.[29] Elsewhere in tragedy and in life it was the proprietor (god or hero) of the sanctuary, very much tied to one place, who protected suppliants in that sanctuary and who punished violators.

Xenoi, as guests/hosts, were owed τιμή and violation of their rights was an impiety. Gods would punish those who dishonored *xenoi*, but in popular religion no particular god's own τιμη was damaged by that impiety. The impiety here was rather a violation of traditional practices.[30] But in the *Agamemnon*, as we have seen, Aeschylus assigns concern for *xenoi* to his Zeus, and this Zeus Xenios, again not a deity of Athenian state cult but of literature, punishes men like Paris who maltreat *xenoi*.[31] Aeschylus has thus gathered two major functions which either were not under another god's authority or were split among various gods and has added them to Zeus' portfolio.[32] In conceptual terms sins against *xenoi* and suppliants are thus much simplified. They become sins against one god, Zeus, and he punishes them. Because he is freed from restrictions of time, place, and circumstances, this Zeus, in these functions, becomes universal.

Aeschylus' Zeus also makes occasional forays into the domain of other deities. In the *Agamemnon* (970–971, 1015–1017) and the *Suppliants* (688–690) his Zeus, beyond simply providing rain and good weather, impinges upon the province of agricultural deities by affecting the produce of the land and "mother earth."[33] For the nether realm Aeschylus proposes an infernal Zeus, identical to Hades, in a specifically Aeschylean role of punishing sinners in the afterlife.[34]

The inspiration for Aeschylus' Zeus came not from cult but from literature. We should not think of Aeschylus as devoted to some exotic, protomonotheistic cult of Zeus which attributed new functions to the father of the gods. There was, so far as I know, no such cult of Zeus in Athens or elsewhere in the classical period or later. Aeschylus did not, and would not have expected his contemporaries to think that he did, "worship" in ways characteristic of practised Greek religion the Zeus he created in his poetry.

Aeschylus was not a prophet of a new Zeus religion. He was not, I think, a religious teacher or reformer.

The genesis of the Aeschylean Zeus is the poet's concern with justice in its many forms, and since in the literary tradition before him, particularly in Hesiod, Zeus had been made *the* protector and dispenser of justice. Aeschylus develops and enriches this association, but he does so for the sake of justice, not for the benefit of Zeus. Under the authority of his Zeus he unites fragmented divine responsibility for suppliants, *xenoi*, oaths, and religious traditions, which, as we have seen, were all matters of justice as well as of piety.[35] He further broadens Zeus' concern by making him the father or throne-mate of Dike, justice personified.[36] He casts the aura of sanctity over his Zeus and Dike with the solemn, sacred, and traditional language of prayer, hymn, and aretology, but both his Zeus and his Dike still remain alien to Greek religious tradition, at home only in the mythological and literary traditions. The audiences of the *Oresteia* and the Danaid trilogy would not have been inspired to found a new cult of Zeus or Dike, but they certainly would have been led to think more deeply and sharply about justice in the human world. This might well have affected their behavior towards one another, but since the Aeschylean Zeus who oversees that process was so remote from cult, the impact on religious belief and practice would have been negligible. The dialogue on the relationship of Zeus and justice was begun in Homer and continuously carried on in literature and philosophy. But to judge from the sources for popular religion, it never penetrated cult and religious practice.

That Aeschylus' Zeus ranges beyond his usual cultic responsibilities, that he oversees all suppliants, all *xenoi*, and all oaths, and that he is the guarantor of justice in general is not a matter of detail, something found, as in Sophocles and Euripides, in only a few lines here and there. Of the six assuredly Aeschylean plays it permeates the *Suppliants*, *Agamemnon*, *Choephoroi*, and, in part through Zeus' daughter Athena, the *Eumenides*. In these plays Aeschylus' conception of Zeus forms and shapes the entire religious structure, and it is that which is so distinctive and so alien from popular conceptions of Zeus, deity, and religion.[37]

Aeschylus' concern for justice also led him, again with literary antecedents, to have men punished in the afterlife for the sins and injustices they committed in this life. The Erinyes describe how Orestes, as he suffers in Hades, will see others being punished, those who were impious towards a god, a *xenos*, or their parents (*Eum.* 269–272). In the *Suppliants* those who take unwilling brides and who violate asylum will suffer similar punishments (227–231, 413–416). The judge there will be another Zeus (*Suppl.* 231), great

Hades (*Eum.* 273). Like many concerned with justice, both before him and after him, Aeschylus saw that not all impious and wicked people suffer in life. If there was to be unerring justice, punishments must remain for them in the afterlife. In tragedy this a uniquely Aeschylean view, and it was not shared by popular religion.

More consistently and more often than in Sophocles and Euripides Aeschylus' gods determine, or are asked to determine, the outcome of war. This too reflects Aeschylus' particular concern with divine justice. The gods gave victory to Agamemnon at Troy (*Ag.* 1335–1336) and to the Greeks at Salamis (*Pers.* 293–294, 454–455, 513–514, 905–906). Athena promises her Athenians military glory (*Eum.* 913–915), and the Thebans repeatedly pray for military victory (*Th.* passim). All the victories to which the Aeschylean gods contribute are in causes presented by the dramatist as just.[38] The Athenian people, of course, sacrificed, prayed, and took omens before battle and erected dedications after victory, but they do not seem so wholeheartedly to have credited their victories to the gods or to have assumed divine support in war because their cause was just.[39]

In the cause of justice Athena in the *Eumenides* institutes for the Athenians the Areopagus court for the trials of homicide. In doing so she establishes the jurors' oath and rules of procedure.[40] In the same play she also gives the Athenians sage political and moral advice for the welfare of their state (681–710). Elsewhere among the tragedians and in the popular tradition human laws and government are solely a human creation and primarily a human responsibility. Aeschylus' devotion to justice, which led him to adopt a universal, just Zeus, to envision punishment for sin in the afterlife, and to have the gods determine the outcome of wars, here brings a wise and just Athena into the early structuring of Athenian law and government.

Aeschylus, it appears, created the *Mischwesen* of Darius and Agamemnon, neither true heroes with public cult whose tombs and relics are sacred and who must be appeased nor ordinary, powerless dead. Capable of assisting family members who invoke them, they command considerable dramatic attention whether they actually appear (Darius) or not (Agamemnon). If there are antecedents for them in the religious tradition or the cult of the dead, they lie in the Dark or Mycenaean ages and have left no clear trace. In the literary tradition there are only imperfect models.[41] It is best, I think, to consider them Aeschylus' creation, a new class of "hero" designed to fulfill his dramatic purposes. And apart from the spectacle, which must have been stunning, these purposes included the implementation and explication of justice. In the *Choephoroi* the dead Agamemnon is repeatedly invoked and asked to assist Orestes in his vengeance on Clytemnestra. As late in the trilogy as *Eumenides* 598 Orestes credits his father for his help. Thus Agamemnon is made by Aeschylus, in the *Choephoroi*, into an agent of justice, but his type of intervention is made obsolete, as is that of the Erinyes, by the establishment of the Areopagus court in the *Eumenides*. In the *Persae* Darius whose ghost appears on the stage, is not an agent but an explainer of justice. He describes with wisdom and authority the injustices and sins of Xerxes and the Persians. We may thus suspect that Aeschylus devised these two unusual "heroes" to serve his cause of promoting justice. His Agamemnon, once established, was imitated, though not always with the same emphasis on justice, by Sophocles and Euripides in their plays on the Orestes theme.

In his vision of the divine world and in his reshaping of religious elements in his poetry, Aeschylus exhibits a boldness which one might compare to Milton's in *Paradise Lost*. His portrayal of the just and universal Zeus is, of course, the prime example of this. Yet even more striking, if the play is his, is the tyrannical Zeus of the *Prometheus*, whose character must have changed substantially in the lost plays of that trilogy if he is to be accommodated to the conception of Zeus we find elsewhere in Aeschylus. Less grand, but no less removed from popular beliefs, are the Erinyes/Semnai Aeschylus created for his *Eumenides*.

From minor cultic deities, the Semnai, Aeschylus created and brought into the theater not only the terrifying, blood-sucking, kin-murder-avenging Erinyes but also the beneficent, much honored, and all-blessing Eumenides.[42] I conclude here with a rather detailed description of them because they illustrate well not only Aeschylus' occasional wide divergences from popular religion in the interest of promoting justice but also some characteristic features of the transformation of popular religion into tragedy.

The Erinyes are variously described from Homer on as the embodiments of curses and of pollution, as avengers of those murdered by kin, and as agents of the justice of Zeus.[43] Although the pre-Aeschylean descriptions of them are not necessarily contradictory, a consistent picture of their functions was clearly not established. So far as we can determine, the Erinyes were, to the Athenians, purely literary creatures. In Athens they had no sanctuaries, received no sacrifices, and performed no functions. In short, they were not worshiped by Athenians. For the Semnai we know, by report if not by exact location, three cults, some characteristic "wineless" offerings, cult officials, and the dark, chthonic atmosphere surrounding their worship.[44] But, as so often in Greek religious history, we know least about their function. Their sanctuaries were popular for asylum. The Oedipus of

Sophocles' *Oedipus at Colonus* takes refuge at one, as did some real Peloponnesians at the time of King Codrus and as did Cylon's followers in the seventh century B.C.[45] Even Aristophanic characters talk of fleeing to the Semnai.[46]

But providing asylum was a secondary function of a deity. A deity existed to protect the city, provide rain, heal diseases, or make olives grow. That god's *temenos*, once established, might provide asylum.[47] Why some sanctuaries were more popular for this, we do not know. But in any case protection of asylum was a general divine function shared by many gods: it was not their *raison d'être*. The one attested function of the Athenian Semnai of the Areopagus concerned the murder court. Witnesses and principals in murder trials there swore by them, and acquitted defendants sacrificed to them.[48] They were involved, at least to the extent of being witnesses to oaths, with legal proceedings of homicide.

It was from this real but very limited role of the Semnai in the proceedings of the real Areopagus court of his time that Aeschylus created both his Erinyes and his Semnai. He expanded this real role backward to the Erinyes and forward to his new Semnai. The Erinyes derive from his attempts to imagine divine embodiments of the murderous form of "justice by vengeance" represented in the *Agamemnon* and *Choephoroi*. To create them he had available, of course, the varying descriptions in Homer and Hesiod, but he gave them a unified character and function suited to his purposes.[49] He also, with typically grand Aeschylean vision, made them represent not only the old style of justice but the "old" order of the gods against the new order of Apollo and Athena. The transformation of these Erinyes into Semnai, not previously attested and surely Aeschylus' own invention, reflects the changing state of human justice—the change from "justice through private vengeance" to "justice through law"[50]—and, concurrently, the change of vengeful deities of the old order into beneficent deities of the new style. As we have seen, the Erinyes lose their τιμή (both as function and as honor based on that function), but that τιμή is replaced by roles and honors suitable to Aeschylus' new order of things.[51]

Apart from their immediate dramatic purposes, changes in cult and deities in tragedy almost always serve as aetiologies. The cult or deity that results from the change is one held in reverence in Athens or elsewhere in the Greek world. Euripides' *Heracles* ends with the establishment of Heracles' cults in Athens in the places and form known to the audience. This is true also of the Hippolytus cult described at the end of the *Hippolytus* and of the cults of Artemis resulting from the action of *Iphigeneia among the Taurians*. The end point, the status after the change, reflects fifth-century reality.[52] In this regard the Semnai of Aeschylus' *Eumenides* are unique. These Semnai will not serve only as witnesses to oaths in murder trials or even as guarantors of asylum. They become deities who promise to Athens virtually all the benefits the Athenians hoped for from their gods: good things from the earth, sea, and sky; fertility of the earth, the herds, and people; freedom from blight, plague, untimely deaths, and civil war; wealth from mines; and husbands for the young women. They omit only success in battle, and Athena reserves that function for herself. Far from limiting themselves to their historic role, these Semnai have appropriated functions of Zeus, Hera Teleia, Demeter, Poseidon, and of virtually all the gods except Athena. These goddesses, as Athena says, have as their allotment to "manage all things that concern human beings" (930–931). Aeschylus has no less boldly created his Semnai than his Erinyes.[53]

Aeschylus' Semnai are an extreme example of what I have termed the economy of Greek tragedy in religious matters.[54] For obvious reasons poets wanted to limit the number of deities they introduced into a single play. One cannot have fifteen or twenty deities crowding the stage. Thus limited, the tragedian may assign, to the deities he does choose, roles and interests well beyond the recognized ones of cult. Here Aeschylus concludes his trilogy with the bestowal of *all* divine blessings on Athens, and as a vehicle for this beatification, however unrealistic it might be, he chose his Semnai. They thus become not merely real witnesses of oaths in the Areopagus court but the bestowers of immeasurably important gifts, all of which were, in real life, credited to a wide variety of other individual and independent gods.

But why were the Semnai chosen for this? It is, I think, because Aeschylus makes them represent the new, enlightened form of justice, the justice to be promulgated by Athena's new Areopagus court. They also reflect in the change of their τιμή (in all its senses) the magnitude of the change from old justice to new justice. The blessings they promise are to come to a *just* Athens. The Athenians will enjoy the blessing of the Semnai only so long as they keep their city "upright in justice" (992–995). There is, throughout, the warning that if the Athenians deviate from the path of justice, they may expect sufferings (927–937). The Semnai, like the Areopagus court (681–706), are to provide to Athens the "mysterious" and the "fear"[55] that keep human beings on the straight and narrow path of justice (517–525). And thus, although Aeschylus' Erinyes have literary antecedents and his Semnai have a cultic base, what alone explains the remarkable form both have in the *Oresteia* is his interest in the changing forms of justice, not in the reformation of religious beliefs and practices of his fellow citizens.

By concentrating on Aeschylus' differences from popular religion I do not mean to suggest that there is little or nothing of popular religion in his tragedies. In chapters 2–5 we encountered numerous instances of his use of popular religion, many in the form and context found in the popular sources. But unlike Sophocles and Euripides, Aeschylus had a systematic theological scheme in mind throughout, the cornerstone of which is the justice of the gods and of Zeus in particular. When we find Aeschylus remodeling beliefs or deities of practised Athenian religion, the explanation usually lies in this theodicy. Aeschylus' theological system, I have argued, is far removed from popular religion, and the study of it and of the particular character of the "religion" it generates are really subjects of literary criticism and intellectual history, not of *Religionsgeschichte*.

SOPHOCLES

Sophocles is commonly imagined a paragon of "piety," but in his plays he often portrays men and women buffeted by what seem to many to be capricious, amoral, but nevertheless exceptionally powerful gods. The Athena of the *Ajax* and the Zeus of the *Trachiniae* have been particularly faulted for turning on or abandoning their former favorites. For some scholars this creates a paradox: how, if Sophocles was so pious, could he have represented the gods in such an unfavorable light? How could an extraordinarily pious Sophocles let Ajax, Electra, Oedipus of the *Oedipus Tyrannus*, and Heracles and Deianira function in a world in which gods, if they are not actively hostile to the heroes, provide little or no assistance or encouragement in the crises of their lives?[56] The choice has seemed to be either to reject Sophocles' claim to piety or to construct elaborate theories to show that his gods are, despite appearances, just and moral.

Let us first assess what we know of Sophocles' personal piety. His reputation for exceptional piety is a product of modern scholarship: no contemporary source praises him for it.[57] A late and often untrustworthy *Vita* of Sophocles gives some information on his religious activities, and there are anecdotes culled from assorted other sources. After the battle of Salamis in 480, for example, Sophocles, a boy of fifteen or sixteen years, naked and anointed with oil, led the chorus which sang the paean at the victory monument (*Vita* 3). He held the priesthood of Halon, who was apparently a healing hero (*Vita* II). In the late 420s he was instrumental in the adoption of the Asclepios cult into Athens. He "gave hospitality to Asclepios" (T67[R]) and wrote a paean for him (T73a[R]). For his reception of Asclepios he himself was, perhaps, worshiped as the hero Dexion ("Receiver") (T69[R]).[58] He is also said to have established a cult of Heracles

Menytes ("The Informer").[59] Sophocles seems to have been particularly drawn to hero cults, and, if these stories are not all fabrications, they may reflect his literary interest in human "heroes" and in hero cults like that of *Oedipus at Colonus*.[60] If we can trust even some of this biographical data, he was very active in some areas of public cult. We today may consider this a sign of exceptional piety. If the ancients did, they left no record of it. We have no reason to doubt Sophocles' personal piety, but we also do not find it especially commended by his contemporaries or in the ancient biographical tradition—as was, for example, that of Nicias or Xenophon.[61]

Even to expect that personal piety would carry over into a poetic representation of the gods as just, moral, and concerned with human beings is to misunderstand the realities of ancient religion and literature.[62] In popular religion the ancient believer was not, I have argued, concerned that the gods be just or moral in ways identical to those of mortals;[63] hence someone could be pious without claiming that gods were perfectly moral and just. And, secondly, the literary and mythological traditions established in the Homeric epics were so separate from practised religion that poets pious in conventional ways could, remaining within the literary tradition, call into question the behavior, justice, morality, and even the existence of the anthropomorphic gods. Comic poets could even ridicule them without risking the charge of impiety. All this was possible because the anthropomorphic gods of literature were so remote from the core beliefs of practised religion.

Sophocles thus may have been the most pious of the dramatists in his personal life, but we need not expect that either modern or ancient concepts of piety be exhibited in his representations of the mythological world of tragedy. In fact he seems the tragedian least interested, in his plays, in popular religion and the one most willing to distort it for literary purposes. Unlike Aeschylus he refashions it not to promote a consistent theological program but for a variety of literary and dramatic effects. Sophocles' primary interest is the human hero, and he uses both mythological and popular religion, in different ways in different plays, to illuminate facets of human character. Religious obstacles or challenges are only one variety among the many complications that Sophoclean heroes encounter. I find Sophocles' use of religion neither pious nor impious, but essentially opportunistic.

Sophocles' concentration of attention on the human, at the expense of the divine, is suggested by the famous "Ode to Man" in the *Antigone* (332–375). There, as we have seen, he has the chorus of Theban elders attribute to humanity alone the responsibility for many human advances which Euripides and Aeschylus credit to a divine benefactor: people sail the seas, work the land with animals, hunt birds, beasts, and fish, speak, think, build shelters, cure diseases, develop crafts, and live in ordered society.[64] Elsewhere in tragedy and in much of the philosophical tradition most or all of these are boons owed to the gods, but Sophocles makes them human accomplishments, without a word of the participation of the gods. The more Sophocles exalts humanity the less he must credit to the gods.

A number of small but unique features in Sophocles' plays suggest, if taken together, that he was less concerned than his fellow tragedians to maintain verisimilitude to popular religion. The first is a willingness to combine or remodel, in ahistorical fashion, elements of popular practice. Particularly remarkable is his use of the corpse of Ajax (*Aj.* 1168–1184). Ajax' son Eurysakes and his mother arrive to assist in Ajax' funeral, and, as Teucer, Ajax' brother, leaves the stage, he bids the boy to guard Ajax' body. But Eurysakes himself is also guarded by the body, because Teucer, by a curse, makes the corpse into a place of asylum. An asylum was always a sanctuary, a "holy place," to which a corpse, as a "polluted object," was the polar opposite.[65] To make such an unsuitable object into a place of asylum, Teucer must invest it with a supernatural sanction which it does not inherently have. Hence the curse:

> If anyone of the army should drag you (Eurysakes) by force
> from this corpse, then may he, evil as he is, be cast out
> evilly and unburied from this land, and may his whole
> family be cut down root and all, in the same way as I cut this lock of
>   my hair.
>
> (1175–1179)

Such a curse was, of course, unnecessary for protection in a true place of asylum, because the sheltering deity would, without such prompting, punish violators. Teucer's lock of hair does threefold service and may have been the link that suggested to Sophocles this unusual, not to say bizarre, combination of rituals. Hair is first and primarily the appropriate offering of relatives at a funeral,[66] and as such the audience would understand it here in the context of preparations for the funeral. Teucer, however, transforms this funerary hair-offering into a token of supplication (1173–1175), like the boughs or garlands which suppliants usually held as they crouched at an altar or cult statue. Finally, Teucer makes the gesture of the cutting of the lock, the lock which is to be both a funerary gift and a token of supplication, into an act of sympathetic magic, commonly used to reinforce curses: the violator and his family are to be destroyed "in the same way as I cut off this lock of hair"

(1179).[67] This threefold use of the lock of hair creates a highly unusual blending of rituals of burial, curse, supplication, and asylum, and by this inventive combination of rites and concepts Sophocles is able to concentrate, dramatically, many of the remaining concerns of the play on one point, the corpse of Ajax.[68]

The puzzling double burial of Polyneices in the *Antigone* (245–258, 278–289, 384–436) may be another example of Sophocles' remodeling of popular ritual for dramatic purposes.[69] Many attempts have been made to understand Antigone's burial and reburial of Polyneices in terms of fifth-century funeral practices, but none has succeeded. Antigone's secret first burial of her brother, the discovery and reaction to it, the second burial, at which she is observed and arrested, and the mysterious, almost supernatural elements attending both burials have a widely recognized dramatic effect and are integral to the structure of the play. But in terms of ritual, questions arise. Was mere covering with dust sufficient to ward off pollution? Did the body need to be ritually reburied, once uncovered? What of the mysterious circumstances—no human traces, no attacks on the corpse by dogs or birds, and the dust storms accompanying the burials? No one of these can be explicated from popular practices or beliefs. The double burial remains unique and mysterious, and I think Sophocles intentionally made it so. To create his dramatic sequence he divided up the usual single ritual of burial, lament, and libations and in the whole went beyond popular practices and even literary conventions.[70] He wanted an intricate, mystery-shrouded structure which would allow him to present the situation and characters from multiple perspectives, and for that he was willing to sacrifice religious verisimilitude.

There are also instances of apparently casual, less purposeful disregard of popular religious beliefs in Sophoclean tragedy. Sophocles offers, in all of tragedy, the one character who violates an oath to no ill effect. He is a minor character, the guard in the *Antigone* (388–396), the oath is only reported, and no gods or curse are introduced.[71] This perjury is unimportant to the action of the play. It may have been introduced to add to the characterization of the guard or to emphasize the great turn of events, but it remains the one exception to an otherwise consistent treatment of oaths in tragedy. In addition Sophocles' Orestes in the *Electra* (47–48) recommends that the paedagogue deceive Clytemnestra with an oath. The recommendation is not followed,[72] but again a Sophoclean character is less concerned about the religious implications of a false oath than were his Euripidean and Aeschylean counterparts.

The contamination of quite distinct rituals in the *Ajax*, the anomalous burials in the *Antigone*, and the disregard of perjury in the *Antigone* and *Electra* may be small points, but their like is not to be found in Aeschylus and Euripides.[73] Together they suggest that Sophocles was less concerned than his fellow dramatists to represent the realities of popular religion. A similar impression, but less subject to proof, arises from the *Trachiniae*.

Sophocles in the *Trachiniae* and Euripides in the *Heracles* both treat the extreme sufferings of Heracles, and in both plays Zeus, as Heracles' father, is prominent. A comparison of their portrayals of Zeus and Heracles[74] offers further indications that Sophocles was less interested in religious verisimilitude and popular religion than, at least, his younger rival. Euripides isolates one cultic aspect of the deity, Zeus Soter ("Savior") and combines that, and that alone, with the epic Olympian Zeus. This Zeus Soter is a deity whose altar (and hence cult) on the stage itself has been established by Heracles (*HF* 48–50; cf. 54, 521–522). The Athenian audience knew Zeus Soter as the proprietor of the Stoa of Zeus in the Agora, the deity who had "saved" their fathers from slavery in the Persian Wars. By assigning him the epithet Soter, Euripides points explicitly to a cultic function of Zeus and to his moral and as it were, professional responsibility to "save" his son Heracles and his grandchildren.

Sophocles, rather than developing a single and unified conception of Zeus, introduces a wide range of Zeuses and then binds them together through the paternity of Heracles. We have Zeus Horkios, the Protector of Oaths (1185–1190), Zeus Sender of Lightning (436–437, 1086–1088), Zeus Kenaios, that is, of Cenaeum, a cape on the northwest tip of Euboea (237–241, 287–288, 750–754, 993–1003), and Zeus Giver of Oracles at Dodona (164–172, 1159–1172)—all expressly labeled the "father of Heracles" and thereby linked together and to the epic Zeus of Heracles' myths. Other clearly definable Zeuses in the *Trachiniae* are Zeus Agonios, that is, of the Contest (26), Zeus Oitaios, of Mount Oeta, site of Heracles' funeral pyre (200–201, 436–437, 1191–1216), and Zeus Tropaios, of Victory in Battle (303–306), and they are also surely meant, though nothing is expressly said, to be subsumed under "the father of Heracles." Of all these Zeuses four are defined primarily in terms of their functions (oaths, lightning, contests, victory in battle), two in geographical terms (of Cenaeum and Mount Oeta), and one in both regards (oracles at Dodona). The play also contains numerous references to a Homeric Zeus who lacks cultic restrictions of function and place.[75] The Zeus of Sophocles is a hybrid, an amalgam of various local cultic (Kenaios and Oitaios), functional (oaths, lightning, etc.), and mythological bits which were never found together in such a combination in practised religion. As such he is the type of deity commonly found in epic and lyric poetry, not in life. Euripides' Zeus, however, has his roots more in the cult and religion of the Athenian audience.

The Heracles of Sophocles, like his Zeus, is also primarily a literary, mythological figure. Sophocles' hero will die on the pyre on Mount Oeta in northern Greece; yet there is no clear mention of the cult myth, commonly known at the time, that on this pyre he experienced apotheosis. Sophocles must have intentionally suppressed this familiar element of the Heracles myth. But even if one should grant that some in the audience thought of the Heracles cult on Oeta as they watched the final scene of the play, that was still, to Athenians, a foreign myth, not one of their national history, and a foreign cult, not one in which they participated. In terms of myth and religion, the Heracles of the *Trachiniae*, like its Zeus, is largely Panhellenic and literary. He is, most definitely, not Athenian. Sophocles makes no effort to link Heracles, his adventures, or his cult to Athens.

Euripides, however, plants his Heracles solidly in the soil and national history of Athens. His Heracles had rescued Theseus, king of Athens, from the underworld, and Theseus comes to Thebes expressly to repay to Heracles the favor he received. Heracles becomes, like a host of other figures of tragedy, a beneficiary of Athenian willingness, even eagerness, to give help and sanctuary to people in distress. He is to reside in Athens and receive precincts of land which the Athenians have set aside for Theseus. When Heracles dies these precincts will become centers of his cult. These sanctuaries were those at which the Athenians of the fifth century regularly worshiped and celebrated festivals. The Heracles whom Euripides presents in the *Heracles* becomes their Heracles, a resident of their land. Euripides is dramatizing an aetiology of how Heracles came to be in Athens and why he is worshiped in the places he is. The Heracles of Euripides, like his Zeus, is much closer, both physically and religiously, to the Athenians than is his Sophoclean counterpart.

In contrast to Euripides Sophocles presents his Zeus and Heracles in a mostly mythological, literary, and Panhellenic context. I chose for comparison the *Trachiniae* and the *Heracles* because they involve the same deity, the same hero, and many of the same issues. I recognize that such a comparison cannot constitute "proof" of these differences between Sophocles and Euripides, in part because it would have been exceptionally difficult for Sophocles to construct an Athenian context for this Theban myth of Heracles, but even more because Euripides' side would have looked very different if we had selected some other play of his, such as the *Andromache* or *Hecuba*, for comparison. Nevertheless the comparison still has

some value, because it highlights Sophocles' usual way of presenting gods
and religion. We find much the same mythological, literary, and
Panhellenic—certainly not Athenian and mostly not popular—approach to
deities and religion in all his surviving plays, save one. Sophocles was, I think,
the least interested of the three dramatists in representing dramatically the
religion of his time. Just as he employed the many and heterogeneous Zeuses
in the *Trachiniae* as need for them arose, so he introduced, for literary
purposes, a heterogeneous mix of mythological, literary, and popular deities,
beliefs, and practices into his other plays, with little concern for religious
verisimilitude. His dominant concern was the individual human hero, and to
that he subordinated everything, including popular religion.

The *Oedipus at Colonus* is the exception, and it shows Sophocles not
only capable of but exceptionally skillful at interweaving into the
mythological world of tragedy popular, fifth-century deities and cults. This
he does not so much for Athens as a whole as for a small district of that
country, his own deme Colonus.[76] Written near the end of his long life, set
in Colonus, the play recreates, albeit in legendary times, the delights and
deities and cults in which Sophocles must have found enduring pleasure and
comfort.[77] The demesmen sing of the nightingales, ivy, grapevines,
narcissus, crocus, olives, and river of their small district (668–719).[78] In this
song and elsewhere are introduced, often with an epithet and description of
function, deities who we know were worshiped in Colonus: Poseidon
Hippios (of Horses) and Athena Hippia; Demeter Euchloös; Zeus Morios
and Athena Moria, protectors of the sacred olives; Prometheus, giver of fire;
Aphrodite and the Muses; and Colonus, the hero who gave his name to the
deme.[79] Other deities appearing in the ode were certainly worshiped in
Athens, some perhaps in Colonus itself: Dionysus, and Demeter and Kore
and their Eleusinian Mysteries.[80] Poseidon Hippios as giver of horses and
the bit, master of the sea, and patron of the whole district, is given a
prominence beyond what his role in the play would require.[81] In this play
Sophocles lovingly recreates the landscape and deities and cults of his
homeland. No surviving Greek tragedy, not even Aeschylus' *Eumenides*, is
more deeply rooted in and more expressive of fifth-century deities and
religion.

The Oedipus whose cult is established in this play praises, more than
any other character in a surviving tragedy, the piety of Athens.[82] He calls
Athens the most pious of all cities, a piety the city demonstrates in protecting
his asylum.[83] For this, for their piety, the Athenians are to be rewarded.
Oedipus' tomb will protect them against invasion from his Theban kingdom,
always a real danger in both legendary and classical times. Like the

Eumenides, Aeschylus' last surviving play, Sophocles' last play is an encomium and beatification of Athens, and for this Sophocles turned, as Aeschylus had, to practised fifth-century Athenian religion.

The *Oedipus at Colonus* is, however, very much the exception among the surviving plays of Sophocles in its presentation of religion. Elsewhere Sophocles seems, relative to Aeschylus and Euripides, less concerned with and less interested in the religion practised by his fellow citizens. However pious he may have been in his private life, in his tragedies the gods and cults are primarily in the literary, Homeric model. He certainly does not exclude elements of popular religion, as we have seen throughout the previous four chapters, nor is he incapable of developing them, as the *Oedipus at Colonus* magnificently demonstrates. But, relatively, his concentration on the human and heroic usually diminishes the role of the divine and popular.

EURIPIDES

"But Euripidean tragedy is strange water in which to fish for examples of orthodox Greek piety." Such is Bernard Knox's colorful contribution to a distinguished scholarly tradition which sees in Euripides the critic and debunker of what it calls traditional, conventional, popular, or orthodox religion.[84] This view predominated in the nineteenth century and has found its most influential proponents in A. W. Verrall, Wilhelm Nestle, and, more recently, Gunther Zuntz.[85] Euripides' life and Aristophanes' criticisms, as we shall see below, afford this scholarly tradition an ancient springboard, but at its heart lie three elements of Euripidean tragedy itself: (1) occasional representation of Olympian gods as immoral or amoral by human standards; (2) occasional questioning of the veracity of myths; and (3) occasional introduction of recent or contemporary philosophical theory about the gods. To these must be added the modern presumption of "deep irony" pervading the plays of Euripides: the belief that the apparent meaning of words, speeches, scenes, and whole plays is undercut by contrasting imagery and ritual, by inconsistencies of word or action, by allusions to other mythical versions or philosophical theories, and by other such devices.

I have explained in chapter I why I reject, for purposes of understanding popular religion, this ironizing approach, which even its proponents recognize would have been intelligible to only a few among the audience.[86] The other three elements are certainly to be found in Euripidean tragedy but have little relevance to the religious beliefs of the audience of the plays. In the first instance, Euripides does present deities—such as Athena and Poseidon in the *Troades*, Aphrodite in the *Hippolytus*, and Dionysus in the

Bacchae—who are cruel and perhaps unjust or immoral by human standards. But there is no evidence to prove that fifth-century Greeks worshiped such gods as these or expected the gods they did worship to be perfectly moral or just by these standards. The major concerns of practised religion in the most general terms were that the gods existed, that they had some concern for humans, and that some reciprocity existed between humans and gods.[87] The morality and justice of the gods was a concern of literature and philosophy, not of cult. Hence criticisms of the gods in this regard did not affect cult and worship. As for the second element, Euripides does have his characters question the truth of myths such as the judgment of Paris (*Tr.* 971–982), the birth of Helen (*Hel.* 17–21), the feast of Tantalus (*IT* 386–391), and the adulteries of the gods (*HF* 1341–1346). But these are myths which, at least by the fifth century, were literary and divorced from cult. He raises no such questions about aetiological myths for practised Athenian cults. And, third. Euripides does occasionally introduce contemporary philosophical theories, but these need not be viewed as attacks on the cults and religious beliefs and practices of Athenian citizens.[88] Theological speculation, of more interest to some than others, is a regular feature of Greek literature. There is no evidence that such speculation penetrated worship or religious beliefs in classical Athens. To think that poets assumed or hoped that their views would change cult is probably to misunderstand both Greek literature and Greek religion.

The claim that Euripides is a critic of traditional, conventional, popular, or orthodox religion rests on the assumptions that in this "religion" the gods worshiped in life were identical or very similar to the gods portrayed in poetry;[89] that the gods were, as Hesiod, Pindar, and Aeschylus presented them, themselves moral and just by human standards and were, on their own initiative, enforcers of morality and justice in human society; and that the myths of Homer and the epic cycle were taken to be literally true. But the evidence from cult and the prose sources give no indication that any of these propositions is tenable. As we change our conception of what was the traditional, conventional, popular, and orthodox religion in the classical period, we will have to reassess Euripides' relationship to it.

In the preceding four chapters we fished extensively in Euripidean waters and, even without the angler's usual exaggeration, can claim to have caught many examples of orthodox Greek piety. An Athenian's major concerns in popular religion were fertility, of self, of family, and of crops and animals; health and security in times of danger; and prosperity, especially economic, for self and country. In chapter 2 we saw that Euripidean gods, no less than those of Aeschylus and Sophocles, provide these services to humans.

When they do not, Euripides offers through his choruses and characters explanations in terms of sin and the resulting punishment. The individual who violates the τιμή of a god (or of the gods) loses divine assistance in just these areas. The punishment for sin may often seem exceptionally severe, but so it was in popular cult. For example, under "old laws" an Athenian could be fined heavily by religious and civil authorities for stealing wood from a sanctuary, whereas a similar crime in a profane setting would be counted only a minor offense.[90]

Piety in popular religion consisted of belief in and reverence for the gods of the city, maintenance of oaths, respect for the rights of asylum and hospitality, observance of tradition and law in cult sacrifices and tendance of the dead, loyalty to country, and proper care of living parents.[91] In Euripides virtually *all* violators in these matters are punished. In chapter 3 we found that all Euripidean characters who commit perjury, who maltreat *xenoi* or those having asylum, who are traitors, or who neglect or violate the rites of the dead eventually suffer. The punishment may arise for other reasons as well, and the human agent of the punishment may be impious too; but in the end *all* violators of conventional, orthodox piety suffer. Conversely those who show exceptional piety in these areas, such as Admetus in the *Alcestis* and Theseus and Demophon in the *Heraclidae* and *Suppliants*, are rewarded. The virtually uniform punishment of sinners and reward of the pious are alone sufficient to belie the notion that Euripides systematically criticizes and debunks the religious beliefs and practices of his audience. They rather point to the conclusion that he is supporting conventional religious beliefs, once these "conventional religious beliefs" are properly understood.

The fundamental error, I have argued, in taking Euripides to be a critic and mocker of traditional religion is mistaking the myths and anthropomorphic gods of literature for the beliefs and deities of practised religion. The view of Euripides as critic of religion is also thought to find support in the testimonia about his life and in the attacks against him by the comic poet Aristophanes, his contemporary. Euripides' biographical tradition, drawing heavily from Old Comedy, is generally unflattering. According to it he had moles, sties in his eyes, and bad breath, was misanthropic and unpleasant to talk to, and hated laughter and women.[92] Given its prejudice, we might expect to find in this tradition some ugly incidents illustrating his alleged impiety. But, to the contrary, we are told that he served as torchbearer in the rites of Apollo on Cape Zoster (*Vita* 17–18) and as winepourer for the dances at rites for Apollo Delios in Athens (Ath. 10.424E–F, citing Theophrastus).

Once, reportedly, Euripides was formally charged with impiety by the

demagogue Cleon (Satyrus, frag. 39, col. x = *P.Oxy.* ix, 1176). We know
nothing more of this charge and can only speculate on its basis.[93] Aristotle
reports a second attack, in his description of methods for countering slander
(*Rh.* 1416a28–35). It seems that in a trial involving liturgies and property, a
certain Hygiainon accused Euripides of impiety on the basis that he had
promoted perjury when, in the *Hippolytus*, he had Hippolytus claim. "My
tongue has sworn the oath, my mind has not" (612). I have twice discussed
this line, showing both that it is unfairly torn from context for criticism and
that Hippolytus eventually exhibits, in the most difficult circumstances,
exceptional piety in maintaining just this oath.[94] The court case, moreover,
was not expressly for impiety but concerned providing expensive financial
services for the state and the value of the principals' property. In this
procedure *(antidosis)* the principals exchanged oaths,[95] and it was no doubt in
this regard that Hygiainon attacked Euripides. Aristotle presents it as
"slander," not as itself a criminal charge. Euripides responded that it was a
matter for the theater, not the law court to decide, and we should remember
that in the festival at which he produced the *Hippolytus* Euripides won one of
the four first prizes he was to receive in his lifetime.[96] The audience must not
have found line 612 as offensive in context as Hygiainon found it in isolation.
We may surmise that ultimately Cleon's charge was rejected, for there is no
evidence that Euripides was punished, and that Hygiainon's accusation
probably failed, for Aristotle cites Euripides' response as a model of
counterattack against slander.

Hygiainon's recourse to *Hippolytus* 612 serves to introduce
Aristophanes' and modern critics' attacks on Euripides' personal piety. The
comic poet alludes to *Hippolytus* 612 three times and no doubt gave it the
notoriety upon which Hygiainon seized.[97] In one other instance, in
Aristophanes' *Thesmophoriazusae* of 411, a widow who has made a "half-bad"
living for herself and her five children by weaving garlands used for festivals
and sacrifices complains that Euripides has ruined her business:

> He, writing his tragedies,
> has persuaded men that gods do not exist.

(450–451)

The Athenians, made atheists by Euripides, have no need for the widow's
garlands. These two Aristophanic criticisms of religious aspects of Euripides'
plays, although the one (on *Hipp.* 612) is unfair and the other isolated, cannot
be ignored. The charge of promoting perjury cuts to the heart of popular
piety, and the gods mentioned in the *Thesmophoriazusae* are those of cult, not

myth. But there is scarcely anything in Euripides' complete plays to justify the widow's charge,[98] and in fact some modern scholars see Euripides as asserting the power and hence existence, if not the morality and justice, of the gods.[99] Without assuming a very deep irony one can hardly think that Euripides meant his audience to imagine that the Athena of the *Troades*, the Aphrodite and Artemis of the *Hippolytus*, and the Dionysus of the *Bacchae* do not, in the tragedies to which they are central, exist. There is likewise no reason to think that he is casting doubt on the Athenian cults of Artemis and Heracles with which he concludes *Iphigeneia among the Taurians* and the *Heracles*.

Support for the widow's claim, like support for modern scholars' attribution of atheism to Euripides, is usually drawn from the fragments.[100] We have seen how misleading this can be in the case of *Hippolytus* 612, and in chapter 1, I pointed out the insurmountable problems in using the fragments of lost tragedies for such purposes. Euripides, somewhat more often than Aeschylus and Sophocles, has characters make blasphemous or impious statements, and from them such fragments have been culled. But in the complete plays, the speakers of such thoughts, when they violate the canons of popular piety, invariably suffer.

The sum of ancient evidence for Euripides' personal impiety comes to little: a charge by Cleon, of which we know nothing; three Aristophanic allusions and one courtroom reference to *Hippolytus* 612; and, last and perhaps alone significant, the widow's complaint in Aristophanes' *Thesmophoriazusae*.[101] Her charge, we must remember, is but a part of a sustained comic assault by women on the "woman-hater" Euripides and, if we are to accept it as historically justifiable, we should do the same for all the attacks on Socrates in Aristophanes' *Clouds*.

Euripides seems, indeed, to have introduced more of the practised religion of his time into his plays than did his fellow tragedians. This includes numerous aetiologies for contemporary cults, maintenance of local particularism of some deities and cults, detailed descriptions of religious rituals, a popular usage of the terms *daimon* and θεός, description of sin and punishment in terms consistent with those of popular religion, and, finally, rewards for conventional piety, especially when Athenians are involved.

Euripidean *del ex machina* close *Iphigeneia among the Taurians* with a description of the future cults of Artemis at Brauron and Halae in Attica, the *Erechtheus* with the cults of the Erechtheum, the *Hippolytus* with the cult of the hero in nearby Troezen, the *Helen* with Helen's cult as protector of sailors, the *Antiope* with the cults of Dirce, Amphion, and Zethus at Thebes, the *Suppliants* with the cult of heroes who fought and died at Thebes, and the

Andromache with the cults of Neoptolemus and Achilles.[102] Similarly the future cults of Heracles, those practised by fifth-century Athenians, are explained in the *Heracles*, as is the Corinthian cult of Medea's children in the *Medea*.[103] In a sense the *Bacchae* is aetiological, explaining not only why Dionysus is worshiped in Thebes but also characteristic features of his ritual and myth. Added to these aetiologies which stand out by emphasis or position within a play are numerous lesser ones: the cult of Eurystheus in the *Heraclidae* (1026–1044), the Athenian Arrephoria in the *Ion* (15–26, 267–273), the rituals of the Choes festival in *Iphigeneia among the Taurians* (947–960), and the founding of the Spartan Hyacinthia in the *Helen* (1465–1475).[104]

These aetiologies, especially the major ones assigned to *dei ex machina*, have proved an embarrassment to scholars who see in Euripides a critic of the religion of his time. They wonder that Euripides is "addicted to such accounts of the legendary origins (αἴτια) of contemporary things" or consider such aetiologies as "bonuses' appended more or less gratuitously to the end of the play" or as sops offered to the unsophisticated among the audience.[105] Some draw, somewhat surprisedly, the seemingly more obvious conclusion: "[Euripides'] fondness for tying his story on to a particular cult at the end of the play surely implies that he perceived some value in traditional religion."[106] I would go further. Although such aetiologies are not unknown in Aeschylus and Sophocles (as, for instance, in the *Eumenides* and the *Oedipus at Colonus*), by comparison Euripides shows far more interest than they in the backgrounds and origins of contemporary cults and religious practices.[107] There is also no evidence from the texts that these aetiologies are being introduced to be criticized or ridiculed.

Complementary to Euripides' interest in cult aetiologies is his somewhat more "realistic" depiction of religion. The representation of the gods in Euripides' plays generally is, like that of Aeschylus, Sophocles, and most Greek poets, Homeric,[108] but Euripides characteristically varies it in the direction of practised religion. Cult aetiologies are part of this, but he also occasionally depicts local varieties of cults, gives detailed descriptions of ritual, assigns divine figures the epithets and functions of real cults, and, finally, usually describes sin, punishment, and wrath of the gods in terms familiar to popular religion. Examples of such things can also be found here and there in Aeschylus and Sophocles, but they are not nearly so common or systematic. They each contribute to the greater realism of Euripides' plays, a realism that has been widely recognized from other, nonreligious elements of his tragedy.[109]

The prominence of Apollo in the Delphic *Ion* and of Athena in the

Erechtheus are only to be expected from any dramatist,[110] but in the *Medea* Euripides gives, beyond what the myth might require, particular attention to Helios and Aphrodite, and it is hardly coincidental that these two deities are central only to the cult of Corinth, the setting of the play. In the *Phoenissae* Eteocles, defending the homeland, appeals to the specifically Theban Athena of the Golden Shield. His brother Polyneices, a Theban too but now living in Argos, turns to Hera, the patroness of the Argolid (*Ph.* 1359–1376).[111] When Euripides set his plays away from the familiar soil of Athens and Greece, he allowed himself greater inventiveness in religious matters. The cult of Artemis in *Iphigeneia among the Taurians*, located at the far shore of the Black Sea, and that of Aether in the Egypt of the *Helen* are described in detail but are very un-Greek in conception. These we shall include among the innovations of Euripides, discussed below.

Earlier in this chapter I described at length how Euripides, in contrast to Sophocles in the *Trachiniae*, created in the *Heracles* a Zeus who had some ties, as Zeus Soter, to Athenian cult. So too the Dionysus of the *Bacchae* is given not only mythological but cultic ties to specifically Theban sacred places and rituals. Such links, established through epithets and references to sacred places and through aetiologies, though not present in all Euripidean plays, are still much more frequent there than in the works of Sophocles and Aeschylus.

Much of what is usually considered the best fifth-century evidence for burial rites, sacrificial ritual, and rites of individual cults is drawn from the plays of Euripides. In chapter 4 we observed how much of the funerary cult is described in the *Alcestis* and *Troades*, whereas such descriptions in Aeschylus seem at variance with fifth-century beliefs.[112] The sacrificial scene in Euripides' ripides' *Electra* 781–843 is the fullest fifth-century account we have of this ritual. The *Ion* (passim, esp. 82–237, 414–420) gives us our most vivid fifth-century picture of Apollo's cult at Delphi. And most of what we think we know of the Theban cult of Dionysus comes from the *Bacchae*. These and other brief descriptions of ritual are integral to the plays, not merely tacked on pedantically, and they reveal Euripides' interest in using ritual, ritual often practised by the audience, as a dramatic device.[113] Also more common than in other tragedians are Euripides' references to a god or the collective of the gods as *daimon* or θεός τις another characteristic of popular religion.[114]

Euripides also, more than his fellow tragedians, describes the complex of sin, wrath of the gods, and punishment in terms common to popular religion. An individual, usually through an act, violates the τιμή (in all its meanings) of a god. Because of this the god becomes angry and punishes the individual. Whether or not one accepts my evaluations of the characters and gods in the *Hippolytus*, *Bacchae*, and *Troades* (see chapter 4), the pattern of violated τιμή wrathful god, and punishment of the human is unmistakable. And it was in these terms that popular religion conceived of the nexus of sin and punishment (chapter 5). Euripides often introduces secular motives in addition to religious ones for the punishment of immoral sinners,[115] but that too is realistic and does not undermine these conclusions. The relative emphasis on the religious and secular varies from play to play, but the religious element is always present to some degree. The net effect is that religious thought in Euripidean plays is much closer to popular thought than is, for example, Aeschylus' framework of Ate, Hybris, and Nemesis. Aeschylus' formulation is literary; Euripides', though certainly not completely popular, lies closer in that direction. It may be partially Euripides' proximity to popular belief, not his remoteness from it, that, at least in Aristophanes, generated such a strong reaction.

As a final consideration in stressing Euripides' support of popular religion we may note that in the *Suppliants* and *Heraclidae* piety and its rewards in conventional forms, such as securing burial rites and protecting suppliants, are central. Some scholars see in these "political plays" a temporary lapse in the Euripidean spirit, a failure of nerve.[116] Some admit that Euripides is placing conventional moral law and national traditions into a favorable light but deny religious background to them.[117] Or else the plays are reinterpreted through deep irony.[118] These approaches are, I think, mistaken. In terms of religion two points are salient for these plays: they are set in Athens and they concern acts of piety, not the anthropomorphic gods of mythology. Throughout tragedy Athens is presented as a model of piety.[119] No Athenian commits the horrible impieties of tragedy. Athens is rather where impieties from elsewhere in the world are resolved, whether the perpetrators be Argive, Theban, or barbarian. One could call it a "convention" that Athens was praised for piety in tragedy, but that is probably to misrepresent what a tragic convention is. Rather, neither Aeschylus nor Sophocles, nor Euripides, chose to portray Athens and Athenians as impious. Athenian tragedians, writing plays set in Athens for an Athenian audience, made their homeland and their ancestors pious. It was for Aristophanes and his fellow practitioners of Old Comedy to reveal the follies of the Athenians in their theater.

In these two political plays the Olympian gods have minor roles, and since most of the "religious" criticism that scholars perceive in Euripides is directed against anthropomorphic gods, there is little for them in these plays. In the *Heraclidae* and *Suppliants* Euripides, as he always does, has rewards for characters pious in observing burial rites, maintaining oaths, and protecting asylum. Therefore, with no problematic Homeric gods present but with pious deeds performed and rewarded, these two plays appear "pro-religious." So they are, but they differ little from other Euripidean plays in their respect for the tenets of popular piety.

To stress the support for popular religion in Euripides' plays is not, however, to claim that this aspect alone of "religion" is to be found there. In terms of literary and mythological religion some deities, such as Athena and Poseidon in the *Troades*, are largely Homeric in form, manner, and concerns. The Aphrodite and Artemis of the *Hippolytus* and the Dionysus of the *Bacchae*, while not merely psychological forces, are certainly more developed along these lines than they were in cult or had been in previous Greek literature.

Another characteristic feature of the Euripidean treatment of deity and belief is the occasional introduction of current philosophical theories.[120] Various philosophical ideas appear in individual plays, but unlike the developed theology of Aeschylus they do not permeate the corpus of Euripides' work.[121] Nor are they mere gratuitous digressions; in the play in which each occurs, it has significance for the meaning of the whole. In the *Heracles* Heracles rejects Theseus' somewhat tentative claim ("If the stories of the poets are not false," 1314–1319) that the gods practise adultery, enchain even their fathers to gain tyrannical rule, and, more generally, "sin." Heracles proposes a conception of deity which goes far beyond traditional mythological and popular ideas:

> I do not think the gods enjoy illicit love affairs.
> I have never thought it right nor will I ever believe
> that they tie up one another or that one god is master of another.
> For god, if he properly is a god, lacks nothing.
> These are the miserable tales of poets.
>
> (1341–1346)

The philosophical tradition from which these statements derive had begun nearly a century before Euripides, with Xenophanes of Colophon, who refused to attribute such moral failings to the gods.[122]

In the *Bacchae* Euripides has Teiresias attempt to explain the myth and importance of Dionysus by both scholarly etymology and current philosophical theory. Dionysus was believed to have been born from Zeus' thigh because once Zeus had created a Dionysus image as a hostage to be given to Hera (286–297). Teiresias seems to be borrowing from the

philosopher Prodicus in having Demeter represent the "dry" of the world
and Dionysus the "wet" wine, and in both being thought gods for their
benefactions (274–285).[123] Hence even someone moved only by
philosophical theory could find cause to render τιμή to this new god. In the
Troades much-suffering Hecuba finally invokes a Zeus who may be Air, or the
Necessity of Nature, or the Reason of Mankind, a Zeus who "guides all
mortal things according to justice" (884–888). The origin of such a Zeus lies
in philosophy, and in Hecuba's invocation scholars have detected ideas of
Anaximenes, Diogenes of Apollonia, Heraclitus, Anaxagoras,[124] and all
those, beginning with Hesiod, who assigned justice to Zeus.[125]

These and similar examples show Euripides' willingness to introduce
contemporary philosophical and theological theory into his plays.[126] Such
allusions are, however, scattered and determined by the particular needs of
the play at hand. They form no systematic whole, and Euripides' apparent
interest in philosophy does not grant us license to read philosophical theories
into the many plays where the text offers no warrant for it. Euripides'
particular innovation in this regard may be his eclectic use of highly specific
philosophical theory for dramatic purposes. Aeschylus was no less a
philosopher, but he followed one consistent theology well-established in the
previous literary tradition.

Euripides' comparatively high respect for the non-Greek, "barbarian"
world and for practised religion may also explain another characteristic: his
creation, for a particular play, of a realistic but essentially non-Greek
religious milieu. For the *Helen*, set in Egypt, he created a religion centered
on a divine Aether (see above, chapter 3). Although Aether as a deity is a
philosophic conception,[127] Euripides brings the religion alive by giving it its
own devotee, rites, and eschatology. He makes this imaginary religion
realistic by introducing rituals and terminology which, though not identical
to Greek popular religion, were sufficiently similar to allow the audience to
recognize it as a religion. Likewise, in *Iphigeneia among the Taurians*, the cult
of the Taurian Artemis, at the far edge of the Black Sea and involving human
sacrifice, is not Greek but has substance and definition because it is Greek-
like. Here we may compare Aeschylus. For the existing cult of the Semnai he
imagined the Erinyes as predecessors. But his Erinyes had no cult, no
worship, and one can hardly speak of them as religious figures. By contrast
Euripides gives to his imaginary predecessor of the Artemis cults in Attica
the seemingly real cult of the Taurian Artemis. But it is "seemingly real" only
because Euripides was attentive to practised religion and gave necessary
elements of that to his imaginary cult.

And, finally, not least among his innovations is Euripides' treatment of

myths concerning the gods. Unlike Aeschylus, who refashioned myths to
reveal the ultimate justice of the gods and of Zeus in particular, and unlike
Sophocles, who employed myths to highlight and challenge human heroes,
Euripides seems often to have let the mythological tales run their course in
traditional form and then drawn the conclusions about mortals and gods that
such tales imply. If one accepts as true the tales of Heracles in the *Heracles*,
of Aphrodite and Artemis in the *Hippolytus*, of Dionysus in the *Bacchae*, and
of Athena and Poseidon in the *Troades*, one can hardly credit these deities
with the same ethics, morality, justice, wisdom, and *sophrosyne* one admires in
human beings.[128] Rather than reshape the myths as Hesiod, Aeschylus, and
Pindar did, Euripides either let them stand or chose versions which cast these
problems into a bright light. As a result, in these plays and others rather
harsh criticisms of *mythological* gods are indeed expressed or implied. It is
from this approach to myth, if not idiosyncratic at least most developed
among the tragedians, that scholars who have equated mythology with real
religion find in Euripides a critic of religion. But—to state it a final time—
their equation is false. However much Euripides may lay open mythological
gods to criticism, he finds no fault with, indeed he supports, the fundamental
beliefs and practices of popular religion.

EXODOS

I conclude with the lines with which Euripides so often closed his plays:

> Many are the forms of the divinities,
> and the gods bring to pass many things contrary to our
> expectations.
> That which was expected was not accomplished,
> and a god found a way to bring forth the unexpected.
> So this work turned out.[129]

In the Greek tradition there are many forms of divinities, some
mythological, some philosophical, and some popular. They should not be
confused. What we had expected to find we did not. Aeschylus, the most
theological, is most removed from the practised religion of his time. The
"pious" Sophocles shows least interest in popular religion and least attention
to its details. Euripides, "the poet of the enlightenment," "the savage critic
of conventional religion," "the promoter of impiety," gives to popular
religion, properly understood, the strongest and most consistent support. So
this work turned out.

A Note on Spelling

The names of ancient authors and their works and the spellings of the names of characters of the tragedies are, with a few exceptions, those of the second edition of the *Oxford Classical Dictionary* (1970). The epithets of deities and some place names are, however, in the Greek, not Latinized, style.

Notes

1. Nilsson, *Geschichte der griechischen Religion*, 1:772.
2. For Artemis and Aphrodite in E. *Hipp.* see above, pp. 146–147.
3. See above, pp. 21–22, 143.
4. See above, pp. 64–68.
5. See above, p. 65.
6. See above, pp. 87–101.
7. See above, p. 26.
8. E.g., in Athens, at least after 420, Asclepios had the healing functions usually given to Apollo in tragedy. Similarly in classical Greece success in seafaring was sought by sacrifices to beneficent deities, especially Poseidon. In tragedy problems with seafaring are usually overcome by appeasing an angry deity.
9. See above, pp. 17–29, 138–139.
10. It seems a convention of tragedy, in fact of all Greek literature, that requests by individuals having asylum are just and are, or should be, granted. See above, pp. 71–72.
11. See above, pp. 129–131.
12. See above, pp. 160–161.
13. See above, pp. 147–151, 158–162.
14. See above, p. 159.
15. See above, pp. 86–87.
16. See above, pp. 86–87, 178–179.
17. See above, pp. 86–87. For arguments that Zeus dispenses justice in the *Iliad* see Lloyd-Jones, *The Justice of Zeus*, 1–27.
18. See above, pp. 29–45.
19. On Apollo's false oracle in the *Ion* see above, pp. 90–91.
20. Cf. Parker, *Miasma*, 15: "while in high literature the seer is always right, in comedy he is always wrong."
21. It is a tragic convention that oracles and *dei ex machina* give prior or immediate validation to new cults. In life such validation was usually sought from Delphi *post factum*. See above, p. 89.
22. It also seems to be a tragic convention that only women have prophetic dreams. See above, pp. 102–103.
23. See above, p. 121.
24. On Antigone in Sophocles' *Antigone* as an exception to this see above, p. 123.
25. See above, p. 291 n. 116.
26. Mikalson, "Religion and the Plague in Athens, 431–423 B.C." On Nicias see above, pp. 162–164.
27. On Zeus, religion, and justice in Aeschylus see Rose, "Theology and Mythology in Aeschylus"; Solmsen, "Strata of Greek Religion in Aeschylus" and *Hesiod and Aeschylus*; Lloyd-Jones, "Zeus in Aeschylus" and *The Justice of Zeus*, 84–103; Winnington-Ingram, "A Religious Function of Greek Tragedy"; Kiefner, *Der religiöse Allbegriff des Aischylos*.

28. See above, pp. 74–75.

29. On Zeus Hikesios see above, pp. 74–75.

30. See above, p. 192.

31. On Zeus Xenios as a literary deity see above, p. 77. Cf. A. *Suppl.* 627–629.

32. See above, pp. 192–193, 194–196.

33. Cf. A. *Suppl.* 583–585.

34. A. *Suppl.* 156–160, 230–231, *Ag.* 1385–1387, *Ch.* 382–385, *Eum.* 273–275, frag. 273a[R]. Cf. S. *OC* 1606; E. frag. 912[N].

35. Among the tragedians Aeschylus alone makes Zeus and Dike authors of τὰ νόμιμα. See above, pp. 194–195. On Zeus Hikesios and Xenios in Homer see Lloyd-Jones, *The Justice of Zeus*, 5. On justice and piety see above, pp. 178–179.

36. See above, p. 178.

37. Cf. A. frag. 70[R]. The justice of Zeus may well have been a central issue also in the lost plays of the Prometheian trilogy.

38. See above, pp. 50–51.

39. See above, pp. 49–53. For the one instance in Euripides where the Athenians expect divine support because their campaign is just see E. *Suppl.* 594–596 and p. 249 n. 148 above.

40. Euripides in *IT* 1469–1472 follows Aeschylus' version of the founding of the Areopagus but does not make it into an exemplum of the justice of the gods. He seems merely to be following Aeschylus' account of the fate of Orestes. See above, p. 254 n. 232.

41. See above, pp. 35–37.

42. According to the *Vita* (9) of Aeschylus, the appearance of the chorus of Erinyes so terrified the audience that children fainted and women miscarried. On the story see Taplin, *The Stagecraft of Aeschylus*, 372, 438 n. 2; Calder, "*Vita Aeschyli* 9."

43. On the Erinyes and Semnai in Aeschylus, literature, myth, and cult see Rose, "Theology and Mythology in Aeschylus"; Solmsen, *Hesiod and Aeschylus*, 178–224; E. Wüst, "Erinyes," *RE* suppl. 8 (1956), cols. 82–166; Winnington-Ingram, "A Religious Function of Greek Tragedy" and *Sophocles*, 205–216; Dietrich, *Death, Fate, and the Gods*, 91–156; Henrichs, "The *Eumenides* and Wineless Libations" and "The 'Sobriety' of Oedipus"; A. L. Brown, "The Erinyes in the *Oresteia*"; Lloyd-Jones, "Les Erinyes."

44. See Paus. 1.28.6–7, 1.30.4, 1.31.4; and above, note 43.

45. Paus. 7.25.2–3; Thuc. 1.126.11; Plut. *Sol.* 12.1; and above, pp. 69–70.

46. Ar. *Eq.* 1311–1312, *Thesm.* 224.

47. See above, pp. 69–77.

48. Paus. 1.28.6; Dinarchus 1.47; schol. to Aeschines 1.188.

49. Solmsen, *Hesiod and Aeschylus*, 178–224; Winnington-Ingram, "A Religious Function of Greek Tragedy," 21; Parker, *Miasma*, 125.

50. For criticisms of this traditional view see Lloyd-Jones, *The Justice of Zeus*, 90–95.

51. See above, pp. 183–185.

52. See above, pp. 13–14.

53. If we accept the contention of, e.g., Dietrich and Lloyd-Jones (above, note 43) that the Erinyes were deities worshiped in archaic Athens, then the Erinyes of the *Eumenides* would not be so much Aeschylus' personal creation as his revival of deities once important to popular religion.

54. See above, p. 11.

55. If we accept δέει, Casaubon's conjecture, in line 522. Cf. Thuc. 2.37.3.

56. For the "classic view" of Sophocles' piety and its relationship to interpretation of the plays see Whitman, *Sophocles*, 4–21. Cf. B.M.W. Knox, *The Heroic Temper*, 52–54.

57. The earliest explicit claim of Sophocles' exceptional piety is apparently the scholion to S. *El.* 831 = T107[R]. Two other such explicit claims are thought to be found in Satyrus' *Vita* of Sophocles (third century B.C.) but are based on misinterpretations of the passages. The most recent detailed study of Sophocles' piety is Lefkowitz's *Lives of the Greek Poets*, 76, 83–84, 86–87. I give her translations of the *Vita* here, with my reservations stated below.

Vita 12: "Sophocles was more pious than anyone else, according to what Hieronymus says (frag. 31, Wehrli) ... about his golden crown. When this crown was stolen from the Acropolis, Heracles came to Sophocles in a dream and told him to go into the house on the right and it would be hidden there. Sophocles brought this information to the citizens and received a reward of a talent, as had been announced in advance. He used the talent to establish a shrine of Heracles Informer." The word translated as "pious" is, however, θεοφιλής, and that is not what it means in classical Greek. It means, rather, "god-loved," and the point of the story (whether it be true or not; see Lefkowitz, 84) is that Sophocles is god-loved because the gods helped him find the crown which he presumably had been awarded and had dedicated to an Acropolis deity. He is not here being labeled pious for founding a shrine. On θεοφιλής see Dirlmeier, ΘΕΟΦΙΛΙΑ-ΦΙΛΟΘΕΙΑ. "

Vita 16: "Lobon says that this epitaph was written on his tomb: In this tomb I hide Sophocles who won first prize with his tragic art, a most holy figure." Σχῆμα τὸ σεμνότατον means, it must be emphasized, a figure "most respected," "most revered." Lobon's Sophocles was the receiver of the σέδας, not the giver of it. The Greek says nothing of Sophocles' own εὐσέδεια.

We may correct one further small misunderstanding arising from mistranslation of the *Vita*. Ister (*FGrHist* 334 F37) and Neanthes (*FGrHist* 84 F18) say that Sophocles died not "at the festival of the Choes" (Lefkowitz, 86) but "about the time of the Choes" (πεοι τοὺς χόας). If we believe their account, we know only the date of his death (ca. 12 Anthesterion 406 B.C.), not that he died while celebrating a sacred festival.

58. On the cult of Dexion see Lefkowitz, *Lives of the Greek Poets*, 84; Ferguson, "The Attic Orgeones," 86–91. For a recent assessment of Sophocles' role in the founding of the Asclepios cult in Athens see Aleshire, *The Athenian Asklepieion*, 9–11.

59. See above, p. 39.

60. See above, pp. 39–41. See also B. M. W. Knox, *The Heroic Temper*, 54–58.

61. See above, pp. 162–164.

62. For the Christian assumptions lying behind such a view see Schlesier's comments on Euripidean criticism in "Götterdämmerung bei Euripides?" 39–40.

63. See above, p. 178.

64. See above, p. 48. Nestle (*Euripides*, 66) notes that from the traditional list Sophocles omits only divination, which of course he would have had to assign to the gods.

65. Even the sanctuary of a hero such as Proteus was exceptional as a place of asylum. See above, p. 259 n. 22.

66. See above, p. 121.

67. Cf. Fraenkel on A. *Ag.* 1602.

68. On this scene see Burian, "Supplication and Hero Cult."

69. On the "double burial" see Winnington-Ingram, *Sophocles*, 125 n. 31; Gellie, *Sophocles: A Reading*, 38–39; Kitto, *Form and Meaning*, 138–158: and, most recently, Rothaus, "The Single Burial of Polyneices."

70. On the ritual elements in the two burials see Bradshaw, "The Watchman Scenes."

71. See above, p. 85.

72. See above, p. 85.

73. For Sophocles' possible manipulation of the Athenian Oedipus cult to achieve unity in the *Oedipus at Colonus* see Pfister, *Der Reliquienkult*, 110–112. To the list of Sophocles' irregularities might be added the prayer (*Ant.* 1126–1152) to a Delphic/Theban/Athenian Dionysus to come and "purify" Thebes.

74. A fuller study of this topic appears in Mikalson, "Zeus the Father and Heracles the Son in Tragedy."

75. E.g., 126–128, 139–140, 251–280, 499–500, 1021–1022, 1278.

76. The praises of deities and Athens may be mixed (see Kamerbeek on 668–670, 707–711), but the focus is usually on Colonus. In 668–719, e.g., the Panathenian deities are introduced through links with flowers and produce of Colonus.

77. Cf. 62–63.

78. According to the biographical tradition (T81–84[R]), the aged Sophocles, as his only defense against charges of senility and incompetence lodged by his son, read this ode to the jury. The charges were judged baseless. For a very skeptical account of this story see Lefkowitz, *Lives of the Greek Poets*, 84–85.

79. Poseidon Hippios and Athena Hippia: 707–719, 1070–1073. Pausanias saw at Colonus, near Oedipus' tomb, altars of these two deities (1.30.4). Cf. Thuc. 8.67; E. *Ph.* 1707. On the cult of these two deities see Farnell, *The Cults of the Greek States*, 1:270–272; Burkert, *GR*, 138, 221. Demeter Euchloös (1600) should be identified with Demeter Chloe ("Of Green Vegetation"). She had a sanctuary near the Acropolis in Pausanias' time (1.22.3), and her sanctuaries, sacrifices, festivals, and priestesses are attested throughout Attica from the fourth century B.C. to the second century A.D. (*IG* II^2 1356, 1358, 1472, 4748, 4750, 5129). From *OC* 1600–1603 some have assigned her a shrine on a hill near Colonus. On her cult see Jacoby on *FGrHist* 328 F61; Nilsson, *Geschichte der griechischen Religion*, 1:151,467; Farnell, *The Cults of the Greek States*, 3:33–48. Zeus Morios and Athena Moria: 694–706. On their cult see Nilsson, *Geschichte der griechischen Religion*, 1:442; K. Latte, "Moria," *RE* 16 (1933), cols. 302–303. Prometheus: 55–56. Cf. Paus. 1.30.2; schol. to S. *OC* 56. Aphrodite and the Muses: 691–693. On their joint cult in Athens, with one site perhaps near the Cephisus River, see above, pp. 63–64. Colonus: 58–61.

80. Dionysus, Demeter, and Kore: 683–684, 1050–1053.

81. Cf. 54–55, 707–719, 887–889, 1070–1073, 1156–1159, 1285–1287, 1491–1495.

82. On the cult see p. 246 n. 105 above.

83. Cf. 258–262, 275–283, 1006–1013, 1124–1127.

84. See B. M. W. Knox, *The Heroic Temper*, 109.

85. For summaries of nineteenth-century views of Euripides see Jenkyns, *The Victorians and Ancient Greece*, 92, 106–110; Henrichs, "The Last of the Detractors"; Calder, "Wilamowitz: *Sospitator Euripidis*"; Michelini, *Euripides and the Tragic Tradition*, 3–51. For more recent proponents see Nestle, *Euripides*; Verrall, *Euripides the Rationalist*; note esp. Zuntz, *The Political Plays of Euripides*; 52: "I for one, though, should very much hesitate ... to credit Euripides with even a passing devotion to the 'popular religion.'" Cf. *Euripide*, 205, 215. See also Klotsche, *The Supernatural in Euripides*, 98; Page, *Euripides: Medea*, ix; Gamble, "Euripides' *Suppliant Women*: Decision and Ambivalence," 405. Such views are also shared by some scholars who specialize in religion, not Greek tragedy—e.g., Rose in *La notion du divin*, 229: "I had always thought of (Euripides) as a man interested in religion as a subject of study and criticism, on occasion of antiquarian research, but personally of a non-religious temperament." Cf. Nilsson, *Geschichte der griechischen Religion*, 1:771–779. For helpful correctives to the tradition of Euripides as antireligious see Schmid and Staehlin, *Geschichte der griechischen Literatur*, 1.3:701–726; Chapouthier, "Euripide et l'accueil du divin"; Grube, *The Drama of Euripides*, 41–62; Dover, "The Freedom of the

Intellectual," 42–46; Lloyd-Jones, *The Justice of Zeus*, 144–155; Schlesier, "Götterdämmerung bei Euripides?"; Lefkowitz, "Was Euripides an Atheist?" and "Impiety and Atheism in Euripides' Dramas"; Yunis, *A New Creed*, passim.

86. See above, pp. 8–9.

87. Yunis. *A New Creed*, passim, esp. 11–58.

88. See below, pp. 233–235.

89. Cf. B. M. W. Knox, *Word and Action*, 326.

90. *IG* II^2 1362 and 1177, lines 17–21.

91. See above, p. 5.

92. On the life of Euripides see Lefkowitz, *Lives of the Greek Poets*, 88–104, 110, 163–169, and "Was Euripides an Atheist?"; Stevens, "Euripides and the Athenians."

93. Avery, "My Tongue Swore, but My Mind Is Unsworn," 22–25; Fairweather, "Fiction in the Biographies of Ancient Writers," 255; Arrighetti, *Satiro, Vita di Euripide*, 125; Winiarczyk, "Wer Galt im Altertum als Atheist?" 170–171; Lefkowtiz, "Was Euripides an Atheist?" 159–160. For the likelihood that the whole incident is a late fiction see Dover, "The Freedom of the Intellectual," 29, 42–46.

94. See above, pp. 5, 85–86.

95. MacDowell, *The Law in Classical Athens*, 162–164.

96. Barrett. *Euripides: Hippolytos*, 13.

97. For the three allusions see Ar. *Thesm.* 275–276, *Ran.* 101–102, 1471.

98. For what evidence some might adduce—namely *IT 570–575, HF 1341–1346, and Tr.* 884–888—see Reinhardt, *Tradition und Geist*, 232–234. On these passages see pp. 107–110, 156, 233–234.

99. E.g., Schlesier, "Daimon und Daimones bei Euripides" and "Götterdämmerung bei Euripides?"; Lefkowitz, "Impiety and Atheism in Euripides' Dramas."

100. On the actual and potential misuse, ancient and modern, of fragments to demonstrate Euripides' impiety see Dover, "The Freedom of the Intellectual," 44–46.

101. Cf. Yunis, *A New Creed*, 14.

102. Collard (*Euripides: Supplices*, pp. 407–408) recognizes that having the *deus ex machina* found or ratify cults is a Euripidean innovation. On *dei ex machina* see above, pp. 64–68. On the relationship of these aetiologies to the actual cults at Brauron and Halae see Lloyd-Jones, "Artemis and Iphigeneia." On *Suppliants* and the Theban heroes see Pfister, *Der Reliquienkult*, 189–190.

103. Cults of Heracles: Pfister, *Der Reliquienkult*, 202 n. 746. Cult of Medea: Pfister, 313–314, 567.

104. For a fuller list of such αἴτια in Euripides, Sophocles, Aeschylus, and other tragedians see Schmid and Staehlin, *Geschichte der griechischen Literatur*, 1.3:705 n. 7. Cf. Barrett on E. *Hipp.* 1423–1430.

105. See Barrett on *Hipp.* 24–40 ("addicted"); Conacher, *Euripidean Drama*, 304 ("bonuses"). On all this see Grube, *The Drama of Euripides*, 78–79.

106. Webster, *The Tragedies of Euripides*, 27. Cf. B. M. W. Knox, *Word and Action*, 326–327.

107. Kamerbeek in *Euripide*, II; Schmid and Staehlin, *Geschichte der griechischen Literatur, 1.3:705 n. 7, 1.2:480*; Pfister, *Der Reliquienkult*, 571–572. Cf. Dodds, "Euripides the Irrationalist," 101, on Euripides: "The state religion meant little or nothing to him."

108. Schmid and Staehlin, *Geschichte der griechischen Literatur*, 1.3:707–708.

109. Diller, "Umwelt und Masse."

110. But on the greater realism, compared to Aeschylus' *Eumenides*, of the place and cult at Delphi see Zeitlin, "The Argive Festival of Hera and Euripides' *Electra*," 645 n. 3.

111. On the deities depicted in the *Medea* and *Phoenissae* see Mikalson, "Unanswered Prayers."

112. See above, pp. 121–123.

113. Cf., e.g., general cult, *Tr.* 1060–1076; birth ritual, *El.* 1124–1133, *Ion* 24–26, and frag. 2[N]; marriage ritual, *IA* 716–723, 1110–1114; festivals, *El.* 171–180, *Ph.* 784–791, *HF* 687–690, *Hec.* 466–474, *IT* 947–960; purifications, *HF* 922–942; initiation rites, *Bacchae*, passim, frag. 472[N]; sacrifice, *IA* 433–438, *Hyps.* frag. I.IV[Bond], 29–32; rites for specific deities, *Hipp.* 1423–1430, *IT* 1449–1467, *Med.* 1378–1383.

114. Schlesier, "Daimon und Daimones bei Euripides," 271.

115. See above, pp. 130–131.

116. On the "unexpected orthodoxy" of the *Suppliants* see Conacher, "Religious and Ethical Attitudes in Euripides' *Suppliants*" and *Euripidean Drama*, 93–108. Cf. Schmid and Staehlin, *Geschichte der griechischen Literatur*, 1.3:723–724; Pohlenz, *Die Griechische Tragödie*, 358, 364.

117. E.g., Zuntz, *The Political Plays of Euripides*, 3–54. Cf. his comment on the *Heraclidae*: "The trust in divine succour which the Chorus bases upon the righteousness of his cause and upon the punctual observance of the national cult could confirm and purify the convictions of the faithful. The ʼσοφοί among the audience might perhaps tend to enjoy the last antistrophos mainly as the piece of beautiful lyric which it is ...; they might also substitute their philosophical concepts for the personal deities to whom the Chorus refers" (48).

118. E.g., Greenwood, *Aspects of Euripidean Tragedy*, 92–120; Conacher, "Religious and Ethical Attitudes in Euripides' *Suppliants*" and *Euripidean Drama*, 93–108. Athenians of the fourth century certainly did not view the events of the *Heraclidae* and *Suppliants* ironically. In much the form in which Euripides presented them these stories became standard features of Athenian self-encomia (Lys. 2.7; Dem. 7.8, Pl. *Menex.* 239B; Isoc. 4.54–56, 12.168–171; cf. Hdt. 9.27.3), and even foreigners wishing to curry Athenian favor could refer to them (Xen. *Hell.* 6.5.46–47).

119. See above, pp. 62–64, 152–153.

120. Dodds, "Euripides the Irrationalist," 97: "While Sophocles is a dramatist, Euripides happens to be, like Bernard Shaw and Pirandello, a philosophical dramatist." For a skeptical account of the biographical tradition linking Euripides to Anaxagoras, Protagoras, and Prodicus see Lefkowitz, "Was Euripides an Atheist?"

121. Chapouthier, "Euripide et l' accueil du divin," 205—225.

122. Xenophanes, frags. A32, B11, B12[DK]; cf. B14–B16, B23–B26[DK]. On possible relationships of these lines to the meaning of the play see Mikalson, "Zeus the Father and Heracles the Son in Tragedy"; Yunis, *A New Creed*, 157–171.

123. On which see Dodds on E. *Ba.* 274–285, 292–294. On *Ba.* 274–285 see also Henrichs, "Two Doxographical Notes," 110 n. 64; Lefkowitz, "Impiety and Atheism in Euripides' Dramas," 74–75.

124. See above, p. 284 n. 122.

125. On the relationship of Hecuba's invocation to the meaning of the play see above, p. 156.

126. Nestle (*Euripides*, passim, and "Untersuchungen über die philosophischen Quellen des Euripides"), Schmid and Staehlin (*Geschichte der griechischen Literatur*, 1.3:315–317), and Webster (*The Tragedies of Euripides*, 295) list numerous references in Euripides' plays to theories of identifiable philosophers (as distinct from passages exhibiting arguments in a "sophistic style"). From the complete plays the likely or even possible ones, in addition to those discussed here, are *Hipp.* 385–387, *Hec.* 798–805, *Suppl.* 201–215, *HF* 757–759, *IT*

389–391, *Ph.* 538–545, *Or.* 982–983, *Ba.* 201–203. Fragments 189[N], 282[N], 638[N], 833[N], and 839[N] may also have a philosophical background.

127. This was a philosophical conception to which Euripides turned several times, sometimes identifying Aether with Zeus (frags. 839[N], 877[N], 941[N], sometimes making Aether the destination of the souls of the dead (*Suppl.* 531–536, 1138–1141, on which see pp. 114–115 above; *Hel.* 1014–1016; frag. 839[N]). But in no surviving play except the *Helen* does he create a cult for Aether. Aristophanes mocks Euripides' frequent references to Aether (*Ran.* 100, 888–894, *Thesm.* 14–15, 43, 51, 272, 1067).

128. See, e.g., Conacher, *Euripidean Drama*, 50–53, 81–83, 312.

129. For defenses of these lines as closing the *Medea, Bacchae, Hippolytus, Andromache, Helen,* and *Alcestis* see Roberts, "Parting Words"; Lefkowitz, Implety and Atheism in Euripides' Dramas," 80–82.

RUTH PADEL

Knowledge That Is Sad to Have to Know

TERRORS OF THE EARTH

To sum up. Greek tragedy represents madness as something temporary, come from outside. It darkens within like a storm, twists how you see. It is inner writhing, expressed externally in dancelike jerkiness. People know you are mad by how you look and move. Madness is associated with "black earth" (a deep Greek image for the mind itself), with what comes out of it (Erinyes, black roots), and with the emotion that does most outside damage: anger. (The West's first sentence asks the Muse to sing of Achilles' anger, that brought pain to the Greeks.)

Madness is an overdetermined black: color of anger, storm, earth, and tragedy itself. In this black, you see differently. You may see true things—but not things it is safe or comfortable to see. Madness isolates. The mad do not look or see like other people. They are dangerous. Self-set apart, walled out by others, madness wanders. It resembles other isolating marks of divine hostility: disease, skin disease, pollution. Madness is mistake, damage, and ultimately self-damage whose cruellest examples are *theomachia* (battle against god) and killing your own children.

This, very roughly, is Greek tragedy's grammar of madness. We inherit it. Its elements have patterned tragedy through centuries. They are at work, for instance, in Shakespeare and our response to him as Lear faces madness:

From *Whom Gods Destroy: Elements of Greek and Tragic Madness.* © 1995 by Princeton University Press.

> I will have such revenge upon you both
> That all the world shall—I will do such things—
> What they are yet I know not; but they shall be
> The terrors of the earth. You think I'll weep.
> No, I'll not weep. [*Storm and tempest.*]
> I have full cause of weeping; but this heart
> Shall break into a hundred thousand flaws
> Or ere I'll weep. O fool, I shall go mad![1]

But why was it tragedy that gave us this? You can see many of these elements in other classical writers, but tragedy is the body of work that established the whole Western grammar of madness. Why? What has madness to do with tragedy, and tragedy to do with madness, that brought this about?

IN THE MAD GOD'S THEATER: TAKING ILLUSION FOR REALITY

> GLOUSTER: Come, cousin, canst thou quake and change thy colour,
>   Murder thy breath in middle of a word,
>   And then begin again, and stop again,
>   As if thou were distraught and mad with terror?
> BUCKINGHAM: Tut, I can counterfeit the deep tragedian....
>   —Shakespeare, *Richard III* 3.5

Tragedy structured itself, I have suggested, round an initially Homeric insight into the world-damage a damaged mind can do. Within that structure, madness has two roles. It is both human—a permanent possibility, a hyperbolic presence against which tragic acts are judged—and divine: a sudden incursion, daemonic destruction of mind or life. Madness takes up this position in a genre which evolved, specifically, in a "mad" god's theater.

Mainomenos Dionusos.[2] Out of all the features of this god's impacted persona, and the relation each of them bears to his madness, tragedy's madness most sharply, I think, mirrors three.

First, his violence. The violence both of madness and of Dionysus mirrors that of tragedy: the reported violence of Greek tragedy, the performed violence of tragedy in other ages. This is particularly clear in the Renaissance, which received the tragic tradition through the prism of Roman violence, especially Seneca, and responded to its violence in a way the nineteenth century did not.[3] Dionysus connects interior violence, hurt mind, mad thought, with violence performed: on stage, in the world. In cult and in tragedy Dionysus is a link between madness and murder.[4]

Greek tragedy's interest in a connection between violence and madness comes over also in its use of Delphi. In many lost tragedies, Delphi purifies madness caused by bloodguilt. Orestes was not the only one. Alcmaeon, Telephus, Athamas: their madness was there in the myths but tragedy kept choosing to stage it; to explore the link between madness and spilled blood.[5]

Second, the relation between Dionysus's madness and his interest in illusion, disguise. Madness involves taking illusion for reality (see Chapter 7). This is what any audience does. "Actors are madmen, playgoers are fools," says an ancient Chinese proverb. In context, this speaks to a traditional Chinese image of the theater's votaries: to an insiderism that has nothing to do with Athenian theater. But the words reflect a strange remove in the bond any theater creates between those who watch and those who play. Athenians sat in the precinct of a "mad" god, with whom it was normal to "be mad." They did so to share illusion as truth, for a while. The theater's truth is illusion, which you treat as reality: doing that is madness.[6]

Feigned madness is another feature of tragedy. The story that Odysseus pretended madness, to duck the Trojan war draft, went back to a Homeric epic, the *Cypria*. The fifth century loved it and Cicero implies he thinks tragedy invented it. Lost plays that used it include Sophocles' *Odysseus Mainomenos*.[7]

Feigning madness became big business in Renaissance tragedy. Asked to seem "mad for grief," Buckingham "can counterfeit the deep tragedian." Madness and feigning belong automatically in "deep" tragedy. Hamlet's madness, interpreted as proving him "mad for love," is tested. What he told Ophelia "was not like madness." Once it is seen through, Hamlet is in danger. Like Edgar's, his madness is disguise. Both fake madnesses have enormous power in their plays, mirroring the genuine madness of other characters.[8]

This is madness as mask. Pretend madness, with imagined sanity behind it: as the Greek audience knows the real actor is behind and in the mask.[9] "Real" madness on stage is the drama itself feigning madness. Illusion, taken for reality, is presented by the illusion of a person, a mask that hides the actor. Madness and feigned madness alike belong with the strangeness of tragic performance: masses of people, collectively taking illusion for reality. Dionysus presides over disguise.[10]

Third, the relation between Dionysus's own madness and his outsider status. Tragic madness evokes images of darkness and nonhumanity, of being "outside," alienated. In several cults and myths, Dionysus's persona had this "outside" status too.[11]

These, I think, are some background reasons for the importance of madness in fifth-century tragedy. Vase-painters reflect this importance, and give tragic madness a high profile. Their market too valued tragedy's madness and its daemons.[12] For the Athenian imagination, Dionysus connected violence, wild madwomen on mountains, death, illusion—and the theater. The fact that this is his theater itself makes madness important for tragedy.

"Tragic Fall"

> The ship, the black freighter....
> —Brecht, *The Threepenny Opera*

Madness is also the perfect image of tragic "fall." In mediaeval Christian Europe, when tragedy is simply the narrative of disaster, laying bare "the universal drama of the fall of man," "fall" resonates with images of Adam, and tragedy is "harm" of the "fallen":

> The harm of hem that stode in heigh degree
> And fillen so that ther nas no remedie.

From the first European account, criticism takes the damage-fall as tragedy's characteristic movement: "Tragedie is noon other maner thing."[13] Even earlier, in Greek tragedy itself, "fall" is an image through which tragedy can see itself. The chorus, faced with Oedipus's "fall" from king to moral outcast, sings

> Mortals, I count you as nothing.
> As dead generations. No one has more
> than this much luck with life and gods: just
> to seem happy. Then, having had that seeming,
> fall away. Oedipus, you, and your *daim?n*,
> I cannot call happy.[14]

In Greek tragedy, vulnerability to "fall" is double. Daemonic agents of harm rush above in the air and "fall" on human heads. "With a great leap from above," say the Furies,

> I bring down my foot's heavy-falling force.
> My limbs make even fast runners fall:
> a terrible disaster. And as he falls,
> he knows nothing, in mad folly.

"Fall" has daemonic resonance. Unseen agents ambush human lives:

> It creeps up on
> the man who knows nothing
> before he approaches his foot
> to the hot fire.[15]

This Greek awareness of chaotic vulnerability to daemons that "fall at" you out of the air, making *you* "fall," became the tragic sense. Conrad, according to Bertrand Russell, thought of "civilized and morally tolerable human life as a dangerous walk on a thin crust of barely cooled lava, which might break at any moment and let the unwary sink into fiery depths."[16] From outer to inner. Daemonic fall in tragedy is answered by, and also explains, fall within. Madness is central to this image: that we live on the edge of chasm. It gives tragic "fall" its inner echo chamber. Greek daemons operate inside as well as outside. Sophocles' image of approaching fire unawares comes from his "*atē*-song."[17] Madness is the inward correlative of external "fall": reason "topples." "What a noble mind is here o'erthrown."

"Disease of Heroes"

In many respects, all tragic heroes are *like* the mad. Or (the other way round) a mad person is image of a tragic hero. There are important similarities between heroes and the mad, as tragedy represents both. What madness does, heroes also do. Even sane, Greek tragic heroes are a destructive and self-destructive lot. They kill others and themselves, blind others and themselves.[18] In tragedy as in cult, a near-animal capacity for violence can make someone a "hero." Tragic madness is violent. It upsets distinctions between human and animal, often violently.[19] Sometimes one violent act was enough to turn a historical figure into a worshipped "hero."[20] Tragic heroes are isolated in their unshareable vision. Antigone the hero rejects, even "hates," the nonheroic sister who loves her but cannot see things her way. Tecmessa begs Ajax to soften, not endanger himself by rebelling. He shakes off her loving plea: "You're a fool if you want to educate my nature now."[21]

If heroes are *like* the mad, they are also the people likely to go mad. From late antiquity madness can be called *to pathos hērōikon*: "the disease of heroes." The thought could be reported ironically, but it was there all along, getting a boost in the Renaissance from the reevaluation of *Problem* 30. Heroes go mad. Not just tragedy's heroes, but those of Arthurian and Irish myth like Lancelot, Tristan, Sweeney.[22] In this relation of tragic heroes and madness, here is another turn of the crystal. Heroes are specially *prone to madness*.[23]

You might say, *Of course* the elements of tragic madness are manifest in tragic heroes. It is they who go mad. The features they demonstrate as heroes match features of madness you found *in them*. Circular, isn't it?

No. On the one hand, tragic heroes display many of the qualities of madness, like aggression or self-destruction, when they are sane. And on the other hand, tragedy does not sign its interest in madness only in its heroes. Madness is everywhere. Lyssa and Erinyes are characters on the stage of some tragedies, and are painted in scenes from other tragedies by vase-painters *as if* they were around, even though the plays themselves had not put them on the stage. Madness is often spoken of, rather than brought on stage. Its hyperbolic presence contributes to a continual sense of madness. In *Antigone*, the chorus hints that Haemon is mad with love. His father calls him "empty of mind," and expects him not to "rave against his sire." *He* says his father is "not in his right mind." The chorus later sings of someone else's madness: Lycurgus opposed Dionysus and maenads, and madly killed his son. As one commentator says, "madness on the one side, madness on the other." Madness is a presence *around* the figures and songs. In one comedy, two characters try to guess the identity of a strange figure. "Perhaps it's an Erinys from tragedy," says one. "She has a mad and tragic look." It is from choral references, hyperbolic accusations of madness, and the identification of Erinyes with tragedy, as well as heroes themselves going mad, that we know madness matters to tragedy.[24]

Madness visits Greek tragic heroes. It is not "in" them as firmly and clearly as it is in later heroes. For the Renaissance, madness is something wrong within. You must get it out: purge the black bile, exorcise the demons. Horrific sixteenth-century drawings and paintings show doctors cutting the "stone of folly" from the forehead of the mad, who queue up for the operation.[25] Greek tragic heroes are marked rather by a *relation* to madness, which is out there in the world: an external possibility that permanently threatens the human interior in its pain.

Maybe being apt for madness, and being *like* the mad, makes them heroes. Maybe tragedy uses madness as a metaphor for a hero. In a sense, the ultimate "hero" of tragedy is its image of consciousness, divided and ambiguous, active and passive in its suffering: something that gets destroyed and yet survives. The "place where the terrible is good," which lives catastrophe, suffers divine damage, and endures.[26] It goes mad, and survives.

Tragedy is about something that goes suddenly wrong—in a house, family, city, and in the inner correlate of this, the mind. One thing wrong in the tragic universe is the permanent possibility of sudden madness, of mind damage leading to outside damage. Madness, the nonhuman inside the human, shatters "human" in outer and inner worlds.[27] It is reversal at every level: reason's polluted shadow; being suddenly hated as much as you were loved by gods; being outside society instead of safe within. It twists and damages seeing, feeling, relating. It is the permanent shadow to ordinary ways of being. Tragedy's compound image of madness belongs with this sense of damage and survival. Madness is the epitome of tragic harm: outer and inner, savage, temporary, daemonic, miraculously survivable, but with enduring terrible results. Apt metaphor for a tragic hero.[28]

TRUTH FROM ILLUSION, TRUTH FROM PAIN

Heroes resemble the mad in one more thing. Both produce truth out of pain. Sometimes the truth is a prophecy; the pain is physical agony, grief, or simply being on the point of death. Polymestor sees his children murdered in front of him, then gets blinded. Then he prophesies the deaths of Agamemnon and Cassandra, and the metamorphosis of his tormentor Hecuba. Oedipus hears gods "herald" his death and sends for Theseus, tified with tragedy: Wilson and Taplin 1993:176. Elizabethan and Jacobean tragedies also make constant side reference to madness, outside madness-scenes: e.g., *Duchess of Malfi* 1.1.505, 4.2.5, 4.2.17, 5.2.8–26, 5.4.15. that Theseus may find him still "straight in his *phrēn*."Before dying, he tells Theseus secret truths, important for Athens.[29]

Truth coming out of pain, or at the edge of death, underpins Athenian torture of slave witnesses. A slave's testimony was not believed unless he was tortured. Physical pain also accompanied prophetic possession.[30] The *splanchna*, innards, were prophetic: animal *splanchna* were consulted in entrail divination, and tragedy often speaks of human *splanchna* as "knowing" and "prophesying." It is as if the gods had a special line to innards, particularly apparent at the moment of death.[31]

Prophecy at the point of death was connected, anciently, with Pythagoras.[32] It had deep appeal throughout the classical period and caught fire in mediaeval and Renaissance imagination:

HOTSPUR: O! I could prophesy,
                  But that the earthy and cold hand of death
                  Lies on my tongue. No, Percy, thou art dust,
                  And food for—

PRINCE: For worms, brave Percy.
                  Fare thee well great heart![33]

The truth produced in agony before death may be prophecy about a particular future (as for Theseus and Hecuba). Mental or moral agony, at the edge of madness, also produces prophecy and true utterance: maybe a moral truth from the brink, like that uttered by Orestes as he feels madness approaching, which embodies a specific view of the past.[34] Truth comes from the edge of the normal, where people do not usually go. Like prophecy *from* madness: the historical truths sung by mad Cassandra.[35]

We have met before the thought that truth may come from madness. Madness is darkness; but Greek thought expects illumination through the dark. Madness takes illusion for truth, yet some of its illusions *are* truth.[36] Some mad illusions are wrong. Agave and Heracles see their children wrongly. But sometimes the mad see more truely. The Erinyes Orestes sees are really there, for the audience sees them in the next play.[37]

Madness has something deeply to do with the illusions of drama itself: masked actors pretending a story, conveying truth to an audience. An important possibility of madness for other people, the not-mad, is that somewhere in the damage and illusion it may get a truth across. This, perhaps, is the tragic value of madness. It was, I guess, at the heart of Plato's response to tragedy's madness and tragedy's mad god. It made possible his alchemy of the tragic tradition: his revolutionary revaluing of madness as a source of goods, of seeing truth.[38]

A tragic hero produces truth out of pain most deeply and simply by embodying it. In the Greek tradition, what is destructive, like Sirens, also illumines.[39] Spectators do come away from tragedy with new insight: even though it is knowledge that is "sad to have to know."[40]

Like the mad, heroes are *outside* normal ways of being human.[41] From that outsideness, they convey something about what lies within human limits. Heroes are ec-centric: from *ek*, "out," and *kentron*, a "sharp point," the fixed "pin" of compasses, the "center" of the circle. Heroes are extravagant: from *extra-vagare*, "to wander outside." From extra-vagance and eccentricity come truth about pain and desolation within the human circuit. Throughout Western literature, especially on stage, insights about men have been communicated through representations of women. Equally, insight into the normal self has been got across by representing what is outside and other. By madness.

Madness stages the possibility that out of ec-centric pain, out of taking illusion for reality, may—for the onlookers—come insight into reality, as tragedy presents it.

MADNESS AND THE TRAGEDY-PRODUCING SOCIETY

In the twenty-five centuries since the Greeks, tragedy has emerged quite rarely, in a handful of different times, languages, and societies. In many ways, it is not a continuous tradition. Tragedy expressed itself at specific moments: fifth-century Athens, Elizabethan and Jacobean England, seventeenth-century Spain and France. Some periods tried it and failed. For the Romantics, tragedy was the supreme goal they never reached (except, for a while, in Germany).[42]

Why should madness resurface in tragedy in these different epochs? Maybe one thing these societies share in common is this: that they were all, in different ways, poised on some momentary cusp between theological, or daemonological, and innovative scientific explanations for human pain.[43] Maybe tragedy lives best through a particular interplay or confrontation between these types of explanation in general, and in particular as this confrontation affects ideas of madness, its most poignant example.

In Britain, for example, in the late sixteenth and seventeenth centuries, there is a tension between theological and scientific perspectives on pain and insanity, which might evoke parallels from fifth-century Greece: another society where vibrant religious life rubbed against developing scientific theories of human hurts.[44] Maybe a medical and theological tug-of-war between religious and scientific explanation encourages an attention to madness as illustration of human suffering that is best expressed in tragedy.

It certainly seemed so in the Renaissance, when madness, perceived in real life as shameful and dangerous, had enormous literary value. Robert Burton was born in 1577 and his formative years were those of *Hamlet*, *Othello*, *Lear*, and *Anthony and Cleopatra*. Burton calls the "melancholy" man "the cream of human adversity, the quintessence and upshot."[45] The cult of melancholy had an impetus of its own, but I suspect Burton's image illustrates a general point: that a time of intense making of tragedy is a time of intense interest in madness.[46] Madness belongs to, and is valued by, tragic literature in some special way.

Violent physical hurt resonates through tragedy wherever it appears. This hurt reflects tragic verbal imagery, in which passion wounds the innards. What tragedy says happens to mind and spirit reflects what happens to its bodies.[47] Tragedy has many forms of extreme pain. You could read its madness as the supreme example of tragic obsession with mutilating hurt, both physical and spiritual. In the early Renaissance, madness is a *speculum*, "mirror," where human nature sees its own self-hurt.[48]

In or out of tragedy, madness is not the only "disaster." Tragedy, staging many disasters, turned *at?* (its model for madness) into a general word for disaster.[49] It is madness's totality, I think, as result and cause of damage—itself damage both inside and outside, damage to the values and perceptions on which human society frailly rests—which makes it so useful to tragedy.

"The Scream"

> Though it is noon, the helmet screams against the light;
> Scratches the eye; so violent it can be seen
> Across three thousand years.
>   —Christopher Logue, *War Music*

The West's images of madness always come back to tragedy and are, essentially, tragic. Madness may be "subversive,"[50] in that it provides *other* people, writers, with ways of challenging safe ways of seeing. But it *is* a tragedy: in our sense, the modern sense, of disastrous pain. These tragic elements of madness are not just a literary construct but part of a syntax that helped to define Europe's images of suffering.

They are ours too. We think of them as (loaded word) "natural." You see them in Munch's *The Scream.* Isolation, distance from people, a single figure set against black freighters in the harbor, against blood-colored sky and a black god-shaped menace in the landscape. Black on the body and in the world; black centered on the open eyes and mouth of a tragic mask.

Grammars change. Modern Greek demotic lost the infinitive. People use the same grammar to say different things. Psychoanalysts use Greek elements of thought to express ideas about madness very different from those of Greek tragedy. But different as modern perceptions are, they rest on a grammar stamped "made in Greece," and put together for the first time, for better or worse, by Athenian tragedy.

Notes

1. *King Lear* 2.4.278–85. Earth and underworld as image of mind: Padel 1992:99–102; above, Chapter 5, n. 26, and Chapter 17, n. 52.

2. Taplin 1978:162 approved the ancient saying that tragedy is "nothing to do with Dionysus," and got a many-voiced indignant response: see, e.g., Seaford 1981; Goldhill 1986:74–78; Zeitlin and Winkler 1990; Padel 1994:132 nn. 28–29; above, Chapter 3.

3. Spencer 1962; Howard 1974:74.

4. Padel 1990:336.

5. See Parke and Wormell 1956 1:305–307. Murder as link between blood and madness: Padel 1992:172–89.

6. See Padel 1981:126–29; Scott 1982; Foucault 1971:35; Segal 1982.

7. Apollod. 3.7; Hyginus *Fabulae* 95. Lucian *De saltatione* 46 follows the story with the typically tragic Philoctetes. Aeschylus probably mentioned it in *Palamedes* (Jebb/Pearson *ad.* S. frr. 462–67). Arist. *Poet.* 1451A26 says Homer avoids it. See Cic. *De officiis* 3.97: *ut quidem poetae tragici prodiderunt.*

8. *Hamlet* 2.1.77–85, 103, 109; 2.2.5, 9, 165–222, 234–306; 3.1.86–172. *Richard III* 3.5.1. *King Lear* 3.4, 3.6. Cf. the flute test for possession, in Men. *Theophoroumen?*: Handley 1969.

9. Cf. Padel 1990b:358–59.

10. See, e.g., Burkert 1985:162, 166; Schlesier 1993.

11. See, e.g., Burkert 1985:163; Segal 1982; Seaford 1993; Cole 1993.

12. See above, pp. 18–20. Lyssa in vase-paintings: Padel 1992:118, 125, 131, 156, 163.

13. Chaucer *The Monk's Tale*, 2–3, 3951. "Fall" is the point of the string of exempla throughout the *Tale*. See G. Steiner 1961:11–16.

14. *OT* 1187–95; cf. Winnington-Ingram 1980: ch. 8. Cf., from an anonymous English tragedy, c. 1591 (quoted in Barton 1962:136):

> O fickle fortune, O unstable world ...
> Wherein as in a glasse we plainly see
> That all our life is but a Tragedie.
> Since mightie kings are subject to mishap.

15. *Eum.* 372–78: see Padel 1992:131; *Ant.* 618–19.

16. Russell 1956:82; cf. above, Chapter 6, n. 47. Daemons "falling at" you out of air: Padel 1992:129–31.

17. Padel 1992:125–29, 138–40, 158–61. *At?*: below, Appendix.

18. *Hec.* 1120–21; *OT* 1276.

19. Mattes 1970:60–63; Girard 1977:40, 128, 164; above, Chapter 3, nn. 4–5, and Chapter 13.

20. Knox 1964:42, 56.

21. *Ant.* 1–93; *Aj.* 596; Knox 1964:32–35.

22. Aulus Gellius 18.7.4. See Padel 1981:122–23; Klibansky, Panofsky, and Saxl 1964:42 n. 100; Kinsman 1974b:20. *Problem* 30: above, Chapter 6.

23. Foucault 1971:108–11 claims the opposite: "The tragic hero can never be mad." But his model of "classic" is seventeenth-century France, not Greece.

24. Ar. *Pl.* 422. See Winnington-Ingram 1980:102–104 on *Ant.* 754, 756, cf. *Ant.* 791–92, 633. Lycurgus: *Ant.* 954–63. "Hyperbolic" madness: above, pp. 194–95. Erinyes iden-

25. E.g., Hieronymous Bosch painting of 1480: see Gilman 1982:38–42, plates 47–53. Purging bile: see Chapter 5, nn. 7–8, 12.

26. *Eum.* 517: see Padel 1992:132–34, 192; above, Chapter 4, n. 49.

27. See Chapter 7, n. 45; Chapter 13 nn. 53–72.

28. In a modern sense of metaphor; cf. Padel 1992:9, 33–34.

29. *Hec.* 1261–80; *OC* 1511, 1456–518.

30. DuBois 1991:37–38; Padel 1983:14.

31. Padel 1992:14–18, 68–75.

32. See Bolton 1962:154, 202 (with n. 16); Brenk 1977:125–26.

33. See Pl. *Apol.* 39C3; Plu. *Mor.* 432C; Shakespeare *Henry IV Part One*, 5.4.83–86.

34. *Cho.* 1026–27.

35. See Chapter 4, nn. 19–29.

36. Padel 1992:112–13; above, Chapters 8, 9.

37. *Ba.* 1107, 1171, *HF* 970–1000; *Cho.* 1048; Padel 1981:126–29; above, Chapter 8, nn. 1, 5–7.

38. See Chapter 8, nn. 28, 46–47.

39. See Padel 1992:113.

40. Howard 1974:70. Cf. *pathei mathos: Ag.* 177.

41. See Chapter 10; cf. Knox 1964:42–43.

42. See G. Steiner 1961:106–107, 123, 126–29. Steiner attributes the Romantics' failure in tragedy to revolutionary ideals fading after the French Revolution, and to optimism about human nature. They put responsibility for crime and evil outside: "Evil cannot be wholly native to the soul." In tragedy, it must be: as well as being abroad in the world. True tragedy, Steiner argues, is anti-Romantic. "Redeeming insight comes too late to mend ... or is purchased at the price of irremediable suffering." There is no "compensating Heaven" like that of which Romanticism dreamed.

43. I first put forward this suggestion in Padel 1981:123–25. It would of course need detailed support, by historians of madness, religion, and science in the societies involved, to make it stick.

44. See Lloyd 1979:37–58; Padel 1992:44, 49–68, 73–75.

45. See Burton, *Anatomy of Melancholy* 1.4.1; Fox 1976:17. MacDonald 1981:147 warns against idealizing Renaissance idealization of madness, or assuming that what they liked in literature they liked in life.

46. This seems to fit Racine's France; does it fit Racine? Cf. above, n. 23.

47. Padel 1992: ch. 6.

48. See, e.g., *The Mirrour of Madness*, translated by J. Fan[ford], (1576).

49. See Appendix.

50. Felman 1985.

NIALL W. SLATER

The Fabrication of Comic Illusion

> But art has no goal. It evolves but it does not necessarily progress. Just as the history of politics isn't simply a progress towards parliamentary democracy, so the history of painting isn't simply a progress towards photographic realism.
> —Sir Anthony Blunt, in Alan Bennett's *A Question of Attribution*

Among the many changes from Old to New Comedy is one basic to the framing of the action on stage and therefore to our interpretation of the plays in their entirety: it is the creation of a consistently maintained dramatic illusion. Gregory Sifakis focused the discussion of this question with his bold claim that "illusion as a psychological phenomenon was entirely alien to Greek theatrical audiences...."[1] While many would regard that now as an overstatement, it was a useful overstatement nonetheless. It liberated us from the view that Aristophanes was groping his way toward nineteenth-century illusionistic comedy, rather like some people's view of an early Renaissance painter, painstakingly working toward vanishing point perspective; we now can see that Aristophanes might rather have his own aesthetic and structural principles in which a striving after illusion played no part.

Whether one then accepts Old Comedy as fundamentally non-illusory drama[2] or prefers still to see breaking of illusion in the parabases and other metatheatrical devices in Aristophanes, it is in any case clear that stage convention and practice have changed significantly by the time of

From *Beyond Aristophanes: Transition and Diversity in Greek Comedy*, edited by Gregory W. Dobrov. © 1995 by the American Philological Association.

Menander's plays. Direct address to the audience essentially disappears, except for the occasional use of ἄνδρες in a soliloquy,[3] as do references to stage machinery[4] and address to the flute-player (an exception being *Dyscolus* 880).[5] Above all, there are no claims about the quality of the play or abuse of the playwright's rivals, such as we know in Old Comedy.

This triumph of illusion is sometimes attributed simply to the influence of Euripides or more generally tragedy, sometimes to a loss of imagination and nerve following the Athenian defeat in the Peloponnesian War. It seems more valuable to examine, not the Zeitgeist, but the changing conditions of production in the Greek theatre. The evidence suggests that several interrelated developments within the period we now dub Middle Comedy, including the repetition of plays, the rise of stock character types, and the decline or at least transformation of the chorus, all contributed to the fabrication of a consistent stage illusion in comedy. Let us look briefly at these in turn.

The simple fact that plays were now being restaged or toured beyond the original Athenian performance encouraged new kinds of comic writing. Certainly some plays in the fifth century had more than one production: we know of Aeschylus restaging a play in Sicily during his lifetime. Evidence for deme theatres in Attica in the late fifth century may not be conclusive proof for touring productions of comedies and tragedies staged earlier in Athens,[6] though we do know that tragedies were restaged in the theatre in the Peiraeus. The real explosion of demand for theatre comes in the fourth century. An anecdote about Anaxandrides, from Chamaileon on comedy, tells us that he was *unusual* because, instead of revising his failed plays and producing them again (for the secondary market?), he simply destroyed them (Athenaeus 9.373f-374b; cf. Eustathius 1834.15):

> Being of a morose disposition, [Anaxandrides] used to do this with his comedies: whenever he failed to win, he took and gave them to the dealers in frankincense to chop up with it, and he never revised them, as most writers did. In this way he destroyed many plays which had been elaborately composed, because his old age made him peevish toward the spectators.[7]

Perhaps Anaxandrides was conservative in other ways too. Nesselrath notes the rarity of anapaestic tetrameters, a characteristic recitative metre of Old Comedy, in the remains of Middle Comedy: two of three examples are in Anaxandrides.[8] Our sample is not genuinely random, and the metre is employed by actors as well as chorus, but its use is nonetheless noteworthy.

A geographically expanded audience had less interest in specifically

Athenian politics. Nesselrath notes this decline: some political comments remain, but they are "local color,"[9] like Attic geographical references. Perhaps these latter were of especial interest on the touring circuit of the deme celebrations of the rural Dionysia. Because such references are inorganic to plot, far from breaking the illusion, they help suture the audience into the play experience. References to demes and demotics seem to be about as frequent in Middle Comedy as in Old, but the names are not the subject of puns, as they were in Aristophanes.[10] Once again, Anaxandrides harks back more to the spirit of Aristophanes, when he makes a joke at the expense of the deme of Sunion, implying that they were careless about citizen registrations.[11]

An export market for comedy grew up as well. There is a growing consensus that the South Italian vases which we conventionally call phlyax vases, based on the notion that they represent native phlyax drama, in fact often depict performances of Greek, indeed specifically Athenian, scripted comedy. Oliver Taplin has given us one of the more striking pieces of evidence with his demonstration that a South Italian vase depicts a performance of Aristophanes' *Thesmophoriazusae*,[12] and more evidence, including the use of Attic (rather than Doric) Greek on vases to indicate what figures are saying, continues to be noted. Richard Green in particular has shown that the Apulian vases showing comic scenes were manufactured primarily in Taranto, which provided a ready audience for Greek touring companies, but such vases were *not* being painted in the South Italian hinterland.[13] The conclusion is clear: what we have been calling phlyax drama is in fact Greek comedy, and primarily Middle Comedy, as produced by Greek touring companies, the forerunners of the Artists of Dionysus.[14]

The international market for plays helps explain the disappearance of direct, metatheatrical references to the comic competition. Stephen Halliwell has recently observed[15] that "gibes and counter-gibes of collaboration, plagiarism and the like, had by [the last third of the fifth century] become a stock comic *topos*—a recurrent motif in the twin techniques of self-promotion and denigration of others that played an explicit part in the rivalry of comic poets competing for public prizes." This motif simply disappears in the next century—though plagiarism does not. Middle Comedy playwrights stole freely from each other without recorded reproach, as Richard Hunter notes in his commentary on Eubulus fr. 67 K [= 67 K.-A.], where line 4 is essentially identical to Xenarchus fr. 4 K.-A. line 6.[16] The seachange in the world of comedy is obvious: charges of plagiarism would simply be unintelligible in a touring production, which may well not have been written for the Athenian market to begin with.

The career of Menander provides striking evidence for the writing of plays for a non-Athenian market.[17] Over one hundred titles of his plays are known, far more than he could have produced at Athenian festivals during his lifetime. The inference that some were written for non-Athenian performances is obvious. The further question arises as to what texts we have. In the absence of positive evidence, we should presume that we have the performance versions of the touring companies (we hear of no state archival copies of comedy, as we do for tragedy).[18]

This does not mean that certain more abstract metatheatrical elements were excluded from the comic stage immediately, but they become rarer and more generalized. One especially interesting fragment is from Timocles' *Women at the Dionysia*, fr. 6 K.-A., lines 8-19, where an unnamed speaker discusses how watching the myths of tragedy is a comfort or perhaps a therapy for the audience in their own personal griefs.

> Consider first, if you will, how the tragedians help everyone. For the man who's poor finds Telephus to be even poorer than himself and so bears his own poverty more easily. The sick man sees Alcmaeon raving mad. Someone has eye disease—well, the sons of Phineus are blind. Someone's child has died—Niobe is a comfort. The lame sees Philoctetes, an old man in misfortune learns about Oineus. So each one, having learned of all the greater misfortunes having befallen others, laments his own lot the less.

Tragedy as the opiate of the people, in other words.[19] Note that nothing in the passage implies that the audience must have seen a *particular* play, that is, a particular author's version of the myth; paradoxically, the tragic myths are viewed as having a comforting reality to them.

More puzzling are two fragments from Alexis' play, *Womenocracy*. The first, fr. 42 K.-A., has often been cited in discussions about whether women attended the theatre in Athens.[20]

> You women must sit there in the farthest section[21]
> to watch, since you're strangers.

We know essentially nothing about this play beyond what the title and the two fragments tell us. Boettiger, who saw this fragment as the strongest evidence against his view that women did not attend the theatre, argued that, like the *Ecclesiazusae*, the *Gynaikokratia* portrayed a topsy-turvy world of women invading what was in fact a male public space.[22] Later Kann also took the view that the *Gynaikokratia* was about women attempting to control a public sphere.[23] Who speaks? To whom? And what are they watching? We simply do not know the answers to the first two questions, but I would agree with Jeffrey Henderson, who says, citing the subject of the next fragment, that "we are entitled to assume that the festival in question was theatrical."[24] That fragment, 43 K-A., deals with an actor.

> This Hippocles of Cilicia,
>   the pickled-fish actor

This is of course the only use of ζωμοτάριχος in this sense, so we are left wondering whether the epithet reflects one of Hippocles' eating habits, or is rather an aesthetic judgement upon his acting style. If the latter, it is doubtless unflattering. In either case, such personal comment is extremely rare in the period of Middle Comedy, and we can only conclude that Alexis was somewhat retrograde in this respect[25] (though we cannot date the *Gynaikokratia* in his long career).[26]

The evolution of stock characters and stock scenes represents a more complex level of borrowing from competitors and simultaneously moves comedy sharply toward illusion. Once again, the archaeological record is particularly helpful: terracotta figurines begin to appear, of which a famous example is the New York Group. As Richard Green has convincingly argued, however, they do *not* represent the cast of a single play; there are simply too many copies, over too long a period of time. As he points out, "No single play or set of plays could have been that popular or had so much re-play."[27] Instead they represent a growing standardization of masks and stock character types, which could be used and re-used in varying plays. Antiphanes (who seems to have averaged 5 or 6 plays a year and was clearly writing for more than the Athenian festival market) is therefore somewhat disingenuous in the famous complaint in his *Poetry* (fr. 189 K.-A.), where it is asserted that writing comedy is harder than tragedy because all the names, characters, and events must be invented anew each time.

> Tragedy's a cushy art altogether,
> since first of all the spectators
> know the plots already, before anyone speaks—
> all the poet has to do is remind them.
> All I need to do is say "Oedipus"
> and they know the rest—his father Laius,

his mother Jocasta, his daughters, sons,
what will happen to him, what he's done. Or again
if someone says "Alcmaeon," in the same breath
he's included all the children, how he
went off his rocker and killed his mother, and how
Adrastus will enter and leave again...
And when the poets can't come up with anything
and have said absolutely everything in their plays
they lift the crane just like a finger
and the spectators get their money's worth.
That's not the way with us comic poets—
we have to invent everything: new names,
set-up, action, second act curtain,
opening.[28] If a Chremes or a Pheidon leaves out
any of this, he's hissed off the stage, but Peleus
and Teucer can do what they please.

Characters and plots were by no means unique. The rise and fall of the boastful cook in Middle Comedy demonstrates the dynamics of the market for comedy: type scenes (arrival, marketing, report on menus) evolve, which can be added to any play the cook appears in, but a decline for this particular figure sets in after mid-century,[29] and parasites, slaves, and young lovers fill the vacuum.

Finally, the decline of the chorus (apparent already in late Aristophanes) goes hand in hand with the fabrication of a comic illusion. Now the decline of the chorus does not mean necessarily the disappearance of the chorus: there were choral performances in late Aristophanes and in Menander,[30] and Kenneth Rothwell (pp. 99–118, below) provides evidence that the Athenians continued to pay handsomely to support tragic and comic choruses. The question is what relation this choral activity had to the plays being written. Richard Hunter has carefully examined the evidence for the chorus during the transition from Old to New Comedy,[31] but several of the passages he discusses appear to be references *to* the chorus, rather than verses actually sung *by* the chorus: his best candidates for the latter are Alexis fr. 239 K.-A. [=237K], Anaxilas fr. 13 K.-A. [=13K], and Eubulus fr. 102-103 K.-A. [=104-105K]. In other words, there is very little evidence to contradict the picture that plays were being written to *allow* for the insertion of choral lyrics when a chorus was available to sing them, but there is also very little to indicate the presence of choruses more specific than Menander's typical drunken revellers, that is, choruses which had characters and verses written for them by the play's author.[32]

This accords well with the picture we have been building up of both a domestic and an international audience for comedy. Plays written for the festivals in Athens could still expect production with a full chorus, and a playwright might choose to write lyrics for such a performance.[33] Most plays, however, were written with an eye on the international market, where production conditions were much more varied. At Delphi in the third century BC, we have inscriptional evidence for a single comic chorus of seven which was shared by three troupes of comic actors. Sifakis assumes that these choristers were professional.[34] That does not mean, however, that these choristers regularly toured with any one of the competing troupes. More likely they were based at Delphi. More commonly the Hellenistic inscriptions mention only chorus trainers,[35] which suggests that touring troupes for major festivals might recruit and train a local chorus. One wonders how much rehearsal time was available and therefore how high a standard such choruses could attain. Even if the playwrights wished to hold onto this oldest element of comedy, amateur choristers were extraneous to the theatre of professionalized and highly specialized comic actors in the great guilds of the Artists of Dionysus. Lesser companies simply did without choruses, and the productions were no less intelligible.[36]

Interconnected with this decline of the chorus was the fundamental change in theatre architecture brought about by the raised stage. Though the stage was never completely cut off from the orchestra level,[37] this change reduced any possible interchange between chorus and actors to the moments of the latter's entrances and exits. If not quite so powerful as the nineteenth-century picture frame proscenium, the raised stage of the Hellenistic theatre ratified the divide of the dramatic world in two, and the actors inhabited a world of consistent verisimilitude.[38]

Before closing, we should cast one glance at the possible influence of tragedy on this process, in particular at an extremely interesting fragment that has only recently come to light. It has most recently been edited by Anton Bierl,[39] who argues that it comes from a comedy, not a satyr play, as Kannicht maintains.[40]

1 ...[he] slipped off into the billowy wave...[41]
4 ...of Semele...hymn...
   ...Arcadian god...
   ...observing...
   ...handed over....
8 ...having fled, as a child I played [in] the caves...
   ...a simple worker..., undefiled by any evil...

...picking the mountain fruit...

...long ago uncultivated, to [?] the approaches of beasts...

12 ...I guarded the young fruit I trained...

...[the fruit] of autumn I carried to deep winepresses...

...to mortals I revealed the drink of Dionysus...

...the initiate never ceasing...to Bacchus...

16 ...and the first [female follower?] of the god bound with curls...

...forgetfulness shone forth in those joys...

...thiasos. I was taught to boast of such things...

...the great bard of Salamis says...

20 ...the steward, and now I've been rolled into deceptions...

...doing little service to the fictions...

...rousing him from that far-off bourne, [he] will send...

...goddesses. The present labor of tragic hymns...

24 ...defines so that justly beautiful things not...with toil...

...scarcely consider third [prize?] a sideline burden...

...Dionysus rightly...

...judging in the competition...

In an important article which lays out the metatheatrical dimensions of this text, Bierl suggests that we may have a spokesman for comedy complaining that, under the influence of Euripides, comedy has fallen into a use of illusion, which is appropriate rather to tragedy.[42] Because all of the lines lack at least one metron at the beginning, some very basic elements of the interpretation are obscure. There may be one, two, or three speakers. The verses may come from a parabasis or an agon. I do accept that the "bard of Salamis" (ἀοιδὸς Σαλαμῖνος) in line 19 is Euripides and that εἰς ἀπάτας κεκύλισμαι in line 20 does refer to theatrical illusion.[43] What is unclear is whether the speaker of line 20 is necessarily acting as a spokesman for, or judge of, the genre of comedy. Certainly the direct reference in line 23 to tragic hymns is at home only in a comedy, not a satyr play. The idea that the speaker is specifically describing the influence of tragic ἀπάτη on the writing of comedy may be more a result of the conventional belief in Euripidean influence on comedy than a direct inference from this tantalizingly fragmentary text. The fragment is also hard to date, but Bierl's suggestion of a turn-of-the-century date, not far from the death of Euripides, seems in keeping with the subject matter. Bierl's interpretation of τρίτα in line 25 as "third prize" does suggest some further support for this date. On the conventional view that the number of competing comedies at the City Dionysia was reduced to three during the war years and only later restored to five, the reference to third prize (as apparently the worst position one could attain) suggests a date at the end of the fifth century rather than in the next.[44]

Such a date too fits the concern over the fates of both tragedy and comedy that is evident in *Frogs*. I believe it is not just the wisdom of hindsight which sees in that play's debates concern both for the political fate of Athens and for the dramatic genres she had so preeminently nourished. Great artistic achievements commanded the attention of an ever-widening public, so large that it was soon beyond any centralized control. The archon basileus could determine what was seen in Athens but not elsewhere.

Illusion triumphed in the fourth century comic theatre not because tragedy was so compelling a model for dramaturgy but because a diverse and internationalized audience created an enormous demand for a standardized and portable product. Illusion may not even have been a conscious goal of the playwrights in this process, and some, including perhaps Anaxandrides and the author of P. Köln 242A, may have resisted the demands of distribution and market forces. Illusion was not inevitable. As much as anything else, it may have been the incidental result of the "framing" of comic action which took place both physically on the raised stage and metaphorically through the abstraction of the comedy from its specifically Athenian festal setting.

NOTES

1. Sifakis, *Parabasis* 7. Green, "Seeing and Depicting" 15–50, esp. 40, has recently pointed out how differently the vase painters see tragedy and comedy. For a succinct bibliography on the question of illusion in comedy, see Green, "Seeing and Depicting" 26, note 37.

2. I use the term of Styan, *Drama, Stage and Audience* (see esp. 180–223).

3. E.g., *Samia* 269. See Gomme and Sandbach, *Menander, ad loc.* for a list of further examples. Frost, *Exits and Entrances* 116–17 ad *Samia* 725 suggests that the μαρτύρων referred to are members of the audience, but the allusion is subtle and not absolutely required.

4. Frost, *Exits and Entrances* 29–31 discusses the use of the *ekkyklema* at *Aspis* 299ff., originally suggested by Jacques, "Mouvement des acteurs" 51–52, and further discussed by S. Halliwell, (cited from *LCM* 8.2 [1983] 31–32 in Frost, *Exits and Entrances* 30, note 28); there is no explicit comment in the text, however. For the use of the *ekkyklema* in *Dyscolus* 690–758, see Gomme and Sandbach, *Menander* 239–41, *ad loc.* and Frost, *Exits and Entrances* 58, with full discussion. Cnemon's line at 758, εἰσκυ]κλεῖτ᾽ εἴσω με seems sufficiently explicit, but there is no parody or play with the convention, as in Aristophanes. See also my review of Frost in "The Players Come Again."

5. See Frost, *Exits and Entrances, ad loc.* and Handley, *Dyskolos* 283–86, *ad loc.* Of interest in this regard is the "Bari Dancers," an Apulian calyx crater dating around

365–350 BC and showing two aulos players with wings dancing around an altar; see the discussion in Taplin, "Auletai" and, more fully, Taplin, *Comic Angels* 70–78. Taplin, *Comic Angels* 105–10, is a very useful survey of possible metatheatrical play with the aulosplayer. It is notable, however, that all of his examples come from Old Comedy, with the sole exception of the only surviving (and quite corrupt) fragment of Antiphanes' *Auletes*.

6. On the late fifth century deme theatre at Trachones see Green, "Seeing and Depicting" 18–19, and the articles by O. Alexandri cited there (from *Ergon* [1980] 24–25, *Praktika* [1980] 64–67, and *Ergon* [1981] 44–45). Taplin, *Comic Angels* 5, makes a good case for interpreting *Clouds* 523, πρώτους ἠξίωσ' ἀναγεῦσ' ὑμᾶς, to imply that Aristophanes had other venues in which he *could* have produced *Clouds*.

7. Translation by C. B. Gulick from the Loeb edition of Athenaeus.

8. Nesselrath, *Mittlere Komödie* 335. We cannot demonstrate that any of these uses was choral or in an epirrhematic exchange with the chorus, but it is tempting to speculate.

9. Nesselrath, *Mittlere Komödie* 335.

10. Whitehead, *Demes* 338–45, esp. 339.

11. Anaxandrides, *Anchises* fr. 4 K.-A. 3–4: πολλοὶ δὲ νῦν μέν εἰσιν οὐκ ἐλεύθεροι, / εἰς αὔριον δὲ Σουνιεῖς. Cf. Whitehead, *Demes* 340. There may have been a similar joke about the deme Potamos in Menander's Διδύμαι since Harpocration says, s.v. Ποταμός· ... ἐκωμῳδοῦντο δὲ ὡς ῥᾳδίως δεχόϋενοι τοὺς παρεγγράπτους, ὡς ἄλλοι τε δηλῦσι καὶ Μένανδρος ἐν Διδύμαις. Whitehead, *Demes* 292, note 7, suggests this joke may go back to Strattis in the fifth century, since he wrote a Ποταμιοι.

12. See Taplin, "Phallology, *Phlyakes,*" "Classical Phallology," and *Comic Angels* 36–41.

13. Green, "Phlyax Vases" 49–56, 55.

14. While the *Thesmophoriazusae* vase is invaluable evidence for Attic drama in South Italy, the concern of Taplin, *Comic Angels* 44–45, over the paucity of other specific associations of surviving vases with known Aristophanes plays seems misplaced. Surely the majority, indeed the vast majority, of Greek performances in South Italy were of contemporary plays. One would assume that Aristophanes was no larger a proportion of the current repertoire in the fourth century than G. B. Shaw is today—a classic, not a staple, in other words.

15. Halliwell, "Authorial Collaboration" 515–28; especially 519. Cf. Slater, "Play and Playwright References" 103–5. See note 25 below on Timocles.

16. Hunter, *Eubulus, ad loc.* Hunter notes that such borrowing was "particularly frequent in the Middle Comedy fragments," and provides this list of examples: Philemon fr. 114 K.-A. [=123K]/Straton fr. 1 K.-A. [=219 Austin]; Eubulus fr. 122 K.-A. [=125K]/Alexis fr. 284 K.-A. [=282K]; Eubulus fr. 109 K.-A. lines 1–2 [=110K]/Ephippus fr. 15 K.-A. lines 3-4 [=15K]; Antiphanes fr. 89 K.-A. [=89K]/Epicrates fr. 5 K.-A. lines 4-9 [=5K]. See also his references to Stemplinger, *Das Plagiat*, and Kroll on the general subject of plagiarism.

17. Since coming to this conclusion on the basis of Menander's career alone, I find that Taplin, *Comic Angels* 94, note 14, argues for an increasing market outside Athens based on the larger outputs of fourth century playwrights (perhaps 130 reported titles each for Antiphanes and Alexis).

18. We must at least consider the possibility that the original productions at the City Dionysia and Lenaia contained references to other comic plays and comic playwrights, but such references were excised from the touring productions which are the source of our texts. Such a system of double texts is rather inefficient, however, and if such ever existed, I would assume it quickly gave way to writing a single, "international" text.

One might point here to the interesting contemporary case of Woody Allen's *God: A Play*, which is virtually unperformable outside New York City, because of its explicit metatheatrical references to things experienced by actors and audience in the subway on the way to the theatre, etc. The few productions that take place tend to re-write the text massively.

19. On the virtually magical view of poetry's powers implied here, see Pohlenz, "Anfänge" 142–78, 168–69. Pohlenz sees in particular here the influence of Gorgias' theory of ἀπάτη.

20. See most recently Henderson, "Women" 133–47, 140–41.

21. Literally, "wedge,"—the outermost wedge of seats (i.e., with the worst sightlines) is meant. See Henderson, "Women" 140–41.

22. Boettiger, *Kleine Schriften* 300–2. The social views which inform Boettiger's scholarship on this point become rather clear with his reference to "dieses neumodische right of Women (um mit der neuesten gro?en Verfechterin dieser Ordnung, der Mi? Wolstonkraft, zu reden)...."

23. Kann, *De iteratis* 78: "Ut in contione feminae in Ecclesiazusis, ita in theatro in Γυναικοκρατία imperium sibi parare volunt."

24. Henderson, "Women" 141.

25. Cf. also Alexis fr. 77 and 113 K.-A., both of which mention a Timocles who *may* be the comic poet. In fr. 77, Timocles is given as the source for a witticism about Chairephilos's sons: this may have been in a play, or it may have been in conversation. If this is the poet, and one of his plays is being quoted, this is most unusual, since even in Old Comedy, one poet rarely quoted another with approbation, due to the competitive mode of play production. In fr. 113, a Timocles is cited as a typical drunkard; Edmonds speculates that this may be the comic poet being criticized as Cratinus was in the fifth century, but again we cannot be sure (and he occurs in a list with two definitely mythical characters, Oinopion and Maron). Alexis fr. 184 K.-A. speaks of water being "ψυχρότερον Ἀραρότος," apparently a reference to Aristophanes' son, who had no particularly distinguished career as a comic poet. The use of the term ψυχρός here is intriguing, in that it echoes Aristophanes' own description of Theognis, the minor tragic poet, in *Thesmophoriazusae* 170: ὁ δ᾽ αὖ Θέογνις ψυχρὸς ὢν ψυχρῶς ποεῖ (cf. also *Acharnians* 11 and 140). We should remember how long the career of Alexis was. Old Comedy elements, such as this kind of personal commentary, may have lingered long in his style.

26. Edmonds, *Fragments*, ad fr. 41 [= fr. 42 K.-A.] speculates that the play might date after the rebuilding of the Theatre of Dionysus in 329 BC, but the division of the theatre into *kerkides* predates that rebuilding, so there is really no evidence for the date. Amphis also wrote a Γυναικοκρατία, of which only one fragment, 8 K.-A., survives, whose subject matter is not theatrical. On the other hand, Amphis's Ἐρίθοι may well be the first evidence for the use of the metaphor of life as theatre. In a contrast between country and city living, Amphis says (fr. 17 K.-A. line 4; see p. 69 below): ἄστυ δὲ θέατρον [ἐστιν] ἀτυχίας γέμον. It is hard to judge from a four-line fragment, of course, but the use of the metaphor does not seem particularly metatheatrical here: rather, the theatre has become the preeminent place of display for the workings of τύχη, so that reference to the theatre is simply a matter of moralizing reflection.

27. Green, "Seeing and Depicting" 32. See also his discussion of the group in Webster, *Monuments*³ 45–47.

28. What I have translated "opening" might or might not be the prologue. The narrative of a conventional prologue would fall under "setup," but the use of the word εἰσβολήν for "opening" seems deliberately vague: a play needed a strong opening which

might be a dialogue scene, followed by a delayed prologue. "Second act curtain" is literally the catastrophe, the turning point of the action, which often comes in the fourth act of a New Comedy.

29. Nesselrath, *Mittlere Komödie* 339, suggests a reading public is responsible. The type never disappeared, as Sikon in *Dyscolus* and various cooks in Roman comedy demonstrate, but their roles were much less prominent.

30. On the chorus in late Aristophanes, see Handley, *Dyskolos* 55–61. For Menander, see Handley, *Dyskolos* 171–74 on lines 230–232 (cf. Frost, *Exits and Entrances* 27) and Gomme and Sandbach, *Menander, ad Epitrepontes* 169. Sifakis, "Aristotle, *E.N.*, IV, 2" 410–32 argues that in Middle Comedy it was common for the chorus to perform the parodos in character and uncharacterized interludes thereafter, with an emphasis on dancing which was "lively and even, in the opinion of some critics, obscene" (432). If this was the case for the performances Aristotle saw, however, it need not have been so outside Athens.

31. Hunter, "The Comic Chorus" 23–38.

32. Maidment, "The Later Comic Chorus" 1–24, does point out one problem for this uniform view. He notes that Aeschines, in a prosecution of Timarchus in 345 BC, refers to a joke made at Timarchus's expense by a comic actor performing at the Rural Dionysia (*In Tim.* 157): πρώην ἐν τοῖς κατ᾽ ἀγροὺς Διονυίοις κωμῳδῶν ὄντων ἐν Κολλυτῷ καὶ Παρμένοντος τοῦ κωμικοῦ ὑποκριτοῦ εἰπόντος τι πρὸς τὸν χορὸν ἀνάπαιστον ἐν ᾧ ἦν εἶναί τινας πόρνους μεγάλους Τιμαρχώδεις…. The actor Parmenon (393 O'Connor) is known and had one Lenaean victory: *IG* II/III^2 2325; see Mette, *Urkunden* 179, and Ghiron-Bistagne, *Recherches* 350. Note that the actor specifically spoke in anapaests, the typical metre of the parabasis. This seems astonishingly late for such direct address to the audience and for such a personal attack. We do not know the playwright or the play. I can only suggest that a parabatic tradition may have survived longer at the Rural Dionysia than at the city festivals, but even this is a rather unsatisfactory explanation, for Kollytus was one of five "genuinely urban demes"; see Whitehead, *Demes* 26. We also know of a fourth century performance of Sophocles' *Oinomaus* there: Demosthenes, *De Corona* 180. Perhaps a certain conservatism was a function of the deme festival differentiating itself from the great city festivals. The passage does not, as suggested by Maidment, "The Later Comic Chorus" 13 (and note 3), necessarily imply that "the chorus in contemporary comedy was present throughout the dialogue [and] also took a definite part in the dialogue."

33. We might note that, the absence of any such lyrics from Menander is not conclusive proof that he never wrote such lyrics. Again, the most likely assumption is that we possess the touring versions of his plays, which would lack such details; cf. note 18 above.

34. Sifakis, *Hellenistic Drama* 72, cf. 116.

35. Sifakis, *Hellenistic Drama* 116–20.

36. The scanty evidence from South Italy is fertile ground for speculation on the questions of whether comic performances there normally had choruses. Taplin, *Comic Angels* 55–60 and 75–78, believes that choruses were part of South Italian performances (though perhaps smaller in number than in Athens), but we should perhaps be a bit more cautious. His belief in choruses allows him to provide an interesting explanation of the so-called "Choregoi Vase," which he himself admits (76) is the best evidence he can provide (nor are the Delphi inscriptions persuasive for choruses in South Italy—see pp. 48–49). An analysis of the "Choregoi Vase" is beyond the scope of this note, but I would suggest that Taplin too easily dismisses the difficulty that the two labelled choregoi are shown on the stage, not on the orchestra level. Might they then be actors playing characters with a

function but not necessarily personal names, much like the Logoi in *Clouds?* Though much later, Plautus may provide evidence for what he and his contemporaries could see performed in Taranto and elsewhere. Hunter, "The Comic Chorus" 37–38, prefers to see Greek choruses behind the *piscatores* of the *Rudens* and the *advocati* of the *Poenulus*. Whether that is so or not, however, nothing persuaded Plautus to attempt any use of a traditional chorus in the orchestra in his plays. I suspect that there were some performances with chorus in the cities of Magna Graecia, but they are likely to have been the exception rather than the rule.

37. Sifakis, *Hellenistic Drama* 130–35.

38. Cf. Slater, "Transformations of Space" 1–10.

39. Bierl, "Dionysos" 353–91.

40. Kannicht-Snell *TrGF* II 217 comments on the metre and gives a list of words which seem too "tragic" for a comedy. The text has also been edited in Gauly, *Musa Tragica* 251–53; See also p. 302 where the editors adopt the suggestion of W. Luppe (cited from *ZPE* 72 [1988] 36) that the verses come from a "parabasenhafte[r] Epilog" to a satyr play (250). The degree of illusion-breaking tolerable in satyr play is open to debate. Interesting in this regard is the discussion in Green, "On Seeing and Depicting" 47–49, of the satyrs' metatheatrical discussion of masks that they carry in Aeschylus's *Isthmiastae*. One can only say that the degree of metatheatricality in P. Köln 242A exceeds anything else in our limited evidence heretofore.

41. My translation is of course deeply indebted to that in Bierl, "Dionysos" 355–56, and his commentary. A number of terms would not in other contexts be unambiguously theatrical, but here it is very tempting to take ἐδιδάχθην as "I rehearsed, learned my part," ψευδομέ να[ις]′ as "fictions, plots," and τρίτα as "third prize."

42. Bierl, "Dionysos" 385 (commenting on line 20): "In our text the comic poet, or the speaker representing comedy, notes in the first person that he has been rolled or has rolled himself into illusion, i.e., the tragic form of Euripides. He may be saying that with the new comic style there is scarcely any distinction between tragedy and comedy. In the following lines he wants to express his opposition to this kind of comic composition."

43. See Bierl, "Dionysos" 365–68 (with notes), for an excellent discussion of ἀπάτη as theatrical illusion; cf. Slater, "Space, Character and ἀπάτη." One point Bierl does not address seems of particular interest to me: why does the speaker refer to ἀπάτας, rather than simply ἀπάτη? Could ἀπάτας mean "plays with illusionistic plots," or could it mean that there are different kinds of dramatic illusions?

44. For my argument in favor of the reduction during the war years (against the proposal of Luppe that five plays continued to compete throughout the war), see Slater, "The Hypotheses to Aristophanes' *Peace*" (with bibliography).

PETER BURIAN

Myth into *Muthos*: The Shaping of Tragic Plot

TRAGEDY AS REPETITION AND INNOVATION

Tragedie is to seyn a certyn storie
as olde bookes maken us memorie
of hym that stood in greet prosperitee
and is yfallen out of heigh degree
into miserie, and endeth ureccedly.[1]

In the Middle Ages, when tragedy as an enactment on stage had been all but
forgotten, Chaucer still knew the right shape for a tragic tale. In such a
scheme, only the names need be changed, for the form of the tale—and its
meaning—always remain the same. Of course, Chaucer's definition is far too
restrictive to describe the shapes that Greek tragic plots actually took, but
even the much more knowing and differentiated analysis in Aristotle's *Poetics*,
from which Chaucer's notion of tragedy ultimately derives,[2] appears to certify
only some of the plots used by the tragedians as properly tragic. Still, it is clear
that in practice not any subject was a tragic subject, not any plot-shape
suitable to the requirements of the tragic stage. First, the plots of Greek
tragedies were drawn largely from a limited repertoire of legends, the great
cycles in which the Greeks came to terms with their own past—the stories of
'a few families', as Aristotle says, above all the legendary histories of Troy and

From *The Cambridge Companion to Greek Tragedy*, edited by P.E. Easterling. © 1997 by
Cambridge University Press.

Thebes.[3] Secondly, as we shall see, it appears that a relatively few underlying plot-shapes ('story patterns') were found particularly congenial for use in the Theatre of Dionysus, and that the old tales were, from the earliest traceable stages in the development of the genre, made into tragic plots by being adapted to these patterns. Finally (and this is also true at least from the time of our first surviving examples), the plots of Greek tragedies are articulated through a limited but highly flexible repertoire of formal units, and we shall need to examine the ways in which the conventions of form create expectations and provide frames for interpretation (see also Ch. 7).

If, from the point of view of its plots, Greek tragedy constitutes a grandiose set of variations on a relatively few legendary and formal themes, forever repeating but never the same, it follows that tragedy is not casually or occasionally intertextual, but always and inherently so. Tragic praxis can be seen as a complex manipulation of legendary matter and generic convention, constituting elaborate networks of similarities and differences at every level of organisation. Such a praxis supplies the poet with constructive elements predisposed to favour certain actions, character types, issues, and outcomes, and provides the audience with a significant frame or control for the interpretation of what they are witnessing. The particular shape and emphases of a tragic plot, as the product of variation in the shape and emphases both of known legendary material and of familiar formal constituents, can forcefully direct or dislocate spectators' attention, confirm, modify, or even overturn their expectations. When this happens, a structure comes into being that depends upon a kind of complicity of the audience in order to be fully realised. Seen in this light, a tragic plot inheres not simply in a poetic text, but also in the dialectic between that text in performance and the responses of an informed audience to the performance as repetition and innovation.[4]

A useful principle can be inferred from observing this interaction between an ongoing series of tragic performances marked by sameness and difference and their reception by the 'interpretive community' (to use Stanley Fish's phrase)[5] of tragedy-goers. Where there is large-scale repetition, even small innovations and minor differences will be disproportionately prominent and emphatic. In comparing, for example, Aeschylus' *Libation-Bearers*, Sophocles' *Electra*, and Euripides' *Electra*, our only surviving group of plays on the same mythical subject by all three tragedians, it would be difficult to overestimate the consequences of the fact that the first two are set, expectedly, before the palace at Argos, the last in the countryside at the house of a yeoman farmer. In the Euripidean version, self-conscious deviation from past presentations becomes the means of forcing the audience to rethink every facet of character, motivation, and the very meaning of the action.[6] The sufferings of Electra, who seems almost to luxuriate in her loss of status and privilege, ask to be understood as at least in part self-inflicted. Orestes, cautiously assessing his situation from the safety of the countryside, emerges as something less than the knight in shining armour Electra is awaiting. Clytemnestra and Aegisthus, away from the scene of their crime, do not seem to fit the vituperation of their enemies; and their deaths—he slaughtered like a sacrificial beast while himself sacrificing at a country altar, she lured to the farmer's house by the ruse of a grandchild's birth—undercut any easy sense of justice being done.

The vagaries of preservation have left the three Electra tragedies as a unique opportunity to observe the play of repetition and innovation at work. It is worth pointing out, however, that if we had more such groups of tragedies based on precisely the same subjects, these three plays would look much less like a special case.[7] Indeed, we should think of their relation as paradigmatic, since it points to the status of any given dramatisation of a segment of legend as one of a number of variations on a theme, to be understood from the outset as a version among other versions—supplementing, challenging, displacing, but never simply replacing all the rest.

MYTH, NARRATIVE PATTERNS, AND THE SHAPING OF TRAGIC PLOTS

Traditionally, the criticism of tragedy has assumed that there is (or should be) something that can be called a 'true' tragic plot. The most widely accepted master narrative is an integral part of the Aristotelian tradition that for centuries dominated tragic criticism and is still surprisingly resilient today. This schema emphasises *hamartia*, generally understood as the 'tragic flaw' of overweening pride, and its punishment.[8] The tragic hero, although caught in circumstances beyond his ken and control, is finally to be understood as destroyed by the gods (or fate) because of his own failings. Even cursory examination of the plots of extant tragedies will suggest some obvious ways in which this schema is inadequate and even irrelevant. After all, a play such as Euripides' *Trojan Women*, for example, makes its devastating effect without peripeteia or even a 'tragic hero' (though it certainly has a wonderful 'star' role; see Ch. 7, pp. 174–5.) It is perhaps more important to observe that the search for a master tragic narrative is itself problematic. It has at any rate created a situation in which the small corpus of surviving Greek tragedy has been further subdivided, leaving only a tiny group universally recognised as 'true' tragedies. The rest are treated as failed attempts at tragedy, relegated to mixed genres invented *ad hoc*, or left to the specialists. We should begin, then, by recognising that there is not a single tragic narrative, but rather a number of story patterns characteristic of tragedy, patterns that tragic practice from an early stage in its development was capable of mixing and even subverting.

1. Conflict

If there is one category that overarches these patterns, it is conflict, the starting-point of all storytelling. 'Conflict' has been a central term in criticism of tragedy only since Hegel's *Vorlesungen über die Ästhetik* of the 1820s,[9] surprisingly, since from our perspective it is in many ways the crucial one. Tragic narrative patterns can usefully be classified by their characteristic conflicts, and something can be said in general about the kinds of conflicts that tragic plots seem to require. The first and most obvious quality of tragic conflict is its extremity: it does not ordinarily admit of compromise or mediation. For Ajax to yield to his enemies, for Medea to accept Jason's new marriage, would be to deny or negate their very natures. Where reconciliation of enemies does occur in tragedy, it is generally the result of direct divine intervention, as when Heracles persuades Philoctetes to fight at Troy or Athena persuades the Furies (themselves divine) to drop their pursuit of Orestes in return for new civic honours at Athens. Odysseus, in *Ajax*, is an eloquent human spokesman for reconciliation, but he achieves only the limited goal of persuading Agamemnon to permit the burial of their old enemy. The other common pattern of reconciliation is that of 'late learning', after the tragic crisis has already and irrevocably occurred. Here, the scope for reconciliation is limited by the very fact that the learning comes too late. In *Antigone*, for example, Creon recognises his mistake only after he has caused Antigone's death, and Haemon and Eurydice have committed suicide. Theseus learns at the end of *Hippolytus* how unjustly he has condemned his son, and Hippolytus forgives him before he dies, but it is of course too late to call back the curse.

Secondly, conflict in tragedy ordinarily involves more than a clash of choices freely taken by human agents. We regularly find such elements as past actions that, whether recognised or not, determine the shape of present choices and even their outcome (e.g. the curse of Oedipus in the *Seven Against Thebes*); ignorance or misunderstanding on the part of the agents that produce or threaten catastrophe (e.g. Ion's and Creusa's mutual attempts at murder in *Ion*); and even the direct imposition of divine will (e.g. the maddening of Heracles in the play that bears his name).

Finally, conflict in tragedy is never limited to the opposition of individuals; the future of the royal house, the welfare of the community, even the ordering of human life itself may be at stake. Oedipus' downfall is not merely, in our common parlance, a personal tragedy. He became ruler of Thebes by saving the state from the ravages of the Sphinx, and now, if the oracles prove true, his undoing threatens Thebes with anarchy. Nevertheless, his citizens, and along with them the audience in the Theatre of Dionysus, cannot simply wish him to escape unscathed and prove prophecy false. 'Why should I dance?' (896) the chorus of *Oedipus the King* sings (and dances) in a famously self-referential moment when it seems that the oracles may fail. In this sense, the fundamental struggle is to wrest meaning from suffering, and the perennial question of tragic pleasure—the exaltation that accompanies the witnessing of awful events—can be related to tragedy's affirmation, despite everything, of both cosmic and social orders against the unknown and against all those 'others' that threaten stability. But tragedy, as a quintessentially dialogic form, is always raising questions about those very foundational assumptions, even as its form tends to their (at least formal) resolution. (See Ch. 5 for a sociological approach to this question; also Chs. 1 and 6.)

In introducing the concept of conflict, I have left unmentioned the element often given pride of place in discussions of tragic conflict: fate. Fate is omnipresent, at least in the sense that the outcome of the story is known, in broad terms, at any rate, and therefore the audience is aware of the overall patterning of events in a way that characteristically eludes the agents until the end. Fate describes the limits of the possible for the action as a whole, because it acts as a 'reality check' for spectators who know that the Trojan War *did* take place, that Clytemnestra *did* kill Agamemnon when he returned home, and so on. The dramatist is, in effect, relieved of the requirement of providing suspense at this level of the plot, but instead he must find ways to make fate work for him as a tool for building dramatic tension. Moreover, the fulfilment of fate can be an essential part of the process of providing satisfaction for the expectations, moral as well as aesthetic, of the community. Apart from such considerations, however, the notion that Greek tragedy is fate-ridden and its characters essentially puppets in the hands of an angry destiny is very far from the mark. I venture to say that in Greek tragedy fate never operates in a simple, mechanical way apart from the characters and decisions of human agents.

2. The legendary subjects

The fourth-century comic poet Antiphanes writes that

> tragedy is a blessed art in every way, since its plots are well known
> to the audience before anyone begins to speak. A poet need only
> remind. I have just to say, 'Oedipus', and they know all the rest:
> father, Laius; mother, Jocasta; their sons and daughters; what he
> will suffer; what he has done.[10]

Antiphanes' point is that tragedy is much easier to write than comedy, in
which everything has to be invented afresh. This is more than a little
disingenuous, as regards both comedy (which is of course a highly patterned
and conventional genre in its own right) and tragedy (which permits and
even encourages much more freedom of invention than Antiphanes allows);
but there is a kernel of truth in it. For our purposes, we may restate the point
by observing that the successful tragedian would have to vary traditional
stories to make new what had been seen before, perhaps many times, in the
Theatre of Dionysus. We might equally well speak of the playwright's
opportunity to give an individual, perhaps highly personal, stamp to a tale
whose outline was already thoroughly familiar to the audience.

   At any rate, on the basis of the surviving victory lists and lists of titles,[11]
we can say that the earliest history of Attic tragedy already shows subjects
repeated by later tragic poets. A late source attributes to the semi-legendary
Thespis a line taken from a *Pentheus*, presumably on the same subject as
Euripides' *Bacchae*. The few surviving titles of Aeschylus' older competitors,
Chocrilus, Phrynichus, and Pratinas, all recur in the works of later
tragedians.[12] Of the close to six hundred works[13] attributed by title to all the
known tragic poets, there are a dozen different plays entitled *Oedipus* (at least
six from the fifth century, including plays by all three surviving tragedians),
eight plays named *Thyestes* (including versions by Sophocles and Euripides),
and seven named *Medea* (Euripides' being the first). Six playwrights entered
the lists with an *Alcmaeon*, a *Philoctetes*, and a *Telephus*; five with an *Alcmena*,
an *Ixion*, and an *Orestes*. All in all, more than one hundred of the titles appear
twice or more, and nearly half of the attested plays have repeated titles.[14]
From the point of view of plot, the history of Greek tragedy is one of
continuously recasting tales already known to the audience, already part of
what we may call a system of tragic discourse.

   In speaking, however, of tales already known, I want to avoid giving the
impression that there was a fixed body of lore waiting patiently for the
playwrights to give it dramatic form. In an important sense, poets were the
mythmakers of Greece. At any rate, there was no mythological 'orthodoxy'
in fifth-century Athens. A play whose plot has become canonical, Sophocles'
Antigone, appears to have had little in the way of literary precedents.[15] Yet,

even Sophocles cannot be said to have given the story its definitive form: we know that Euripides went on to write an *Antigone* in which the heroine survived to marry Haemon and bear him a son.[16] This state of affairs is typical. As regards the actual structures and details of plot, there are few tragedies that retell a familiar story in a familiar way.[17] The very fact that the same material was dramatised again and again must have encouraged the impulse to vary and reshape so as to outmanoeuvre expectation. Evidently, it would make no more sense to show an Oedipus who did not kill his father and marry his mother than it would to show a Napoleon who triumphed at Waterloo.[18] That is to say, myth is subject to interpretation and revision, but not to complete overturn, because it is also history. But within the limits of a living, fluid, intensely local tradition, plot stood open to invention, most obviously in the areas of motivation and characterisation, but also in such features as location and sequence of events.

This invention could extend, in Euripides, at any rate, to the self-conscious highlighting of deviation from earlier tragic versions (e.g. the Euripidean Electra's rejection of the recognition tokens from Aeschylus' *Libation-Bearers*; cf. p. 196 below) and to the almost novelistic fleshing out of the received mythical tradition (e.g. the account of the events between Orestes' murder of his mother and his departure from Argos in *Orestes*). But with few exceptions, the tragic poets developed their plots within the framework of the legendary tradition, taking 'slices from Homer's great banquets', as Aeschylus is reported to have called his own plays.[19]

We know that fifth-century tragedians did experiment with plays based both on recent history and on entirely invented tales, but neither could find a firm foothold. The latter class is known to us from a reference in Aristotle's *Poetics* to Agathon's *Antheus*, a play 'in which the names and the happenings were made up, and [which] is none the less enjoyed' (1451b21–3). Aristotle, although urging poets of his own day to follow the example of this late fifth-century innovator, admits that they do not. We can, I believe, deduce that both the crucial civic functions of the dramatic festival and the literary traditions that inform the tragic text would make the purely 'fictional' plot appear at a disadvantage. It is not merely that the great cycles of myth have a certain prestige; they have become an integral part of the system of tragic discourse.

As regards tragic plots based on recent history, the poets seem to have discovered at an early point that their ability to comment on civic life and the affairs of the Athenian state was impaired rather than enhanced by direct depiction of events from the immediate past (see Ch. I, pp. 24–5, for further discussion of early tragedies based on contemporary themes). Aeschylus'

Persians, the only such tragedy to survive, and as far as we know the last of its kind, dates from the 470s and dramatises the recent defeat of the Persian invader. It is fascinating, among other things, for the degree to which it has been accommodated to what we might call the mythic mode, with the full panoply of dreams, portents, and prophecy emphasising a pattern of divine punishment, while at the same time its focus on the hopes, fears, and sufferings of the Persians compels compassion for the vanquished foe.

3. Story patterns

By story pattern, I mean the shape of a narrative, constructed according to the rules of its own inner logic as storytelling rather than the probabilities of everyday life, and capable of generating indefinite numbers of variants.[20] To begin with a familiar example: romance, fairy tale, and legendary history offer a large number and variety of stories in which royal children are exposed, survive, and eventually return to claim their birthright. Notice first that the story pattern reverses ordinary expectations. Whereas exposure of children in real life must usually have ended in death, the logic of the story pattern demands the child's survival—no child, no story. Second, the logic of the plot coincides with clear moral and even social predispositions. We are invited to expect the child not only to live but to obtain what is rightfully his or hers by birth, and in particular to view the restitution of the birthright as an act not only of justice but of legitimation.[21]

Why might such a pattern appeal to a tragic poet? The answer, I suspect, is that both its narrative inevitabilities and its moral directionality can easily be made problematic. Since the inner logic of the story pattern inevitably sets up expectations that must be met or disappointed, the poet can direct our responses to the unfolding drama by meeting or disappointing them, or more precisely by controlling just how and to what extent the drama does so. And, since the outcome has moral and even social dimensions, more than just the aesthetic sensibilities of the audience can be engaged. Such patterns also participate in broader ritual paradigms. The pattern of the foundling's return, for example, clearly reflects the well-known *rite de passage* marked by separation from normal society and a period of liminality and testing, which, if successful, finally leads to reintegration into the social order at a new level. Patterning of this kind links the success or failure of tragic agents to the fate of the community as a whole.

We find characteristically complex adaptations of this story pattern in two surviving tragedies, Euripides' *Ion*, where it retains in a somewhat muted form the expected happy ending, and Sophocles' *Oedipus the King*, where it forms a crucial element in the irony for which the play is famous. In *Ion*, Creusa's attempt to murder her son, a young temple servant of Apollo at Delphi whom she believes to be her husband's bastard, is thwarted, and Ion, discovering that she is his mother and Apollo his father, at last assumes his destined role as prince of Athens and coloniser of Ionia. In *Oedipus*, the foundling plot reappears with ironic inversion, since Oedipus learns that he is hereditary king of Thebes only by discovering the double secret of his hideous pollution, and loses his kingship in the act of recovering his birthright.

In speaking of story patterns, I am not claiming to isolate a set of master plots to which all the narrative forms of tragedy can be referred; I am simply highlighting particular forms used repeatedly by the tragic poets in shaping their plots. Each involves a characteristic type of conflict, each presupposes a particular storytelling logic. We will examine a number of ways in which these patterns inflect spectator response, above all by forming frames of reference and what we might call frames of expectation for the experienced Athenian tragedy-goer. Even as story patterns are manipulated and combined to meet the needs of a particular tragic subject, they still retain sufficient identity as shared and even conventional elements to provide significant interpretative pointers. Their interest, then, lies largely in the ways they meet, deflect, or defeat the expectations that they themselves arouse. The commonest of these story patterns are those I shall refer to as retribution, sacrifice, supplication, rescue, and return-recognition. At the risk of making them seem far more mechanical and less problematical than they are as the tragedians deploy them—sometimes singly, but often in combinations and with surprising twists—to articulate their plots, let us take a brief look at each.

The *retribution* pattern is organised around punishment for past offences. It may involve conflict between gods and mortals, with the mortals' challenge to divine supremacy leading to their destruction. Aeschylus' *Persians*, the sole surviving tragedy based on contemporary events, is such an action in its simplest form, but divine retribution also plays a central part in the more complex actions of Sophocles' *Ajax* and Euripides' *Hippolytus* and *Bacchae*. *Prometheus Bound* represents an interesting special case, since the punishment is inflicted by one god upon another over whom he has seized control, and since we know that his victim will not in the end be destroyed but reconciled to him. The other form of this pattern provides an analogous conflict between human agents, although divine interest and participation is by no means excluded. The Electra dramas of all three tragedians provide clear examples of plays whose plots are constructed around this form of retribution, as do Euripides' *Hecuba* and *Medea*. Aeschylus' *Seven against Thebes* shows retribution at work through Oedipus' curse of his sons, which they themselves bring to fruition by their own choices. In Sophocles' *Women of Trachis*, retribution takes the form of a malign trick: the centaur Nessus, as he was dying, gave Deianeira blood from the wounds made by Heracles' poisoned arrows, telling her to use it as a love charm if her husband should ever prefer another to her. The 'charm', of course, is deadly, and when Deianeira uses it, she unwittingly carries out the centaur's revenge against her husband.

The *sacrifice* pattern entails conflict between the needs and desires of the individual and those of a community in crisis, resolved in favour of the community through the willing participation of the sacrificial victim. Euripides' *Alcestis* and *Iphigeneia at Aulis* are organised around this pattern, more often in Euripides developed as a subsidiary motif (e.g. the self-sacrifice of Macaria in *Children of Heracles* or Menoeceus in *Phoenician Women*).

The *supplication* pattern involves a triangular confrontation: a suppliant or group of suppliants, pursued by an implacable enemy, seeks and obtains protection from a ruler who must then defend them, by force if necessary. There are four full-blown suppliant dramas in the corpus of extant tragedy: three involving suppliant bands, Aeschylus' and Euripides' *Suppliant Women*, whose choruses represent, respectively, the fifty daughters of Danaus and the mothers of the Seven who fell at Thebes, and Euripides' *Children of Heracles*; and one whose central figure is a lone suppliant, the aged Oedipus of Sophocles' *Oedipus at Colonus*. Supplication and rescue from an implacable and violent enemy are also primary plot elements of several other plays, notably Euripides' *Andromache* and *Heracles*. In *Orestes*, Euripides goes so far as to allow a suppliant action to fail when the intended saviour rejects the suppliant's suit.[22]

The *rescue* pattern enacts a struggle whereby the principals, unexpectedly reunited, defeat a common foe and work their own salvation. Here the typeplays are the closely related Euripidean *Iphigeneia among the Taurians* and *Helen*, in which pairs of clever Greeks (brother and sister in one case, husband and wife in the other) outwit barbarian oppressors and win freedom. Once again, the pattern can be used as one episode in a compound plot, as it is in Euripides' *Andromache*.

In the *return—recognition* pattern, conflict arises from the central character's ignorance of his own true identity. By labouring against inner and outer opposition to establish that identity, he is able to reclaim his proper inheritance. We have already noticed how the two chief surviving examples of return—recognition tragedy, *Ion* and *Oedipus the King*, illustrate the degree to which a given story pattern can be made to serve disparate dramatic ends. But the pattern is a variant of one of the most common plot elements in tragedy (and comedy and romance, for that matter): recognition of another, as in the three *Electra* plays, Euripides' *Helen*, and many others.

These tragic story patterns, of course, are special cases of narrative forms that are widely used in storytelling of many kinds. As story patterns, they control the overall shape of the tragedy, providing a satisfying logic for the adaptation of myths to the stage; and the same narrative forms are also deployed in tragedy as subsidiary elements and to articulate individual episodes. We cannot assume that the tragic poets inherited them already connected to the segments of heroic legend that they proposed to dramatise. In some cases, no doubt, the shape of the plot was largely given by the matter. In others, it seems clear that the poet has adapted a story pattern to a particular myth for specific dramatic ends. It is hard to imagine composing a *Medea* that is not structured as a drama of retribution, whereas the suppliant pattern of *Oedipus at Colonus* was presumably not part of the local legend of Oedipus' death in Attica, but rather Sophocles' means of giving it a suitable dramatic form.

Tragic plots often combine two or more underlying patterns in unexpected and disturbing ways. Sometimes it is a matter of an action adhering to one pattern but achieving its particular effect by the inherence of another. In Sophocles' *Electra*, for example, the revenge tragedy is modulated by an emphasis on the recognition of brother and sister and on the rescue of Electra effected by Orestes' return. In *Antigone*, a pattern of divine punishment involving Creon emerges from the action shaped by Antigone's self-sacrifice. In other cases, brief but complete actions based on one pattern may be inset into a central plot structure of a different kind: Euripides, for example, repeatedly constructs willing sacrifice actions as episodes within the larger plots of his dramas. The extreme cases are the Euripidean dramas that more or less abruptly allow patterns to succeed one another to form complex plots. There are three such patterns in *Heracles*: a suppliant action ending in the saving of Heracles' family, an action of divine punishment resulting in his destruction of that same family, and a rescue action, in which Theseus brings the abject hero to Athens.

Surprising and unsettling effects arise also from the deflection of expectations built into the story patterns themselves. Sophocles' *Philoctetes* is an extraordinary example of a rescue plot played, as it were, against type: Philoctetes, offered rescue from his agonised exile on Lemnos, does not wish it on the terms that are available and finally refuses it on any but his own, setting himself firmly against what we know to be the 'right' outcome of his story, his necessary part in the sack of Troy. And the drama is played out as if Philoctetes can indeed set his own terms—and thereby prevent Troy's fall—until Heracles intervenes *ex machina* to set the myth back on track. The effect is a double dislocation: Neoptolemus finally 'saves' the narrative form by offering to take Philoctetes home, but this alternative rescue must fail if the myth is to be saved. Something analogous happens in Euripides' *Suppliant Women*, in which Theseus, against all the expectations aroused by the suppliant pattern, initially rejects the plea for aid of the mothers of the Seven who fell at Thebes, until his own mother puts the plot back on track by persuading him to change his mind; and in *Orestes*, where the suppliant action actually fails when the suppliant's putative saviour, Menelaus, refuses to take any action on his nephew's behalf, and an entirely different rescue plot has to be substituted.

In cases such as these, the interesting thing is not just the flexibility of story patterns, but the tensions generated by gaps, real or potential, between the expectations raised by the patterns and their fulfilment in specific plots. The dissonance thus generated invites the audience to consider anew what the myth enacted before them really means. Breaches in the conventions of storytelling make the myths themselves problematic and open their religious and ethical, social and political meanings to question. In a system of production based on almost constant repetition of legends and story patterns, in which every version is a variant, the disruption of expectations is a crucial element of tragic plots.

4. The mythic megatext

This repertoire of narrative forms is part of what we might call the tragic matrix; some legendary subjects are congenial to these forms, while others require greater effort to adapt them for the tragic stage. Tragic plots, then, are not supplied ready-made in myth, but they are also not invented from scratch each time a poet composes a new drama. The intersection in tragedy of a relatively small number of well-known legendary subjects and a limited repertoire of narrative forms helps to clarify the way in which tragedy participates in what has been called the 'megatext' of Greek myth, the repertoire of legendary subjects seen not as a corpus of discrete narratives, but as a network of interconnections at every level, from overtly shared themes, codes, roles, and sequences of events to the unconscious patterns or deep structures that generate them.[23]

Myth functions as a system whose signifiers are closely aligned to the central values (and therefore the central conflicts) of a culture. It is engaged, among other things, in a struggle to validate cultural norms. Tragedy uses myth, and thus itself inflects the mythic megatext, through a specific complex of narrative forms that is hospitable to specific cultural issues, and those issues in turn become, as it were, canonical in tragedy. The obsessive way in which tragedy keeps reworking female threats to male power, whether figured as the murderous assault of a Clytemnestra or the political defiance of an Antigone, offers an obvious, and suitably complex, example of tragedy going about this cultural work (cf. Chs. 1 and 5 above). Tragedy in such instances acquires a particular valence as an intervention in the production of the mythic megatext, one which countenances a threat to order and reinscribes it in a larger affirmation of cultural values.

The fact that threats to order and its reaffirmation are at the centre of the tragic use of myth helps explain why we can and must read tragedy both as challenging and as justifying established power structures, practices and beliefs; neither challenge nor justification is unequivocally asserted to the exclusion of the other. Evidently, this observation is related to dramatic form as well, since tragedy lacks the single, authoritative voice of a bard, the authorised voice of truth, as it were. Rather, the multiple voices of tragedy can all claim their own truths, assert their own rights, and all—even divine voices—may be subject to doubt, contradiction, accusation of wrongs. The dramatic mode itself is particularly receptive to a dialectic of criticism and affirmation. Greek comedy, especially the political and cultural satire of Attic old comedy, shares this critical/affirmative stance.[24]

The cultural work of tragedy may be briefly illustrated with reference to the pattern of transition of the young male to adulthood found in many of the myths that it dramatises. This pattern encodes the marginality of adolescence in a series of narrative structures that express the underlying cultural values at stake. The rite of passage involves, among other things, wanderings outside the city (not fixed abode within it), virginity (not marriage), absence of the father (but presence—often baneful—of the mother). In other words, the liminality of the youth is figured precisely in the symbolic set of exclusions that he must overcome. But this set of structures is not itself a story pattern, for its shape is indeterminate. The passage may succeed (as it does, finally, for Orestes), or fail (as in the case of Pentheus), or even both succeed and fail (as happens with Oedipus), and therefore it is invested with both hope and danger. The rite of passage, like the rites of sacrifice and purification, is one of the narrative elements of tragedy that adumbrate the great rituals of communal propitiation and therefore evoke the welfare of the community. Just as initiation into adulthood entails the dangers of passage from one state to another, purification presupposes the threat of pollution, and sacrifice often implies a civic crisis. Tragedy as a genre accommodates both mythical narratives that show the threat realised in all its destructiveness and those that show it safely negotiated, but in either case the outcome is not to be understood simply as the fate of an individual. Its meaning for the continued life of the community is always part of tragedy's concern.

In Aeschylus' *Oresteia*, Orestes' plight is presented in terms suggestive of the initiation pattern not once but twice. Having been cast out of the city at the time of his father's murder, Orestes attempts to reclaim his patrimony and re-establish the primacy of the male line by returning as armed warrior and killing his mother. He is then driven out once again as a hunted victim of the Furies, who seek vengeance for his mother's blood; this time, however, with the intervention of Apollo and Athens, he wins his freedom and establishes his claim to his father's place in Argos. But the trial in which Orestes is absolved of guilt for his mother's death takes place in Athens, and its consequences for Orestes are given far less emphasis than those for the polis. These include, in the first instance, the reaffirmation of the primacy of the male in the structure of household and state, and secondly Athens' assurance of the Furies' favour as Eumenides, granted a new home and honours and a role in the democratic order of persuasion and law whose symbolic birth the trilogy has dramatised (cf. Ch. 1 above).

In Euripides' *Bacchae*, the same matrix of male transition yields an action of a very different shape, but concern for larger civic consequences can still be observed. Pentheus' initiation is marked as a failure in its every detail: he leaves the city disguised as a female worshipper of Dionysus, and instead of trials to prove his right to rule the city in patrilinear succession, he is hunted and defeated by women, dismembered and symbolically devoured by his own mother. But his horrifying death is also marked as a sacrifice on behalf of the community.[25] Before Pentheus leaves for the mountains, Dionysus tells him, 'alone you wear yourself out on behalf of this city, alone' (963)—and indeed his suffering does benefit the city, by deflecting punishment upon himself as a kind of scapegoat for the city's guilt, and by providing the starting-point for a communal cult of the god.

Pentheus' death is also a prime tragic example of the 'perverted sacrifice' that constitutes a prominent tragic theme. He is identified by his killers as an animal and explicitly described as a sacrificial victim (1246), adorned for the sacrifice, led in procession, and slaughtered in a sequence that reproduces the stages of animal sacrifice, with his mother as priestess (1114) making the kill.[26] The overt Dionysiac content of this sacrifice accounts for its detail and emphasis, but the representation of killing as sacrifice is a repeated tragic trope—in every case connected with the deformation and perversion of ritual practice.[27] The subversion and distortion of marriage ritual is similarly widespread.[28] Such elements have importance not only because of the intrinsic emotive power connected with the representation of religious ritual in distorted and aberrant forms, but also because such representations produce a sense of danger for the well-being of the community, a precarious imbalance that calls out for redress.

METATHEATRE AND THE PRESSURE OF PRECEDENTS

Given the character of the tragic corpus as a set of variations on mythological themes, we may expect to discover traces of both theatrical and nontheatrical (chiefly Homeric) antecedents inscribed in our tragic texts. The centrality of theatrical performance in Athenian civic and cultural life during the fifth century makes it equally likely that we will find reflections of theatrical practice. Such elements do not constitute primarily a form of literary allusion, but a resource for inflecting and extending the possible meanings of a given situation, a means of directing and modulating audience response. The traditions in (and also against) which the poets write do not constitute mere background, but a dialectic of assimilation and opposition out of which much of tragedy's social meaning is constituted.[29]

The mythological cross-references of tragedy are nothing new. The Greeks employed them constantly from Homer onwards—one need only think of the sustained parallels in the *Odyssey* between the homecomings of Odysseus and Agamemnon, between what has already become of Clytemnestra, Orestes, and Agamemnon, and what may yet happen to Penelope, Telemachus, and Odysseus. Tragedy, especially in its choral lyrics, is full of such mythological comparisons and exempla, but for our purposes the interesting phenomenon is the covert or implicit cross-reference, such as is found, for example, in the well-known and striking use of *Iliad* book 6 in Sophocles' *Ajax*.[30] The memorable scene of Hector's farewell to Andromache serves as model for the episode in which Ajax takes leave of Tecmessa, though to call it a model is to understate the richness of Sophocles' allusive technique. His audience knew their Homer intimately, and he expects them to recognise his use of Homer and to use it in turn to interpret the scene they are witnessing. Hector, whose sword will kill Ajax, looms behind him as husband, father, warrior, and enemy; Andromache, whose husband is her all, conditions our perception of the despairing Tecmessa; even the child Astyanax informs the figure of Eurysaces (cf. Ch. 6 above).

It is not the parallels, however, but the differences that emerge once the parallels have been recognised that carry the interpretative burden, as in the striking contrast of the heroes' hopes for their sons. Hector, returning from the battlefield, only thinks to take off his helmet when it frightens his son. Gently lifting the child into his arms, he prays that Astyanax will grow to be as great and strong as he is, indeed better by far (*Iliad* 6.476–81). Ajax, emerging from his tent after his mad slaughter of the flocks, grasps his son in his bloody arms, saying that a child of his should be broken in to his own raw ways, and wishes for the boy to be in every way like himself—only luckier (*Ajax* 550–1). It is by such adaptation and inversion of Homeric situations and even locutions that Sophocles prompts his audience to compare characters, relationships, tones, outcomes. The allusion makes for a brooding richness hardly imaginable without it, appropriating Homer and as the same time inverting the Homeric value structure.

The fact that such cross-references can remain implicit and still be present for the spectator as interpretative frames suggests that they should be understood not with reference to the author, according to the traditional philological paradigm of source study, but with reference to the audience. Allusions call on a cultural competence that the author counts on spectators to share. Implicit relations among texts can thus be understood as part of a formal design that depends for its full realisation upon an act of recognition—a form of audience complicity in the making of meaning.

Another form of intertextuality depends not so much upon recollection of parallel narratives as upon the evocation of prior theatrical experience. Here, the very conventions of tragedy are used to overturn audience expectations. As an example, let us look briefly at the end of Euripides' *Medea*, a sequence both powerful and disturbing. Medea's final entrance is not unexpected; on the contrary, everything has been pointing to a last confrontation with Jason, and he arrives to pound on the door of her house and demand it. But the manner of Medea's entrance—above the scene building, on a chariot provided by her grandfather Helios—is a carefully calculated and prepared surprise. Jason is told that Medea has killed their children. 'Open the door and you will see the corpses' (1313), says the chorus leader, and an audience of tragedy-goers knows what happens next. They have seen those doors swing open to reveal the bodies of Agamemnon and Cassandra, Clytemnestra and Aegisthus, and no doubt many equally terrible spectacles before the production of *Medea* in 431. So every eye is fixed on the doors—but they do not open. Instead, Medea swings into view on high, and her scornful words draw attention to the spectacular breach of expectations: 'Why do you batter and unbar these gates seeking the bodies and me, who did the deed?' (1317–18). This spine-chilling moment takes Medea literally out of range, but the point is not just in the scenic effect. Medea appears *ex machina* like a goddess, because, against all expectations, that is what she turns out to be, or something very like it. Her dreadful wrath has made her an elemental power, destroying everything in her wake and then flying from the ruin she has wrought.[31]

This example, in its grim play with the conventions of the tragic stage, introduces a note of metatheatricality that we find again and again in Euripides. Two passages that have traditionally been treated as cheap shots at Aeschylus are worth mentioning in this context. In the great central scene (369–685) of Aeschylus' *Seven against Thebes*, Eteocles carefully and elaborately chooses warriors to meet the challenge of the Argive captains attacking each of the city's gates, and finds in the end that he alone is left to defend the last gate against his own brother, thus fulfilling his father's curse. In the *Phoenician Women*, Eteocles simply agrees to Creon's suggestion that he should select a captain to stand at each gate, adding that it would be too time-consuming to name their names, but that he hopes to find his brother opposite him (748–55). Euripides marks his difference from his predecessor in no uncertain terms (and Aeschylus' play was evidently a famous one, since Aristophanes is still citing it in his *Frogs* in 405), but he does so not so much to score a stray critical point as to mark his vastly different purpose: his characters consciously pursue destructive and self-destructive ends rather than struggle with destiny.

The second 'critique' of Aeschylus, and the self-conscious outer limit of this form of intertextuality, is the notorious recognition scene of Euripides' *Electra*, in which the old servant trots out the tokens by which Aeschylus' Electra had recognised the return of Orestes, only to have Electra dismiss them with scorn. His hair would be a man's, not girlish curls like hers; his footprint would naturally be bigger than hers; he could not still be wearing some piece of weaving she made for him as a child (525–46). Commentators have tended to take this as a Euripidean critique of Aeschylus' lack of realism, but it is not simply an isolated bit of literary criticism. Euripides' mocking exposure of the incongruity of Aeschylus' tokens is also an exposure of the machinery of theatrical recognition, which only functions smoothly when it is hidden.[32] (Ironically, in the end, Orestes' identity is proved by the even hoarier, but incontestable, Odyssean token of the childhood scar—albeit one acquired in a fall in the courtyard while chasing a tame fawn!) Euripides is interested precisely in the arbitrary and theatrical character of the convention of recognition, because by highlighting it he can call its conventional satisfactions into question. The essential further irony is that the old man is right to deduce that Orestes has returned, and Electra is wrong. She impugns the tokens because she cannot believe that her high-hearted brother would cower in the countryside in fear of Aegisthus, and we immediately see how self-delusive that view is. Although this quintessentially Euripidean self-reflexiveness has traditionally been a sticking-point for critics, it is the logical conclusion of the intertextual development of the genre, an assertive response to the burden of tragic precedents.

The conventions of tragedy did not permit the overt breaking of the dramatic frame, direct audience address, or other forms of theatrical self-reference available to Old Comedy. Nevertheless, such theatrical elements as role-playing and disguise are commonplace, and by the time of Euripides' later plays, we occasionally find what amounts to tragic parody within the frame of tragedy itself. Already in Aeschylus' *Oresteia*, we find Clytemnestra shamelessly 'acting' her cunning welcome of the returning Agamemnon and Orestes' impersonation of a Daulian stranger announcing his own death to his mother. Sophocles' *Philoctetes* is organised around a kind of play-within-a-play staged by Odysseus to bring Philoctetes to Troy. (On the most strikingly metatheatrical moment of this play, the scene involving a 'trader' whom the spectators know to be a sailor sent by Odysseus to aid the inexperienced Neoptolemus, see Chapter 7, pp. 169–70.)

Even more elaborate is the role-playing in Euripides' *Helen*, a drama that takes as its leitmotif the gap between appearance and reality. Helen stages the central intrigue in a way reminiscent of the Orestes story, by having Menelaus announce his own death. Here, however, that by now hackneyed device becomes not merely a way into the palace but the fulcrum of the whole escape plot, with the king, hoodwinked into helping with Menelaus' burial honours, providing the ship and resources needed. Euripides was notorious for bringing heroes on stage in rags, and in a number of plays, *Helen* among them, costuming becomes a major preoccupation. The shipwrecked Menelaus' rags, at first a disconcerting symbol of his loss of place and power, become a useful element in Helen's scheme, since they add credibility to the tale that Menelaus is merely a sailor who survived his commander's disaster. Only when the escape plot has been set in motion does Menelaus reappear in the armour that suits his reputation; but we are made to see this, too, as a costume, designed first to make him seem a participant in the rites for the dead, and only then to serve his 'true' role as scourge of the barbarians who stand in the way of his and Helen's freedom.

Euripides' *Bacchae* constitutes the supreme example of tragic metatheatre, not surprisingly, perhaps, since its central character is the god of theatre.[33] The whole play is staged for us by Dionysus, who announces at the outset that he is playing the role of his own priest in order to punish Pentheus. He has already maddened the women of Thebes and sent them to the mountains as maenads. In his mortal disguise, he plays along with his own entrapment and then uses his divine powers to escape and to stage a horrible masque—the sacrificial procession to the mountains where Pentheus, attired as the god's surrogate, becomes surrogate victim of a mad sacrifice at the hands of his mother and the other Theban Bacchantes. In the end, he appears *ex machina* in his 'true' guise—one wishes it were possible to know just how this appearance of the god differed from that in his role of mortal priest. Altogether, costuming in this play has a far more complex function than in any other surviving tragedy. In a bleakly comic vein, Cadmus and Tiresias appear in maenadic costume, unsuccessfully trying to negotiate a Dionysiac deconstruction of the boundaries of age and gender. Pentheus mocks them but obviously feels threatened by the blurring of gender identity in the feminine garb and long hair of Dionysus. This feeling is intensified for us when the god breaks down the young ruler's last resistance by feminising him, robing him in full Bacchic regalia in a scene (912ff.) that endows the transvestitism of the theatre—men acting women's roles—with a real threat to sexual identity and male domination.[34]

TRAGIC FORM AND THE SHAPING OF TRAGIC PLOT

The conventions of the tragic stage form the matrix in which a given segment of legend takes shape on its way to becoming a plot. Chapter 7 examines conventions in detail, and I limit myself here to a few observations on the relation of plot and tragic form. Along with endless variations on a limited repertoire of heroic legends, the tragic poets generated enormously inventive permutations and combinations of a limited repertoire of closed forms, to some extent analogous to those of opera. From the formal point of view, the crucial fact is the alternation of speech and song, out of which each play makes its own distinctive musical patterns.[35] We should not think of these poetic forms as moulds into which a given story is poured, but rather as flexible and expressive devices for developing and articulating tragic plots out of the materials of the legendary tradition.

The choice of a chorus is one obvious way for the poet to articulate his approach to a legendary subject. The chorus, after all, constitutes not only a collective character standing in a defined relation to the other characters of the drama, but also an intermediary between the world of the play and the

audience whose perspective it helps to shape. Thus, for example, Aeschylus'
decision to use Theban women rather than elders for the chorus of the *Seven
Against Thebes* permits him to give voice to desperate fears for the fate of the
city against which we can measure the resolve of Eteocles, its defender.
Sophocles' choice of Theban elders for the chorus of *Antigone*, rather than
companions or servants of the heroine, initially furthers her isolation but
then permits a dramatically crucial shift in their understanding and
sympathy.[36]

From the parodos (entrance song) to the end of the play, the chorus is
continually present in the orchestra, with rare and noteworthy exceptions,
making palpable the communal and public character of tragic drama. One
consequence of this convention is that, apart from prologue speeches that are
in effect addressed to the audience to set the scene, there is practically no
soliloquy in Greek tragedy, for at least the chorus is there to listen. (The
great suicide speech in Sophocles' *Ajax*, 815–65, is one of the exceptions.)[37]
The chorus does take part, through its leader, in the dramatic dialogue, as
well as participating in lyric exchanges with other characters. The odes,
however, stand apart from the action. Actors often remain on stage during
the odes, but do not directly acknowledge their performance or contents.
(The only exceptions constitute special cases.)[38] As moments of lyric
reflection, choral odes draw the spectator away from the immediate concerns
of the plot, while at the same time they inevitably have an effect on dramatic
mood, providing a kind of objective correlative for the spectator's responses
to the action.

Greek tragedy is essentially a drama of words. Characters enter, talk
with each other, exit. Very little 'happens' on stage—no battles and no
blindings as in Shakespeare. Physical action, though sometimes dramatically
crucial, is usually limited in scope and relatively static—acts of supplication,
gestures of affection or pity or lamentation. Violent events tend to be
described in messenger-speeches, a convention that has often been
interpreted as a matter of decorum, but more likely stems from the
realisation that, within the conventions of the fifth-century theatre, such
things can be made far more vivid through narration than through stage
presentation (on this point, see Ch. 7, pp. 154–5). The confrontations of
tragedy are also essentially verbal, although they very occasionally spill over
into the physical, and when they do, the effect in context is shocking (for
example, Creon's seizure and abduction of Antigone in Sophocles' *Oedipus at
Colonus*, 818ff.). But the threat of physical violence is one of tragedy's
important verbal tools, and in general what we may call verbal violence is a
regular feature of tragic discourse. Confrontation is not merely a matter of

angry, emotional exchanges of insults. More often it is staged as a formal debate, with the whole panoply of opposing speeches and rancorous stichomythia, extended alternation between two speakers by single lines or pairs of lines (cf. Ch. 6 above, pp. 127–8).

The primacy of the word in tragedy is not, however, merely a function of the resources of the theatre or conventions of the genre. Words are tools of power in tragedy. Tragic discourse is still responsive to a notion of the ominous quality of language itself, as can clearly be seen, for example, in the constant etymologising of names like Ajax (from *aiai*, 'alas') or Pentheus (from *penthos*, 'grief'). The ominous refrain of the great opening chorus of *Agamemnon*, 'Sing sorrow, sorrow: but good win out in the end',[39] comes as the Argive elders discover that their song keeps turning unbidden to dark events in the recent past, which they try to counter with the power of positive speech. As the fifth century wore on, it might be argued, the discursive powers of speech, logical argument, sophisticated techniques of persuasion, came to have the upper hand over this archaic view of language. But, in whatever form, the power of words—intended or otherwise—remains one of tragedy's enduring themes in the form of prophecy, vow, curse, riddle, lie, and incantation.

The power of such words is not easily controlled, and it should come as no surprise that their effects are often diametrically opposed to what the speaker intended or the hearer understood. A familiar case is Oedipus' curse on the slayer of Laius, who turns out to be himself (*O.T.* 222–75). Even more arresting is the succession of speech-acts that produce the peripeteia of *Oedipus the King*: for Oedipus' downfall is constituted not by deeds, the killing of the father or wedding of the mother (outside the drama, as Aristotle would say), or even the self-blinding (after the fact and off stage), but by a dialogue sequence that puts special emphasis on the code of communication. I summarise the scene beginning at line 1146, with particular attention to the thematics of speech. The old shepherd, realising that the garrulous messenger from Corinth may inadvertently reveal the awful secret of Oedipus' origins, *orders* him to be silent. Oedipus *countermands* his order and *threatens* punishment. The shepherd *asks* how he has erred, and Oedipus *reproaches* him for *refusing to tell* about the child of which the messenger has *spoken*. The shepherd attempts to allay Oedipus' suspicion by *alleging* that the messenger is *speaking nonsense*. Oedipus again *threatens* torture, the old man *begs* to be spared, Oedipus *orders* his arms to be twisted. Again Oedipus *asks*, and this time the shepherd *answers*, adding the *wish* that he had died on the day he gave up the baby. Another round of *threats* and *laments* leads to the further *question*, 'Where did you get the child?', which the shepherd *evades* by the vague 'From someone.' To Oedipus' repeated *question*, the shepherd *answers* with a desperate *plea* to *ask* no more. But Oedipus *threatens* his destruction if he must be *asked* again, and he *admits* that the child was from the house of Laius. On the verge of the terrible recognition, Oedipus *asks* the final question, 'A slave, or one born of Laius' own race?' To the shepherd's *lament* that he is now about to *speak* the dread thing itself, Oedipus responds with one of the most memorable lines of the play (line 1170): 'And I to *hear*—but *hear* I must.' This is certainly an extraordinary passage, but in precisely the respects we have been attending to it is characteristic, even paradigmatic, for Greek tragedy in general. Discourse, verbal interaction, *is* the essential action, not a mere reference to or representation of the action. The issues of tragedy, lodged as they may be in political, moral, and/or personal conflicts, are enacted through speech-acts.

THE EXAMPLE OF EURIPIDES' *HIPPOLYTUS*

A closer look at one play may help to bring together some of the central themes of this chapter. I have chosen Euripides' *Hippolytus*, in part because of the many ways in which it typifies tragic practice and in part because of something that makes it unique. *Hippolytus* is the only known instance of a second dramatisation of the same subject by the same poet.[40] We know enough about the lost first version to trace two very different ways of telling the 'same' story, and by comparing them we can clarify the distinction between myth as the body of lore available to the tragic poet and *muthos*, Aristotle's term for plot as a structure of events embodied in a particular drama. The chief thing we know about the first *Hippolytus* is that in it Phaedra made a deliberate attempt to seduce Hippolytus, who responded by covering his head in horror (thus the lost play's distinguishing title of *Kalyptomenos*, 'Hippolytus Veiling Himself'). That is to say, this version conforms to the pattern of the biblical tale of Joseph and Potiphar's wife, in which a shameless advance by the woman was met with rebuff and followed by a false accusation of (attempted) rape. Our evidence permits us to deduce a few more things about the first *Hippolytus* with reasonable certainty. The scene of the play was probably Athens, not Trozen as in the surviving play. Phaedra's nurse may have tried to restrain her mistress's passion, rather than encourage its expression. After Phaedra made her accusation to her husband Theseus, there was a confrontation between him and Hippolytus, concluding as in the surviving play with the curse that Poseidon fulfilled by sending a bull from the sea to kill Hippolytus. The truth was revealed, perhaps through a confession on Phaedra's part, and she then killed herself.

This first version of *Hippolytus* apparently shocked and offended its audience through what our version's *hypothesis* (a brief synopsis and critique offered by the manuscript tradition) succinctly calls the 'unseemliness and blameworthiness' of its portrayal of woman's desire. Rethinking the subject, Euripides is able to present the same outline (approach—rebuff—accusation—double death) in a frame that 'saves' the character and motivation of Phaedra. He makes Phaedra a woman fighting to suppress and conquer her passion, who, when she finds that she cannot do so, is ready to die rather than bring dishonour upon herself and her children. The nurse in this version becomes the figure of seduction, at least vicariously, as she wheedles and supplicates in order to force her mistress to reveal the secret source of her 'illness', then betrays her by approaching Hippolytus in her stead. Hippolytus' shock is here answered by Phaedra's shame and the suicide with which she plots to salvage her reputation. Phaedra leaves a written accusation of rape against Hippolytus for Theseus to find, and on its strength the king curses his own son, only to discover his innocence as he lies dying.

No doubt there were many other changes from the first to the second *Hippolytus*, but even what little we can affirm with some assurance suffices to make clear that, within a frame that prescribes only the barest outline of the story, the poet is free to vary not only the place and the sequence of events, but the characters and motivations of the central figures. And precisely because not only the bare outline, but also previous versions theatrical and otherwise are known to all or most of the audience, he can gauge his effects in relation to that knowledge, and to expectations based on it as to how the story will be told. It is in playing with these expectations that new emphases, new centres of gravity, new meanings can emerge from the old myths. All of this seems to be at work in the second *Hippolytus*, where Phaedra's attempts to resist her passion and the nurse's betrayal emphasise the extremity of Hippolytus' scathing denunciation of Phaedra and change the emotional and moral balance between them, and where the new manner and timing of her death permit the final scenes of the drama to focus entirely on Hippolytus.

We can now turn to some of the ways in which this play typifies features of Greek tragedy that I have discussed in this chapter.[41] The first of these involves an interesting and rather special case of metatheatricality. This is the introduction of Aphrodite herself as speaker of the prologue, matching the appearance at drama's end of Artemis. In all probability, we are dealing here with another change from the first to the second *Hippolytus*. Unlike the earlier play, this version insists on the secret nature of Phaedra's affliction, so that neither Phaedra nor anyone else at Trozen can reveal it, and Euripides brings on a god to set the scene. But theatrical convenience becomes metatheatrical coup; Euripides uses the occasion of the exposition to make the drama itself a kind of play-within-a-play staged by the goddess of love, just as Dionysus stages the action to come in the prologue of *Bacchae*. At the end of *Hippolytus*, Artemis foretells the next such divine drama when she promises to destroy one of Aphrodite's favourites in revenge for the loss of her own (1420–2). By such means is the plot drawn into the orbit of the pattern of divine retribution.

The plot of *Hippolytus* can also be seen in the light of an overriding ritual pattern, that of passage. The Potiphar's-wife story of attempted seduction here becomes symbolic of the failure of the male to reach sexual maturity through the transition to adulthood. This is accomplished in a number of ways, but is rooted in the feminisation of Hippolytus that accompanies his desire to remain a virgin, a status associated in Greece primarily with the female. Hippolytus' cultivation of the virginal Artemis to the exclusion of Aphrodite puts him in the position of the reluctant maiden, like Persephone, who must finally relinquish her maidenhood even against her will. In the end, ironically accused of the violation of his father's marriage bed, he sacrifices not his virginity but his life to his father's curse and Aphrodite's anger. But the refusal of adult sexuality is not merely destructive to Hippolytus; in its blurring of distinctions between male and female it represents a danger to the community, and in death Hippolytus partakes of another civic rite, that of the scapegoat, the liminal figure who is expelled from the polis to remove some threat to its safety. To the extent that the bull from the sea represents both the granting of Theseus' curse by Poseidon and the culmination of Aphrodite's wrath, responsibility for the violent death is transferred to the gods. To the extent that it also symbolises the passion that Phaedra recognised and resisted, Hippolytus denied and repressed, it expresses the human truth of the power of *erōs*. In a last ironic reversal, Hippolytus is associated for ever in Trozenian cult with Aphrodite (and the story of Phaedra's love) as the cult-figure to whom maidens on the eve of marriage dedicate locks of their hair. His heroic status corrects—tragically too late and for others, not himself—the imbalance of his life.

Finally, the nature of confrontation and conflict as verbal—the character of Greek tragedy as a drama of speech-acts—can nowhere be better illustrated than in *Hippolytus*. Bernard Knox's isolation of the choice between speech and silence as the motor of the plot provides a useful starting-point.[42] The drama proceeds as a series of encounters in which misguided estimations of the power of words successively produce omissions, repressions, indiscretions, irrational outbursts, and lies in a concatenation that brings destruction on all the parties. Phaedra and her old nurse, in very different ways, overvalue speech. In Phaedra's case, this verges on fetishisation when she can think of no way of speaking compatible with her honour and takes refuge in silence. The nurse, on the other hand, is a great believer in the ability of *logos* to solve any problem. Her mistress' silence exasperates her, and she wheedles a confession from her. Having ground down Phaedra's resistance with rhetorical cunning, she goes straight to Hippolytus, and when we next see her, she is begging the enraged youth to be silent about what she has told him (603). Yet, despite the disastrous failure of her speech, she does not lose faith in its power. Her final words to Phaedra are, amazingly, an offer of further machination, to which Phaedra replies by telling her one last time to stop talking and dismissing her with the tragic formula for sending an enemy packing, 'Get out of my way!' (708). Having fully grasped the extremity of her situation, Phaedra takes full charge, and her remaining speech-acts are decisive, efficient, indeed (in the case of her final written message, the indictment of Hippolytus) masterful and devastating. As she becomes Aphrodite's agent in the destruction of Hippolytus, she assimilates a divine ability to make her words achieve her ends.

Theseus and Hippolytus may be called, by contrast, men who undervalue the word, repeatedly misapprehending its relation to its conventional opposite, the deed. Hippolytus, comfortable only among the age-mates who share his values, leads them in hymning Artemis but refuses even the *pro forma* prayer to Aphrodite urged upon him by his old retainer. Unmindful of the danger of withholding honour from so powerful a god, a perfunctory 'fond farewell to your Cypris' (113) is all he can muster. His response to the nurse's pleading of Phaedra's suit is the opposite of reticent, however. He launches on an extraordinary tirade against all womankind, a heady mixture of absurd hyperbole, offended sensibilities, and assorted male anxieties (616–68). Theseus trusts the truth of Phaedra's written accusation so much more than any word Hippolytus might speak that he launches his curse even before hearing what his son has to say (887–90). Ironically, Theseus appears to doubt the efficacy of his own curse, since he adds exile as the alternative punishment should it fail, and later tells Hippolytus that swift death would be too easy (1047). He displays a complete unwillingness to consider Hippolytus' solemn oath. Like his son, he knows what he knows and refuses to acknowledge that what he doesn't know is of any consequence. When Hippolytus suggests that he at least consult the utterances of soothsayers, the King replies, 'As for birds flying overhead, a fond farewell to them!' (1059). This is the very same phrase of dismissal with which, at the beginning of the play, Hippolytus 'greeted' Aphrodite.

In the end, only the gods can line up their words infallibly with the results they wish to achieve. (Even Phaedra's apparently authoritative writing can only destroy Hippolytus, not save her own reputation.) Both Aphrodite and Artemis assert, reveal, promise, predict, damn with a certainty unknown to mortals, while the mortals make the best they can of a world of uncertain meanings, broken promises, unrealisable wishes, ineffectual regrets. After Theseus' curse has mortally wounded his son and Artemis has arrived to instruct and rebuke him, the King can only wish that the curse had never come to his lips; it cannot be called back. The only effective human speech left comes from the dying Hippolytus, the words with which he frees his father from blood-guilt (1449). Like Phaedra, he finally makes the word do his bidding, but too late, when death is upon him.

CONCLUSION: MYTH, INNOVATION, AND THE DEATH OF TRAGEDY

The great period of Greek tragedy seems to have lasted less than a century. The extant plays date from a period of roughly seventy years (except for the *Rhesus* ascribed to Euripides, which may well be a fourth-century play), and it is admittedly risky to make guesses about what we have lost. Nevertheless, if it is true, as Aristotle tells us, that Aeschylus added the second actor, then tragedy in its fully developed form began with him and as far as we can tell the cultural dominance of tragedy did not survive Athens' loss of the Peloponnesian War. Of course, new tragedies continued to be produced, and we know that a number, such as the *Hector* of Astydamas (a great-grandson of Aeschylus!), had enormous success[43] but tragedy never again attained the centrality that it maintained in Athens through the fifth century. Nietzsche, in *The Birth of Tragedy*, offered perhaps the most influential explanation for tragedy's death: the poison of Socratic reason, administered by Euripides. The decline of tragedy as a creative force is, however, as complex a phenomenon as its meteoric rise. I want to suggest that the intertextual play of innovation and repetition that we have seen as an important feature of tragedy can help us understand both the intense flowering of the genre in the fifth century and its subsequent fading.

Recent scholarship has rightly emphasised the close relation between fifth-century tragedy and Athenian civic life (cf. Ch. 1 above). The rise of tragedy as an art-form gave Athens a powerful instrument for the celebration, criticism, and redefining of its institutions and ideals, for examining the tensions between heroic legend and democratic ideology, and for discussing political and moral questions. This civic role was intensified and focused by the continuity and concentration of tragic production. As we have seen, tragedy revolved around a restricted repertoire of subjects; it was embedded in the ritualised framework of the Dionysiac festivals and the resources of a particular theatre.[44] At the same time, both as the vehicle of an important competition and as a form of popular entertainment, tragedy had to meet a constant demand for novelty. The extent of this demand is made clear when we remember that each year saw the production of nine new tragedies, not allowing for the fact that earlier tragedies were occasionally revived, but also not counting satyr drama, formally and thematically linked so closely to tragedy (cf. Ch. 2 above). Furthermore, while tragedy enjoyed the highest civic prestige, it was also (as Aristophanes makes clear) the centre of passionate controversy. Intellectually, tragedy embodied the traditional wisdom of the culture at the same time as it lay open to the new languages of persuasion and philosophy that threatened the overturn of traditional values. Socially, it could be seen as validating the established political and religious order in its role as an institution charged with inculcating civic virtue, and equally as expressing the unresolved tensions within the polis and therefore breaching the armour of the establishment. Thus, tragedy's repetitions and innovations reveal themselves as symptomatic of a deeply rooted doubleness, bringing past into confrontation with present, staging in ever new guises the immemorial conflicts of male and female, of parent and child, of rival siblings, of individual and community, and of mortal and god. In this sense, innovation serves not only its obvious function of differentiation among repeated enactments of myth in the ritualised setting of tragic performance, but also pushes to the limit the search for truth in myth, for the authentic token of cultural identity and meaning.

So far as we know, the conditions of tragic performance in Athens remained essentially unchanged after the Peloponnesian War, but such evidence as we have suggests that even after the restoration of democracy the tragic theatre lost its intimate relation to public issues and political life (a process that can be much more fully documented for comedy by comparing Aristophanic 'old' comedy to the 'new' comedy of Menander). A typically laconic passage of Aristotle's *Poetics* informs us that the 'old' poets (i.e. the tragedians of the fifth century) had their characters speak 'politically', whereas the new poets make theirs speak 'rhetorically' (1450b7–8). The contrast implies a distinction between political discourse (the oratory of assembly and public ceremony) and the argumentation of the courtroom, with its litigation of personal disputes. In addition, the chorus, in many ways the voice of the community in fifth-century tragedy, is often removed from the action by the substitution of ready-made 'insert songs' (*embolima*) for the odes formerly composed for a particular dramatic context.

As long as it commanded the serious and thoughtful attention of the citizens of Athens by the solemnity of its production, the intensity of its poetry, and the expressiveness of its music and choreography, tragedy remained an important formative experience. It is all too easy to write off as insignificant the large body of tragedy from the fourth century that has not survived. But we can reasonably speculate that the concerns of the later tragedians were more private and psychological than those of their predecessors, and that they emphasised emotional effect over intellectual challenge. Freed from the expectation of comment on public affairs but caught in an increasingly complex interplay of repetition and innovation, involving both their own contemporaries and the classical repertoire of the preceding century, now regularly performed at the festivals, tragedians would inevitably gravitate to sensational situations and theatrical display. At the same time, the increased professionalisation of acting, about which we are reasonably well informed,[45] no doubt made its own demands on the tragic poets. Again, the evidence of Aristotle's *Poetics* is telling: good poets, he says, write in an episodic style 'for the benefit of actors; writing for the dramatic competitions, they often stretch a plot beyond its possibilities and are forced to dislocate the continuity of events' (1451b35–52a1).

To what extent might the very intensity of the repetition and innovation necessary to sustain tragedy be responsible for its ultimate decline? Charles Segal calls tragedy 'simultaneously a commentary on the megatext of the mythic system and the final text of the system; simultaneously the culmination of the system and its dissolution'.[46] Culmination, certainly; but should we make tragedy, no matter how extreme the innovations to it or how frantic their pace, responsible for the dissolution of myth? That tragedy was inextricably wedded to myth seems clear from the failure of Agathon's attempt to free tragedy from the traditional tales; and by the end of the fifth century, powerful new forms of discourse were competing successfully with myth in the search for meaning. The opening of tragic discourse to sophistic rhetoric and Socratic rationalism may be seen not as the assault on myth that Nietzsche deplored but rather as a recognition that myth had already lost much of its prestige as a tool for the discovery of truth and the advancement of social dialogue. Once myth is in doubt, tragedy becomes marginal.

BIBLIOGRAPHICAL NOTE

Many general books on Greek tragedy deal with the subject matter of Chapters 7 and 8: earlier bibliography can be found in Lesky (1983); *CHCL*

1; *Métis* 3.1–2 (1988). See also Goldhill (1986); Zimmermann (1991); Rehm (1992); and three collections of essays by Charles Segal: *Interpreting Greek Tragedy* (Ithaca 1986); *Euripides and the Poetics of Sorrow* (Durham, NC, 1993); *Sophocles' Tragic World* (Cambridge, MA, 1995). A new edition of Richard Buxton's *Sophocles* (*Greece & Rome* New Surveys in the Classics, no. 16) appeared in 1995. For tragedy's links with other artistic genres see Herington (1985); *Arion* 3rd series 3.1 (1995); Nagy (1996).

On performance criticism cf. Ch. 12, with bibliography, and O. Taplin, 'Opening performance: closing texts?', *Essays in Criticism* 45.2 (1995) 93–120.

On music in tragedy: W. C. Scott, *Musical Design in Aeschylean Theater* (Hanover and London 1984) and *Musical Design in Sophoclean Theater* (Hanover and London 1996); West (1992).

On myth and drama see Foley (1985); Buxton (1994); Seaford (1994).

NOTES

1. Geoffrey Chaucer, *Canterbury Tales*: 'The Monk's Prologue' 85–9. That Chaucer is here thinking of epic is made clear from the next lines: 'And they ben versifyed comunly / Of six feet, which men clepe *exametron*.'

2. For the development of the idea of tragedy from Aristotle through the Middle Ages, see Kelly (1993); for Chaucer's importance in the tradition, esp. 170–5.

3. *Poetics* 1453 a19. Aristotle is speaking of a restriction in subject matter that in his view characterises the best recent tragedies, but what we can learn of all but the earliest tragic practice suggests a similar concentration of subjects. Among the surviving thirty-two tragedies, fifteen deal with the 'matter of Troy', seven with Theban saga, and in addition four (all by Euripides) dramatise episodes in the legendary history of Athens. Of course these categories are not exclusive; Sophocles' *Oedipus at Colonus* brings Oedipus to his final resting-place in Attic soil and Euripides' *Suppliant Women* shows the Athenians risking war to bury the Seven who fell at Thebes.

4. It should be added that tragedy is not unique in this respect; something similar could be said of New Comedy and, e.g., Greek temple architecture, or the iconography of vase-painting.

5. Fish (1980) esp. 171–2.

6. I assume that Euripides' *Electra* is later than that of Sophocles, although neither play can be dated with certainty, and the responsive relationship among the versions would be of equal interest and importance if the order were Aeschylus-Euripides-Sophocles. For arguments in favour of a relatively early dating of Euripides' *Electra*, see Zuntz (1955) 63–71, Newiger (1961), and Burkert (1990). For another important scenic link between the three plays, see Ch. 7, pp. 168–9.

7. There is some further overlap in subject among existing plays which confirms this view: Euripides' *Phoenician Women* corresponds in subject—though hardly in treatment—to Aeschylus' *Seven against Thebes*; Euripides' *Orestes* may be said to open up a subject in the space between the end of *Libation-Bearers* and the beginning of *Eumenides*. A tantalising bit if evidence is provided by *Orations* 52 and 59 of Dio Chrysostom (first century AD), the first of which provides a comparison of Sophocles' *Philoctetes* and the lost Philoctetes plays

of Aeschylus and Euripides, the second a prose version of the Euripidean prologue. See Bowersock (1994) 55–9.

8. On the traditions of interpreting *hamartia*, see Bremer (1969) 65–98.

9. For the question of conflict in tragic theory and criticism, see Gellrich (1988).

10. Fr. 191 Kock 1–8.

11. Records of the dramatic competitions were systematically kept, and fragments of inscriptions that contain these *didaskaliai*, literary sources in which they are excerpted, and comments appended to many of the surviving dramatic texts (*hypotheses* and scholia) contain information concerning playwrights, titles, dates of production, and awarding of prizes. The evidence (in Greek) is published most accessibly in Snell (1986); for full publication of the sources for the *didaskaliai*, see Mette (1977).

12. Chocrilus: *Alope* (also Euripides and Carcinus, fourth century); Pratinas: *Perseus* (presumably the same subject as the *Andromeda* tragedies of Sophocles, Euripides, and Lycophron, third century), *Tantalus* (Phrynichus, Sophocles, and his contemporaries Aristias, son of Pratinas, and Aristarchus); Phrynichus: *Actaeon* (also Iophon, son of Sophocles, and Cleophon, fourth Century), *Sons of Aegyptus* and *Daughters of Danaus* (Aeschylus), *Alcestis* (Euripides), *Antaeus* (Aristias). For Phrynichus' tragedies on contemporary events, see Ch. I, p. 24.

13. Including numerous plays bearing the same title as well as titles that certainly or probably belong to satyr plays.

14. I hasten to point out that these figures are meaningful only in an exemplary way. It is not possible to be sure that plays with shared titles actually share legendary subjects as well. Thus, for example, there are seven reported *Achilles* plays and an equal number of *Bacchae*, but they need not all have dealt with the same legendary episodes. On the other hand, different titles may well hide the same basic material (e.g. Euripides' *Phoenician Women* recasts the subject of Aeschylus' *Seven Against Thebes*).

15. Unless, that is, one accepts the authenticity of the received ending of Aeschylus' *Seven Against, Thebes*. It seems not unlikely that the nucleus of the story was known to the playwrights from a Theban tradition not fixed in literary form. A brief, judicious discussion in Kamerbeck (1978) 5 concludes that 'even if the core of the fable was to be found in epic tradition (or elsewhere) and even if the authenticity of the final scenes of the *Septem* deserves more belief than they are nowadays generally credited with, we may safely state that in the *Antigone* the handling of the story ... [is] as original as anything in Greek Tragedy'.

16. Sophocles' *Antigone*, Hypothesis I and schol. 1351; discussion in Webster (1967) 182. This process of adaptation continues of course to our own day: see Steiner (1984).

17. On the transformation and criticism of myth in tragedy, see Vickers (1973) esp. 295–337.

18. Euripides' *Helen*, whose heroine never went to Troy, comes close, but had precedents in earlier treatments. Poets can also play with overturn of the legendary tradition, as in Sophocles' *Philoctetes*, where the conclusion of the action itself, which would result in the indispensable man not going to Troy, is 'corrected' by Heracles' intervention as *deus ex machina*. But history is never simply overturned, as in the notorious modern example of Schiller's *Maid of Orleans*, in which Joan of Arc dies heroically on the field of battle.

19. Athenaeus, *Deipnosophistae* VIII 347e.

20. I adopt the term from Lattimore (1964). Two studies of Euripides are of special interest for their treatment of typology of plot: Strohm (1957) and Burnett (1971), from which my pattern-categories are adapted.

21. The pattern is thus at least as suited to comedy as to tragedy; we find a version of it in a fragmentary fourth-century comedy, Menander's *Epitrepontes (Arbitration)*.

22. See below, p. 190 and Burnett (1971) 184–7.

23. Segal (1983) esp. 174–6.

24. See Henderson (1990) and (1993).

25. On this element, as well as interpretation of the ritual elements, see Seaford (1994) 280–301.

26. Seidensticker (1979). It should perhaps be added that the reconstitution of the body in the last scene of the play may restore—or attempt to restore—Pentheus symbolically to the status of human being. On the complexity of the relation between tragedy and ritual, see Easterling (1988).

27. For Aeschylus, see Zeitlin (1965); for Euripides, Foley (1985).

28. See Seaford (1987); Rehm (1994).

29. On this subject, see Goldhill (1986) esp. 138–67.

30. See Easterling (1984c). Segal (1983) points out the interesting case of Sophocles' *Women of Trachis*, in which the central figures oscillate between Odyssean and Oresteian paradigms, Heracles appearing first as an Odysseus, then an Agamemnon, Hyllus as a Telemachus and then a kind of Orestes, Deianeira as a Penelope who becomes an inadvertent Clytemnestra. For discussion of this kind of intertextuality in Euripides, see Zeitlin (1980). For general discussion of allusion in Greek tragedy, see Garner (1990).

31. On Medea as daimon, see Knox (1977), esp. 206–11.

32. Goldhill (1986) 249.

33. See Segal (1982) 214–71 and Foley (1980).

34. Even Pentheus' mask seems to play a special metatheatrical role in the equally chilling 'unmasking' of the horrible killing. Agave is made to see that the *pros?pon* ('face' or 'mask') that she carries is her own son's severed head, not the lion she has imagined.

35. A detailed study of types and development of lyric exchange in tragedy can be found in Popp (1971). On the relation of lyric forms in tragedy to earlier Greek song traditions, see Herington (1985) esp. 103–50.

36. This play provides one of the striking exceptions to the convention that choruses do not intervene directly in the action: after Teiresias has revealed that Creon's entombment of the living Antigone and failure to bury the dead Polyneices have caused ominous signs of divine anger, the leader of the chorus takes it upon himself to tell Creon in no uncertain terms that he must now try to undo his errors; Creon yields, but too late (1091–114).

37. The earliest instance we have of a chorus exiting and re-entering involves the only scene change in an extant play, that from Delphi to Athens in Aeschylus' *Eumenides*. The chorus of *Ajax* leaves the *orch?stra* to search for Ajax, allowing him to enter an empty stage and die undisturbed. The other cases (in Euripides' *Alcestis* and *Helen* and the *Rhesus* attributed to Euripides) similarly serve to facilitate a scene that would be difficult or impossible to play in the presence of the chorus.

38. In Aeschylus' *Suppliant Women*, Danaus, the father of the suppliant maidens who are both chorus and *de facto* protagonists, explicitly praises the song of thanks they sing when the Argive assembly has voted to accept their plea and protect them. In Sophocles' *Oedipus the King*, Oedipus appears to respond directly to the prayers of the choral parodos, and does so in language that claims oracular knowledge and power; see Knox (1957) 159–60.

39. Lines 121, 139, 159; quoted in Lattimore's translation.

40. There is also a *Phaedra* of Sophocles, which may well have intervened between the

first and second *Hippolytus*. Discussion and fragments of both lost plays in Barrett (1964) 10–45.

41. The following remarks are by no means intended to constitute even the sketchiest interpretation of *Hippolytus*, merely to show some elements of its construction. The English-language reader can consult a number of recent interpretative essays on this play, from which I single out as particularly useful Segal (1965), Reckford (1972) and (1974), Zeitlin (1985), Goff (1990), and Mitchell (1991).

42. Knox (1952b).

43. For a positive view of such successes and the state of tragedy in the early fourth century, see Easterling (1993a) 559–69 and Ch. 9 of this volume.

44. However, the growing performance of tragedy outside Athens, both at the Rural Dionysia of Attica and in centres elsewhere in the Greek world, needs to be taken into account; see further Ch. 9 below.

45. See Pickard-Cambridge (1988) 279–305.

46. Segal (1983) 184–5.

Chronology

All dates are approximations.

600 B.C.	First dithyrambic chorus is introduced on stage by Arion at Corinth and Sisyon.
534 B.C.	Tragedy is introduced at City Dionysia Festival.
C. 525	Aeschylus is born.
510	End of tyranny in Athens.
C. 500	Pericles is born.
C. 501	Satyr plays are added to City Dionysia Festival.
C. 496	Sophocles is born.
490	First Persian invasion.
486–487	First comic dramas are performed at the City Dionysia Festival.
484	Aeschylus achieves first victory in dramatic competition.
480	Euripides is born. Second Persian invasion.
477	Delian League is created.
472	Aeschylus exhibits *Persians* and wins first prize.
470	Socrates is born.
468	Sophocles wins first prize for the first time in drama competition with *Triptolemus*.

462–429	Age of Pericles.
458	Aeschylus exhibits *Oresteia* and wins first prize.
C. 456–455	Aeschylus dies.
449–C. 420	Building of the Parthenon and Precinct of Dionysus takes place.
C. 448–445	Aristophanes is born.
440	Euripides produces *Rhesus*. Sophocles exhibits *Antigone*.
431	Peloponnesian War between Athens and Sparta begins. Euripides produces *Medea*.
C. 430–428	Plague strikes Athens. Sophocles produces *Oedipus the King*.
C. 429	Pericles dies. Plato is born.
C. 425–413	Euripides, *Electra*.
423	Aristophanes, *Clouds*.
421	Aristophanes, *Peace*.
C. 415	Euripides, *Heracles*. Euripides, *Trojan Women* and *Iphigeneia*. Sicilian Expedition. Aristophanes exhibits *Birds*.
411	Revolution of the Four Hundred at Athens overthrows democracy. Aristophanes, *Lysistrata*.
C. 410	Sophocles exhibits *Electra*.
408	Euripides, *Orestes*.
C. 405	Euripides and Sophocles die.
405	Aristophanes, *Frogs*. Euripides's *Bacchae* is produced posthumously and wins first prize.
404	Sparta defeats Athens, ending Peloponnesian War; rule of the Thirty Tyrants.
403	Civil war in Athens restores democracy.
401	Sophocles's *Oedipus at Colonus* is produced posthumously.
399	Socrates is executed in Athens.
388	Aristophanes, *Plutus*. Aristophanes dies.
387	Plato founds the Academy.
386	Regular revivals of tragedy are introduced at the City of Dionysia.
C. 386–380	Aristophanes dies.
384	Aristotle is born.

367	Aristotle joins the Academy.
360	Accession of Philip of Macedonia.
350	Theatre of Epidaurus is built.
347	Plato dies.
342	Menander is born.
C. 336	Aristotle, *Poetics*. Philip is assassinated.
336–146	Hellenistic Age.
330	Lycurgus builds first stone theater in Athens.
323	Alexander the Great dies.
322	Aristotle dies.
316	Menander exhibits *The Malcontent*.
305	Menander, *The Woman from Samos*.
291	Menander dies.
254	Plautus born.
250	Theatre at Syracuse rebuilt. Theatre at Ephesus built.

Contributors

HAROLD BLOOM is Sterling Professor of the Humanities at Yale University. He is the author of over 20 books, including *Shelley's Mythmaking* (1959), *The Visionary Company* (1961), *Blake's Apocalypse* (1963), *Yeats* (1970), *A Map of Misreading* (1975), *Kabbalah and Criticism* (1975), *Agon: Toward a Theory of Revisionism* (1982), *The American Religion* (1992), *The Western Canon* (1994), and *Omens of Millennium: The Gnosis of Angels, Dreams, and Resurrection* (1996). *The Anxiety of Influence* (1973) sets forth Professor Bloom's provocative theory of the literary relationships between the great writers and their predecessors. His most recent books include *Shakespeare: The Invention of the Human* (1998), a 1998 National Book Award finalist, *How to Read and Why* (2000), *Genius: A Mosaic of One Hundred Exemplary Creative Minds* (2002), and *Hamlet: Poem Unlimited* (2003). In 1999, Professor Bloom received the prestigious American Academy of Arts and Letters Gold Medal for Criticism, and in 2002 he received the Catalonia International Prize.

FRIEDRICH SCHILLER was a dramatist, poet, essayist, and translator. A major figure in German literature's Sturm und Drang period, some of his plays are Mary Stuart and Wilhelm Tell, with his masterpiece being the Wallenstein cycle.

LANE COOPER was a classics Professor at Cornell University. Some of his titles include *The Poetics of Aristotle: Its Meaning and Influence* and *A Concordance to the Poems of William Wordsworth*. He also edited a work of Aristotle's.

ARISTOTLE (384–322 B.C.) was a student of Plato's who became a philosopher and taught students of his own. His famed classic *Poetics* established him as a preeminent literary critic and inspired such titles for him as the "czar of literary criticism." He also wrote on logic, philosophy, natural science, ethics, and politics.

WILLIAM ARROWSMITH had taught at a number of schools such as Emory, NYU, Princeton, and Yale. He translated many titles and was the general editor of a multi-volume set of translations of the complete Greek tragedies. He edited or co-edited work by Aristophanes and Nietzsche and in addition to being a scholar was an educational theorist, film critic, and poet.

JOHN JONES has been Professor of Poetry at the University of Oxford. He is a translator and has written books on Wordsworth, Keats, and Dostoevsky.

FRIEDRICH NIETZCHE, philosopher, poet, and critic, was a Professor of classical philology and then devoted himself exclusively to his philosophical studies. Some of his many works include *On the Genealogy of Morals*, *Philosophy in the Tragic Age of the Greeks*, and *The Will to Power*.

R.P. WINNINGTON-INGRAM is Emeritus Professor of Greek Language and Literature at King's College, University of London and the author and/or editor of several books, such as *Euripides and Dionysus* and *Studies in Aeschylus*.

C.M. BOWRA was warden of Wadham College from 1922–71, Professor of Poetry at Oxford, 1946–51, and Vice Chancellor from 1951 to 1954. He was the author or editor of numerous texts, including *Sophoclean Tragedy* and *Greek Lyric Poetry*.

W. GEOFFREY ARNOTT has been Professor of Greek at the University of Leeds and has published *Menander*.

E.T. KIRBY has taught at the State University College at Brockport, N.Y. He is the editor of *Total Theatre*.

FRANCES MUECKE has taught at the University of Sydney and is the author of *Plautus: Menaechni: A Companion to the Penguin Translation*.

JACQUELINE DE ROMILLY has been a Professor at Collège de France in Paris. She has written many books, including *A Short History of Greek Literature* and *Time in Greek Tragedy*.

MALCOLM HEATH has been Lecturer in Classics at the University of Leeds. He has translated and written the introduction for a book of Aristotle's and has translated a text by Hermogenes.

JON D. MIKALSON teaches at the University of Virginia. He is the author of *Athenian Popular Religion* and *Religion in Hellenistic Athens*.

RUTH PADEL has taught at Cambridge, Oxford, and London Universities. She is the author of several texts, among them *In and Out of the Mind: Greek Images of the Tragic Self* and *Whom Gods Destroy: Elements of Greek and Tragic Madness*. She is now a poet, journalist, and reviewer.

NIALL W. SLATER has been an Associate Professor of classics at the University of Southern California. He has published Plautus in Performance: The Theatre of the Mind and Reading Petronius.

PETER BURIAN is Professor of Classical and Comparative Literatures at Duke University. He is the editor of Directions in Euripidean Criticism and a translater and co-translater of ancient literature.

Bibliography

Arnott, P.D. *Greek Scenic Conventions in the Fifth Century B.C.* Oxford: Clarendon Press, 1962.

Arnott, W. G. "Off-Stage Cries and the Choral Presence." *Antichthon* 16 (1982): 35–43.

Aylen, L. *The Greek Theater*. Cranbury, NJ: Associated University Presses, 1985.

Bacon, Helen. *Barbarians in Greek Tragedy*. New Haven: Yale University Press, 1961.

Baldry, H.C. *The Greek Tragic Theatre*. London: Chatto & Windus, 1971.

Berington, David. "The Uses of Contemporary History in the Greek and Elizabethan Theatres." *Proceedings of the Comparative Literature Symposium 12* (1981): 31–50.

Bowie, A.M. *Aristophanes: Myth, Ritual, and Comedy*. Cambridge: Cambridge University Press, 1993.

Case, Sue-Ellen. "Classic Drag: The Greek Creation of Female Parts." *Theatre Journal* 37, no. 3 (October 1985): 317–27.

Csapo, E. and W.J. Slater. *The Context of Ancient Drama*. Ann Arbor: University of Michigan Press, 1994.

Else, G.F. *The Origin and Early Form of Greek Tragedy*. Cambridge, Mass.: Harvard University Press, 1967.

Goff, Barbara. *History, Tragedy, Theory: Dialogues on Athenian Drama*. Austin: University of Texas, 1995.

Goldhill, S. *Reading Greek Tragedy*. Cambridge: Cambridge University Press, 1986.

Green, J.R. *Theatre in Ancient Greek Society*. London: Routledge, 1994.

Greene, William Chase. *Moira: Fate, Good, and Evil in Greek Thought*. Cambridge, Mass.: Harvard University Press, 1944.

Henrichs, Albert. "Why Should I Dance? Choral Self-Referentiality in Greek Tragedy." *Arion* 3, no. 1 (1995): 56–111.

Hubbard, T.K. *The Mask of Comedy*. Ithaca, NY: Cornell University Press, 1991.

Hunter, R.L. *The New Comedy of Greece and Rome*. Cambridge: Cambridge University Press, 1985.

Kernodle, George R. *The Theatre in History*. Fayetteville: Arkansas University Press, 1989.

Kitto, H.D.F. *Greek Tragedy*, third edition. London: Methuen, 1961.

Lattimore, R.L. *Story Patterns in Greek Tragedy*. London: Athlone Press, 1964.

Lefkowitz, M.R. *The Lives of the Greek Poets*. London: Duckworth, 1981.

Lesky, A. *Greek Tragedy*, translated by H.A. Frankfort, third edition. London: Benn, 1978.

McDowell, D.M. *Aristophanes and Athens*. Oxford: Oxford University Press, 1995.

McLeish, Kenneth. *A Guide to Greek Theatre and Drama*. London: Methuen, 2003.

Meier, C. *The Political Art of Greek Tragedy*, translated by A. Webber. Cambridge: Polity Press, 1993.

Moulton, Richard. *The Ancient Classical Drama*. NY: Russell & Russell, 1890.

Patsalidis, Savas. "The Revival of Ancient Drama and the Rage of the Critics." *Text & Presentation* 11 (1991): 75–81.

Pickard-Cambridge, A.W. *The Dramatic Festivals of Athens*, second edition, revised by J. Gould and D.M. Lewis. Oxford: Clarendon Press, 1988.

———. *The Theatre of Dionysus in Athens*. Oxford: Clarendon Press, 1962.

Platnauer, M., ed. *Fifty Years of Classical Scholarship*. Oxford: Oxford University Press, 1954.

Rosenmeyer, T.G. *The Masks of Tragedy*. Austin: University of Texas, 1963.

Rosslyn, Felicity. *Tragic Plots: A New Reading from Aeschylus to Lorca.* Aldershot; Brookfield, VT: Ashgate, 2000.

Sandbach, F.H. *The Comic Theatre of Greece and Rome.* London: Chatto & Windus, 1977.

Scodel, R., ed. *Theatre and Society in the Classical World.* Ann Arbor: University of Michigan Press, 1993.

Segal, C. *Interpreting Greek Tragedy.* Ithaca, NY: Cornell University Press, 1986.

Segal, E., ed. *Oxford Readings in Aristophanes.* Oxford: Oxford University Press, 1996.

Self, David, ed. *Classic Drama.* Cheltenham: Thornes, 1998.

Stanford, W.B. Greek Tragedy and the Emotions. London: Routledge, 1984.

Stinton, T.C.W. *Collected Papers on Greek Tragedy.* Oxford: Oxford University Press, 1990.

Taplin, O. *Greek Tragedy in Action.* London: Methuen, 1978.

Walcot, P. *Greek Drama in Its Theatrical and Social Context.* Cardiff: University of Wales Press, 1976.

Walton, J.M. *The Greek Sense of Theatre: Tragedy Reviewed.* London: Methuen, 1984; second edition, Amsterdam: Harwood, 1996.

———. *Greek Theatre Practice.* London: Methuen, 1991.

Webster, T.B.L. *Greek Theatre Production.* London: Methuen, 1956.

Wiles, D. *Greek Theatre Performance.* Cambridge: Cambridge University Press, 2000.

———. *Tragedy in Athens.* Cambridge: Cambridge University Press, 1997.

Winkler, J.J. and F.I. Zeitlin, eds. *Nothing to Do With Dionysos? Athenian Drama in Its Social Context.* Princeton: Princeton University Press, 1990.

Wise, Jennifer. *Dionysus Writes: The Invention of Theater in Ancient Greece.* Ithaca, NY: Cornell University Press, 1998.

Zimmermann, B. *Greek Tragedy.* Baltimore: Johns Hopkins University Press, 1985.

Acknowledgments

"The Use of the Chorus in Tragedy" by Friedrich Schiller. From *The Maid of Orleans, The Bride of Messina, Wilhelm Tell, Demetrius*, translated by Sir Theodore Martin, Anna Swanwick, and A. Lodge: 223–233. © 1903 by John C. Nimmo, Ltd. Reprinted by permission.

"Introduction" by Lane Cooper. From *Ten Greek Plays*, translated by Gilbert Murray and others: ix-xx. © 1929 by Oxford University Press. Reprinted by permission.

"Poetics" by Aristotle. From *The Poetics and Longinus of the Sublime*: 11–35. ©1930 by The Macmillan Company. Reprinted by permission.

"The Criticism of Greek Tragedy" by William Arrowsmith. From *The Tulane Drama Review* 3, no 3 (March 1959): 31–57. ©1959 by *The Tulane Drama Review*. Reprinted by permission.

"Sophocles's Electra: The Orestes Myth Rephrased" by John Jones. From *On Aristotle and Greek Tragedy*: 141–158. ©1962 by John Jones. Reprinted by permission.

"The Birth of Tragedy" by Friedrich Nietzsche. From *The Complete Works of Friedrich Nietzsche, The Birth of Tragedy*, Vol. 1, translated under the General Editorship of Oscar Levy. (New York: Russell & Russell, 1964). Reprinted with the permission of Scribner, an imprint of Simon & Schuster Adult Publishing Group.

"Tragedy and Greek Archaic Thought" by R.P. Winnington-Ingram. From *Classical Drama and Its Influence*, edited by M.J. Anderson: 29–50. ©1965 by Methuen. Reprinted by permission.

"The Antidote of Comedy" by C.M. Bowra. From *Landmarks in Greek Literature*: 191-209. ©1966 by C.M. Bowra. Reprinted by permission.

"From Aristophanes to Menander" by W. Geoffrey Arnott. From *Greece & Rome* 19, no. 1 (April 1972): 65–80. ©1972 by Oxford University Press. Reprinted by permission.

"Greece: The Forms of Dionysus" by E.T. Kirby. From *Ur-Drama: The Origins of Theatre*: 90–140. ©1975 by New York University. Reprinted by permission.

"'I Know You—By Your Rags,' Costume and Disguise in Fifth-Century Drama" by Frances Muecke. From *Antichthon* 16 (1982): 17–34. ©1982 by the Australian Society for Classical Studies. Reprinted by permission.

"Fear and Suffering in Aeschylus and Euripides" by Jacqueline de Romilly. From *Greek Tragedy*, edited by Erich Segal: 390–395. ©1983 by Jacqueline de Romilly. Reprinted by permission.

"Aristophanes and His Rivals" by Malcolm Heath. From *Greece & Rome* 37, no. 2 (October 1990): 143–158. ©1990 by Oxford University Press. Reprinted by permission.

"The Tragedians and Popular Religion" by Jon D. Mikalson. From *Honor Thy Gods: Popular Religion in Greek Tragedy* 203–236. ©1992 by The University of North Carolina Press. Reprinted by permission of the publisher.

"Knowledge That Is Sad to Have to Know" by Ruth Padel. From *Whom Gods Destroy: Elements of Greek and Tragic Madness*: 238–248. ©1995 by Princeton University Press. Reprinted by permission of Princeton University Press.

"The Fabrication of Comic Illusion" by Niall W. Slater. From *Beyond Aristophanes: Transition and Diversity in Greek Comedy*, edited by Gregory W. Dobrov: 29–46. ©1995 by The American Philological Association. Reprinted by permission.

"Myth into Muthos: The Shaping of Tragic Plot" by Peter Burian. From *The Cambridge Companion to Greek Tragedy*, edited by P. E. Easterling: 178–208. ©1997 by Cambridge University Press. Reprinted by permission of Cambridge University Press.

Index

DATE DUE			

DEMCO